MW01070043

THE HOUSE

OF

AUGUSTUS

FRONTISPIECE The Palatine and its environs in 1888; detail of the 'panoramic view of Rome' by H. E. Tidmarsh and H. W. Brewer, published in *The Graphic*, a London journal, on 24 May 1890 (Ravaglioli 1981).

THE HOUSE
OF
AUGUSTUS

A HISTORICAL DETECTIVE STORY

T. P. Wiseman

PRINCETON UNIVERSITY PRESS

PRINCETON AND OXFORD

Copyright © 2019 by Princeton University Press

Requests for permission to reproduce material from this work
should be sent to permissions@press.princeton.edu

Published by Princeton University Press
41 William Street, Princeton, New Jersey 08540
6 Oxford Street, Woodstock, Oxfordshire OX20 1TR

press.princeton.edu

All Rights Reserved

Library of Congress Control Number: 2019933155
ISBN 978-0-691-18007-6

British Library Cataloging-in-Publication Data is available

Editorial: Ben Tate and Charlie Allen
Production Editorial: Leslie Grundfest
Cover and Text Design: C. Alvarez-Gaffin
Jacket/Cover Credit: *front*: Roman coin featuring Augustus, 12 BC. 1867,0101.596
© The Trustees of the British Museum. *Background image*: Detail of "panoramic view
of Rome," H.E. Tidmarsh and H.W. Brewer, *The Palatine and its Environs*, 1888.
Production: Jacqueline Poirier
Publicity: Alyssa Sanford and Amy Stewart

This book has been composed in Minion Pro

Printed on acid-free paper. ∞

Printed in the United States of America

1 3 5 7 9 10 8 6 4 2

For Anne

CONTENTS

ABBREVIATIONS

CIL   *Corpus inscriptionum Latinarum* (ed. T. Mommsen et al., Berlin 1863–)

FGrH   *Fragmente der griechischen Historiker* (ed. F. Jacoby, Berlin 1923–)

FRHist   *The Fragments of the Roman Historians* (ed. T. J. Cornell et al., Oxford 2013)

ILLRP   *Inscriptiones Latinae liberae rei publicae* (ed. A. Degrassi, Florence 1957–63)

ILS   *Inscriptiones Latinae selectae* (ed. H. Dessau, Berlin 1892–1916)

ILLUSTRATIONS

PREFACE

Caesar Augustus died on 19 August AD 14. His almost-last words were a question to the friends and family at his bedside: 'Do you think I played my part all right in the comedy of life?' His life had indeed been dramatic, but unlike the man whose name he bore, his great-uncle and adoptive father Julius Caesar, he did at least achieve a happy ending.

Caesar had been empowered by the Roman People to break the domination of an arrogant aristocratic oligarchy. He defeated them in three military campaigns, but spared and honoured the survivors; then, when the wars were over and his bodyguard dismissed, they murdered him. His great-nephew was eighteen at the time, studying oratory in Greece. When the young Caesar came to Rome to claim his inheritance, and his duty of vengeance, a comet appeared in the northern sky and remained visible for seven days. His entry on to the stage of history could hardly have been more spectacular.

Now, fifty-five years later, he came to Rome again, in solemn procession from the country estate where he died to the forecourt of his town house on the Palatine hill, where his coffin would stay until the funeral, on display for public veneration.

A grandly formal colonnaded space, the forecourt opened on to the most historic square in Rome, site of the 'august augury' (by Romulus at the foundation of the city) which had given the young Caesar his honorific name 'Augustus'. But the house whose entrance door the forecourt framed was not grand at all. It was respectable but not luxurious, an object lesson in restraint and moderation. Luxury and extravagance were what characterised the arrogant aristocrats whose power had been broken by the Caesars, father and son, in the name of the Roman People.

Two thousand years on, 'The House of Augustus' has claimed a place among the leading tourist attractions of modern Rome. Excavated between 1958 and 1984, it includes four relatively well-preserved rooms with extensive wall-paintings, which required the most careful modern techniques of restoration and conservation to make public exhibition possible. The site was eventually opened to visitors in 2008, but it soon became clear that the paintings were inadequately protected. The project had already cost nearly two million euros, and another two and a half million would be needed to create the display environment that visitors can now enjoy. It was reopened in 2014 as part of the Augustus bimillennium celebrations, and in the nearby Museo Palatino, reorganised and refurbished as part of the same programme, there are brilliantly evocative digital reconstructions that explain the significance of Augustus' house in the context of the history of the Palatine.

What is not explained (and one could hardly expect it) is how we know the history of the Palatine in the first place. How can we tell, at a distance of two thousand years, that out of all the people who ever lived on the hill in the long history of ancient Rome, *that* particular person owned *that* particular house? This book is an attempt to provide an explanation.

What we think we know about the distant past can only be inference from the evidence that happens to survive, and the evidence that matters most is textual. Without the huge corpus of 'classical literature'—texts that were written in the ancient world and kept and copied long enough for the advent of the printing press to preserve them for scholarly consultation—the remains revealed by archaeological excavation would have no story to tell.

But texts rarely tell us exactly what we want to know. Finding our way to Augustus' house will be a long, circuitous journey through time, and at every stage we shall be trying to make sense of obscure bits of evidence, looking for ways to turn inadequate information into a properly intelligible narrative. We have to go where the evidence leads, however unexpected the result may be.

Unless otherwise stated, all the translations of sources, ancient and modern, are mine; the texts in the original languages can be found in the Notes section at pp. 169–223.

* * *

The first germ of an idea for this book goes back to a conversation with Amanda Claridge at the Durham Classical Association conference in 2011; I am very grateful to Amanda for much patient discussion of archaeological matters since then, but it should not be assumed that she agrees with everything I have done with it.

Chapter 1 originated as a paper given at the Augustus conference at the University of Lisbon in September 2014, and the original version ('Augustus and the Roman People') is due to appear in *Saeculum Augustum: New Approaches to the Age of Augustus on the Bimillennium of his Death* (ed. Cristina Pimentel, Rodrigo Furtado, Nuno S. Rodrigues, and Ana Lóio); I am very grateful to the editors for allowing me to reuse it here.

Particular thanks are due to Seán Goddard, for painstakingly turning my crude spatial ideas into proper plans; and to Albert Ammerman, Andrew Burnett, Amanda Claridge, Jonathan Hall, Daria Lanzuolo, Stefania Peterlini, Lorenzo Quilici, Marco Ravaglioli, Valerie Scott (with her colleagues in the BSR Library), Elizabeth Jane Shepherd, Julia Sorrell, and Mariantonietta Tomei, for generous help with the illustrations. My greatest debt, for a lifetime's loving support, is expressed in the dedication.

THE HOUSE
OF
AUGUSTUS

I

UNDERSTANDING AUGUSTUS

The first subject of our enquiry must be Caesar Augustus himself. He is often de-scribed as the first Roman emperor, but that is a wholly misleading description. What causes the misunderstanding is the simple-minded idea that the Roman republic came to a sudden end in the civil wars of the forties BC, and that what followed was the imperial monarchy. That was not what happened.

To understand Augustus, we need to understand the late republic. To under-stand the late republic, we need to take seriously what the ancient sources say about it. Those sources are uniquely authoritative and well informed, consisting as they do of the writings of contemporary participants whose understanding of the political culture of their time is, I think, beyond challenge. So the argument in this chapter will depend entirely on primary evidence, presenting a picture of Augustus' life and times through the words of contemporaries—including, of course, Augustus himself.

1.1 THE OLIGARCHY

Our first witness is Cicero, in the famous description of republican politics that he stitched into the text of his speech in defence of Sestius in 56 BC:

> In this state there have always been two sorts of people who have been ambitious to engage in politics and distinguish themselves there. They have chosen to be, re-spectively, by name and by nature either *populares* or *optimates*. Those who wanted their words and deeds to be welcome to the multitude were considered *populares*, and those who acted so as to justify their policies to all the best people were con-sidered *optimates*.

Cicero *Pro Sestio* 96

Of course Cicero was not going to say in a public speech that the term *optimates* was a euphemism for oligarchy, but he was perfectly well aware of the fact, and in a philosophical dialogue a couple of years later he was even prepared to admit it:

Cicero *De republica* 3.23
But when certain people control the republic by reason of their wealth or noble birth or resources, that is a faction, but they are called *optimates*.

What these abstract definitions conceal is the violence with which, on the one hand, 'all the best people' defended their oligarchic privilege, and on the other, 'the multitude' supported their elected champions in trying to abolish it. The most effective of those champions were Gaius Julius Caesar, as consul in 59 BC, and Publius Clodius, as tribune in 58.

The climax came in 52, with the cold-blooded murder of Clodius on the Via Appia, and the symbolic burning of the Senate-house by the Roman People at his funeral. Caesar, the People's chosen commander, was away in Gaul, and the *optimates* were determined to prevent him from coming straight back to another consulship.

Our next witness is Aulus Hirtius, narrating Caesar's support in 50 BC for Marcus Antonius' election as augur:

Hirtius *De bello Gallico* 8.50.2
He was glad to make the effort, both readily to help a close friend whom he had earlier sent on ahead to begin canvassing, and keenly to oppose the powerful faction of a few men who were eager to see Antony defeated and thus undermine the influence of Caesar on his return.

That faction of a powerful few were the *optimates*, as described by their opponents. A similar phrase appears in a text of great historical importance, Caesar's own self-reported speech at Corfinium in February of 49 BC:

Caesar *De bello ciuili* 1.22.5
'I left my province not for any criminal purpose, but to defend myself against the slanders of my enemies, to restore to their proper place the tribunes of the *plebs* who had been expelled from the city for that reason, and to bring about the freedom of myself and the Roman People from oppression by the faction of a few men.'

The Roman People, in a special law sponsored by all of the ten tribunes, had given Caesar the right to stand for his second consulship in absence, but the oligarchs frustrated that by getting the Senate to declare him a public enemy, and then driving out the two tribunes who tried to veto it. So there is no reason at all to reject Caesar's presentation of the crossing of the Rubicon as an episode in the ongoing ideological struggle. Certainly he had the enthusiastic support of the People, as even Cicero privately conceded at the time.

Our next witness is Gaius Sallustius Crispus, who had been tribune at the time of the riots after Clodius' murder in 52. Writing his historical works ten to fifteen years later, and insisting on the claims of truth over partisanship, Sallust too saw the politics of the late republic as a struggle between the many and the few. The Roman People and a powerful aristocratic oligarchy had been at odds ever since the murderous events of 133 BC:

> After Tiberius and Gaius Gracchus, whose ancestors had contributed much to the republic in the Punic and other wars, began to bring about the freedom of the *plebs* and expose the crimes of the few, the aristocracy, guilty and therefore on the defensive . . . opposed the actions of the Gracchi.

Sallust *Bellum Iugurthinum* 42.1

The same phraseology is used of events seventy years later:

> After Gnaeus Pompeius was sent to the wars against the pirates and Mithridates [66–65 BC], the resources of the *plebs* were diminished, and the power of the few increased.

Sallust *Bellum Catilinae* 39.1

Note that both these passages are in the author's own voice; many more such statements could be added from the speeches Sallust put into the mouths of the People's champions, Gaius Memmius in 111 BC, Gaius Marius in 108, Licinius Macer in 73, and Catiline in 63. Moreover, at the start of his monograph on the Jugurthine war Sallust made it explicit that this ideological struggle had led seamlessly into the civil wars of his own time:

> I propose to write the history of the war the Roman People waged with Jugurtha, king of the Numidians . . . because that was the first time a challenge was offered to the arrogance of the aristocracy. The conflict threw everything human and divine into confusion, and reached such a level of madness that the hostility between citizens ended in war and the devastation of Italy.

Sallust *Bellum Iugurthinum* 5.1

That was evidently written in 41 BC, during the civil war that saw the destruction of Perusia and the sacking of other Italian cities.

When Sallust wrote of 'the crimes of the few' and the 'guilty' aristocracy, he was no doubt referring to the murder of Tiberius Gracchus and his supporters by a group of senators led by Scipio Nasica, whom the *optimates* regarded as a national hero. But we can be sure that his readers would think also of more recent murders, equally celebrated by the *optimates*—those of Clodius and of Caesar himself.

Similarly, Sallust's identification of arrogance as the defining characteristic of the aristocracy will have made perfect sense to anyone who had been in Rome in the months after the Ides of March 44 BC. The key witness here is Gaius Matius, replying to a letter in which Cicero had expressed the opinion that Caesar had been a tyrant (*rex*):

I'm well aware of what they've said against me since Caesar's death. They consider it an offence that I find it hard to bear the death of a friend, and that I'm angry that someone I loved has died. They say patriotism should be put before friendship—as if they've already proved that his death was of benefit to the republic. . . . 'You'll suffer for it, then,' they say, 'for daring to disapprove of what we did.' What unheard-of arrogance!

[Cicero] *Ad familiares* 11.28.2–3

Not unheard-of, in fact, but familiar: it was the arrogance of men who claimed the right to decide who should or should not be allowed to live, without reference to the laws that bound the rest of the Roman People.

At this point we can recall our first witness, Cicero, and this time not as a theorist of the republic but as a suspect for the crime of helping to destroy it. Here he is as praetor in 66 BC, explaining to a jury the nature of the rule of law:

This is the constraint of the status I enjoy in public life, this is the foundation of liberty, this is the fountain-head of justice: the mind and heart and judgement and verdict of the citizen body is placed in the laws. As our bodies cannot employ their parts—their sinews, blood, and limbs—without a mind, so the citizen body cannot do so without law. The magistrates administer the laws, the jurors interpret the laws, all of us in fact for that reason are slaves of the laws so that we can be free men.

Cicero *Pro Cluentio* 146

By contrast, here he is in 44 BC, writing to one of the assassins, Decimus Brutus:

So you of all people don't need encouragement, if you didn't require it for that deed you carried out, the greatest in human history. . . . You liberated the republic without any public authority, which makes the deed even greater and more glorious.

Cicero *Ad familiares* 11.5.1, 11.7.2

For both men, and for all *optimates*, it was self-evident that Caesar had been a 'tyrant', and his murder therefore both legitimate and heroic. But what criterion of 'tyranny' were they applying?

All Caesar's powers and honours had been voted to him by the Roman People, usually in his absence; and despite what Cicero later claimed, the People were not coerced by military force. Caesar's rule was not tyrannical: on the contrary, it was conspicuously humane, as Cicero himself knew better than anyone. He had made the point explicitly in a letter to his fellow-optimate Aulus Caecina in the autumn of 46:

I'm constantly surprised by Caesar's seriousness, fairness, and wisdom. He never refers to Pompey except in the most honorific terms. You'll say he did him a lot of harm—but those were the acts of warfare and victory, not of Caesar himself. And how he has embraced us! He's made Cassius his legate; he's put Brutus in charge of

FIGURE 1. Murder as 'liberation': *denarius* issued in Greece in 43 or 42 BC by BRVT(*us*) IMP(*erator*), 'commander Brutus', whose portrait is on the obverse; L. PLAET(*orius*) CEST(*ianus*) was presumably the quaestor responsible for paying the troops. The reverse image is of two short swords (*pugiones*) flanking the 'cap of liberty' (*pilleus*) worn by freed slaves: the legend reads EID(*ibus*) MAR(*tieis*), 'on the Ides of March'. *BMCRR* East 68; Crawford 1974.518 no. 508.3. © The Trustees of the British Museum. All rights reserved.

Gaul, and Sulpicius of Greece; he's recalled Marcellus, who especially angered him, with all possible respect.

Cicero Ad familiares 6.6.10

But clemency and generosity were soon forgotten. The only thing that mattered to the *optimates* was that Caesar's authority was something they didn't like. As with Tiberius Gracchus, it was enough to say 'He wants to be king', and the murder of an unarmed man, in defiance of religion as well as law (for both Gracchus and Caesar were protected by *sacrosanctitas*), could be defined as the liberation of the republic.

Fig. 1

That was not how the Roman People saw it. When the assassins eventually held a public meeting in the Forum on the Ides of March, they needed an armed escort of professional gladiators. But if the many were angry, the arrogant few were exultant. Six months later Cicero could casually refer to Caesar's victory in the civil war as 'fouler than Sulla's', and feel no need to justify the judgement.

1.2 THE YOUNG CAESAR

Why does all this matter for Augustus? It matters because it was happening while he was growing up.

Young Gaius Octavius lost his father when he was four years old, and thereafter he was brought up by his mother Atia, who was Caesar's niece. He was ten years old when the Roman People burned down the Senate-house for Clodius' funeral pyre. He was thirteen years old when his great-uncle crossed the Rubicon to reinstate the People's tribunes. He was sixteen years old when Caesar put him in charge of the Greek theatre at the great triumphal games of 46 BC. And he was eighteen years old, studying the arts of war and oratory in Epirus, when the news came that Caesar had been murdered, and that he himself had been adopted as Caesar's son.

Six months later, not long after his nineteenth birthday, the young Caesar addressed the Roman People from the temple of Castor, next to the place where the People had burned Caesar's body and demanded vengeance on his murderers. Cicero was away at Arpinum, but he heard all about it:

Cicero *Ad Atticum* 16.15.3
> Although for the moment that boy's doing a fine job of blocking Antony, still, we ought to wait and see what happens. But what a speech! (A copy was sent to me.) He swears 'So may I be allowed to attain my father's honours' as he holds out his right hand to the statue! I'd rather not have the help of *that* sort of person.

Six months later again, after Cicero had indeed used the boy's help to get Antony defeated at Mutina, he got a warning letter from Decimus Brutus:

[Cicero] *Ad familiares* 11.20.1
> Here's something I've often been told, and I think it's worth taking seriously. Just now Segulius Labeo, a very reliable person, tells me he's been with Caesar and talked much with him about you. Caesar himself didn't actually complain about you—except for something he says you said, that the young man ought to be praised, honoured, and got rid of. He said he didn't intend to make it possible to get rid of him.

Given the long-standing optimate tradition of killing politicians they disapproved of, no one could have been in any doubt what Cicero had meant.

Decimus Brutus wrote that letter on 24 May, 43 BC. On 19 August the young Caesar was elected consul. On 27 November, along with Antony and Lepidus, he was elected Triumvir 'for the establishment of the republic' (*triumuir rei publicae constituendae*). On 7 December, Cicero was killed at their order. However much we admire Cicero, and however brutal we know the proscriptions were, it is still hard to disagree with the verdict of Augustus' friend the historian Titus Livius:

Livy fr. 50 (Seneca *Suasoriae* 6.22)
> On an honest estimate his death might seem less undeserved, in that he had suffered at the hands of his victorious enemy nothing more cruel than he himself would have inflicted if he had had the same chance.

And it is important, if uncomfortable, to remember that Cicero was killed legally.

The Roman People set up the Triumvirate, by a tribunician law. The Roman People elected the Triumvirs, and their remit was to re-establish the *res publica*. Only the People were competent to legislate and empower. They had empowered Caesar, and the *optimates* had killed him on the arrogant claim that *they* had the right to determine what was good for the republic. Now the young Caesar and his colleagues were the People's agents in restoring the People's authority, and they acted with a ruthlessness that reflected the People's anger.

As always, proper understanding requires contemporary evidence, and here our witnesses are the Triumvirs themselves:

> 'Edict of Marcus Lepidus, Marcus Antonius, and Octavius Caesar, elected to regulate the republic and set it right: if evil men had not, by treachery, begged for mercy when they needed it, and when they obtained it become enemies of their benefactors, and then conspirators, Gaius Caesar would not have been killed by those to whom he showed compassion when they were his prisoners of war, whom he made his friends, and whom he favoured collectively with magistracies, honours and personal gifts.'

Appian *Civil Wars*
4.8.31–2

The *optimates* had had their chance. Caesar's clemency and generosity had been abused, and would not be repeated.

The People's vengeance was carried out at Philippi (42 BC), and completed by the war in Sicily (36 BC). To describe the Triumvirs' opponents in those campaigns as 'the republicans', as modern historians often do, seems to me a gross distortion of the truth. Brutus and Cassius and the men who fled to Sextus Pompey were fighting not for the republic, a body of equal citizens under the rule of law, but for the continued power of the *optimates* and the right of the few to dictate to the many.

The Greek historian Appian was surely right to end his history of the civil wars in 36 BC. The war against Cleopatra and Antony (31–30 BC) was much more like a traditional campaign against a foreign enemy, supposedly defensive and leading to conquest; Antony was regarded not as the leader of a political faction but as a renegade in alliance with a foreign ruler. Since the Triumvirs' powers lapsed at the end of 33, Commander (*Imperator*) Caesar, as he now called himself, needed an *ad hoc* 'oath of all Italy' to justify his command of the People's forces, but the outcome shows clearly enough that his ideological position was the same as it had always been.

It was the Roman People who established by a law that conquered Egypt was to be governed by an equestrian Prefect; that must be the origin of the remarkable rule prohibiting any senator from setting foot in Egypt without permission. A similar point was made by the *cistophoroi* coins that were minted in Asia after the victorious Commander Caesar had completed his reorganisation of the eastern provinces in 28 BC. The legends announced:

> [*obverse*] Imperator Caesar Divi filius, consul for the sixth time, champion of the liberty of the Roman People. [*reverse*] Peace.

Sutherland
1984.79 (no. 476)

The phraseology is precisely what Sallust had used of Tiberius Gracchus and the elder Caesar had used of himself. Also in 28 BC, an issue of *aurei* reminded the users of gold coins that now the Roman People had got their republic back:

FIGURE 2. The return of the rule of law: *aureus* of 28 BC. The obverse shows the young Caesar (soon to be Augustus) wearing a laurel wreath; on the reverse he sits on a chair of office holding a scroll in his right hand, with a box at his feet containing further scrolls. British Museum, CM 1995-4-1-1. © The Trustees of the British Museum. All rights reserved.

British Museum
CM 1995-4-1-1
Fig. 2

[*obverse*] Imperator Caesar Divi filius, consul for the sixth time, [*reverse*] has restored laws and justice to the Roman People.

On 13 January of the following year, the restoration of their powers to the sovereign People was formally completed, and Commander Caesar was honoured with a new name. His house too received a mark of honour:

Degrassi 1963.113
(*Fasti Praenestini*,
13 Jan.)
Fig. 3

Oak Crown: the Senate decreed that it be placed above the door of Imperator Caesar Augustus because he restored the republic to the Roman People.

The sovereign People entrusted their champion with military command over a large but limited *prouincia*, for a long but limited period. He then left, as Julius Caesar would have left if he had lived, to fight their wars and secure their empire, and in his absence the proper business of the republic resumed.

One example of that was the conduct of elections in the traditional way, as we know from a contemporary poet's observations:

Horace *Odes*
3.1.10–14

Of the candidates coming down to compete in the Campus, A is more aristocratic, B has a better character and reputation, C's crowd of clients is more numerous.

If appearance and influence make a man fortunate, then let's buy a slave as a name-prompter—his dig in the ribs will get us crossing the cobbles with hand outstretched. 'This chap's big in the Fabia tribe, that one in the Velina. This one will give the *fasces* and curule chair to whoever he likes, and deny them to whoever he likes if he wants to be awkward.'

Horace *Epistles*
1.6.49–54

The elections were working as usual—and if Caesar Augustus and his trusted allies were regularly elected as consuls, that was by the will of the People, as we can infer from their riotous indignation when Augustus refused to stand for the consulship after 23 BC. In the traditional Roman republic, as a Greek observer

FIGURE 3. The 'civic crown' of oak-leaves: *aureus* of 12 BC. 'In my sixth and seventh consulships [28–27 BC], after I had extinguished the civil wars, although I had power over everything by universal consent I transferred the republic from my power into the control of the Senate and People of Rome. In return for my action I was named Augustus by a resolution of the Senate, the doorposts of my house were publicly decorated with laurels, and a civic crown was fixed above my door' (Augustus *Res gestae* 34.1–2); for 'civic crown' (*corona ciuica*) the Greek version of the text has 'the oak wreath which is given for saving citizens'.

The obverse of the coin shows AVGVSTVS DIVI F(*ilius*), Augustus the son of the deified Caesar; on the reverse, the doorway has laurels at either side and the oak wreath above, with the legend OB C(*iues*) S(*eruatos*), 'for saving citizens'. L. CANINIVS GALLVS was the magistrate responsible for minting the coinage. *RIC* I² Augustus 419: Sutherland 1984.74. © The Trustees of the British Museum. All rights reserved.

noted, 'the People bestow office on the deserving', and that is what was now happening again.

A more unexpected indication of the way things were comes from a neglected fragment of Livy, which happens to be preserved in a fifth-century biblical commentary:

> Caesar Augustus, as Livy relates, on his return from the island of Britain, reported to the Roman People at the spectacles that the whole world had been subdued to the Roman empire in the abundance of peace, either by war or by treaties.

Livy fr. 55
(Apponius
*In Canticum
canticorum* 12.53,
CCL 19.291–2)

The reference to Britain is garbled (Augustus never went there in person), but otherwise this is a recognisable description of something Livy must have witnessed himself, Augustus' return in 24 BC from his Cantabrian campaigns. He had also settled affairs in Gaul and re-established the tribute from Britain, so 'peace either by war or by treaties' was a precisely accurate phrase. What matters for our enquiry is 'at the spectacles' (*in spectaculis*): Caesar Augustus was in the theatre, or perhaps the Circus Maximus, addressing the Roman People *en masse*. He had received his command from them, and it was to them that he chose to report.

In the light of all this, it is not surprising that after Augustus refused to accept election to the consulship he used the tribunician power, granted in 23 BC by a law of the People and conspicuously numbered year by year. Its purpose, as always, was 'to protect the common people', and once again Horace provides contemporary confirmation:

> While Caesar is the guardian of our affairs, no civil madness or violence will drive out peace, nor anger that forges swords and brings wretched cities to enmity.

Horace *Odes*
4.15.17–20

Because Augustus, in the People's name, had tamed the arrogant aristocrats, there would be no more of the faction-fighting that had led to armed conflict and the sacking of cities. It was the *optimates* who had corrupted the republic, but now that their arbitrary power was held in check by tribunician authority, the conditions that had developed into civil war no longer applied.

1.3 THE AUGUSTAN AGE

Horace wrote those lines a few years after the celebration of a new era (*saeculum*), and he called the new age the age of Caesar. I think it makes historical sense to use the 'Secular Games' of 17 BC as a convenient chronological marker. From now on, this restored republic, with Caesar Augustus empowered by the People as its guardian, may be regarded as no longer provisional but an established fact.

For this more stable period too, we must look for contemporary evidence. The best evidence of all is provided by Augustus' own words, and we are fortunate that our sources quote surprisingly often from his speeches, letters, and edicts. Suetonius, for instance, gives us a wonderful extract from the proceedings in 2 BC, when Messalla Corvinus spoke on behalf of the whole Senate:

> 'The Senate, in consensus with the Roman People, joins in saluting you as *pater patriae*.' Augustus had tears in his eyes as he replied in these words (and I give them verbatim, like Messalla's): 'Now that I have achieved all I have prayed for, members of the Senate, I have only this to ask of the immortal gods, that I may be permitted to extend this consensus of yours to the very end of my life.'

Suetonius *Diuus Augustus* 58.2

Consensus between Senate and People would mark the end of the enmity that Cicero and Sallust had taken for granted as inherent in the republic (**1.1** above). That was what Augustus hoped he had achieved.

Fig. 4

Later that same year, at the dedication of the new 'Augustan Forum', he carefully explained why it featured statues of the great commanders of the past, 'who had changed the *imperium* of the Roman People from very small to very great':

> He dedicated statues of all of them in triumphal costume in the two porticos of his forum, declaring also in an edict that he had designed this so that he himself, while he lived, and the *principes* of later ages, might be held by the citizens to the standard of those men, as an example to imitate.

Suetonius *Diuus Augustus* 31.5

Note that the initiative lay with the citizens. Augustus evidently thought of the Roman People not as passively obeying their rulers, but as actively demanding the highest standards from the leaders they had empowered.

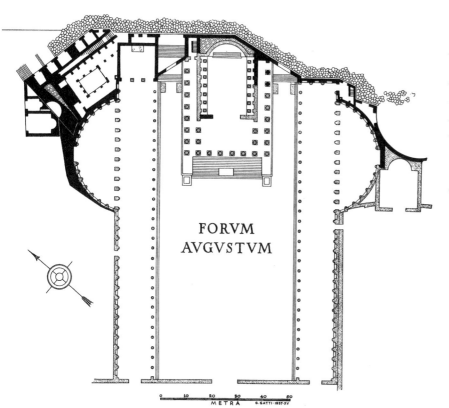

FORVM
AVGVSTVM

FIGURE 4. The 'Augustan Forum' and the great temple of Mars Ultor, 'the Avenger': plan by Guglielmo Gatti (Degrassi 1937.xxv). The temple was vowed before the avenging of Caesar at the battle of Philippi in 42 BC (Ovid *Fasti* 5.551–78, Suetonius *Diuus Augustus* 29.1–2), but the project was long delayed (Macrobius *Saturnalia* 2.4.9) and completed only in 2 BC (Cassius Dio 55.10.1–3).

Where was the Senate in all this? Fifty years before, Cicero had put into the mouth of his own 'example to imitate', the orator Marcus Antonius (consul in 99 BC), an eloquent statement of the Senate's right to rule. Antonius was objecting to a phrase in a famous speech by his great contemporary Lucius Crassus (consul in 95):

'As for your further statement, that the Senate not only can but should serve the People—what philosopher could be so soft, so languid, so feeble, so ready to refer everything to the criterion of pleasure and pain, as to approve the idea of the Senate serving the People, which itself has handed over to the Senate the power—the reins, as it were—to guide and regulate it?'

Cicero *De oratore* 1.226

Even at the time, that was a partisan view. The phrase 'senator of the Roman People' was used by Cicero himself when he was a young outsider attacking the corrupt aristocracy, and that alone is enough to show that Crassus was right: the Senate answered to the sovereign People.

The formal description of the Senate as *senatus populi Romani* is attested not only in late-republican authors (Varro and Sallust) but also in the proceedings of the decurions of Pisa after the death of Lucius Caesar in AD 2:

> Inasmuch as the Senate of the Roman People, among the very many and very great other honours to Lucius Caesar, augur and consul designate, son of Augustus Caesar *pater patriae*, *pontifex maximus*, in the 25th year of his tribunician power, by the consensus of all classes and with enthusiasm [has decreed . . . .]

CIL 11.1420.9–12
= *ILS* 139.9–12

Note again the emphasis on consensus. As for the Senate, the decurions' phraseology shows how the constitutional proprieties of the republic were observed; the only thing that had become obsolete was the *optimates*' own tendentious assertion of senatorial supremacy.

Even in the last decade of his life, when everything seemed to be going wrong, the ageing Augustus still kept faith with his vision of the republic as literally 'the People's thing' (*res publica*). Suetonius quotes two extracts from his letters to Tiberius, now his adopted son, who was fighting difficult campaigns in Illyricum and then Germany:

> 'Please look after yourself. If we heard you were ill it would be the death of your mother and me, and the Roman People would be risking the whole of their empire.' . . . 'I pray the gods, if they don't simply hate the Roman People, to preserve you for us and allow you good health, now and always.'

Suetonius
Tiberius 21.7

It may be doubted whether Tiberius saw it in quite the same way. He was a patrician, and his father had voted in 44 BC that the assassins should be honoured by the Senate for their deed. It seems clear that the Roman People didn't like Tiberius, despite Augustus' best efforts to persuade them. His biographer believed that

> Augustus weighed up Tiberius' faults and virtues and decided the virtues were more important, especially as he testified on oath at a public meeting that he was adopting him for the sake of the republic. . . . Augustus noted these unpleasant and arrogant characteristics in him and often attempted to excuse them to the Senate and the People, claiming they were faults of his nature, not his attitude.

Suetonius *Tiberius*
21.3, 68.3

Strictly speaking this is not contemporary evidence, since Suetonius does not give verbatim extracts from those speeches; but there is no reason to doubt that he had read them and reported their meaning correctly. The brute fact was that the successor to Augustus' position—his *statio*, as he put it—had to be a Caesar, but in AD 4 the only person he could safely adopt seemed to have the characteristics of an old-fashioned optimate.

At this point we must listen to Augustus' final assessment, composed in AD 14 (or possibly late 13), of the achievements 'by which he subjected the world to the *imperium* of the Roman People'. This is how he began it:

> At the age of nineteen, on my own initiative and at my own expense, I raised an army with which I brought about the freedom of the republic from oppression by a dominant faction. On that account the Senate adlected me into the order with honorific decrees in the consulship of Gaius Pansa and Aulus Hirtius, giving me at the same time consular precedence in stating my opinion, and granted me *imperium*. It instructed me as pro-praetor, together with the consuls, to see to it that the republic suffered no harm. In the same year, when both consuls had fallen in war, the People elected me consul, and Triumvir for the establishment of the republic.

Augustus Res gestae 1.1–4

The first sentence repeated Caesar's declaration of 49 BC (**1.1** above), except that Augustus claimed to have freed not just the *populus Romanus* but the whole *res publica* from the domination of a faction. The Senate is the subject of the second and third sentences, the People of the fourth, and the phrase *res publica* is conspicuously repeated in the terminology of the Senate's decree and the title of the Triumvirate. Throughout the text the idea of consensus constantly recurs, culminating in the grant of the title *pater patriae* by the Senate, the equestrian order, and 'the entire Roman People' (*Res gestae* 35.1).

Nevertheless, the ideology of Augustus' republic is clear from the start. The first two sentences do not encourage readers to remember the *real* details of November 44 BC, when the young Caesar was challenging Antony (**1.2** above), or of January 43 BC, when the Senate's decrees were to cement an alliance of convenience between the young Caesar and the *optimates* for the war of Mutina. The message of the first sentence is explicitly *popularis*: the many were freed from the domination of the few. In the Greek version, *factio* is translated as 'the conspirators', and that is surely how the Latin version too was meant to be read. The assassins' power was illegal, and as the fourth sentence specifies, the Roman People, by election, gave the young Caesar constitutional authority against them.

'Poor Roman People!', the dying Augustus is supposed to have said after his final conversation with Tiberius in August AD 14. Of course the story is apocryphal, but one can see why it was told in those terms.

One can also see why Tiberius was so contemptuous of the Senate's refusal to take responsibility. 'These men deserve to be slaves', he is supposed to have said. The reason is that they were accustomed to a republic of consensus, where Caesar Augustus and his body of advisers would convey to them what the Roman People wanted. Tiberius abandoned that system; he took everything to the Senate, and he expected them to make the decisions. It looks as if he shared the view of Cicero's Marcus Antonius, that the Senate's job was not just to advise but to make policy, without any input, mediated or otherwise, from the Roman People.

The result was a return to late-republican conditions—angry crowds shouting round the Senate-house, and in AD 31 an orgy of violence on the streets after the fall of Sejanus. But by then Tiberius had done what aristocrats like him normally did at his age; he retired to the peace and quiet of his palatial country estate. When he died, the Roman People were jubilant.

What they got was Gaius 'Caligula'—a true Caesar, the Dictator's great-great-grandson. Like him, and for much better reason, he was assassinated (AD 41), and by great good fortune we have a contemporary eye-witness account of the event and its aftermath, transmitted in the nineteenth book of Josephus' *Jewish Antiquities*. It contains a very revealing analysis:

> A clear difference had emerged between the attitude of the senators and that of the People. The aim of the senators was to regain their former dignity; they owed it to their pride to free themselves, now that it was possible at last, from the slavery imposed on them by the tyrants' insolence. The People, on the other hand, resented the Senate; they saw the emperors as a curb on its arrogant behaviour and a protection for themselves. They were delighted at the seizure of Claudius [by the Praetorians], believing that if he became emperor he would save them from the sort of civil strife there had been in the days of Pompey.

Josephus *Jewish Antiquities* 19.227–8

What this well-informed observer reveals is how much ground the People's cause had lost since the death of Augustus twenty-seven years before. In AD 41, the senators were again thinking like Brutus and Cassius (and Cicero): for them, it was self-evident that all the Caesars from the Dictator onwards had been 'tyrants'. The People were again fearful of optimate arrogance, and anxious to be protected against it. The only thing different now was the role of the Praetorian Guard in finding them a new protector.

To understand Augustus properly, it is necessary to consider Roman history over a long period of time, from Tiberius Gracchus to Claudius Caesar. To assume, as so many do nowadays, that the republic simply came to an end and power passed to the first of the emperors, is to be content with a historical travesty that misses all the essentials. The *optimates* of the late second and first centuries BC were not 'the republic', but a murderous corruption of it. Augustus was not 'the emperor', but a commander empowered for limited periods of time, with renewal not automatically assumed. The time of *emperors* began when the Praetorians chose the ruler, when his house on the Palatine was a purpose-built palace, and when 'Caesar' was no longer an inherited or adoptive name but a title bestowed on whoever succeeded.

If, broadly speaking, Augustus presided over a period of peace and stability, and Tiberius over one of strife and discontent, perhaps that is because Augustus thought and acted like a *popularis*, and Tiberius like an optimate. The terms themselves may have gone out of use, but there is no reason to suppose that the ideologies they described suddenly become obsolete in 49 or 42 or 27 BC.

Let's look back at Cicero's classic definition, in the first passage quoted in this chapter. What Augustus did, and Tiberius failed to do, was keep the interests of 'all the best people' subordinate to those of what Cicero disdainfully called 'the multitude'. Augustus was Julius Caesar's son, and for fifty years, with conquests, spectacles, and grand public works, Caesar Augustus gave the Roman People the confidence to believe that the *res publica* really was their thing: it belonged not to the few, but to the many.

2

HISTORY AND ARCHAEOLOGY

If you believe, as most people do, that Augustus was an emperor, you will naturally assume that he lived in a palace. If on the other hand you accept the view of people at the time, that he was a popular leader opposed to an oligarchy of the rich and powerful, then your idea of what his residence was like may be rather different.

The question is complicated by the fact that our understanding of the ancient city of Rome depends on two quite different types of professional expertise, that of the classicists, who know the texts, and that of the archaeologists, who know the sites. Archaeology is the more glamorous and exciting of the two professions, but the evidence it uncovers cannot speak for itself. Identification of an excavated building necessarily depends on the archaeologist's own historical knowledge, and that knowledge is itself dependent on texts collected and interpreted by classical scholarship.

My aim throughout this book is to make the methodology as transparent as possible, by presenting the reader with the texts I think are important, and explaining as clearly as I can what I think they imply.

2.1 PUBLIC AND PRIVATE

'The Roman People hate private luxury, but love public magnificence.' Cicero made that observation as consul in 63 BC (when the future Augustus was about three weeks old), and his own experience showed how right he was.

The young Cicero had been a *popularis*, lending his eloquence to the exposure of oligarchic corruption and the defence of reforming tribunes. As consul, however, he took a decisive step in the other direction: he ordered the execution of five Roman citizens without trial, on the authority of the Senate alone. The following year, as if to advertise his newly optimate position, he bought a very expensive house on the north slope of the Palatine.

He knew it was a controversial move. In April 59 BC, when Caesar as consul had put the *populares* briefly back in the ascendancy, Cicero shared his anxiety with his friend Atticus:

> In times like these, when life is so uncertain for the best people, I value even one summer's enjoyment of my Palatine *palaestra*.

Cicero *Ad Atticum* 2.4.7

The Greek term was a learned allusion to the Athenian exercise grounds where some of Plato's Socratic dialogues were set; but Cicero's cultural interests did him no good with the ordinary populace. His fears were justified: a year later a law of the Roman People banished him and declared his house public property. It was demolished, and the public portico erected on the site incorporated a shrine to the goddess *Libertas*.

To understand why it mattered so much, we must remember that in the Roman republic all citizens were supposed to be equal. Romulus himself, dividing the new city's land into equal lots, had aimed to achieve 'the greatest public equality', and the expulsion of the Tarquins had restored 'equal liberty for all'. Since economic inequalities were regarded as dangerously divisive, conspicuous expenditure was penalised by the censors. This set of values was most clearly articulated by Manius Curius and Gaius Fabricius in the third century BC, and forcefully restated by Marcus Cato as censor in 184 BC, attacking, as he put it, the hydra-headed monster of luxury.

The great overseas conquests of the second century BC brought about a huge influx of wealth, and a huge inflation of both public and private expenditure, on which repeated legislation to regulate private spending had little or no effect. The secret of Rome's success had always been the consensus of her citizens, their willingness to subordinate private interest to the public good. But sudden riches changed all that:

> Desire increased, first for money and then for power; those were the building material, so to speak, of every kind of evil. For avarice destroyed honesty, integrity, and all the other virtues; instead of them, it taught arrogance, cruelty, neglect of the gods, the belief that everything can be bought.

Sallust *Bellum Catilinae* 10.3–5

One of the results was the uncontrolled privatisation of public land by the rich, an abuse countered by Tiberius Gracchus in 133 BC with an explicit appeal to traditional ideology. 'Shouldn't the property of the community be divided among the community? It's a bad example to hold more land than the holder himself can cultivate.'

It was the murder of Gracchus—and its brazen justification as the defence of the republic against tyranny—that brought about the politically polarised society in which, in successive generations, Cicero and Augustus both grew up (**1.1** above).

In public, Cicero honoured the memory of Manius Curius and Gaius Fabricius and paid proper respect to the traditional values they exemplified:

> The good sense and high principles of our ancestors led them to be content with very little in the expenses of their private life, and to live in a most unpretentious style.

Cicero *Pro Flacco* 28

But that was just lip service. Cicero's private correspondence is full of contemptuous comments about the ordinary citizens of Rome ('the wretched starving *plebs*, that bloodsucker of the public purse'), and his treatise *On the Republic* describes political equality as unjust 'because it has no distinctions of status'. It was precisely 'in order to attain a certain status' that Cicero had borrowed the money to buy his grand house on the Palatine.

In effect, it was a symbolic demonstration of inequality, and in their law for his banishment the People were determined to reverse it. When he was recalled eighteen months later, and the college of *pontifices* had to decide whether the *Libertas* shrine could be removed for the rebuilding of his house, Cicero made it clear that what was at stake was not just bricks and mortar but his own status or humiliation. The *pontifices* found in his favour and the portico and shrine were demolished, but there was noisy opposition to what the People saw as an affront to 'their own Liberty'.

Cicero's status was restored. 'I live in a somewhat more expansive style than I used to,' he wrote to his brother; 'it was necessary.' Another letter referred to the enviable 'splendour and show' of his life at that time. But he had to pay for his recall and reinstatement with a political shift in favour of Caesar, whose *popularis* policies he had previously deplored.

Caesar's Gallic command, granted by the People in the teeth of optimate hostility, was producing enormous profits, which would be spent in the traditional way, not on private luxury but on public magnificence. Cicero would now be part of that. In 54 BC he wrote to Atticus, knowing his friend would not approve:

> Caesar's friends, I mean myself and Oppius (you're allowed to explode!), have casually spent sixty million sesterces on that project you used to praise so much, widening the Forum and extending it to the Atrium Libertatis. Dealing with private owners meant it couldn't be done for less. We're going to create something really glorious.

And there was another project, in the Campus Martius:

Cicero *Ad Atticum* 4.6.8

> We shall make voting enclosures for the Tribal Assembly, in marble with a roof, and surround them with a lofty portico a mile in extent, and attach the Villa Publica to the complex at the same time. You'll say 'What good will that project do *me*?', but why should that bother us?

Cicero's enthusiasm for public works didn't last long (in a couple of years he was back in the optimate camp), but together with the saga of the Palatine house it provides vital contemporary evidence for how the ever-changing cityscape of late-republican Rome reflected competing political ideologies. Understanding that is fundamental to the question of Augustus' house.

2.2 MATERIAL EVIDENCE

Gaius Octavius, the future Augustus, grew up in his stepfather's house at the 'Carinae'. When he was eighteen, just back from service with his great-uncle Caesar in the war in Spain (45 BC), he moved to a house of his own nearby. It was near the Forum, which was appropriate for a *popularis*; indeed, Caesar's own modest house was nearby, in the Subura, though as *pontifex maximus* he now occupied the 'public residence' on the Sacra Via. As Augustus' biographer tells us, the young Caesar

> lived first near the Roman Forum above the Scalae Anulariae, in a house which had belonged to the orator Calvus, and afterwards on the Palatine, but in the no less modest house of Hortensius, which was distinguished for neither space nor elegance, having as it did only short porticoes with columns of Alban stone, and rooms without any marble or handsome pavements. And for more than forty years he remained in the same bedroom for winter and summer, although he found the city unfavourable to his health in winter and yet consistently wintered there.

Suetonius *Diuus Augustus* 72.1

The message is very clear: yes, he moved to the Palatine, but no, he did not live like an ostentatious optimate.

What he did not do is vividly described by contemporary eye-witnesses like Sallust and Horace. The arrogant aristocrats of Rome were constantly building, demolishing, and rebuilding, joining properties together to create houses 'like palaces or whole cities', with columns of marble imported from Asia or Africa. The magnificence appropriate to public architecture was consciously applied to private dwellings, and the contrast with the traditional values of the republic was painfully clear:

> This is not what was prescribed by the auspices of Romulus and unshorn Cato and by the rule of the ancients.
>
> Their private wealth was small. Their public wealth was great. No portico laid out by the ten-foot rod caught the dense northern shade for private citizens,
>
> And laws commanded them not to despise the turf beneath their feet, but to beautify at common cost their towns and the temples of their gods with freshly-quarried stone.

Horace *Odes* 2.15.10–20 (trans. David West)

Horace's readers were well aware that 'the auspices of Romulus' had given Augustus his honorific name. But the young Caesar had made his point long before that.

Most of the grand houses of the optimate oligarchy became public property in November 43 BC, when the Triumvirs published their proscription list. All those who had conspired to murder Caesar, and those who had approved the deed, were named as public enemies, and their property was sold at auction to raise funds for the war of vengeance. It was probably at that time that the young Caesar acquired 'the house of Hortensius' on the Palatine: Quintus Hortensius was an ally of the assassins, and fought for Brutus at Philippi.

It took six years, and a hard-won victory over Sextus Pompey in Sicily, before the oligarchs were finally defeated. The civil wars were over, or so it seemed, and in 36 BC the young Caesar could turn his attention to the city of Rome:

> Victorious, Caesar returned to the city and announced that he was marking out for public use several houses which he had brought together by purchase through agents in order to give his own more space; and he promised to build a temple of Apollo and porticoes round it, a work that was constructed by him with remarkable munificence.

Velleius
Paterculus 2.81.3

> Also at that time [the People] resolved that a house should be given to him at public expense. For he made public the place on the Palatine which he had bought in order to build something, and consecrated it to Apollo after a thunderbolt had fallen on it.

Dio Cassius
49.15.5

While 'Commander Caesar' was away fighting the People's wars, those acting on his behalf had evidently bought up several adjacent Palatine houses, thus creating a substantial extended property. This property he now handed over to public ownership. In return, the grateful People gave him back one of the houses, presumably that of Hortensius, and the rest of the site was reserved for the Apollo temple and the magnificent portico that would surround it.

FIGURE 5. Western edge of the Palatine summit, during the early stages of Pietro Rosa's excavations in the 1860s: Tomei 1999.45 fig. 32. The grass-covered masonry in the background is the concrete core of the platform on which the Apollo temple stood, showing the proximity of the remains to the slope of the hill. Rosa's excavation is discussed at **8.1** below.

Fortunately, we know where the Apollo temple was. The remains of the concrete core of the rectangular podium on which it was built were uncovered in 1865 at the south-western edge of the hill, immediately above the slope overlooking the Circus Maximus. Although at first the podium was attributed to the temple of Jupiter Victor, which was also on the Palatine, the correct identification was made in 1910 and has never been doubted since.

Its hilltop site is best illustrated by the newly discovered circular domed chamber that was partly inserted into the slope at the bottom of the hill: about forty metres south-west of the temple podium on a horizontal plan, the chamber is more than thirty-one metres below it. The space needed for the temple and its porticoes was created by extending the summit level of the hill by means of an artificial platform, the substructure of which incorporated the masonry of all pre-existing buildings at the top of the slope at that point.

Fig. 5

Fig. 6

Fig. 7

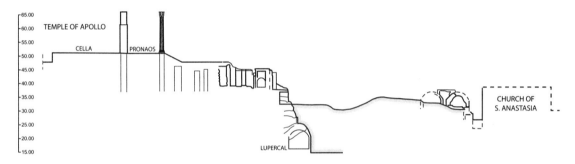

FIGURE 6. Section through the slope of the Palatine below the Apollo temple, by Irene Iacopi and Giovanna Tedone (redrawn). The identification of the constituent parts of the temple is conjectural, and I believe mistaken (**8.1** below). The chamber at the foot of the hill (so-called 'Lupercal') is at 16.23m above sea level; the platform on which the temple was built is at 47.60m.

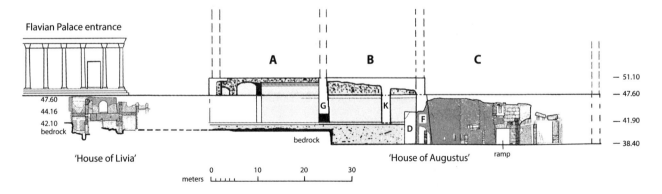

FIGURE 7. The Apollo temple and its platform (Claridge 2014.149 fig. 5). The 'summit level' of the hill is at 47.60 masl (see also fig. 60 below). A and B: the two masses of concrete that formed the core of the podium for the Apollo temple; G marks the robbed-out foundations of the entrance wall of the *cella*. C: the mass of concrete that supported the extended platform; at the far right are the remains, incorporated into the platform foundation, of the building identified by Carettoni as the house of Augustus.

FIGURE 8. The house below the Apollo temple platform (Hall 2014.173 fig. 93). For the layout of the temple, see on fig. 6 above.

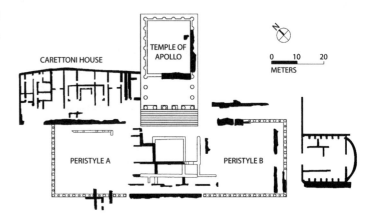

Understandably, there has been intense archaeological investigation of those lower areas, resulting in the identification of a very substantial house occupying about 140 metres of the upper slope at a level nine metres below that of the platform; it featured two matching peristyle courts and between them a sequence of rooms, still uncompleted at the time of the destruction, with wide doors offering a panoramic view to the south. 'Palace' is the word repeatedly used to describe it.

Fig. 8

This material evidence provides a perfect example of the triumph of public magnificence over private luxury, precise confirmation of what Velleius Paterculus and Dio Cassius say the young Caesar did in the thirties BC on behalf of the Roman People. What the archaeologists have discovered are the remains of one of the houses he bought up 'in order to build something', part of the residential area he 'marked out for public use'.

But that is not what the archaeologists themselves say. On the contrary, they insist that the splendid mansion that was destroyed to create the platform for the Apollo temple and its portico was built by the young Caesar himself. As they see it, it was literally a palace, *il palazzo di Ottaviano*, designed in deliberate imitation of Hellenistic monarchs. No evidence is offered, just a repeated rhetorical question:

Carandini 2010.176

Who else in Rome, at that time and at that address, could have allowed himself a building fit for a king, if not the quasi-monarch Octavian?

Coarelli 2012.378

Who else, even as a pure hypothesis, could have carried out a development on such a scale, in this vicinity, in these years?

Hall 2014.182

One wonders precisely who, in the 40s BCE, would have had the overweening confidence to begin work on such a prodigious residence in so exalted a location.

Some archaeologists take it as axiomatic that 'Octavian' was a despot wielding unlawful power, an autocratic megalomaniac.

One might pose a question in return. Who commanded the forces fighting the young Caesar in the civil wars of 42–36 BC? The answer, of course, is the optimate oligarchs, the men Sallust (at that very time) described as 'the powerful few', the arrogant aristocracy, forever building and rebuilding at enormous expense. It was *their* houses and villas that Horace likened to the palaces of Hellenistic kings; it was against *them*, the assassins of Caesar, that the Roman People had legally and constitutionally voted power to the Triumvirs; and it was *their* luxurious property that could now be demolished to make room for magnificent public projects like the Apollo temple and its porticoes. 'Commander Caesar' was not like them. As his biographer Suetonius succinctly put it, 'he disliked grand palaces'.

2.3 THE WRONG TRACK

Astonishing though it may seem, the archaeologists' idea of the historical context is totally mistaken. How could that have come about? The rest of this chapter tries to document the cumulative effect of a succession of particular misinterpretations.

Excavation of the level nine metres below the summit began in January 1958, in the area immediately north-west of the temple podium. Gianfilippo Carettoni soon uncovered the surprisingly well-preserved remains of a Roman house with extensive wall-painting surviving in two of the rooms. He knew, of course, the potential importance of this discovery. 'The exploration of this part of the Palatine is of great interest,' he wrote in 1960, 'since it involves the problem of identifying the temple of Apollo and the residence of the Emperor Augustus.' By 1963 he already thought it 'probable' that that residence was the very site he was excavating.

What made him think so was simply the layout of the house, with the main suite of rooms spacious and symmetrical, looking out on a peristyle court, and a smaller set of rooms near the entrance, opening off a separate corridor:

> The particular character of the building, its aspect of official premises together with private living space, cannot fail to call to mind the characteristics of Augustus' residence.

Carettoni 1966–7.67

He went into a little more detail in 1969, by which time he regarded the identification as certain:

Fig. 9

> The clear distinction between living quarters and rooms for public functions shows that the object was to keep the family deliberately apart from the area designed for public and official use.

FIGURE 9. Identifying 'the house of Augustus': Carettoni 1969.24 (redrawn). The site is terraced on two levels, with a vertical difference of 9m. The upper level was evidently entered from the street by the 'house of Livia'; the entrance to the lower level, from the lane that led down the side of the hill, was at the bottom left-hand corner. The rooms marked 'a'-'c' and 'o' are interpreted as 'rooms for public functions', those marked 'd'-'e' as a separate suite 'clearly meant to be the most private part of the house'.

Traces of a wooden staircase are visible on the back wall of the 'd' rooms (which is also the terracing wall); according to Carettoni, the staircase 'joined this suite to an upper floor and also probably to the terrace of the little portico (P)'. But what makes it 'probable'? Nine metres is a lot for a wooden staircase. In the absence of any other internal access from one terrace to the other, there is no good reason to think that the two levels were parts of the same house.

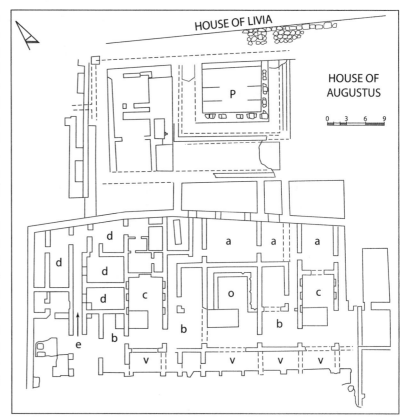

From what we know, this corresponds to the view of the house of Augustus, who lived according to Dio Cassius, 'in a modern house which was both public and private', while the simplicity of the private wing with 'rooms without marble or expensively paved floors' certainly befits a head of state who, according to Suetonius, was satisfied with a house 'scarcely fit for a private citizen'.

Carettoni 1969.24

Three separate arguments need to be disentangled here: the 'rooms for public functions', the supposed quotation from Dio Cassius, and the genuine quotations from Suetonius.

The rooms off the corridor by the entrance are small and unimpressive, much more like servants' quarters than the family's own living space. The other rooms are much more spacious, but still not the grand chambers that were thought necessary for the transaction of public business. For the latter we have the best possible contemporary evidence, the recommendations of an architect:

For aristocrats, who are required to be of service to the citizens by holding honours and magistracies, we must make lofty, regal forecourts, grand atria and peristyles, groves and spacious covered walks completed to a high standard of majesty;

also libraries and basilicas designed in a way comparable to the magnificence of public buildings, because in their houses both public deliberations and private judgements and decisions are frequently carried out.

Vitruvius 6.5.2

As we shall see in a later chapter (**8.3** below), Augustus did indeed provide such spaces, but not inside his own house: it was his private, not his public life that he wanted to differentiate from that of the Roman aristocracy. Looked at without prejudice, the layout of the house Carettoni excavated seems to be evidence for the difference between the family's accommodation and the service area, not between 'official premises' and private living space.

Carettoni's alleged quotation from Dio Cassius is simply baffling. It seems to be a garbled reference to what the historian said about Augustus' election as *pontifex maximus* in 12 BC:

> He did not accept an official residence, but since it was absolutely necessary that the *pontifex maximus* should reside in public, he made part of his own house public property.

Dio Cassius
54.27.3

Dio also reported the rebuilding of the house after a fire in AD 3:

> When Augustus [re]built his house he made it all public property, either because of the contribution made by the People [to the cost] or because he was *pontifex maximus*, so that he might live in premises that were simultaneously private and public.

Dio Cassius
55.12a.5

But these were changes in legal ownership, nothing to do with the original design of the house.

Carettoni's Suetonius quotations are at least accurate, though the second refers to Augustus' furniture, not the house itself. But this evidence of modest living would become seriously problematic as the further progress of his excavation revealed the full extent and 'palatial' nature of the property. It is to Carettoni's credit that he never engaged in the kind of evasive special pleading that came to be required; but he never explained the contradiction either.

A momentous discovery in 1970 seemed to make all such doubts irrelevant. Exploration of the range of rooms on the south-east side of the peristyle court revealed that one of them gave access to a broad ramp leading upwards at an angle of about 12 degrees from the horizontal. Since the platform on which the Apollo temple stood was nine metres directly above, Carettoni was in no doubt about the ramp's purpose:

Fig. 10

> Given Augustus' particular devotion to Apollo, one can understand why there was at first a direct communication route between the emperor's living quarters and the terrace of the temple.

Carettoni 1983.9

FIGURE 10. The 'house of Augustus' and the ramp: Zanker 1988.52 fig. 40 (after Carettoni 1983.8). A: 'upper terrace', accessible from the street next to the 'house of Livia'. B: 'lower terrace', accessible from the stepped street to the left ('Scalae Caci'). R: ramp. Accurate spot heights are now available (Tomei 2014b.45 fig. 25): A is at 47.71 masl, about the same level as the platform on which the Apollo temple was built (Fig. 7 above); B is at 38.65 masl, which means that the ramp would have to rise nearly thirty feet from the peristyle at B level to reach the temple precinct.

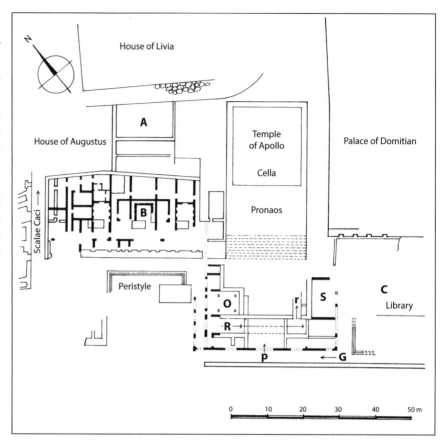

Why only at first? Because Carettoni knew that the ramp had a short life; it was interrupted by the foundations of a subsequent building scheme and taken out of use.

That inconvenient detail did not prevent Paul Zanker, the world's leading authority on Roman art and architecture, from using the idea of 'house and temple as a unit' as evidence of the future Augustus' 'autocratic self-presentation':

> The victor of Actium lived not just near, but by and with his guardian deity . . . .
> Hardly anyone has thought about this before, and asked what precedents there
> could be for this architectural concept that bound temple and residence together.
> The answer is obvious: Hellenistic royal palaces.

Zanker 1983.23–4

Once repeated in Zanker's great book *Augustus und die Macht der Bilder* (1987), translated as *The Power of Images in the Age of Augustus* (1988), this idea became an accepted part of mainstream scholarly opinion.

Zanker offered three supporting examples, all exactly contemporary with the Apollo temple, for his notion of Augustus as a quasi-monarch. They were the

Mausoleum, the temple of Divus Julius, and the Pantheon. These were indeed dynastic monuments—but the whole point about the Caesars, father and son, was that their private expenditure was modest and their public expenditure was colossal. These buildings were demonstrations of public magnificence, not private luxury. The Mausoleum, for instance, was much more than just a family tomb:

> He had built this in his sixth consulship [28 BC], between the Via Flaminia and the Tiber bank, having already made the groves and covered walks that surrounded it public property for the People's use.

Suetonius *Diuus Augustus* 100.4

> It is a great mound near the river on a high podium of white marble, thickly shaded all the way up with evergreen trees. On top there is a bronze statue of Caesar Augustus; beneath the mound are the tombs of himself, his family and friends, and behind it there is a large grove that contains wonderful covered walks.

Strabo 5.3.8 (C236)

'Groves and covered walks' (*siluae et ambulationes*) were exactly what Vitruvius recommended for a grand aristocratic house. Augustus made them available to everyone.

Paul Zanker knew perfectly well, and clearly stated, that the future Augustus' house was 'relatively modest'; Suetonius said so, and Carettoni's early results seemed to confirm it. Where he went wrong was in accepting Carettoni's idea of the purpose of the ramp, without also taking into account Carettoni's knowledge that the ramp had very soon been put out of use. Zanker assumed that the house-temple connection was what defined the house of Augustus, and the very weight of his authority caused the archaeologists themselves to make that assumption too.

In her article for the authoritative *Lexicon topographicum urbis Romae* (1995), Irene Iacopi put it like this:

> The connection existing between the *domus* and the temple building, something unique to the Palatine complex—even though precedents for it have been suggested in the Pergamene palaces of the Attalids connected to the *temenos* of the temple of Athena (Zanker)— provides evidence for the construction context of the two buildings; besides, the ancient authors too clearly attest that they were contemporary.

Iacopi 1995.48

This passage was closely based on Carettoni's own resumé, then still unpublished. However, Iacopi did not mention that 'the ramp that provided the direct connection between the house and the cult site' was only in use for a very short time.

Worse was to come. Ten years later, in a thorough re-examination of the whole archaeological context, Iacopi and her co-author Giovanna Tedone demonstrated that the two buildings were not contemporary after all. Not only that, but the ramp never led to the temple area anyway:

It is not, in fact, thought that this access [the ramp] could have been relevant to the temple, (a) because of the lack of space necessary for the insertion of a stair or ramp in the direction of the temple, considering the substantial difference in level; (b) because of the inevitable interference that would have resulted between the parts reserved for the occupants of the house and the temple areas intended for public use; and (c) because, again for lack of space, an important element of the cult complex, the *temenos*, would have been reduced.

Iacopi and Tedone
2006.366–7

The ramp was simply a structural element joining upper and lower levels within the unfinished 'palatial' house that was destroyed for the construction of the platform for the temple. The key argument for the identification of the house at the nine-metre level with the house of Augustus had now evaporated.

It made no difference. Iacopi and Tedone continued to treat the identification as a fact, and so the '*palazzo di Ottaviano*' was born—a completely unattested and inherently improbable luxury dwelling created for his own use by the young Caesar in the early thirties BC and then destroyed before completion by the young Caesar himself, as part of the Apollo temple project. This chimerical idea has now been elaborated in imaginative detail by Andrea Carandini and Daniela Bruno in their book *La casa di Augusto dai 'Lupercalia' al Natale* (2008), and subsequently enshrined in the monumental *Atlas of Ancient Rome* by Carandini and Paolo Carafa (2012 and 2017).

It is a remarkable story of misinterpretation, overconfidence, and wishful thinking, and it all began when a cautious, scrupulous archaeologist made an uncharacteristic historical guess, that the house he was excavating was that of Augustus himself.

Half a century later, the chief proponent of the '*palazzo di Ottaviano*' is a very different sort of archaeologist. For Andrea Carandini, making historical guesses is what archaeology is all about:

> Ancient realities generally reach us in an incomplete and discontinuous form, but for that very reason reconstructions must aim at rediscovering the lost totality, avoiding the scepticisms of hyper-critics who wouldn't want to reconstruct anything because of a vow of chastity they have made to 'the Data'. The fillings of gaps should not be concealed, in fact they must be illustrated, demonstrating by graphic means the judgement of probability that the author has made about them. There is no 'art of knowing' and 'art of not knowing', as pusillanimous empiricists think.

Carandini
2008.148

The *ars nesciendi* (art of not knowing) is indeed basic to the empirical method, and it applies very precisely to the ownership of the 'palatial' house that was still under construction when the young Caesar destroyed it in order to create the public magnificence of the Apollo temple and its porticoes.

Carandini is contemptuous of empirical method, and finds it intolerable merely to attribute the house to one of the optimate grandees. For him, that makes it 'nobody's house'. As for the literary sources, 'they are scanty, and show just selected moments of a much more connected and surprising history, which only a professional archaeology is qualified to uncover'. By 'professional' he means an archaeology unfettered by rules of empirical enquiry that matter only to 'traditional classicists locked into an insufferably snobbish scepticism'.

I leave it to the reader's judgement whether the argument presented thus far deserves that description. To understand Augustus and the Roman People we have to collect all the evidence we can find, and take seriously what it tells us. Andrea Carandini is right to describe his method as 'free thinking' (*libero pensiero*); it is freedom to ignore the evidence, freedom from historical responsibility. In our search for the house of Augustus it offers only a route to avoid.

3

THE PALACE

Nowadays visitors to the Palatine have to reach it via the Roman Forum. Once through the turnstile by the Forum ticket office, we walk down the ramp that brings us to the ground level of Augustus' time, about 30 feet below the modern city's street-level.

Fig. 11

Directly in front of us are the ruins of two buildings. To the right is the concrete core of the podium on which stood the temple of Divus Iulius, the deified Caesar, looking out across the Forum piazza to the Capitol; to the left, the remains of the archaic *regia* ('king's house'), as rebuilt in Augustus' time. Beyond, we can see the marble columns of the round temple of Vesta, a modern reconstruction on foundations uncovered in the 1880s. Behind Vesta rise the substructions of later imperial buildings on the steep north side of the Palatine.

The ancient sources regularly describe the Divus Iulius temple as 'in the Forum' (*in foro*); the *regia*, however, was 'at the foot of the Palatine at the edge of

FIGURE 11. The Forum and modern access to the Palatine.

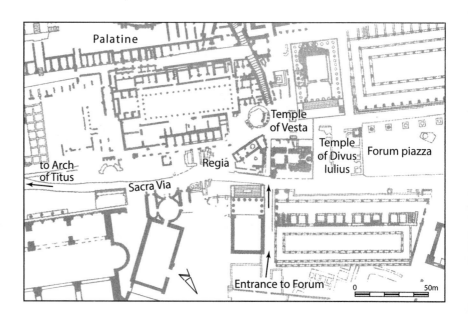

the Roman Forum', and the Vesta temple, with which it was always associated, is similarly described as 'close to the Forum', but never *in foro*.

Where we are standing is, in fact, the boundary between two zones of the ancient city. If we turned right we would enter the Forum piazza, created in the valley between the Palatine and the Capitol. For the Palatine itself we must turn left, on the ancient street that at this point starts to rise towards the ridge where the Arch of Titus stands. A right turn at the Arch will bring us up to the summit of the hill. At most stages of the city's history, thanks to the lie of the land, that ridge has been the main access route to the Palatine, either from the 'valley of the Forum' to the west, or from the 'valley of the Colosseum' to the east.

3.1 NERO'S URBAN LANDSCAPE

What we see around us is the result of the most important event in the history of the Palatine, the great fire of Rome in July of AD 64. Fortunately, what happened on that occasion is very well attested:

> It began in the part of the Circus [Maximus] that adjoins the Palatine and Caelian hills, among shops containing flammable merchandise; a powerful fire right from the start, it was stirred up by the wind and immediately took hold of the whole length of the Circus. With no mansions or temples surrounded by protecting walls, or anything else in its way to hinder it, the advancing blaze spread through the low-lying area first, then surged up to the heights and down again, devastating everything. The speed of the disaster outran all resistance, and the narrow winding streets and irregular neighbourhoods, typical of old Rome, made the city defenceless.

Tacitus *Annals*
15.38.2–3

The Palatine was not yet threatened, but it soon would be. Tacitus goes on:

> Nero was staying at Antium at the time. He didn't come back to the city until the fire was approaching the property with which he had linked up the Palatine with the Gardens of Maecenas. Even so, it couldn't be stopped from engulfing both the Palatine and the property, and everything else around.

Tacitus *Annals*
15.39.1

There is a tricky problem of translation here, which it is important to get right.

The word I translate as 'the property' in the two final sentences is *domus*. That ought to mean 'the house', but since the Gardens of Maecenas were on the Esquiline, about eight hundred metres from the nearest part of the Palatine, it clearly cannot refer to a single building. The true sense is indicated by Tacitus' use of the verb *continuare* ('link up'), which is the usual term for extending one's house or land by acquiring those adjacent. Suetonius too uses *domus* in the context of Nero's project:

Suetonius
Nero 31.1

> He made a *domus* from the Palatine as far as the Esquiline, which he called first the 'passage house' and then, when it was restored after being destroyed by the fire, the 'golden house'.

A little earlier, Josephus had made a point of explaining the usage in his narrative of the killing of Gaius 'Caligula' on the Palatine in AD 41:

Josephus *Jewish Antiquities* 19.117

> [The assassins] went by other streets, and reached the house of Germanicus, father of Gaius whom they had just killed, which was adjacent. This was because the residence, though a unity, was made up severally of the buildings belonging to each one of those who had been born in the imperial power, named after those who had built them or even begun building any of the parts.

Both Gaius and Nero were extravagant property developers, and the effect of their linking up sequences of adjacent houses was described by one eye-witness as 'encircling the whole city'. But none of it survived the fire. As Dio Cassius emphatically states, 'the Palatine hill was destroyed in its entirety'.

The rebuilt Palatine would look very different. Nero's architects were not interested in recreating the old city. On the contrary, they were going to straighten out those 'irregular neighbourhoods' and widen those 'narrow winding streets', limiting the height of construction and leaving open spaces with porticoes to protect the buildings. There had certainly been narrow streets on the Palatine, and some of the houses they served had belonged to Roman senators; but now, with the entire hill suddenly available, Nero could redevelop it to suit himself alone.

Fig. 12

The grand scale of the restructured Neronian Palatine is best seen from the air. Four huge rectangular features are still clearly visible after nearly two thousand years. The first is a platform about 100 metres by 145 metres in size, built out on substructures from the ridge towards the eastern valley. Its purpose may be inferred from Suetonius' description of the 'golden house':

Suetonius
Nero 31.1

> Let this be enough evidence for its size and splendour: the forecourt was big enough for a colossal statue of Nero himself, 120 feet high, to stand in it.

Since other sources tell us that the colossus was 'on the Sacra Via', and that the Sacra Via ran from the Forum to the Esquiline, it is clear that the platform on the ridge was created to support the hugely grandiose forecourt of Nero's hugely grandiose extended property.

The old Sacra Via was realigned as a broad, straight avenue leading directly up from the Forum to the centre of the platform, with the colossus dominating

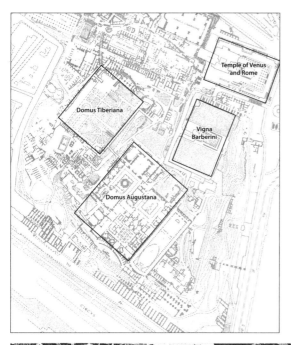

FIGURE 12. The footprint of Nero's Palatine, as visible on an air photograph of about 1932, looking from south-west to north-east. The 'temple of Venus and Rome' platform, identifiable by the campanile of S. Francesca Romana, is immediately to the right of the three great vaults of the Basilica of Maxentius. © ICCD Aerofototeca Nazionale: Fondo A.M., foglio 150, negativo 87623.

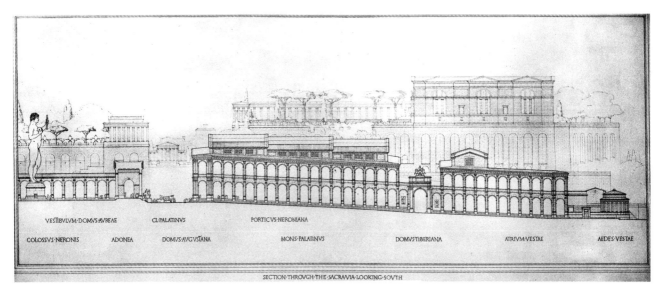

FIGURE 13. The approach to Nero's forecourt: 'Section through the Sacra Via looking south', reconstruction drawing by Albert G. Glay (Van Deman 1925, plate 64), Photographic Archive, American Academy in Rome. To the right, the temple of Vesta just outside the Forum piazza; to the left, the forecourt and colossal statue; in the background, the northern part of the Palatine, represented as it appeared after Hadrian's extension of the Domus Tiberiana.

Fig. 13

the view. Two right angle turns took the public road round the platform on the north side, where the grand forecourt opened on the right for privileged visitors to enter the imperial domain. Once through the forecourt, they could turn left, down the slope to the ornamental lake and gardens in the valley between the Esquiline and the Caelian, or continue straight ahead southwards to the Palatine. Now, for the first time in Roman history, the Sacra Via became the route from the Forum to the Palatine; in effect, Nero had made the whole ridge part of the hill.

Fig. 12

Of the other Neronian rectangles, the one on the summit plateau of the Palatine was the main palace building. Rebuilt on the same layout by Domitian twenty years later (probably to make it more secure), it is generally known nowadays as 'the Flavian palace', or even *domus Flavia*, as if that were its Roman name. In fact, its Roman name was *domus Augustana*.

Modern scholarship wants this to mean 'the emperor's residence'. As the standard history of Roman architecture puts it,

> the legal and spatial entity of the palace, considered in its official representative function, can only be the *domus August(i)ana*, since it is under that name that it has gone through the centuries: whatever the dynasty, it remained the seat of the *Augusti*.

Gros 2001.252

I think that is a misreading. The use of *domus* (or *aedes*) with the adjectival form of a proper name was a common Latin idiom for 'the house where X lived'. Besides, the post-Neronian sources also refer frequently to a *domus Tiberiana* on the Palatine. The natural inference is that two of the constituent parts of Nero's palace complex were named from where his great-great-grandfather and his great-grandfather had lived, respectively, 'the house of Augustus' and 'the house of Tiberius'.

The *domus Tiberiana* is now securely identified as the rectangular platform at the north-west corner of the Palatine. It was, and is, a huge structure, originally 135 by 120 metres (later extended), standing six metres high even on the summit plateau and up to seventeen metres over the north-west slope of the hill. And the fourth Neronian rectangle was a similar platform of similar size, 160 metres by 110 metres, with equally towering substructions over the north-east slope; evidently known as 'the court of Adonis', it was probably a garden terrace with apartments and offices at the lower levels along the sides. The purpose of both these enormous developments was to extend the horizontal space available at the summit level of the hill, and what made them possible was a combination of two things: the devastation caused by the fire, and Nero's spectacularly extravagant self-indulgence.

Fig. 12

Nero was away in Greece while all the reconstruction work was going on. When he returned early in AD 68, he is reported to have said, 'At last I can start to live like a human being'. About six months later the Praetorian Guard decided he wasn't worth protecting, the Senate declared him a public enemy, and the man who wanted Rome to be 'Neropolis' was dead by his own hand.

3.2 THE EMPEROR AND ROME

Nero sealed his own fate by disregarding the fundamental distinction, so well understood by Augustus, between public magnificence and private luxury (**2.2** above). The Roman People resented the extension of his property across to the Esquiline: 'Rome,' they said, 'is becoming just one house.' They even believed (however unjustly) that Nero had started the great fire himself, in order to create the space he wanted.

The civil wars that followed Nero's fall brought Vespasian to power, a man whose old-fashioned frugality put him at the opposite extreme from Nero. Vespasian and his elder son Titus took care to return the extended part of the property to public use, by building a huge new amphitheatre (what we call the Colosseum) and a bath complex. Martial makes it clear what was at stake:

> Here, where the awe-inspiring mass of the amphitheatre rises in the sight of all,
> Nero's ornamental lake once was. Here, where we admire the baths (a speedy gift),

Martial *De spectaculis* 2.5–8, 11–12

his haughty estate had robbed the poor of their homes. . . . Rome has been restored to herself, and under your protection, Caesar, the People now enjoy what was once their master's.

The colossal statue of Nero remained, but it was now remodelled as an effigy of the Sun-god.

Nero's grand forecourt had lost its *raison d'être* when the ridge and the valley beyond were reclaimed as public space. But the platform could not be used for other purposes while the huge statue was still standing there. A solution was only found two generations later, when Hadrian and his architect Decrianus, using twenty-four elephants, managed to move the statue, still upright, and thus free the site for a spectacular double temple of the emperor's own design. It was dedicated in AD 131 to the goddesses Venus and Roma, or as Hadrian's coin issues named them, Venus the Fortunate and Rome the Eternal.

It was two temples back to back. Venus looked east, to faraway Mount Ida where she had given birth to Aeneas, the ancestor of the Romans. Roma herself looked west, down the broad avenue of Nero's Sacra Via to the Roman Forum; her temple came to be known as 'the temple of the City', and just in front of it the street—now public again—led up to the Palatine, where the city had been founded.

Hadrian made a great point of that. His coinage also celebrated Romulus the Founder, and he instituted a new festival on 21 April, the supposed date of the foundation. That day, traditionally called *Parilia*, had always been sacred to the shepherds' goddess Pales, after whom the Palatine was named. From now on, it would provide the Roman People with a noisy annual party in honour of their ancient city. Our evidence for that comes from a very unexpected source.

Some time around AD 200, a learned Greek called Athenaeus, from Naucratis in Egypt, wrote a vast fifteen-volume account of a dinner party supposedly held at the town house of his patron Larensis, a wealthy Roman of equestrian rank. The guests, Greeks and hyper-Hellenized Romans, were all experts in one branch of learning or another, and the whole point of the work was to show off virtuosic literary erudition, on all subjects, but particularly on food. At one point in Book Eight, a detailed discussion of fish has just been diverted on to the ancient history of the city of Rhodes:

While many such observations were still being made, throughout the city sounds could be heard—the booming of pipes, the clash of cymbals, the beating of drums—accompanied by song. It happened to be the festival called in the old time *Parilia*, now 'Rome's day', the day when the temple of the goddess of the city was founded by that wholly admirable and most cultured emperor Hadrian, the special day for all inhabitants of Rome and visitors to the city.

Athenaeus *Deipnosophistae* 8.361e–f

'What's that noise?' asks Ulpianus, the most assertive of the diners, quoting some appropriate lines of Homer. When someone replies 'The whole city's having a ball for the goddess', Ulpianus deplores such colloquial language, and the discussion moves off in a different direction. (Nobody suggests they go out and join the fun.)

Like Vespasian's Colosseum, Hadrian's 'temple of the City' was—and in its ruined state, still is—a gigantic monument to the traditional ideal of public munificence. The dominating site on the ridge, no longer 'the fierce tyrant's hateful hall', was now a glorious symbol of what all Romans had in common. The Palatine itself remained firmly in the emperor's possession. Indeed, the emperor's possession was now what defined it, as a third-century historian helpfully explains:

Fig. 12

> The royal residence is called 'Palatium', not because it was ever decided that this should be so, but because the emperor lives on the Palatium and has his headquarters there. . . . For this reason, if the emperor resides anywhere else, his stopping-place receives the name of 'Palatium'.

Dio Cassius 53.16.5–6 (trans. Fergus Millar)

That, of course, is the origin of the modern word 'palace'.

Hadrian's building programme included an extension of the *domus Tiberiana* platform to the north, aligning it with the Neronian Sacra Via and creating the great cliff of brickwork, thirty-five metres high, that looms over the Forum even today. The Palatine looked like a fortress or citadel, and in a way that is what it was. The emperor was *imperator*, 'the commander', rarely seen without a military escort. When Dio Cassius described the Palatine as his headquarters, he meant it in a military sense. There was always a cohort of the Praetorian Guard on duty there, a reassurance or a threat to ordinary citizens.

Throughout the literature of the Roman Empire we find poets and orators describing what an intimidating place the Palatine *used* to be, so different from the welcoming palace of the *present* emperor! Discounting the flattery, it is easy to see what the norm must have been. 'Uneasy' was the word a more honest poet chose to describe the Palatine. Certainly its architecture was designed to be overpowering. Domitian's *domus Augustana* was so tall that its roof was the first to catch the light of the rising sun; awestruck poets described it as reaching through the clouds to the vault of heaven itself. The audience chamber was over 100 feet high from floor to ceiling, as was the banqueting hall, which was called 'Jupiter's dining-room' (*cenatio Iouis*).

Fig. 14

The emperor on the Palatine was like Jupiter on Olympus. The analogy was so compelling that it outlasted the very conditions that made sense of it. Once again literary evidence provides a vivid insight, but it comes now from a Rome already Christianised, where all-powerful emperors were nothing but a memory.

FIGURE 14. The imperial palace from the south-west, conjectural reconstruction by Alan Sorrell (Sorrell and Birley 1970.38–9). The view shows the rear part of the *domus Augustana*, including its third-century extension eastward (Hoffmann and Wulf 2004), overlooking the Circus Maximus.

In AD 402, the emperor Honorius had lost control of Italy. With the north in the power of Alaric's Goths, he took refuge in Ravenna, protected by marshes with the sea as an escape route. When a short-lived victory provided a respite, Honorius made a symbolic visit to Rome to receive his sixth consulship in the ancient capital, a city he had seen only once before, when he was five years old. Celebrating the occasion on the Palatine in January 404 was the poet Claudian, an experienced panegyrist, who began by telling his distinguished audience about a dream he had had:

Claudian *De sexto consulatu* pref.11–16

> I seemed to be presenting my songs before the feet of supreme Jupiter in the centre of the citadel of the starry sky, and in my happy dream the gods and the sacred company all around were applauding my words.

He dreamed he was singing of Jupiter's victory over the monstrous giants Enceladus and Typhoeus, and his joyful return to heaven after the war.

> Behold, it is true! No illusion has deceived me, nor has the false gate sent a fallacious dream. Here is the emperor, here is the summit of the world, the equal of Olympus! Here are the gods, an awe-inspiring audience, just as I remember!

Nothing greater could sleep have invented. The lofty palace has provided the poet with an assembly to match heaven itself.

Claudian *De sexto consulatu* pref. 21–6

It was the buildings themselves, the towering architecture, that made this fantasy intelligible.

Claudian's main performance referred constantly to the scene of its own delivery, the Palatine itself. What better omen could there be, he asked, than the emperor on high at his own Latin palace, like a star of power at the zenith of the Zodiac?

See, Mount Palatine has gained in reverence, exults that a god resides there, spreads wide throughout the suppliant peoples oracles more powerful than Delphi, and bids its laurels grow green again for military standards. This is certain: nowhere else has ever been a fitter home for the rulers of the world. On no other hill does power more measure itself and feel the grandeur of supreme authority. The palace raises its pinnacle above the lowly *rostra* [where Honorius had just addressed the Roman People], and sees so many temples all around, encircling it with such a guard of gods!

Claudian *De sexto consulatu* 35–44

The poet went on to present the goddess Roma, 'coming forth from her high sanctuary' (Hadrian's temple) to summon Honorius to her own Palatine, where Hadrian himself had dwelt. She also mentioned Nerva, the Antonines, and the Severi, but not Constantine or any other Christian emperor. One wonders what Pope Innocentius, the forty-first successor of St Peter, thought about that.

Of course it was all a gross anachronism. Six years later Alaric's Goths would be plundering the Palatine, and in 455 Gaiseric's Vandals would be plundering it again. The great buildings still stood, but the power they symbolised had passed away.

3.3 DECAY AND REDISCOVERY

More than any other people we know of in the world, the Romans love their city. They take great trouble to protect and preserve their whole heritage, so that none of Rome's ancient splendour may be lost. Even when they were under barbarian rule for a long time, they preserved the buildings of the city and most of their decorative features, which thanks to the excellence of their construction were able to withstand such a long period of neglect.

Procopius *Wars* 8.22.5–6

This Byzantine historian knew what he was talking about: he was in Rome in 537–8 during Justinian's war of reconquest. Prominent among the preserved buildings was the palace on the Palatine, which for the next two centuries resumed its function as an imperial headquarters and a symbol of sovereignty. It now contained a chapel, appropriately dedicated to a saint called Caesarius, where images of the reigning emperor and empress were displayed.

Archaeology, however, complicates the picture. Excavation in the last fifty years has revealed that from the fifth century onward parts of the Palatine became derelict, fit only for dumping rubbish and burying the dead. Old grandeur survived amid modern squalor. The Romans' love of their city now expressed itself in different ways: about AD 630 the emperor Heraclius gave the Roman Church permission to remove the bronze tiles from 'the so-called temple of the City' and use them on St Peter's basilica. Hadrian's great temple would remain unroofed.

The palace itself survived another loss of imperial power, as the Byzantine empire left the West to look after itself. Even in the eleventh century, when 'the emperor' meant the man on Charlemagne's throne, not Constantine's, the Palatine was still his base in Rome, as we know from two rescripts of Otto III dated AD 1000 from 'the Palatine monastery' (evidently that of St Caesarius). How much of the original structure was still inhabitable, no one knows.

Fast forward two more centuries, and the Palatine is already a tourist site. Our next witness is Master Gregory, an Englishman who went to Rome on ecclesiastical business probably about 1230, and wrote an account of the wonderful remains of the ancient city that he saw there, 'built either by magical art or by human labour'.

> I shall not omit the palace of the deified Augustus. This most ample dwelling was particularly excellent, matching the excellence of its founder, Augustus. However, the building, being wholly of marble, has provided valuable material, and plenty of it, for building the churches that are in Rome. Since so little is left of it, let this brief account suffice.

Magister Gregorius Narratio 17

Since Gregory goes on to describe the nearby aqueduct arches, what he took to be Augustus' residence was evidently the Severan extension of the palace at the south-east corner of the Palatine. The true *domus Augustana*, the main palace building on the summit of the hill, is referred to a few paragraphs later:

Fig. 12

> Who could describe the palace of the sixty emperors? Although it is largely ruined, they say that all the Romans of our own time cannot dismantle what still remains of it, so substantial is its totality.

Magister Gregorius Narratio 20

Gregory did not have a high opinion of the Romans of his own time, and was obviously well aware of their use of the ancient buildings as a quarry for marble and other reusable stone.

Petrarch took the same dim view a century later. 'Nowhere,' he wrote, 'is Rome less known than in Rome itself.' But he meant *classical* Rome, and how many people now cared about that? There is no reason to suppose that the Romans of the fourteenth century were any less proud of their city and its buildings than those of the sixth century had been when Procopius was there. It's just that the buildings were very different. Throughout the thousand-year history of papal Rome it was obvious to the great majority of people that the fabric of the pagan past was valuable only in so far as it provided the material for constructing magnificent churches.

Procopius would not have recognised the city Petrarch knew. It was much smaller, mainly confined to the low ground within the bend of the Tiber, and with two-thirds of the area inside the Roman walls almost unpopulated:

Fig. 15

> To the east, south and north a wasteland extended to the walls, where formerly tenement houses had stood in popular quarters and great mansions had risen in the greenbelt. The contrast between the *abitato* and the *disabitato*, as the sixteenth century called them, had become apparent. Starting from the fifth century, and progressively ever more clearly marked, it persisted until the late nineteenth century: a large expanse of vineyards, fields, and ruins, interspersed with small settlements and a few farms surrounding a small densely populated nucleus.

Krautheimer
1980.68

The Palatine was part of the *disabitato*, not only quarried but mined as well, with tunnels dug horizontally from the side slopes in search of stone blocks even from the foundations of the Roman buildings.

On the north side of the hill, the rectangular platforms provided ready-made terraces for gardens and vineyards. Elsewhere, what was left above ground was an overgrown wilderness of brick and concrete, the chaotic remains of walls and substructures too solid to be broken up and reused. Once again, we can see it through the eyes of an English visitor.

Fig. 16

Lord Byron was in Rome in 1817. Thinking of Rome as 'the mother of dead empires', he described the Palatine appropriately at dusk, as owls hooted in the fading light:

> Cypress and ivy, weed and wallflower grown
> Matted and massed together, hillocks heaped
> On what were chambers, arch crushed, column strown
> In fragments, choked-up vaults, and frescoes steeped
> In subterranean damps, where the owl peeped,
> Deeming it midnight: – Temples, baths, or halls?
> Pronounce who can; for all that Learning reaped
> From her research hath been, that these are walls.
> Behold the Imperial Mount! 'tis thus the mighty falls.

Byron, *Childe Harold's Pilgrimage* 4.107

He added a footnote to repeat the point about scholarly ignorance:

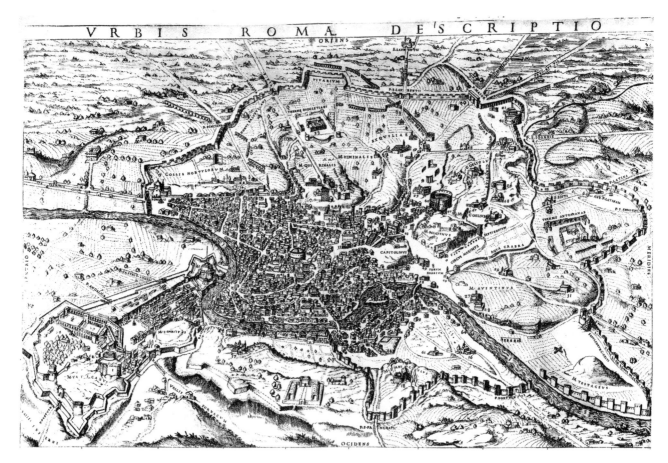

FIGURE 15. Plan of Rome by Mario Cartaro, 1575: Biblioteca di Archeologia e Storia dell'Arte, Rome (Roma X.650). North is to the left; the Palatine, with its standing ruins, is visible below the Colosseum.

> The Palatine is one mass of ruins, particularly on the side towards the Circus Maximus. The very soil is formed of crumbled brickwork. Nothing has been told— nothing can be told—to satisfy the belief of any but the Roman antiquary.

So forget real history, just think of the vanity of ambition and the passing of empires. 'Where are its golden roofs? Where those who dared to build?'

It wasn't just the Romans he had in mind. Napoleon had been crowned as emperor by the Pope, and then as king of Italy as well. And where was he now? St Helena. Dying young, Byron was spared the knowledge that another Napoleon would crush the Roman republic of 1849, garrison Rome to prop up papal rule, and reimpose the French Empire.

Unlike the dismissively rhapsodic English poet, His Majesty the Emperor Napoleon III took real history very seriously, and understood what

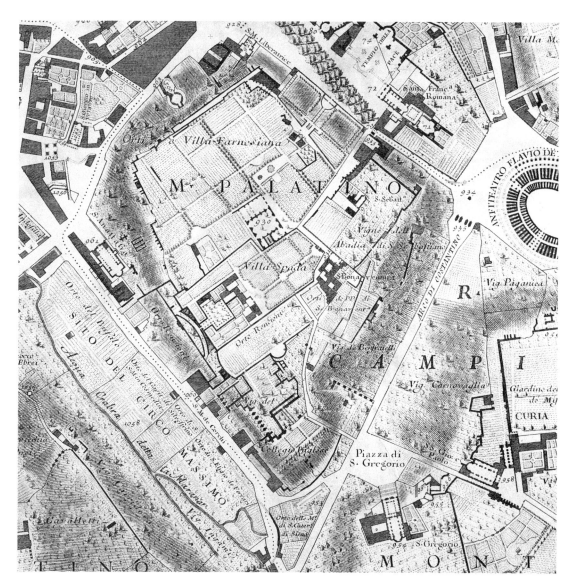

FIGURE 16. The Palatine, in Giambattista Nolli's *Nuova pianta di Roma*, 1748: British School at Rome Library. The Farnese gardens ('Villa Farnesiana') exploited the platform of the *domus Tiberiana* (Fig. 12).

archaeology could contribute to it. In 1861 he purchased the Farnese gardens on the Palatine, and put Pietro Rosa in charge of an ambitious programme of excavation.

Fig. 16

Rosa went to work energetically, making sure as he did so that the site would be accessible to the public; paths and steps were provided, with helpful signage, and there was even electric light in the underground galleries. The effect was greatly appreciated:

Boissier
1880.47 (trans.
D. Havelock
Fisher)

This hill, formerly occupied by the villas of great lords and the gardens of monasteries, where nobody might penetrate, has become one of the most interesting walks of Rome. I do not believe there is a spot where recollections of the past so crowd upon the memory, and where one more lives in mid-Antiquity. It must, however, be owned that this Antiquity was only given back to us in a very sorry plight, and persons allowing themselves to be beguiled by the tablet placed above the entrance to the Farnese Gardens, and believing that they were really going to find the 'Palace of the Caesars' again, would run the risk of being greatly surprised on seeing what really remains of it. There are only a few ruins left, and, in order to see it such as it was, we must make a great effort of the imagination.

It was now a suitable place of resort for characters in Henry James:

Roderick Hudson (1875) ch. xviii

There came a morning that they spent among the ruins of the Palatine, that sunny chaos of rich decay and irrelevant renewal, of scattered and overtangled fragments, half excavated and half identified, known as the Palace of the Caesars. Nothing in Rome is more interesting than this confused and crumbling garden, where you stumble at every step on the disinterred bones of the past . . . and where in the spring-time you may sit on a Latin inscription in the shade of a flowering almond and admire the composition of the Campagna.

In those days you could still see open country from the Palatine.

And now it was under new ownership. In three tumultuous weeks in September 1870, the Prussians defeated the French at Sedan, the Second French Empire was abolished, and the forces of the kingdom of united Italy marched into Rome. In December of that year the exiled Napoleon III sold the gardens to the new government in Rome for 650,000 lire.

The Italian state was much more enthusiastic about archaeology than the papal one had been, but at first its efforts were mainly concentrated on the Forum. Between 1871 and 1885, a series of campaigns by Rosa, Giuseppe Fiorelli, and Rodolfo Lanciani uncovered the full width of the Forum piazza and the whole of the slope up to the Arch of Titus, eventually linking up with Rosa's Palatine to create a unified archaeological site.

Fig. 17

These excavations revealed, in its late-imperial form, the broad avenue of the Neronian Sacra Via. The remains of it were removed by Giacomo Boni in 1899 in order to expose the paving, two metres below, of an earlier street on a different alignment. That caused some controversy—'the queen of streets' destroyed to reveal 'a narrow, crooked lane'—and in fact it is one of the reasons why modern tourists find that part of the site so confusing. We walk up the slope on paving of the time of Augustus, and on either side the grand late-imperial buildings have their foundations exposed. The street the Basilica of Maxentius opened on to was above our heads.

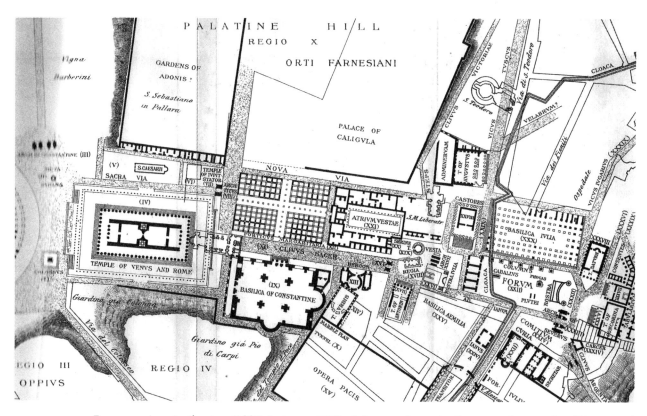

FIGURE 17. Lanciani's plan (1897, facing p. 190) of the area from the Forum to the temple of Venus and Rome (Fig. 12), reconstructed in the light of the new excavations; south is at the top, and the Colosseum is just off the plan to the left. The Neronian Sacra Via is marked as 'Clivus Sacer', a phrase found in Martial (1.70.5); Lanciani wrongly believed that the Sacra Via passed south of the Venus and Rome temple, and identified the Hadrianic extension of the *domus Tiberiana* platform as the 'palace of Caligula'.

As for the Palatine itself, there was one part of the imperial-palace site to which Pietro Rosa had not had access. The one-time Villa Spada, rebuilt in the 1820s in exuberant neo-Gothic style by a wealthy Scotsman called Charles Mills, was acquired in 1856 as a convent for the Sisters of the Visitation, and extended with a new wing, of more sober appearance, in 1868. For Rosa and Lanciani, this was the site of the house of Augustus.

At the turn of the century the Villa Mills was still there, blocking further exploration. The nuns left in 1909, but it was only in 1926 that the old Gothic pile was demolished and the new wing converted into the Palatine Museum. Four years of excavation by Alfonso Bartoli effectively created the site that tourists have visited ever since.

Not all of them have appreciated the archaeologists' efforts. Sixty years ago, the journalist and travel writer H.V. Morton had this to say:

Fig. 16

Fig. 18

FIGURE 18. Part of the *domus Augustana* palace after Rosa's excavations: *Illustrated London News*, 27 January 1872, p. 97 ('The Basilica Jovis, Palace of the Caesars'). In the background is the new wing of the convent, with the Gothic pinnacles of Villa Mills just visible to the left; the wall marks the boundary of the Farnese Gardens property; the pavilion in the right background is the sixteenth-century *'casino del belvedere'*.

I climbed the Palatine Hill and found myself in the loneliest and most ghostly place in Rome. Stone pine and ilex cast their shade upon uneasy mounds where the skeleton of a palace thrusts a marble bone into the light; steps lead into grassy cellars; long, dank passages which once linked hall to marble hall stand like the gaunt remains of an underground station; and the sun has cracked and split pavements of coloured marble that once had known the footsteps of the Caesars. . . . I came to the site of the palace of Domitian: but instead of the marble corridors which these words suggest—the soldiers on guard, the silent slaves passing across floors of inlaid silver, the fountains in courtyards, and vistas of onyx and porphyry—all I could see were many acres of rubble.

Morton
1957.146–7, 155

Whatever did he expect? At least nowadays he would be able to enjoy the digital reconstructions in the Museum.

I hope this eclectic canter through the centuries has given the reader some idea of how the Palatine came to look the way it does today. What matters for our argument is the point at which this chapter began—the great fire of AD 64 that enabled the construction of the imperial palace in the first place. For the Palatine, the fire of Nero was Year Zero. Nearly all the existing structures were destroyed. So if we want to understand the Palatine *before* AD 64, there is no point working back from what survives now. We must try to imagine the very beginning of Rome, and work forward from there.

4

PALATINE PREHISTORY

As the longest river in sub-Apennine Italy, the Tiber was always both an asset and an obstacle to travel. Navigable for a long way upstream, it formed a natural route inland from the coast; but land traffic up and down the western side of the peninsula had to find a way to cross the marshy flood-plain through which its lower course meandered. The point at which that could most conveniently be done was about 36 km upstream from the ancient coastline, where there was an island in the river and three steep-sided hills just below it, providing firm ground close to the left bank.

Fig. 19

FIGURE 19. The physical geography of the surroundings of Rome: drawn by Lorenzo Quilici in 1967 (Cristofani 1990.30). The Capitol and Palatine are just to the right of the Tiber island.

Those hills were the later Capitol, Palatine, and Aventine, and it is from the Capitol that we have our earliest evidence for the inhabitants of what would one day be Rome. Sherds of Middle Bronze Age pottery prove that this defensible site at a strategic route crossing was occupied from at least the fourteenth century BC. Similar evidence from the Palatine is a century or so later. More extensive than the Capitol and more easily defensible than the Aventine on the landward side, the Palatine must always have been an attractive settlement site.

4.1. GEOMORPHOLOGY

It is surprisingly difficult to discover what the physical shape of the Palatine was. It used to be thought that the hill had two separate summits, as shown on Quilici's plan, and though that idea is now rejected, those who assume a single summit do not agree about its size or shape or exact position. We can only be sure of one thing: none of these approximations can accurately represent the hill as it was when it was first inhabited.

Fig. 20

In geological terms this landscape is very recent, probably shaped in the last Ice Age no more than 20,000 years ago. The valleys were at first very much deeper—that between the Palatine and the Capitol, for instance, as much as twenty-three metres below the present sea level—and the hillsides were correspondingly steep. Over the millennia the rising sea level lessened the gradient of the river-flows, and erosion began to soften the outline of the hillsides and build up the valley levels. How far that process had gone by the Middle Bronze Age is a question not easily answered.

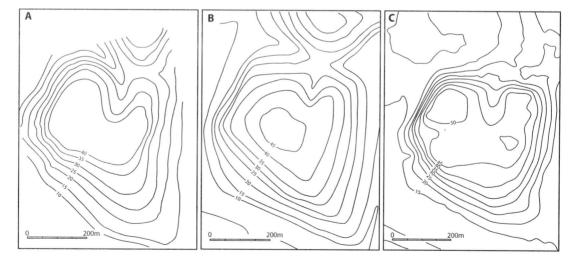

FIGURE 20. Different contour plans of the Palatine: redrawn from (*a*) Mocchegiani Carpano 1984.186 fig. 1, (*b*) Carandini 1990.83, and (*c*) Haselberger, Romano, and Dumser 2002.37 fig. 6.

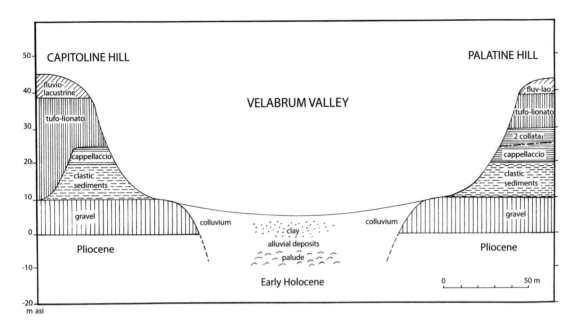

FIGURE 21. Schematic cross-section of the valley between the Capitol and the Palatine: Ammerman 1998.218 fig. 3. The vertical scale is twice the horizontal scale.

Our knowledge of the prehistoric environment of this area has been enormously increased in the past thirty years by the work of Albert Ammerman, whose fieldwork programmes have succeeded in obtaining deep-core samples from a large number of sites between the Capitol summit and the Arch of Titus. One of the earliest results was a new understanding of the valley between the Capitol and the Palatine.

Fig. 21

The gravel beds that once presented themselves as outcrops at the base of the Capitoline and Palatine hills . . . played a significant role in the early environmental setting of the area. The tops of the two gravel beds—each at a height of around 10m above sea level and each in a position elevated above the valley bottom—offered good lines of communication along opposite sides of the valley.

Ammerman
1999.102

These 'elevated shoulder areas', forming natural routes inland from the river, would eventually become the Roman streets called Vicus Iugarius (on the Capitol side) and Vicus Tuscus (on the Palatine side).

The geological structure of the hills themselves is also now much better understood:

The slopes of the Capitol and the Palatine reach heights of the order of 40m above sea level at the summit. These hillsides, which in later times were regularised and at some points substantially modified, must originally have been quite steep and irregular, with fallen rocks scattered along the slope.

Ammerman 1992.108

One important type of human agency was the exploitation of the pebbly volcanic stone called *cappellaccio*, which occurs at a level of about nineteen to twenty-five metres above sea level in both the Capitol and Palatine geological strata.

> *In situ* this lithoid tuff must have been used at an early period to cut blocks for the construction of walls and paving; its exploitation must have brought about complex and far-reaching modification of the slope itself. In fact the course of this stratum must originally have been much more irregular, and there must have been detached masses both from this and from the higher tuff strata, creating a band of distinctly chaotic appearance at the base of the slope. We may suppose that one of the first human interventions in the area was to try to exploit these fallen rock formations and create a usable space.

Ammerman 1992.110

Confirmation of this idea has come from recent deep excavations near the temple of Vesta, which reveal large sporadic boulders of unworked *cappellaccio* incorporated into structures of the eighth and seventh centuries BC.

For the Palatine in particular, two historically important results have emerged from this recent research. The first is the discovery that the north side of the hill was cut off from the Velia to the north by a 'deeply incised gully' (*fossato* in Italian) running down from the site of the Arch of Titus into that of the Roman Forum. A torrent of water during wet seasons, it formed a natural boundary, effectively isolating the Palatine except for the one access route along the ridge near its source. This gully was filled in about the middle of the sixth century BC, but its course was still marked by the Sacra Via, which must originally have been the path along its north side.

The second result has not yet attracted much attention, but is, I think, of fundamental importance for the whole pre-Neronian topography of the Palatine. To understand the context, we must go back for a moment to the early years of Roman archaeology (**3.3** above).

In 1883 Rodolfo Lanciani excavated the post-Neronian House of the Vestals (*atrium Vestae*), a big rectangular building 115 x 53 metres in extent, for which space had been created by cutting away a substantial part of the lower Palatine slope. The ground floor is about 15.80 metres above sea level, but the street immediately behind the building, terraced into the side of the hill, rises from 22.72 to 25.67 metres west to east. The cutting was therefore seven to ten metres deep. The effect of this restructuring of the landscape was to remove for ever the entire pre-Neronian topography of that part of the Palatine slope—not just the ruined buildings (that was to be expected) but even the very ground on which they stood.

Fig. 22

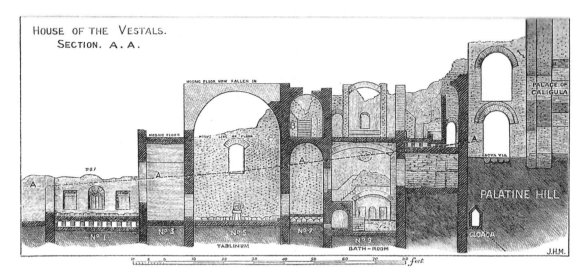

FIGURE 22. Cross-section of the *atrium Vestae*, excavated in 1883: Middleton 1885.189 fig. 22 = 1892.308 fig. 42. Note the dashed line indicating the approximate profile of the pre-existing hillside.

Archaeologists can only guess what that ground might have revealed; but Ammerman's core samples from north and south of the *atrium Vestae* site do at least allow one important inference. Just north of the site an outcrop of *cappellaccio* was found unexpectedly low down, between 13.30 and 14.48 metres above sea level:

> The presence of *cappellaccio* here is due to a landslide of the rock down from the north slope of the Palatine hill in geological time. In its original emplacement, this tuff once stood at 20–25m in elevation on the north side of the Palatine hill.

Ammerman
2009.160

Part of that outcrop was uncovered in excavation: a large flat slab at least 4 × 14 metres in extent, of which the artificially-levelled top surface was at a height of between 13.80 and 14.41 metres above sea level.

A very similar phenomenon was already known from the eastern slope of the Capitol, where *cappellaccio* dislodged from its natural level at 20–25 metres above sea level ended up as two outcrops, one at 15–17 metres and the other at 10–12 metres:

> In fact, on the lower slope of the Capitoline hill . . . there was a series of large stepping stones, as it were, on the landscape. The tops of these masses of *cappellaccio* offered themselves as elevated, rostra-like structures that readily could be used for ritual or ceremonial purposes.

Ammerman
1996.134–5

The lower one became part of the Comitium, the ancient assembly-place for the citizens of Rome. On the Palatine too, the *cappellaccio* outcrop was exploited as a significant site: already in the eighth century BC, the flat slab formed a sort of forecourt for an unusual rectangular building which clearly had some formal public purpose.

At each of these sites the landslide must have left a gap at the twenty to twenty-five metre level, providing an opportunity both for quarrying the exposed *cappellaccio* and for creating an access route up the hillside at that point. Both these phenomena are securely attested at the Capitol site, where Rome's prison (*carcer*) was built on the slope at a place called 'Stone-quarry' (*lautumiae*); the surviving remains of it, under the church of S. Giuseppe dei Falegnami, are indeed at the twenty-metre contour. Next to the *carcer* was the direct stepped route up to the north summit of the Capitol, later called 'the Stairs of Lamentation' (*scalae Gemoniae*) because the corpses of executed malefactors were exposed there. The route still exists, in the form of the steps south of S. Giuseppe that lead up to S. Maria in Aracoeli and the piazza del Campidoglio. We should expect the same thing to have happened at the Palatine site.

Putting all this new information together, we can make a reasoned guess about how the Bronze Age settlers found their way from the river to the hilltops. What the river level was at that time is not known, so we can't tell how much of a scramble it would be to get up from the muddy bank on to the firm gravel 'shoulders' of the valley at the ten-metre level; once there, however, it was an easy level walk on either side, leading in each case to a landslide site that offered a manageable ascent to the high ground.

Fig. 23

Fig. 21

That's how it was for many centuries, and how it still is on the Capitol side. But the Palatine lost its access route when Nero's architects, restructuring Rome on a grand scale after the fire, cut back the hillside to make room for the House of the Vestals. The slope created by that primeval landslide was destroyed, and has had to wait nearly two thousand years to be detected again.

4.2 LEARNED GUESSWORK

Augustus understood very well the importance of the history of Rome, and most of what he knew about it must have come from a great lost work of Roman learning, the *Antiquities* of Marcus Varro, which came out when he was about twelve years old.

Varro's work was epoch-making, its impact best expressed in Cicero's famous tribute:

As we wandered like travellers abroad as strangers in our own city, your books have, so to say, led us back home, enabling us at last to recognise who we are and

FIGURE 23. Access from the river: the stream valley between the Capitol and the Palatine, with contours as in Filippi 2005.95 fig. 1. The extent of the river is conjectural; in the second millennium BC the Tiber bank was about 100m further east than its present line (Ammerman 2006.307). V: position of the Velabrum (S. Giorgio in Velabro), where Varro believed there had once been a landing-stage (*De lingua Latina* 5.43). CL: position of known *cappellaccio* landslides. F: the *fossato* (gully) that defined the Palatine to the north.

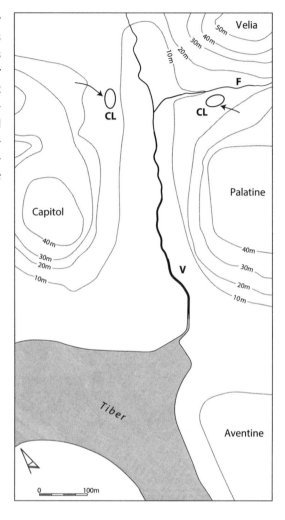

Cicero *Academica* 1.9 (trans. P.G. Walsh)

where we stand. You have revealed to us the age of our native land, its chronological divisions, its laws governing rituals and priests, the training in family and civic life, the locations of regions and sites, and the names, categories, roles and origins of things divine and human.

Among the countless subjects covered in his forty-one volumes, Varro paid serious attention to the prehistory of the site of Rome. Despite the loss of the *Antiquities*, we can recover some of Varro's arguments from quotations in other authors, and also from details in books 5 to 7 of his own work on the Latin language, which do happen to survive, though in a very corrupt text. But this precious information has to be handled carefully.

Both in the *Antiquities* and in the *De lingua Latina*, Varro divided up his material into four conceptual categories: who, where, when, and what; persons, places, times, and actions. In book 5 of the latter work, explaining how places get their names, Varro used the toponym 'Seven-Hills' (*Septimontium*) as an example:

> Where Rome now is, 'Seven-Hills' was named from that number of hills which the city later included within the walls.

Varro *De lingua Latina* 5.41

But *Septimontium* was also the name of a festival day, so in book 6, on how units of time are named, he has this:

> The day 'Seven-Hills' was named from these seven hills on which the city is placed; it is a holiday not for the [whole] people, but only for the *montani*.

Varro *De lingua Latina* 6.24

The *montani* seem to be those who lived on the hills that were called *montes* (the Palatine, Capitol, Aventine, Caelian, Oppian, and Cispian) and not on the hills that were called *colles* (the Quirinal and Viminal); though that's not quite consistent with the first passage, since the *colles* were also included within the walls.

The question of the seven hills of Rome was already controversial in the time of Augustus, and has remained so ever since. But that has not prevented modern archaeologists from citing Varro as if he were documentary evidence for 'proto-urban Rome'. That phrase is currently used to describe the situation in the ninth century BC, when the individual settlements on the Palatine, Capitol, and other hills were apparently no longer independent villages but had become parts of a larger whole. An authoritative recent account puts it like this:

> The 'unity' of the settlement in this phase, or at least a very strong link between the communities in the area of the Roman hills, is assumed on the basis of the location of funerary areas all around the supposed inhabited area.

Fulminante 2014.79

But what was the nature of that 'very strong link'? Varro's evidence is only that the hilltop sites shared a common festival. He assumed it dated to before Rome existed as a city, and he may have been right in that conjecture. But those who want to find evidence for 'proto-urban Rome' attribute much more to him than that.

According to Andrea Carandini, the eighth-century BC wall excavated in 1988 below the north slope of the Palatine has proved the Roman foundation story essentially true. On the other hand, the Roman historians' notion that Romulus founded the city from nothing is inconsistent with the 'proto-urban' archaeology. So Carandini appeals to Varro as the transmitter of 'a more ancient memory', one that 'must have left sufficiently substantial traces of itself' but of which the historians were unaware; 'in the rich reservoir of Roman cultural memory' he found evidence of 'an organisation earlier than the city'.

It's an exciting idea, and some archaeologists have allowed themselves to be seduced by it. But it won't do: you have only to compare what Varro actually says with the intellectual house of cards that has been built on it to see that it's no more than wishful thinking. The problem with the 'proto-urban' concept is its implication that Rome was somehow already there, in embryo. If Varro's guess was right, then the hilltop villages collaborated in a joint festival; but there is also evidence, from a festival at the Latins' communal cult-site on the Alban Mount, that the villages had their own names and their own identities.

What Varro transmits is not, of course, authentic information based on ancient memory, but conjecture based on intelligent observation and enormously wide reading. He himself had no illusions about the nature of the task:

> There are few things that time does not corrupt, and many that it takes away completely. . . . What oblivion already robbed from our ancestors, not even [learned men like] Mucius and Brutus, diligently hunting for what got away, can ever bring back.

Varro *De lingua Latina* 5.5

'If I can't attain knowledge,' he says, 'I shall try to catch an opinion.' The important thing for us is to see what he based his opinions on.

His view of the prehistory of the Capitol is a good example. He explained how the hill got its name, and then, fortunately for us, added a digression that went beyond his etymological argument:

> [Authors] have asserted that this hill was previously called 'Saturnian', and that from it Latium was 'the Saturnian land', as Ennius too calls it. It is written that on it there was an ancient walled town, Saturnia, of which three indications remain even now: the fact that the temple of Saturn is at the entrance [to the Capitol]; the fact that the 'Saturnian Gate' of which Junius writes is there, the one they now call the 'Open Gate'; and the fact that in private building legislation rear house-walls behind the temple of Saturn are written of as 'Saturnian walls'.

Varro *De lingua Latina* 5.42

Varro makes a point of citing written sources, and yet he is conspicuously silent on the reason some of those sources must have given for the name *mons Saturnius*. It's a story we know from Virgil and Ovid: the god Saturn, expelled from Olympus by his son Jupiter's coup d'état, established himself on the hill that would one day be the Capitol, and brought the local inhabitants together under the rule of law.

Varro didn't believe that—it was one of the 'tales unworthy of the gods' deplorably propagated by poets and dramatists—and all he took from the story was the report, unexplained, of the old name of the hill. That much he could accept, because of the three 'indications' that the Capitol had indeed been an ancient walled town (*antiquum oppidum*): the temple placed at the 'entrance', the gate that implied a wall, and the reference in legal documents to what might be the wall itself.

Varro believed there had also been an *antiquum oppidum* on the Palatine. He refers to it three times, though the poor state of his text makes one of the passages hard to understand.

In his book on words for times, Varro offers a derivation of 'February' from *di inferi* (gods of the underworld, whose expiation rites lasted from the 13th to the 21st of the month), only to reject it in the next sentence:

> I prefer to think that 'February' is from *dies februatus* [purification day], because it is then that the population is purified—that is, the ancient Palatine walled town ringed with human flocks[?] is cleansed by the naked Luperci.

Varro De lingua Latina 6.34

The reference is to the *Lupercalia* festival on 15 February. The phrase marked with a query is probably a textual corruption (if it meant 'surrounded by crowds of people', why should he use such an odd metaphor?)— but in any case there is nothing here to indicate why Varro believed there was an *antiquum oppidum Palatinum*.

His reason becomes clear in the other two passages, one of which is an appendix to Varro's explanation of the names of the gates in the city wall of Rome:

> Besides [these gates], I observe that gates are named *within* the walls, on the Palatine: the Mugionis, from *mugitus* [the lowing of cattle], because by it they used to drive the herds out into the cow-pastures that were in front of the ancient walled town; and a second, the Romanula, named from Rome, which has steps on the Nova Via[?] at the shrine of Volupia.

Varro De lingua Latina 5.164

The third reference expands on the name of the festival called *Larentalia*:

> This sacrifice [to Acca Larentia] takes place in the Velabrum, at the exit into the Nova Via. Some say it is at the tomb of Acca, on the grounds that near there the priests sacrifice to the departed spirits of slaves. Both sites were outside the ancient city, not far from the Romanula Gate, about which I spoke in the previous book.

Varro De lingua Latina 6.24

Fig. 23

Since the Velabrum was certainly not outside the city of Rome, the 'ancient city' of this passage must be the same as the 'ancient walled town' of the other two. The two gates, Mugionis and Romanula, were clearly Varro's evidence for its existence.

And that makes them our evidence too. Varro was a highly intelligent observer, incomparably better informed about the realities of his own world than we can ever hope to be. He saw those gates, still surviving in some form in his own time, and he drew his own conclusions from them. (He clearly didn't see a wall, or that would have been evidence enough.) Gates often survived in the urban fabric of historic cities long after the fortifications of which they were part had become obsolete; the six gates of Roman London, for instance, repeatedly rebuilt in the Middle Ages, were demolished only in 1761. So Varro's inference about an ancient walled town is something that demands respect.

As with the Capitol, so too with the Palatine. Varro paid no attention to myth-historical accounts of how the *antiquum oppidum* came to be built. He also ignored a famous story about the Mugionis Gate—how Romulus' great battle with the Sabines was fought in the valley between the Capitol and the Palatine, how the Sabines forced the Romans back to 'the old gate of the Palatine', the *porta Mugionis*, and how Romulus vowed a temple there to Jupiter Stator ('the Stayer') if his men would stand their ground. Varro wasn't interested in that. For us, on the other hand, this aetiology of the temple by the gate is a key document for understanding the topography of the Palatine.

Actually constructed about 290 BC and destroyed in the fire of AD 64, the Jupiter Stator temple was an important building, large enough to house meetings of the Senate. We know that it was near the Forum, at the foot of the Palatine but in an elevated position, and that you reached it by turning right from the Sacra Via just after the Vesta temple and the Regia. But when all that area was excavated in the 1880s, no trace of a temple was found. Only one explanation is possible: the temple must have stood on the slope of the hill that was cut away to make room for the Neronian *atrium Vestae*. And that must be where the *porta Mugionis* was too.

Fig. 22

So Marcus Varro's conjectures about Rome's deep past, 'trying to catch an opinion' in the absence of knowledge, have led us to the place where Albert Ammerman's deep-core samples detected a landslide of *cappellaccio* in geological time. This was where dislodged masses of rock formed 'a series of large stepping stones, as it were, in the landscape', and where the gap in the natural stratum from which they came offered an easier route to the summit for the first prospectors of the site. And here, precisely, well over a millennium later, Varro was able to deduce the existence of a fortified settlement from the anomalous survival of one of the gates.

4.3 RECONSTRUCTING THE TOPOGRAPHY

The other surviving gate was significant too, though Varro's derivation of the name can hardly be right: 'Rome' didn't yet exist, and it's possible that *Romanula* came from a corruption of *rumon*, an old name for the Tiber. Varro seems to say (though the text is uncertain) that the Romanula Gate 'had steps on to the Nova Via'; and he certainly says that it was 'not far from the Velabrum at the exit into the Nova Via'.

In his time the Velabrum was an open marketplace on the Vicus Tuscus, which ran from the Forum to the Circus Maximus; the toponym survives today in the church of S. Giorgio in Velabro. From its name, and that of the Aventine, Varro inferred that there had once been a landing-stage there:

Fig. 23

> I am strongly of the opinion that 'Aventine' is from *aduectus* [transport towards], for in the past the hill was cut off from the others by marshes, and so they were transported there from the city by rafts. The evidence for it is that the [*text lost*] by which at that time [*text lost*] is called Velabrum, and the place from which they came up to the bottom of the Nova Via is the shrine of the *uelabra*[?]. 'Velabrum' is from *uehere* [to transport]. Even now, those who do this for hire are said to perform *uelatura*. The fare for this 'transporting' of those who crossed on the rafts was a *quadrans*; that is why Lucilius writes of a 'raft-copper'.

Varro *De lingua Latina* 5.43–4

One tiny detail in this dense and difficult paragraph—'the place from which they came *up* to the bottom of the Nova Via'—is enough to show that when Varro was writing the difference in level between the bottom of the valley and the gravel 'shoulder' at the base of the Palatine was still perceptible. Whatever was in the missing part of his text must have referred to the ferry passengers disembarking at water level.

Fig. 21

We may imagine the Velabrum as a historic nodal point on the firm gravel at about ten metres above the present sea level, with four separate routes leading from it in Varro's time: two along the ten-metre contour, north to the Forum and south to the Circus Maximus, a third down to the lower level where Varro thought the landing stage had been, and a fourth by the supposed tomb of Acca Larentia, 'at the exit into the Nova Via'. If the Romanula Gate did indeed have 'steps on to the Nova Via', we must assume they led up the side of the hill from the Nova Via (at the Velabrum) to the surviving gate that was part of Varro's evidence for the 'ancient walled town'.

Fig. 24

The route of the Nova Via used to be an insoluble topographical problem, because it was firmly believed to have 'branched off from the Sacra Via'. But Adam Ziółkowski has demonstrated that the supposed evidence for that belief is illusory, and the deep gully (*fossato*) north of the Palatine is now known to have formed a natural topographical boundary with the route of the Sacra Via on one side and the route of the Nova Via on the other. That makes the situation much easier to understand.

Varro knew that the Nova Via, despite its name, was very ancient, and as an experienced soldier he knew all about approach routes to fortified *oppida*. The usual layout was an inclined causeway leading up to the entrance gate in a clockwise direction, so that attackers would find it hard to use their shields against missiles from the fortification above them to their right. It must have

Fig. 25

FIGURE 24. Sketch-plan of the Velabrum, the Nova Via, and the gates of Varro's 'ancient walled town' (*antiquum oppidum*) on the Palatine. As always, the contours are approximate and the line of the river bank conjectural. V: Velabrum, as in fig. 23. The position of the *porta Mugionis* is now, I believe, firmly established (Wiseman 2017), but we can only guess at that of the *porta Romanula*, with its 'steps on the Nova Via' (Varro *De lingua Latina* 5.164).

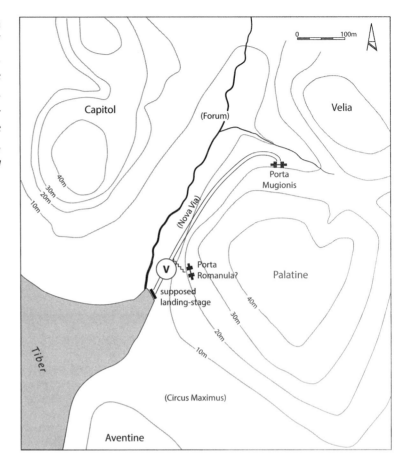

been self-evident to Varro that the Nova Via was just such a causeway, the main approach to the 'ancient walled town' on the Palatine.

You came up from the riverbank—though he didn't know it was that—to 'the bottom of the Nova Via' (*infima noua uia*), on the gravel shoulder about ten metres above modern sea level. From there you went up the causeway incline round the side of the hill, and at 'the top of the Nova Via' (*summa noua uia*) was the Mugionis Gate, which stood on your right at roughly seventeen metres above sea level. Both those toponyms are securely attested, the bottom of the slope by Varro himself and the top of it by Julius Solinus, for whom we know Varro was an important source.

It's worth emphasising again that all this is the result of Varro's intelligent interpretation of what he could see with his own eyes. He did not, of course, have *knowledge* of the distant past, and the idea that he, or anyone in the first century BC, had authentic information from some undefined 'ancient tradition' is (to put it frankly) an absurdity. 'Cultural memory' is a fashionably evasive term

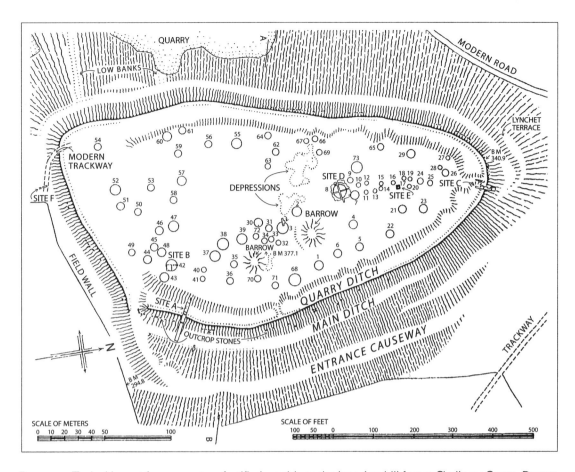

FIGURE 25. Typical layout for access to a fortified *oppidum*: the Iron Age hill fort at Chalbury Camp, Dorset, England (Whitley 1943.100). The 'entrance causeway' is analogous to the line of the Nova Via proposed in fig. 24.

for oral tradition, which cannot transmit accurate information for more than four or five generations at the most. Varro was trying to reach an undated time at least thirty generations before his own. No one was better qualified to make sensible conjectures, but even he couldn't get it right every time.

For instance, we now know that Varro was wrong to believe that the Palatine and Aventine were largely surrounded by marshes. Ammerman's deep-core samples show that the valleys between the Capitol and Palatine and between the Palatine and Aventine, though regularly flooded by the river during the winter months, were otherwise dry. But there was a reason for Varro's idea. He could see the significance of the routes converging at the Velabrum; his inference that there was a landing stage there was a good one; and he needed the marsh and the ferries to make sense of it. He was quite unaware that a thousand years before his time, that was where the riverbank was. No-one knew that until Ammerman's results revealed it.

Admirably, Varro did not link his detection of the 'ancient walled town' on the Palatine with any of the Roman foundation legends. The loss of the *Antiquities* prevents us from knowing what he thought happened between its construction and the supposed foundation of Rome by Romulus, which he dated to 753 BC. His treatment of *Septimontium* (**4.2** above) suggests that for him 'Rome' meant seven hills with a wall round them, and we know that in his version of events Romulus controlled at least the Capitol, the Aventine, and the Caelian, as well as the Palatine. What we do not know is how and when he thought that had come about.

A modern answer to the question is now available, thanks to Ammerman's reinterpretation of a very deep excavation in the Forum by Giacomo Boni in 1903–4:

> The new interpretation I should like to propose here is that the layers in question [strata 23–28, from 6.9 to 9.0 masl] are fills: fills that were intentionally deposited in the center of the basin in order to build up the ground level. This would account for the rapid rate of inflation of the land surface. Once the ground level had been raised to an elevation of about 9 masl, the first gravel pavement of the Forum was laid down on top of this landfill. . . . When the task of filling in and levelling out the area was completed, the surface of the new Forum would have stood at almost the same ground level as the Comitium and the Lacus Iuturnae on the opposite sides of the basin [respectively 9.5 and 10.0 masl].

Ammerman
1990.641

The approximate date of this 'major public works project' was evidently some time in the seventh century BC. A similar communal effort would have been required in the sixth century BC, when the gully (*fossato*) to the north of the Palatine was filled in for building development, and the stream culverted.

This hypothesis is now very widely accepted, and in two respects it is historically momentous. First, the sheer scale of the projects, the manpower and organisation required to carry them out, are enough to show that the hilltop settlements were acting together for a common end:

> The calculated geographical transformation reveals a momentous shift in Roman civilization, not only because it was a vast communal effort, but also because it indicates a radical shift in resources. The project was perhaps the first truly monumental architectonic undertaking in Rome, and it is certainly the first for which archaeological evidence exists.

Hopkins 2016.37

Rather than just a 'momentous shift', perhaps we should see it as the actual *beginning* of Roman civilisation:

> The landfill is the first archeologically attested sign of a community that . . . sought to promote a single topographically connected polity.

Hopkins 2016.34

And that is the second historical implication: these great public enterprises created a common ground. The streams were no longer barriers and boundaries. In particular, the new proto-Forum 'connected the slopes of the Palatine, Capitoline, Velia, Esquiline and Quirinal'. It was now possible to enclose seven hills within a single city wall, just as Varro believed had happened (whichever seven hills he thought they were), and it is generally believed, though not certain, that such a circuit wall was indeed built in the sixth century BC.

If we are looking for a historical moment when the city of Rome came into being, the creation of the Roman Forum is surely it. In Greek terms, it was the *agora* of a *polis*, the communal space of a city-state, and Greek experience may well have been the inspiration behind it. Greek-speakers had been regular visitors in Latium since the ninth century BC, and the earliest evidence for art and architecture in Rome shows very clear influence from the Greek world, particularly Ionia. It is not surprising that the new city, with all its communal resources, called itself *rhōmē*, the Greek for 'strength'.

As for the Palatine, this marks the end of its conjectural prehistory as an independent community. From now on, *Palatium* was part of a greater whole, with a consequent shift in its orientation. The filling of the gully and the development of the area below the north slope made access to the new Forum very straightforward. Once, coming out of the Mugionis Gate had required an immediate left turn on to the Nova Via, which took you down to the river; now, you could go straight down the side of the hill (that primeval landslide site) and turn left at the bottom to reach the Forum by the Sacra Via.

Fig. 26

The Sacra Via was the new city's ceremonial way, made possible by the creation of the Forum: it ran down from 'the citadel' (*arx*, the north crest of the Capitol) across the Forum and up the slope north of the Palatine, along a line that had originally been the northern bank of the gully. That line, and the direct descent from the Palatine, fixed the topography of the area from the sixth century BC to the fire of AD 64.

Two contemporary authors confirm it for Augustus' time. First, the historian Dionysius, relating Romulus' promise to the god who stopped the rout:

> Romulus [vowed the temple] to Jupiter Stator at what is called the Mugionis Gate, which leads to the Palatine from the Sacra Via.

Dionysius of Halicarnassus *Roman Antiquities* 2.50.3

And second, the exiled poet Ovid, imagining his book asking the way to the Palatine and being guided by a friendly passer-by:

FIGURE 26. The *fossato* filled in, the Palatine no longer isolated: contrast fig. 24.

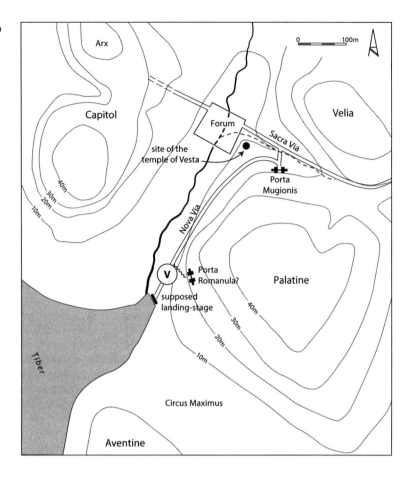

Ovid *Tristia*
3.1.28–32

'This is the street named from sacred things; this is Vesta's place, where she keeps the Palladium and the sacred fire; this was the tiny palace of ancient Numa.' Then he turned right. 'That is the gate of the Palatine; here is [the temple of] Stator.'

It was a route Augustus must have taken a thousand times, returning from the Forum to his house on the Palatine.

5

PALATINE LEGENDS

Augustus chose to live on the Palatine because Romulus had lived there. Indeed, as a young man he thought of using the name 'Romulus' himself, and it would have been a reasonable thing to do, since Romulus had become part of his adoptive family. According to Ennius' *Annales*, the great national epic that provided most of what Romans knew of their own history, Romulus' mother Ilia was the daughter of Aeneas; for the young Caesar, that meant she was the sister (or half-sister) of the Iulus from whom the patrician Iulii claimed descent.

He had second thoughts about calling himself Romulus, but the name he did assume was still an allusion to the legend, and in particular to Ennius' line 'after famous Rome was founded by *august* augury'. Romulus consulted the gods by augury on two significant occasions: first from the Aventine (according to Ennius), to confirm that he, and not his twin brother, would choose the site of the new city and give it its name, and then from the Palatine, to confirm his authority as ruler of the city he would found there. Augustus took augury very seriously, and his choice of where to live was clearly significant.

Fig. 27

Augustus and the Romans of his time regarded Romulus as a historical figure, and the foundation as a historical event. Recently some archaeologists have come to believe that too, and in the last thirty years several books have been written on the origin of Rome which take that assumption for granted. However, such accounts simply ignore all the other origin legends that existed, privileging one version of the Romulus story as if it were somehow 'authentic'. As I hope the next two chapters will show, the real history of Roman foundation legends is more complicated than that, and much more interesting. And it involves the Palatine at every stage.

5.1 PALLANTION

Right from the start, Rome was part of the Greek world. The first known name of an inhabitant of the new city-state is in fact Greek, *Kleiklos* or *Ktektos*, scratched on a Corinthian oil-flask that was buried with him in the mid-seventh

FIGURE 27. Part of a bronze equestrian statue of Augustus, retrieved
from the Aegean Sea in 1979; the
left hand wears a ring with an image
of the augural staff (*lituus*). Athens:
National Archaeological Museum,
inv. X 23322.

Fig. 28

century BC. Two generations later (c. 590–580 BC), one of the earliest public
buildings was decorated with terracotta plaques showing a minotaur processing
with panthers, an iconographic feature paralleled on contemporary Corinthian
painted pottery. The cult-site of Vulcan on the slope of the Capitol contained a
huge Athenian black-figure mixing-bowl of 570–560 BC showing the return of
Hephaistos to Olympus, clear evidence of the identity of the Greek god with the
Roman one. And this archaeological evidence is entirely consistent with what
the literary sources tell us.

Fig. 29

Already in the seventh and sixth centuries BC, Odysseus' adventures in books
9 through 12 of Homer's *Odyssey* were located off the western coast of Italy, in
waters long familiar to Greek traders and colonial settlers. In particular, the 'island' of Circe the witch-goddess was identified as *Kirkaion*, modern M. Circeo
on the coast of Latium. Hesiod, the *Telegony* (a post-Homeric epic sequel to the
Odyssey), and a succession of poets and mythographers building on their material, created a complex story-world that derived the peoples of Latium, Rome
included, from children fathered on Circe by Odysseus. At Rome, Circe lent her
name to the chariot-racing track (*circus*) in the stream valley south of the Palatine; her father, Helios the Sun-god, was the charioteer *par excellence*.

FIGURE 28. Fragment of a terracotta frieze from the Regia,
mid-sixth century BC. Rome, Antiquarium forense, inv. 1918: Soprintendenza per i Beni Archeo-
logici di Roma.

After Homer and Hesiod, the next great narrative poet of the archaic Greek world was Stesichorus of Himera, working evidently in the first half of the sixth century BC. He composed not in hexameter lines, as they had, but in complex lyric stanzas corresponding to dance movements. The dancers would be the young people of the community at whose festival the poet was hired to perform. The Latin city-state with the Greek name (*rhōmē*, 'strength') was certainly prosperous enough at that time to attract a famous performer from northern Sicily, just an easy sail away.

Stesichorus' best-known poem, *Geryoneis*, told the story of Hercules' tenth Labour—to capture the cattle of the monstrous Geryon at the western edge of the world, and bring them back to Argos. The hero killed Geryon and drove the cattle down the length of Italy, thus giving the poet ample opportunity to make flattering connections with whatever host city he was performing in. The story he told about Hercules at the site of Rome explained the origin of the Palatine.

Seeking pasture for the herd, Hercules halted in the rich grass of the Tiber flood-plain. The small fortified settlement on the hill close to the river turned out to be occupied by fellow-Greeks. They welcomed him warmly, and their leader Evander, whose very name was a good omen (*Euandros*, 'Goodman'), told him how they came to be there.

They were Arcadians, from the mountainous interior of the Peloponnese in southern Greece. Their home had been the town of Pallantion, a small place but

FIGURE 29. The Tyrrhenian Sea, sixth century BC. Agylla was the Greek name for Etruscan Caere (modern Cerveteri, 35 km northwest of Rome); about 650 BC a Greek vase-painter called Aristonothos worked there, whose painting of the blinding of Polyphemus is our earliest evidence for knowledge of the plot of the *Odyssey*. Rome, Ardea, Antium, Tusculum, and Praeneste were Latin city-states that were given Greek foundation stories connected with Odysseus and Circe.

All the other city-states marked were Greek colonial foundations. Kyme (Latin Cumae) was ruled in the late sixth century by Aristodemus, with whom the last king of Rome Tarquin 'the Proud' (himself of Corinthian descent) took refuge after his attempts to re-establish himself failed. Elea and Kroton were important centres of Greek philosophy in the sixth century BC; the latter was the home of Pythagoras, to whom, according to one Greek author ('Epicharmus' *PCG* fr. 296), the Romans granted their citizenship.

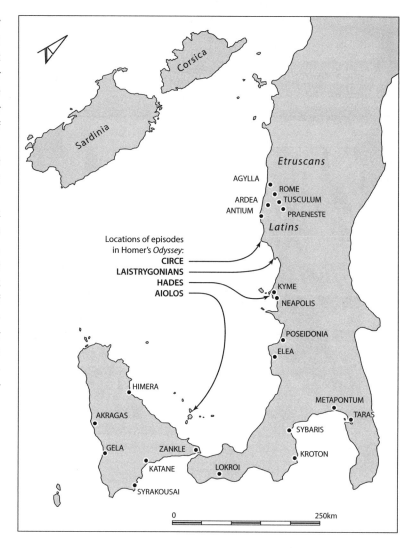

big enough for fierce political disputes in which Evander and his friends were on the losing side. They had taken their families into exile, hiring two ships and sailing to the west. Guided by Evander's mother Themis, a Sibyl or prophetess, they had hauled their ships up the Tiber to the crossing place by the island. That, she said, was the place for them. They built their little town on the top of the hill and named it after their old home—Pallantion, which in the local dialect became *Palatium*.

This is the earliest of the foundation stories. If the name 'Rome' appeared in it at all, it can only have been in Themis' prophecy of a distant future. In the sixth century BC the city-state with its Forum and its new stone buildings was still a recent creation. The flattering legend of Hercules and Evander exploited

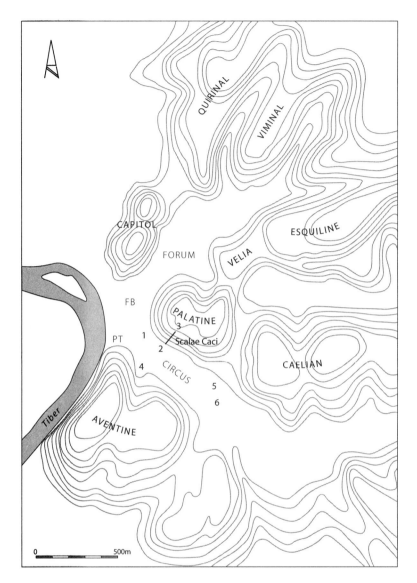

FIGURE 30. Cult-sites associated with the legend of Evander and Hercules. 1. Hercules (*ara maxima*). 2. Pan (Lupercal). 3. Nike (temple of Victoria). 4. Demeter (temple of Ceres, Liber, and Libera). 5. Poseidon Hippios (altar of Consus = Neptunus Equester). 6. Hermes (temple of Mercurius). FB: the Forum Bovarium, where Hercules grazed the cattle (Propertius 4.9.15–20). PT: the Porta Trigemina, where there was an altar dedicated to Evander (Dionysius of Halicarnassus *Roman Antiquities* 1.32.2) and where Cacus, the brigand or monster killed by Hercules, was supposed to have lived (Solinus 1.8).

something much older, the now obsolete walled settlement on the Palatine, remains of which were still detectable five centuries later (**4.2** above).

Several ancient cult sites in Rome were attributed to Evander and his Arcadians. They were nearly all in the valley of the *circus* south-west of the Palatine, and since one of them was the altar of Poseidon Hippios, for whom the Roman games were first established, it may be that these attributions date back to the creation of the legend. Like other poets in the archaic Greek world, Stesichorus would no doubt have made complimentary reference to the particular festival context in which he was performing.

Fig. 30

One of the sites, not in the valley but overlooking it from the top of the Pala-tine, was the temple of Nike (Latin Victoria), an Arcadian goddess who might well be invoked by competing performers at an archaic festival. Two and a half centuries later she would symbolise Rome's victory in the critical battle for con-trol of Italy; three centuries later again, Augustus would give her credit for his stepson's conquest of Germany. The area where the temple stood has been very thoroughly explored, and one particular feature may help us to understand something of its early history.

In 1907, excavating in front of the temple site at a level about seven metres below the crest of the hill, Dante Vaglieri was able to get right down to the bed-rock. Dug into it were the post-holes for an overlapping series of timber and thatched dwellings, and immediately next to them a rectangular grave 2.05 me-tres long and 0.80 metres wide, cut 0.75 metres deep into the rock. The grave contained some bones, not *in situ* but pushed to one side, and a cup (*skyphos*) that is now identified as Etruscan ware of the late sixth or early fifth century BC. The grave had been covered with a carefully-cut slab of Monteverde tuff, from quarries the Romans did not exploit before the fourth century BC at the earliest; at some point this slab had been broken in two.

From these archaeological clues a clear chronological sequence can be inferred:

1. At some early stage in the occupation of the hill, this marginal space was evidently used as a necropolis, of which our grave is the most conspicuous indication. Cur-rent scholarship assigns it to *Cultura laziale* IIA, roughly 900–830 BC on the con-ventional dating, 1020–950 BC according to the 'high' chronology.

2. Later the burial ground went out of use and the area was used for habitation. The hut village is assigned to *Cultura laziale* IIB and III, respectively 830–730 BC or 950–750 BC according to the two rival dating systems.

3. By about 500 BC the hut village had been demolished. Major urban development was taking place, including new artificial terracing at this point of the hill and the construction of a substantial temple, attested by surviving terracotta plaques and antefixes. The *skyphos* cup is clear evidence that the grave had been uncovered during the work. We cannot know whose grave the Romans of the time thought it was, but the disturbance of it must have required an expiatory ritual of some sort.

4. Two centuries later the area was redeveloped again, with new and more elaborate terracing and substructions. The temple was replaced by a new one, dedicated to Victoria by the consul L. Postumius Megellus in 294 BC. Once again the grave was disturbed; this time it was evidently re-covered with the tuff slab, and marked with a monument of some sort on the terrace level directly above it (the core of the monument was discovered by Vaglieri in 1907). It must be significant that the new temple, unlike its predecessor, was aligned on almost the same axis as the

grave. It is possible, though we cannot know, that Postumius took it to be the grave of Evander, supposed founder of the victory goddess's original temple.

5. In 204 BC the cult of the Great Mother of the Gods (Magna Mater) was introduced to Rome, and a temple, completed in 191 BC, was constructed for her on the terrace next to Victoria; it was destroyed in a devastating fire in 111 BC, but immediately rebuilt. Major reconstruction took place in front of the two temples at both dates, which may have caused the breaking of the slab. Perhaps the grave's occupant seemed less significant now: for the Great Mother, as we shall see, Troy and Mount Ida mattered more than Arcadia.

To make historical sense of these complex archaeological data, we need to plot them chronologically against the development of the Pallantion legend. The end of the long history of the mysterious grave more or less coincides with the beginning of Roman historical writing.

The first history of Rome was written (in Greek) by Fabius Pictor, probably in the final decade of the third century BC, and since Fabius was an aristocrat whose family claimed descent from Hercules himself, he naturally began his narrative with the hero's arrival in Italy. Later authors produced rival versions and elaborations, deriving the name of the Palatine from Evander's daughter Pallantia, or from a woman called Palantho, taken hostage by Hercules from the Hyperboreans, on whom he fathered Latinus, eponym of the Latins. The historian Gnaeus Gellius, writing about a century after Fabius, had a story that a brigand called Cacus attacked 'the lands which had passed into the control of the

Fig. 31

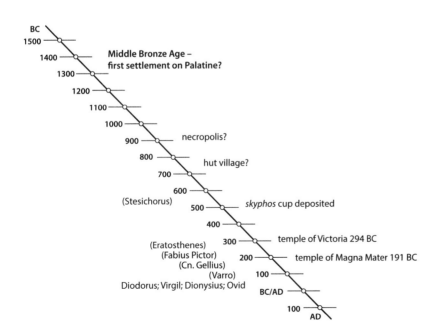

FIGURE 31. Time-line of the Vaglieri 1907 excavation site, and of the authors who are known to have written about Evander and/or Hercules at 'Pallantion'. Names in brackets are of authors whose works are known only from quotations: Stesichorus fr. 21 D-F, Fabius Pictor *FRHist* 1 T7, Cn. Gellius *FRHist* 14 F17, Varro fr. 398 Funaioli; Eratosthenes is quoted by the scholiast on Plato *Phaedrus* 244b (Wiseman 2008.55).

Arcadians', but was defeated and killed by Hercules, 'who happened to be there at the time'. A poetic version of that, well known to modern readers of Virgil and Ovid, made Cacus a fire-breathing monster, son of Vulcan, who tried to steal some of the cattle.

It is possible that Fabius Pictor's Hercules story ignored Evander's Arcadians entirely. We know his history was used by Diodorus of Sicily, a Greek historian contemporary with Virgil and the young Augustus, and Diodorus told the tale like this:

> Passing through the lands of the Ligurians and Tyrrhenians [Etruscans], Hercules came to the river Tiber and made his camp where Rome is now. Rome itself was founded many generations later by Romulus, the son of Ares [Mars], but at that time some of the indigenous people lived on what is now called *Palatium*, occupying a very small town. Cacius and Pinarius, who were among the leading men there, received Hercules with conspicuous hospitality and honoured him with generous gifts. Commemoration of these men exists at Rome to this day. The family of those called Pinarii survives among the present Roman aristocracy, the most ancient still in existence, and as for Cacius, there is on the Palatine a route down with stone steps, called after him 'the Cacian stairs' and close to where his house was at that time.

Diodorus Siculus
4.21.1–2

That 'route down' was an ancient thoroughfare that needed explanation, the only attested descent down the steep south-western slope of the Palatine into the valley of the Circus Maximus.

Fig. 30

Its Latin name was *scalae Caci*—either 'the stairs of Cacius' (the generous host) or 'the stairs of Cacus' (the monstrous brigand). We know quite precisely where it was, and Rosa discovered the upper part of it in 1870, the final season of his work for Napoleon III (**3.3** above). A century and a half later, it is where visitors to the modern Palatine walk down a covered path to the house Carettoni excavated in 1958–1984 (**2.3** above), now confidently entitled 'The House of Augustus'. The entrance to the house is to the left; immediately opposite, also covered over, is the dusty, neglected area explored by Vaglieri in 1907, where that repeatedly rediscovered grave was first dug into the bedrock three thousand years ago.

5.2 THE TROY CONNECTION

Tracing the story of Hercules and Evander has taken us from the sixth century BC to the first, from Stesichorus to Virgil, from the early years of the Roman city-state to the time of Augustus himself. Exactly the same chronological range covers the creation and elaboration of a quite different foundation legend, one that connected Rome with the Trojan War.

Already in the *Iliad* it is fated that the Trojan hero Aeneas will not be killed in the war: the surviving Trojans will be ruled by him 'and his children's children born in future time'. According to Stesichorus, Aeneas and his followers escaped from the destruction of their city and sailed 'to the West'. Someone at some time connected that story with Rome, just as Rome had earlier been brought into the story of Odysseus; when Hellanicus of Lesbos, the great mythological sys- Fig. 29 tematiser of the mid-fifth century BC, wrote that Aeneas and Odysseus founded Rome together, that unnatural pairing was probably the artificial combination of two pre-existing tales.

By the time Hellanicus was writing, the idea of Rome as a Greek city founded by Greeks was much less satisfactory than it had once been. The Corinthian ruling family of Rome had been expelled in 507 BC, and the city was now in alliance with Carthage, the 'barbarian' adversary of the Greeks in Sicily. It made more sense to think of the Romans as descendants of Trojan refugees, still part of the legendary past but hereditary enemies of Troy's Greek conquerors.

A century and a half later (281 BC) Rome was in conflict with the most power-ful of the Italian Greek cities, Taras. The Tarentines sent an embassy to ask for the help of Pyrrhus, king of Epirus in north-west Greece:

> The ambassadors' speech reminded Pyrrhus of the capture of Troy, and he ex-pected his own expedition would have the same outcome, since he was a descen-dant of Achilles making war on a Trojan colony. Pausanias 1.12.1

The Romans themselves took a similar view, as we happen to know from a pre-cious surviving fragment of first-hand evidence:

> Then again, in his history of Pyrrhus, [Timaeus] says that the Romans still in his time commemorate the destruction of Troy: on one particular day they kill a war-horse with spears outside the city in what they call the Campus, because of the tradition that the capture of Troy was due to the wooden horse. Polybius 12.4b.1

Timaeus of Tauromenium (modern Taormina in Sicily) was a famous Greek his-torian whose long writing career spanned at least the first three decades of the third century BC; so his history of Pyrrhus was a narrative of his own times. His works are lost, but we know he was sufficiently interested in the Aeneas legend to go to Latium and ask local people about it. In particular, as his use here of the Latin toponym *Campus* suggests, he went to Rome and asked the Romans.

In conspicuous contrast with Hercules and Evander, Aeneas left no trace at Fig. 30 all in the city of Rome. His role in the 'Trojan' foundation story was always at one remove. Some said the city was named after Rhomos, one of his compan-ions; others, after Rhome, his wife; a third version made Rhome the daugh-ter of his son Ascanius. More interesting than these merely mechanical Greek

FIGURE 32. Two of the eight issues of 'Romano-Campanian' silver issued in the period c. 312–270 BC (Coarelli 2013.31–57). Above, Crawford 1974.137 no. 20.1 (c. 290 BC?): obverse, victorious Hercules, with a ribbon round his head and his club below; reverse, she-wolf suckling twins, ROMANO in exergue. Below: Crawford 1974.138 no. 22.1 (c. 272 BC?): obverse, head of Roma in a Phrygian helmet; reverse, winged Victoria attaching ribbons to a palm-branch, ROMANO. © The Trustees of the British Museum. All rights reserved.

aetiologies was the account in Alcimus, a Sicilian historian of the generation before Timaeus: he claimed Aeneas' wife was called Tyrrhenia (the Etruscans were *Tyrrhenoi* in Greek), and their son was Romulus. This is the first appearance in our sources of the man who would one day be known as the undisputed founder of Rome.

The name 'Romulus' was a Latin eponym (unlike 'Rhomos' and 'Rhome'), and provided a way of explaining why Rome was called Rome without deriving it from Greek. Giving him a Trojan father and an Etruscan mother was another way of making the same point. But it would be a mistake to suppose that the Romans had suddenly made a collective decision to abandon their previous view of themselves. These were rival stories competing for attention; no-one in this cultural marketplace had yet established a monopoly.

Fig. 32

The contemporary evidence of Rome's first coinage—the 'Romano-Campanian' silver didrachms produced intermittently in the early third century—may help to give us a sense of how variously the city chose to present itself to the world. Hercules and Victoria are reminders of the Evander legend, but the goddess Roma is portrayed in a Phrygian helmet, evidently alluding to Troy, and the she-wolf suckling twin boys is a new story altogether.

In Sicily in the fourth century BC, Alcimus had written of Romulus as a single individual, not one of a pair. But by 296 BC the Romans knew the story of the she-wolf and twins:

In that year the curule aediles Gnaeus Ogulnius and Quintus Ogulnius put several moneylenders on trial and confiscated their property. From this revenue to the public treasury they installed . . . statues at the Ficus Ruminalis of the founders of the city as infants beneath the she-wolf's teats.

Livy 10.23.11–12

The Ficus Ruminalis, an ancient fig-tree, grew at Evander's Lupercal, where the miraculous suckling of the twins was supposed to have taken place.

Fig. 30

That site was evidently also relevant to the new cult of the healing god Aesculapius, who was brought from Epidauros in 292 BC and established in a temple on the Tiber island. The evidence is late and difficult, but not to be ignored:

> Even before Romulus there was Roma, and [Rome] took its name from her, as Marianus, poet of the *Luperci*, shows as follows:

> The goddess fair and beautiful,
> Roma, Aesculapius' daughter,
> Made for Latium a new name.
> Everyone now calls it Rome
> From her name, who founded it.

Philargyrius
on Virgil
Eclogues 1.19

Who Marianus was, when he wrote, and where he found this legend, nobody knows. But Rome in the late fourth and early third centuries BC was a ferment of innovation—political, military, religious—and every new cult and temple will have had a story-telling poet or hymnodist to explain its significance.

One such temple on the Palatine was built for 'victorious Jupiter' (*Iuppiter Victor*), in return for his granting the Romans victory in the battle at Sentinum in 295 BC that secured their dominance in central Italy. It too may have generated a foundation myth, picked up by a contemporary Greek historian:

> Antigonus, the writer of an Italian history, says that someone called Rhomus, born of *Jupiter*, founded a city on the Palatine and gave it the name Rome.

Festus 328L

In the precinct of the Jupiter temple was the thatched hut where the founder grew up—but the later source that gives us that information says it was the hut of Faustulus, the shepherd who rescued Romulus and Remus. The story of the twins, progressively developed at just this time, proved much more popular and more durable than those of Jupiter's son or Aesculapius' daughter.

Meanwhile, for the first time ever, a date had been put on the foundation of Rome.

A Greek historian of Augustus' time, having reported all the legendary stories he could find, including of course those of Evander and Hercules and Aeneas and his Trojans, eventually turned to what for him was proper history:

Dionysius of
Halicarnassus
Roman Antiquities
1.73.5-74.1

I have said enough now about the ancient foundations. As for the final settlement of Rome, or foundation or whatever one should call it, the Sicilian Timaeus (by what measure, I don't know) says it took place at the same time as the foundation of Carthage, in the thirty-eighth year before the first Olympiad [814/13 BC].

Timaeus was well known as an expert on chronology, and since he had gone to the trouble of consulting the public records of Tyre, the Phoenician city of which Carthage was a colony, his date for the Carthaginian foundation was probably accurate. On the other hand, as we have seen, he believed that the Romans were descended from Trojan refugees, and he dated the fall of Troy to 1193/2 BC. Perhaps his synchronism of the two great non-Greek powers predated his discovery that the Romans commemorated the Trojan horse.

The most authoritative research on ancient chronology was that done by the great polymath Eratosthenes of Cyrene, working in Alexandria in the second half of the third century BC. He gave a similar date (1183/2 BC) for the fall of Troy, but his account of the foundation of Rome implies a date very different from Timaeus'. We know of it from a late source which also reveals how Roman poets in the generation after Eratosthenes connected the story of the twins with the Trojan legend:

Servius *auctus*
on Virgil *Aeneid*
1.273

Eratosthenes says the [founding] father of the city was Romulus, son of Aeneas' son Ascanius. Naevius and Ennius tell us that Romulus, founder of the city, was Aeneas' grandson by his daughter.

For Gnaeus Naevius (late third century BC) and Quintus Ennius (early second), the story of Romulus and Remus was already canonical. The twins were the sons of the god Mars by Aeneas' daughter Ilia, 'lady of Troy'. We know that other Roman authors, unfortunately not named in our sources, left open the possibility of a mortal father but agreed that the mother of the twins was Aeneas' daughter.

The epic poems of Naevius and Ennius became classics of Latin literature, still read and listened to with enjoyment and respect for centuries after their own time. Thanks to them, most Romans took it for granted that their city was founded two generations after the fall of Troy. They didn't worry about dates.

For serious historians, on the other hand, the dates were now a problem. Eratosthenes calculated the fall of Troy as 407 years before the first Olympiad, and the invasion of Greece by Xerxes as 297 years after it. If the first of the Roman kings was born (say) sixty years after the former date, and the last of them was expelled, as he was, 28 years before the latter, then the regal period was more than six centuries long (in our terms, c.1123–507 BC). But even the most creative reconstruction could find no more than five names of kings to fill the gap between Romulus and Tarquin.

The problem was solved by making the Troy connection much less direct. Aeneas founded a city (Lavinium) in the maritime plain of Latium; his son Ascanius then founded another city (Alba Longa) in the Alban hills, the ancient cult centre of the Latins, where Silvius, half-brother or son of Ascanius, gave his (Latin) name to the royal dynasty.

Fifteen generations later, the Alban king Numitor was deposed by his brother Amulius, who made Numitor's daughter a Vestal Virgin, thus preventing—or so he thought—the birth of an avenger. But she conceived the twins, by Mars or some mortal rapist. Miraculously rescued from being exposed at birth, they grew up, killed Amulius, reinstated Numitor, and at eighteen years of age went off to found a city of their own at the place by the Tiber where they had been left to die. In this story the mother of the twins was no longer the 'lady of Troy'. She was now called Rhea Silvia, a strikingly significant change of name.

This mythographic innovation was created during the late stages of Rome's titanic sixty-year struggle with Carthage. It was first exploited in the histories of Fabius Pictor and Cincius Alimentus, Roman senators writing in Greek for an international Greek-speaking audience, in the last decade of the third century BC. It not only distanced the Romans from the Greek-hating Trojans (Rome was the colony of a *Latin* city); it also respected Eratosthenes' newly calculated chronological scheme. Fabius and Cincius put the foundation of their city in the first year of the eighth Olympiad (748/7 BC) or the fourth year of the twelfth (729/8 BC), respectively.

It was during the time they were writing that the cult of the Great Mother of the Gods was brought to Rome, in 204 BC. Her full Roman title, *Magna Deum Mater Idaea* (in ordinary speech just *mater Idaea*), referred to Mount Ida, south of Troy, where Aeneas was born and where he gathered the surviving Trojans and built the ships that would take them to safety. In traditional Greek theology she was *Rhea*, daughter of Ocean and mother of the Olympian gods. Now the Romans built a temple for her on the Palatine, and learned historians even gave her name, as 'Rhea Silvia', to the mother of Romulus and Remus.

5.3 ALBA LONGA AND THE IULII

This 'long chronology' of the Troy connection, involving an imaginary mother-city with an imaginary dynasty of rulers, probably had little effect on ordinary Romans, who knew their early history from Ennius' epic poem. But it was of very great significance for one particular Roman family, the patrician Iulii. Their ancient family cult centre was at Bovillae, twelve miles south-east of Rome beneath the slopes of the Alban hills, and the god they honoured there was Vediovis, identified as the young Jupiter. The earliest known members of the family, magistrates in the fifth and fourth centuries BC, used the name *Iullus*, which

Fig. 33

Fig. 34

FIGURE 33. Time-line of historical and pseudo-historical events, and of authors who wrote about the legend of Aeneas in Italy. As in Fig. 31, names in brackets are of authors whose works are known only from quotations.

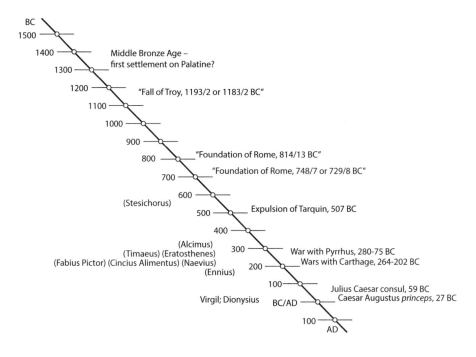

BC
1500
1400   Middle Bronze Age –
1300   first settlement on Palatine?
1200   "Fall of Troy, 1193/2 or 1183/2 BC"
1100
1000
900
800   "Foundation of Rome, 814/13 BC"
700   "Foundation of Rome, 748/7 or 729/8 BC"
600
(Stesichorus)
500   Expulsion of Tarquin, 507 BC
400
(Alcimus)
(Timaeus) (Eratosthenes)   300   War with Pyrrhus, 280-75 BC
(Fabius Pictor) (Cincius Alimentus) (Naevius)   Wars with Carthage, 264-202 BC
(Ennius)   200
100   Julius Caesar consul, 59 BC
Virgil; Dionysius   BC/AD   Caesar Augustus princeps, 27 BC
100
AD

FIGURE 34. Altar from Bovillae, now in the Colonna gardens in Rome (*CIL* 14.2387, *ILLRP* 270): photo H. Behrens, neg. D-DAI-ROM-2013.2466. The original inscription was symmetrical: *Vediovei | genteiles Iuliei,* 'The members of the *gens Iulia* [dedicate this] to Vediovis'. At a later stage, (*a*) the epithet *patrei*, 'Father', was added, emphasising the claim of the Iulii to divine descent, and (*b*) the upper line of the inscription was extended round the side and back of the altar: *Vedi[ovei] aara leege Albana dicata,* 'Altar to Vediovis, dedicated under Alban law', which presupposes the legend of Rome's Alban origin. The date is probably second century BC, before the duplication of long vowels (*aara* for *ara*, *leege* for *lege*) went out of fashion.

meant the same thing ('little Jupiter'). Since Aeneas was the son of Aphrodite (Latin Venus), and Aphrodite was the daughter of Zeus (Latin Jupiter), the Trojan story offered them a direct descent from the king of the gods.

How they exploited it may be seen from an anonymous late text (probably fourth century AD), which was based on an antiquarian work of Augustan date and repeated the original source references that work contained. This text

Figure 35. *Denarius* of L. IVLI L.F. CAESAR, c. 103 BC (Crawford 1974.325 no. 320.1): obverse, helmeted head of Mars; reverse, Venus holding a sceptre, standing in a chariot drawn by two winged Cupids. © The Trustees of the British Museum. All rights reserved.

The moneyer was evidently the later consul of 90 BC, father of the L. Iulius Caesar who was consul in 64 BC. The sceptre, symbol of regal authority, must allude to the descent of the Iulii from Ascanius/Iulus, grandson of the goddess and ruler of Alba Longa. The line of ancestry could be brought through Bovillae, the family's ancestral home, by the assertion (*Origo gentis Romanae* 17.6) that Bovillae was an ancient colony of Alba Longa. Years later, the inhabitants of the town called themselves *Albani Longani Bouillenses* (*CIL* 6.1851a, 14.2405, 2409, 2411).

reports that after Aeneas' death his son Ascanius heroically beat off an attack on Lavinium by the Etruscan king Mezentius:

> Mezentius then sent ambassadors asking for a treaty of friendship with the Latins, as we are told by Lucius Caesar in his first book and Aulus Postumius in the volume he wrote about the coming of Aeneas. And so the Latins, on account of Ascanius' outstanding bravery, not only believed that he was descended from Jupiter but even called him by a somewhat diminutive version of the name—first Iolus, and then afterwards Iulus. It is from him that the Julian family descended, as Caesar writes in his second book and Cato in his *Origines*.

Origo gentis Romanae 15.4–5

From other citations in the same text we can see that Lucius Caesar was a major source of information on Aeneas' journey to Italy, the foundations of Lavinium and Alba Longa, and the kings who supposedly ruled the latter city.

He was probably son of the Lucius Iulius Caesar whose coin issue showed Aeneas' mother Venus holding a sceptre, and cousin of the young Gaius Iulius Caesar who in 69 BC addressed the Roman People in the Forum at the funeral of his aunt Iulia (widow of the popular hero Gaius Marius). By paternal descent, he told them, she was related to the immortal gods, 'for the *gens Iulia*, of which our family is a part, descends from Venus'. That was the start of the uniquely spectacular career—populist politician, imperial conqueror, autocratic ruler, murder victim, dynastic god—that changed the way the Roman People chose to be ruled.

Fig. 35

Acceptance of the Trojan legend meant that all Romans were now in one sense 'sons of Aeneas' (*Aeneadae*) and therefore descendants of Venus. It was Caesar who brought that about, as Mark Antony explained:

Dio Cassius
44.37.3–4

'He is the kinsman of our entire city, for we were founded by those from whom he is descended. . . . So even if anyone once argued that Aeneas could never have been born of Venus, let him believe it now!'

It mattered for Caesar that the Trojan connection was via Alba Longa and its long dynasty of kings. As dictator he made a visual point of it:

Dio Cassius
43.43.2

At that time and later he sometimes wore high red shoes as used by the ancient kings of Alba, since he was related to them through Iulus.

Alba Longa and its kings were a late creation, a chronological contrivance of learned historians which the classic poets Ennius and Naevius, who went straight from Aeneas to Romulus in two generations, wholly ignored. But now they had become part of history, accepted as part of Augustus' ancestry, and it was time for modern poets to fill the gap.

Some classicists nowadays find it hard to believe that 'their' authors should have lent their talents to such an enterprise. In fact they did—or at least, they made the attempt:

Virgil *Eclogues*
6.3–4, with
Servius'
commentary

When I was trying to sing of kings and battles
Cynthian Apollo pulled my ear and warned me . . .

['Kings and battles'] means . . . the deeds of the Alban kings, a subject he began and then abandoned, put off by the harshness of the names.

A few years later Propertius too was tempted to try it:

Propertius 3.3.1–4

I dreamed that, lying in Helicon's soft shade, where the spring flows that Bellerophon's horse created, I was able to sing to my lyre a mighty theme —Alba, your kings and the exploits of your kings.

But he too claimed that Apollo warned him off the grand style.

The great Roman epic of the new era, when it finally appeared, was not about the exploits of the Alban kings. It did, however, presuppose at every stage the Julian vision of the past.

Virgil *Aeneid* 1.1–
3 and 6–7 (trans.
David West)

I sing of arms and of the man, fated to be an exile, who long since left the land of Troy and came to Italy to the shores of Lavinium . . . This was the beginning of the Latin race, the Alban fathers and the high walls of Rome.

Soon Jupiter was revealing what the Fates had in store: three years of Aeneas, who would found Lavinium, thirty years of Ascanius, who would found Alba Longa, and three hundred years of their descendants before the birth of Romulus.

From this noble stock there will be born a Trojan Caesar to bound his empire by Oceanus at the limits of the world, and his fame by the stars. He will be called Julius, a name passed down to him from the great Iulus.

Virgil *Aeneid* 1.286–8 (trans. David West)

And at the midpoint of the whole great structure, where Anchises in Elysium showed Aeneas the souls of his descendants awaiting their time on earth, Silvius and his Alban dynasty were the first in the parade.

In a brilliant stroke of narrative innovation, Virgil brought Aeneas up the Tiber to Pallantion (spelling it *Pallanteum*), where the Trojan hero met the now aging Evander and heard the story of Hercules' arrival. Now, for the first time ever, Aeneas was on the Palatine, where Caesar Augustus had his house.

As we saw in the second chapter (**2.2** above), the young Caesar went out of his way to distance himself from the conspicuous luxury expenditure of the Roman aristocracy. He spent lavishly on public building, but his own house was deliberately modest. Virgil's Evander now brought Aeneas from the riverbank and the great altar of Hercules, by a route his readers could easily follow, through the site of the future Forum to the way up to the Palatine (**4.3** above), noting en route that in those days 'luxurious Carinae' was merely a cow pasture.

Fig. 30

When they arrived at his house, Evander said: 'The victorious Hercules of the line of Alceus stooped to enter this door. This was a palace large enough for him. You are my guest, and you must have the courage to despise wealth. Come into my poor home and do not judge it too harshly.' With these words he led the mighty Aeneas under the roof-tree of his narrow house.

Virgil *Aeneid* 8.362–7 (trans. David West)

The long history of the Troy legend had been given a new ending, on the Palatine in the time of Augustus.

6

THE ROMULUS PARADIGM

Romulus too had a proverbially humble dwelling, as his father Mars pointed out to the poet Ovid:

Ovid *Fasti*
3.183–6

'If you ask what my son's palace was, look at the house of reed and straw. On stubble he would enjoy the gifts of peaceful sleep, and yet from that bed he reached the stars.'

Whether they were Aeneas' grandsons, as in Ennius, or his distant descendants in the seventeenth generation, as implied by the Alba Longa story, Romulus and Remus were exposed as infants and left to die, but miraculously suckled by a she-wolf. In all the many variants of their story, that fundamental datum remained fixed.

So too did the place where the miracle happened. The twins were set adrift in the flood-waters of the Tiber, and the vessel that held them came to rest at the foot of the Palatine, next to the ancient fig-tree by the Lupercal. At that time it was a deserted place visited only by shepherds and their flocks. One of them, Faustulus, rescued the twins, and he and his wife brought them up in his humble hut. The fact that they grew up among shepherds explains the god's description of Romulus' 'palace', since reeds and straw were always used for shepherds' huts in the Roman *campagna*, an immemorial construction method that survived well into the twentieth century.

Fig. 36

Fig. 37

When they were eighteen, they resolved to found their own city 'at the place where they were brought up', Faustulus' hut on the Palatine. Their first citizens were just their fellow-shepherds, augmented by anyone who wanted to join them. When Romulus offered a 'safe haven' (*asylum*),

Livy 1.8.6 (trans.
T.J. Luce)

a motley mob from the neighbouring peoples flocked to the spot, with no distinction whether they were free or slave, and all eager for a new start in life.

Ovid *Fasti*
3.432–4

'Whoever you are,' he said, 'take refuge here. You'll be safe.' Oh, from how poor an origin have the Romans risen, how unenviable the ancient populace was!

FIGURE 36. Wall-painting on the north wall of the *tri-clinium* in the House of M. Fabius Secundus (V.4.13) in Pompeii, as reproduced in Pais 1906, frontispiece; for discussion see Cappelli 2000.166–76 (with Wiseman 2001.188 for some reservations). The scene is the south-western slope of the Palatine, with the Tiber below and the river-god at bottom left. In the upper register Mars descends from heaven to impregnate the sleeping Ilia (this is evidently not the version of events in which Rhea Silvia was made pregnant in Alba Longa); at the left, below what must be the temple of Vesta (and partly lost in the damage), the erring Vestal is led off to execution by being thrown in the river, as in Ennius (Porphyrion on Horace *Odes* 1.2.18); below, Mercury as *psychopompus* shows her shade the survival of the twins at the Lupercal.

FIGURE 37. A shepherd's hut in the Roman *campagna* (Cervesato 1913.187). 'If the shepherd does not actually pitch his tent, as in the days of Abraham, his dwelling is not much more permanent. It is a hut built of logs, stakes, straw, and reeds. . . . . The shepherds are obliged, by the necessities of their work, to erect huts of straw, or of reeds and grasses, wherever their flocks may be grazing' (Cervesato 1913.159, 176).

Since shepherds and brigands were overlapping categories in the ancient world, it is not surprising that the Romans' enemies despised them for their humble origins.

In or about 239 BC, when a Roman embassy sought to intervene in the politics of north-west Greece, the Aetolians replied with contempt:

> What sort of people were the Romans, anyway? Just shepherds, holding land taken from its rightful owners by brigandage!

Justin 28.2.8

It was to counter that sort of attitude that Fabius Pictor and Cincius Alimentus wrote their Greek histories of Rome (**5.2** above), narrating Rome's foundation as a formal colony in the Greek manner. But they never succeeded in making the twins' foundation story fully respectable. As Juvenal put it much later, addressing the Roman aristocrats of his own time,

> However far you trace back your name, however far you unroll it, you still derive your family from the disgraceful refuge. The first of your ancestors, whoever he was, was either a shepherd or something I don't want to say.

Juvenal 8.272–5

6.1 HUTS

When Gaius Octavius, the future Augustus, was growing up in the forties BC, the latest thinking on the origins of Rome was that of Marcus Varro (**4.2** above). It mattered to Varro that the founders were poor men, so unlike the landowning super-rich of his own time:

> Who denies that the Roman People is sprung from shepherds? Who doesn't know that Faustulus, who fostered Romulus and Remus and brought them up, was a shepherd? Isn't it proof that they too were shepherds themselves, that they chose to found the city on the *Parilia* [the festival day of the pastoral goddess Pales]? . . . On the land where the shepherds who founded the city taught their offspring agriculture, *their* offspring, on the other hand, out of avarice and in defiance of the laws, have made pasture-land out of tilled fields.

Varro *Res rusticae* 2.1.9, 2 pref.4

Twenty years later, when Caesar Augustus, now in his thirties, was fighting to secure the Roman People's dominions in Spain and Gaul, two other (very different) authors independently attested the admirable simplicity of the age of Romulus. First there was the architect Vitruvius, discussing primitive house construction:

So too the hut of Romulus on the Capitol and the thatched roofs of shrines on the citadel can bring to mind and demonstrate the customs of antiquity.

Vitruvius *De architectura* 2.1.5

Then there was Virgil, slowly putting together the great epic on Aeneas that Augustus was anxiously awaiting. He included the hut in the prophetic pageant of Roman history sculpted on Aeneas' shield by the god Vulcan:

> At the top [of the shield] Manlius, guardian of the Tarpeian citadel, stood in front of the temple and guarded the lofty Capitol, and the newly roofed palace bristled with Romulus' straw. Here a silver goose, flapping in gilded porticos, warned that the Gauls were at the threshold.

Virgil *Aeneid* 8.652–6

The precious metals used by the divine craftsman were a reminder of the recently gilded bronze roof-tiles of Jupiter's temple on the Capitol, referred to by Virgil earlier in the same book. What a contrast with the simple thatch of Romulus' 'palace'!

Although the thatched hut on the Capitol was a favourite object lesson for Roman moralists, it was never exploited by the historians in their narratives of the foundation. Since Romulus founded his city on the Palatine, the Palatine was where he lived as king. That was probably how Varro told it, and it was certainly how the young Caesar understood it when he bought a house on the Palatine because Romulus had lived there.

A 'hut of Romulus' on the Palatine is listed in the fourth-century gazetteer of the regions of the city of Rome. Despite its late date, that is good documentary evidence: the content of the gazetteer, though much amended in its surviving form, probably originated in 8 BC, when Caesar Augustus created the fourteen *regiones* as the basis of the city's administration. And it is not the only evidence we have. Let's see what the poets and historians had to say about huts on the pre-Neronian Palatine.

The Greek poet Philodemus, writing in Rome perhaps in the fifties BC, mourns the death of a *Gallus*, one of the eunuch priests of the Great Mother (*Magna Mater*):

> Here lies the soft body of the delicate one, here lies Trygonion, devotee of the effeminate hermaphrodites, who made famous the hut and the synod, who enjoyed playful gossip, whom the Mother of the Gods loved . . . .

Anthologia Palatina 7.222.1–4

The temple of the Great Mother, dedicated in 191 BC and rebuilt after a disastrous fire in 111 BC, stood at the south-western edge of the Palatine, facing almost due south towards the Circus Maximus and the Aventine. The hut was evidently where the *Galli* held their 'synod' (or 'holy assembly', as the standard commentary puts it) at the Great Mother's festival each April. We might expect it to be within her sight, in front of the temple rather than behind it—and as it happens, in front of the temple was exactly where traces of an archaic hut village were discovered in 1907 (**5.1** above). Those huts had been destroyed, and the area redeveloped, about five centuries before Philodemus' time, but it is possible that a later hut was kept there to indicate the antiquity of the site.

Next to the Great Mother was the temple of Victoria, from where the ancient route called 'the stairs of Cacus' (*scalae Caci*) descended into the valley of the Circus Maximus. As we saw in the last chapter (**5.1** above), the victory goddess and Cacus (or Cacius) were features of the Arcadian foundation story. But the same steep slope below the two temples was associated even more closely with the legend of Romulus and Remus.

The earliest sign of that is in Varro's fifth book *On the Latin Language*, illustrating ancient Roman place-names:

Fig. 31

Fig. 30

> To this [*Palatium*] they joined *Cermalus* and *Veliae*, because in [the list for] this region is written: 'At *Germalus*: the fifth [site of sacrifice] at the temple of Romulus.' [It is called] 'Germalus' after the brothers Romulus and Remus, because it is at the Ruminal fig-tree and they were found there, where the Tiber's winter flood had brought them when they were exposed in a hollow vessel.

Varro *De lingua Latina* 5.54

Varro was quoting from an old liturgical document, usually attributed to the third century BC, in which the place-name *Cermalus* was spelled *Germalus*, as if from *germani*, 'brothers'. The Ruminal fig-tree (*ficus Ruminalis*) was at the Lupercal, at the very bottom of the Palatine hillside, where Romulus and his brother were washed ashore by the river in flood. We know there was a sacred precinct there, with an old bronze statue-group of the she-wolf and twins; no doubt that was the 'temple of Romulus' referred to in the document Varro used.

Some archaeologists believe, for no good reason, that *Cermalus* was the name given to part of the Palatine summit, and that the *aedes Romuli* named in the document was identical with the 'hut of Romulus' on the hill. But that is impossible. *Aedes* in the singular is the Latin for 'temple', not 'house', and if the place called *Cermalus* was within reach of the Tiber's flood waters, it must have been at a low level beneath the Palatine on its western side. We should look for Romulus' hut at the top of the hillside, not the bottom.

The clearest indication comes from Dionysius of Halicarnassus, writing in the time of Augustus himself. His description of the upbringing of Romulus and Remus no doubt reflects Augustus' approval of traditional simplicity:

> Their way of life was that of herdsmen, living by their own labour on the hills, mainly in roofed huts built from wood and reeds. One of them still existed down

to my own time on the slope of the Palatine facing the Circus Maximus, called [the hut] of Romulus; those responsible preserve it as sacred, taking nothing away to make it more dignified, but if ever any of it suffers from weather or the passage of time, they repair it and make it as close as possible to its original condition.

Dionysius of Halicarnassus *Roman Antiquities* 1.79.11

According to Plutarch, that was where Romulus lived as king of his new city after sharing the royal power with the Sabine leader Titus Tatius:

Tatius lived where the temple of Moneta is now, and Romulus beside the steps called 'the stairs of Cacus'[?]. These are at the descent from the Palatine to the Circus Maximus.

Plutarch *Romulus* 20.4

The name of the steps is a modern emendation (the text is corrupt), but a plausible one in view of what Julius Solinus wrote about the foundation in the third or fourth century AD:

For as Varro, a most careful author, asserts, Romulus the son of Mars and Rea Silvia, or as some say Mars and Ilia, founded Rome. It was first called 'square Rome' because it was placed at the balancing-point. It begins from the grove which is in the precinct of Apollo, and has its end at the brow of the stairs of Cacus, where the hut of Faustulus was.

Solinus 1.17–18

We shall return to this text (more than once); for the moment, we can take it as evidence that there was indeed a hut at the top of the stepped route—therefore in front of the temples of Victoria and Magna Mater—which was attributed either to Faustulus or to Romulus himself. Perhaps it was the one the *Galli* used at the Great Mother's festival.

No doubt the hut gave rise to the story of Cacius, who welcomed Hercules to Pallantion; his house there was 'close to the route down with stone steps, called after him "stairs of Cacius"' (**5.1** above). As we noted in the previous chapter, the Hercules legend, with or without Evander's Arcadians, was particularly associated with the valley of the *circus*, between the Palatine and the Aventine. Later, the same hut could be exploited for the Romulus story. Its position 'at the brow of the stairs of Cacus', 'at the descent from the Palatine to the Circus Maximus', was directly above the place where the she-wolf suckled the twins. That may have seemed more appropriate than the Capitol for the founder's humble 'palace'.

Fig. 30

To Augustus, however, what mattered about Romulus was not the she-wolf but the 'august augury' that gave the founder's rule divine approval. For that, the hut 'on the slope of the Palatine facing the Circus Maximus' was no help at all.

6.2 FAUSTULUS AND THE *AUGURATORIUM*

Augurs faced east. For Romulus' augury that rule is stated explicitly. In Dionysius' narrative Romulus asked the assembled shepherds to choose a form of constitution for the city he had founded. Monarchy, they replied, with himself as king. Romulus accepted, but only if the gods would give their approval:

> Having announced, according to their will, a day on which he would take the auspices for his rule, when the time came he rose about daybreak and came forth from the hut. Standing under the open sky in a clear space, he made the preliminary sacrifice according to custom; he prayed to King Jupiter, and to the other gods whom he had made the sponsors of his foundation, that if it was their will that the city should be ruled by him as king, favourable signs should be manifest in the sky. After the prayer lightning flashed from left to right. The Romans, whether taught by Etruscans or following their own ancestors, consider that lightning from left to right is auspicious, for this reason (as I believe), that the best place to stand or sit for those consulting the gods by means of birds is looking to the east, from where the risings of both sun and moon take place, and of the planets and fixed stars.

Dionysius of Halicarnassus Roman Antiquities 2.5.1–2

The hut from which Romulus came forth into that clear space cannot have been on the slope of the hill facing south-west to the Circus Maximus.

It was in fact on the summit of the hill, as shown by an episode later in Dionysius' history, when the Gauls had burned the city in 387 BC:

> In Rome a certain sacred hut of Mars, set up near the summit of the Palatine, was burned to the ground along with the houses around it; but when the sites were being cleared for rebuilding it preserved intact, in the middle of the burned ashes all around, the symbol of the synoecism of the city—a staff curved at one end, such as herdsmen and shepherds use (some call them *kalauropes*, others *lagobola*), with which Romulus in his capacity as augur marked out the regions for the signs when he was about to found the city.

Dionysius of Halicarnassus Roman Antiquities 14.2.2

A generation earlier, in 44 BC, Cicero had referred to the same event in his dialogue on divination. Quintus Cicero is addressing his brother:

> 'What about that *lituus* of yours, the most famous symbol of the augurship? Where did you augurs get it from? Well of course, it's what Romulus used to mark out the *regiones* at the time when he founded the city. When that *lituus* of Romulus—which is a bent rod, slightly curved at the top, and takes its name from its similarity to the *lituus* [trumpet] with which the signal is sounded—was stored in the *curia Saliorum* on the Palatine, and the building was burned down, it was found unharmed.'

Cicero De diuinatione 1.30

Cicero's *curia Saliorum*, the chapel of the ancient priesthood of Mars, was evidently identical with Dionysius' 'hut of Mars near the summit of the Palatine'. The similarities between the two passages clearly imply a common source, no doubt Varro's *Antiquities*, with which both authors were thoroughly familiar.

At this point we must revisit the text of Julius Solinus, and extend the quotation a little:

> For as Varro, a most careful author, asserts, Romulus the son of Mars and Rea Silvia, or as some say Mars and Ilia, founded Rome. It was first called 'square Rome' because it was placed at the balancing-point. It begins from the grove which is in the precinct of Apollo, and has its end at the brow of the stairs of Cacus, where the hut of Faustulus was. That was where Romulus stayed overnight. After receiving good auspices he laid the foundations of the walls at the age of eighteen years.

Solinus 1.17–18

It seems clear that Solinus' narrative of the origins of Rome was primarily based on Varro, but with many details interpolated from other authors. This passage is a good example, since the precinct of Apollo on the Palatine did not yet exist at the time Varro was writing. And that solves a problem, because the passage only makes sense if the adjacent reference to the 'stairs of Cacus' is also non-Varronian.

Without it, the train of thought is clear. Romulus founded Rome 'at the balancing-point' (*ad aequilibrium*), which ought to mean at the ridge or summit of the hill. He 'stayed overnight' (*mansitauit*) in the hut of Faustulus, from where, as in Dionysius, he emerged at dawn to test the gods' will by augury, looking east. He built his walls 'after receiving good auspices' (*auspicato*), a term repeatedly used by Cicero with reference to the foundation—but only in texts composed *after* the publication of Varro's *Antiquities* in the mid-fifties BC.

The purpose of this complicated little argument is to show that Varro's lost masterpiece is not totally beyond our knowledge. We can rescue enough of its Romulus narrative to guess what the young Caesar believed about it when he came to Rome to avenge his adoptive father. Like Romulus, he was eighteen years of age, and to him too the gods sent a sign in the sky (the comet of July 44 BC). Once empowered by the Roman People (**1.2** above), he chose to live on the Palatine because Romulus had lived there. What mattered to him was evidently not the thatched 'palace' hut on the Capitol, but the hut of Faustulus where Romulus and Remus grew up.

Two Byzantine texts reveal the significance of the site:

> Romulus had been registered as eighteen years old when he synoecised Rome. He founded it around the dwelling of Faustulus, and the place was called 'Palation'.

Zonaras 7.3

Tzetzes on
Lycophron
Alexandra 1232

Having entrusted the kingship of Alba to their grandfather Numitor, they themselves began to found Rome in the eighteenth year of Romulus' age. Before this great
Rome, which Romulus founded around the house of Faustulus on the Palatine hill,
'square Rome', older than these, had also been founded by Romus or Romulus.

Zonaras and Tzetzes, like Solinus centuries earlier, were learned authors trying to combine various different sources into a single coherent story. What they
knew about the dwelling of Faustulus is consistent with Solinus' quotation from
Varro, once we detach the reference to the 'stairs of Cacus'. If Faustulus' hut was
the site of Romulus' augury (Varro in Solinus), and if Romulus founded his city
'around it' (Zonaras and Tzetzes), then the hut was on the summit of the hill,
with usable space all round and a view to the east. The hut on the steep slope
facing south-west had nothing to do with it.

We have just one other reference to Faustulus' hut. It comes in the work of a
mythographer called Conon, who was writing in the time of Augustus himself,
but not at Rome. His patron was the king of Cappadocia in Asia Minor, and all
but one of his fifty chapters were stories of Greek mythology. The one exception
was 'Faustulus, or Ilia', which told the story of Romulus and Remus. Set adrift on
the swollen river, the vessel containing the twins hit the roots of a great fig-tree
and tipped them out on dry land; Faustulus saw them being suckled by the she-
wolf and took them to bring up as his own children:

Conon *FGrH* 26
F1.48.7–8

Evidence of what happened then is displayed by the Romans—a sacred fig-tree
in the Forum, enclosed by the bronze railings of the Senate-house, and a hut in
the precinct of Jupiter which they preserve as a memorial of Faustulus' dwelling,
repairing it with scrap material and new sticks.

Conon evidently cited his sources, but unfortunately the late author who
abridged his work did not reproduce them. For this passage Varro is certainly a
possibility, but in any case we can be reasonably sure that the new information
provided by Conon —that Faustulus' hut was 'in the precinct of Jupiter'—comes
from a pre-Augustan Roman source.

To understand what it means, we return to the regionary gazetteer, the fourth-
century document that evidently contains information dating back to Augustus'
original creation of the city regions in 8 BC. For the tenth region, *Palatium*, the
gazetteer lists fifteen items, as follows:

1. Hut of Romulus
2. Temple of the Mother of the Gods
3. Temple of Apollo Ramnusius
4. *Pentapylum*
5. House of Augustus

6. House of Tiberius

7. *Auguratorium*

8. *Area Palatina*

9. Temple of Jupiter Victor

10. House of Dio

11. *Curia uetus*

12. Temple of Fortuna Respiciens

13. Septizonium of Divus Severus

14. (temple of) Victoria Germaniciana

15. Lupercal

Items 1–3, 5–6, and 11–15 are identifiable sites; items 4 and 10 are otherwise unknown; the sequence of items 7–9 is what concerns us here.

Fig. 38

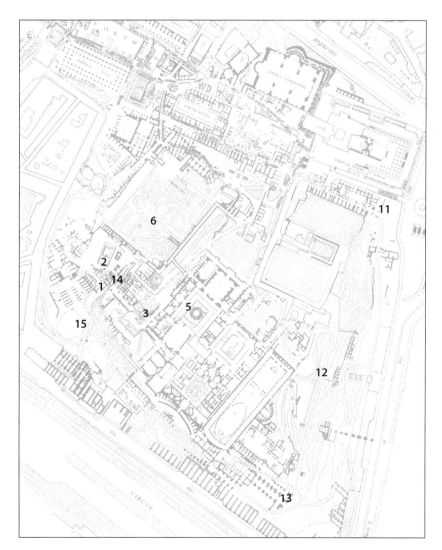

FIGURE 38. Plan of the known sites on the *Notitia* list for *regio X*. Item 1 (*casa Romuli*) is taken to be the hut by the 'stairs of Cacus' discussed in 6.1 above.

It is an obvious first step to identify item 7, the *auguratorium* or 'seat of the augur', as the place where Romulus made his 'august augury'—that is, a hut in a clear space with a view east at the summit of the hill (Dionysius), the hut of Faustulus 'at the balancing-point' (Solinus) around which Romulus founded his city (Zonaras, Tzetzes), situated in the precinct of Jupiter (Conon). It was to Jupiter that Romulus prayed first, and Jupiter's lightning gave him his sign.

Next, we may note that *areae*, open spaces, were often in front of temples, where room was needed to accommodate the altar and the ceremonies that took place there. The classic example is the *area Capitolina* in front of the temple of Jupiter Optimus Maximus on the Capitol, big enough to accommodate crowded voting assemblies. The space was often named after the temple or the divinity, and might be seen as an integral part of the divinity's domain. So the 'precinct of Jupiter' in Conon's Roman source may well have been a pre-Augustan *area Iouis*, identical with items 8 and 9 on the list in the gazetteer, the Augustan *area Palatina* adjacent to the temple of Jupiter Victor.

Corroboration comes from an unexpected witness, a Jewish historian writing in Greek about the death of a Roman emperor. Flavius Josephus—to give him his name as a Roman citizen—inserted into his *Jewish Antiquities* a long digression on the assassination of Gaius Caesar ('Caligula') in AD 41. Gaius was killed on the Palatine, in the complex of imperial properties that had developed since Augustus' time, which twenty-three years later would all be destroyed in the great fire (**3.1** above). When Josephus was writing, the grandiose post-Neronian palaces were already in place, but he was using well-informed sources who could still describe the Palatine in essentially its Augustan form.

Fig. 12

In the chaotic aftermath of the killing, some soldiers of the Praetorian Guard found Gaius' uncle Claudius hiding in one of the buildings, and brought him out:

Josephus *Jewish Antiquities* 19.223

> Being in an open space of the Palatine (the legend says that this part of the city of Rome was the first to be settled), they had already reached the public area, where a much larger assembly of soldiers greeted the sight of Claudius with joy.

We are lucky to have Josephus' parenthetical note about the foundation legend, since it had nothing to do with his story. It evidently referred to the tradition transmitted by Zonaras and Tzetzes, that the city was 'founded around the hut of Faustulus'. If the hut was 'in an open space of the Palatine'—a phrase that obviously refers to the *area Palatina*, and may be a simple translation of the name from Josephus' Latin source—then our conjecture about Conon's 'precinct of Jupiter' is confirmed. It was identical with the piazza later known as the *area Palatina*.

A few hours earlier on that fateful day in AD 41, the piazza had been crowded with people attending the *ludi Palatini*. These 'Palatine games' were a theatrical festival instituted in memory of Augustus by his widow in AD 15. Josephus' source (it is in the present tense) carefully explained the arrangements:

There is a wooden hut just in front of the residence, and the audience consists of the Roman nobility with their wives and children, and Caesar. It would be easy [for the assassins], with so many thousands of people crowded in a narrow space. . . . The theatre was a wooden structure, put up every year in the following way. It had two doors, one leading into the open, one into a portico where people could go in and out without disturbing those segregated inside, and within from the hut itself, which separated off another one by partitions as a retreat for competitors and performers of all kinds.

Josephus Jewish *Antiquities 19.75–6 and 90*

'People could go in and out' of the residence, not the theatre. The portico mentioned here is probably the Ionic colonnade around the forecourt of the house of Augustus, that famous space with the laurels flanking the door, the oak-leaf crown above it, and the shrine of Vesta 'at the threshold'. The easiest way to imagine the temporary theatre is to suppose that the seating for the audience was out in the piazza, and the stage building, incorporating the hut 'just in front of the residence', was close to, or even inside, the forecourt itself.

Fig. 39

Where was 'the residence'? Once we rid ourselves of the modern notion that the house excavated by Carettoni below the temple of Apollo was part of the *casa di Augusto* (**2.3** above), the answer is inevitable. The real house of Augustus was where, after the fire, Nero's architects created the palace called the *domus Augustana* (**3.1** above). We know where the upper entrance to the *domus Augustana* was, and it is natural to suppose that it matched the site of Augustus' historic forecourt.

Fig. 40

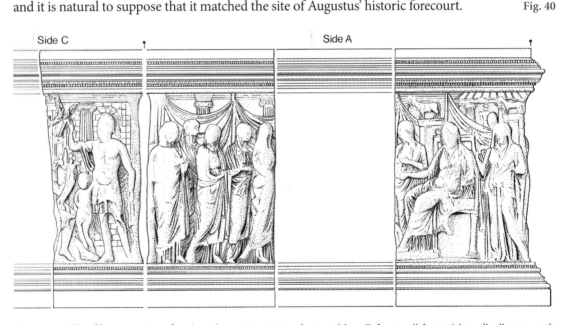

FIGURE 39. The 'Sorrento base', a late-Augustan statue-base with reliefs on all four sides alluding to cult sites on the Palatine (cf. Fig. 55 below): this combined view of two sides, drawn by Seán Goddard, shows the forecourt (*uestibulum*) of the house of Augustus. Far left (only half this side survives): the doorway with the oak-wreath above it. Far right: the shrine of Vesta, installed in 12 BC (*Fasti Praenestini*, Degrassi 1963.132–3). Background: the Ionic colonnade that links the two sides into a single scene.

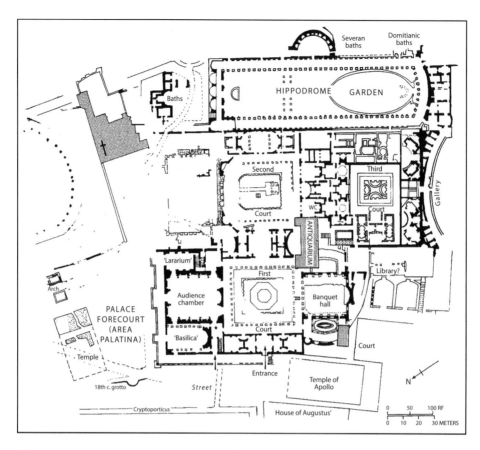

FIGURE 40. Plan of the *domus Augustana* palace: Claridge 2010.146–7, fig. 55. The upper entrance is on the north-west side, at the bottom of the plan; we may imagine the original house of Augustus occupying the area marked as 'first court', behind a substantial forecourt (Fig. 39) facing on to the pre-Neronian *area Palatina* (marked as 'street'). I assume that the building of the palace complexes caused the piazza to be displaced to the north (bottom left), facing the main entrance of the *domus Augustana*.

See Fig. 18 above, where the visitors are in the 'Basilica'; part of the convent building visible there was converted into the Palatine Museum (marked as 'Antiquarium').

Only one piece of the jigsaw is missing, the temple of Jupiter Victor. It must have been destroyed in the fire of AD 64 and rebuilt elsewhere. The *area Palatina* itself was relocated, below the new formal entrance at the north end of the *domus Augustana* palace, and it may well be that the Jupiter temple was moved with it, to preserve the god's traditional association with the piazza; one of the discoveries of Pietro Rosa's excavations for Napoleon III (**3.3** above) was the concrete podium of a substantial temple, precisely at the entrance to the post-Neronian *area Palatina*.

Fig. 41

The original temple was probably built in the third century BC, when Jupiter Victor was popular with the victorious Romans, and so there was no tell-tale

FIGURE 41. The concrete temple podium found by Rosa in 1866 (see Fig. 40, bottom left): Tomei 1999.69 fig. 45 (foto Tuminello 134). Rosa believed it was the temple of Jupiter Stator, but that cannot be right (Wiseman 2017); more probably it was the post-Neronian rebuilding of the temple of Jupiter Victor.

mass of concrete to reveal its position to the excavators. Its podium of rectangular tuff blocks (*opus quadratum*) will have been totally dismantled, and the blocks reused in the huge foundations needed for Nero's palace-building programme. But if it faced the old piazza, of which two sides are accounted for by known buildings (the Apollo temple and the forecourt of Augustus' house), its possible position is not beyond conjecture.

Fig. 42

6.3 REMUS AND 'SQUARE ROME'

What happened to Remus? In early versions of the legend (third and second century BC) Rome was founded by both the twins together; having tested the gods' will by augury, they had amicably decided which of them would rule as king. But when the republic turned murderous (**1.1** above), the story changed. One late-republican historian told of a power struggle between the twins, with Remus killed in a battle between their respective followers. A haunting poem by the young Horace saw it as the origin of the civil wars:

FIGURE 42. Suggested sites for the temple of Jupiter Victor, and approximate position of the original *area Palatina*.

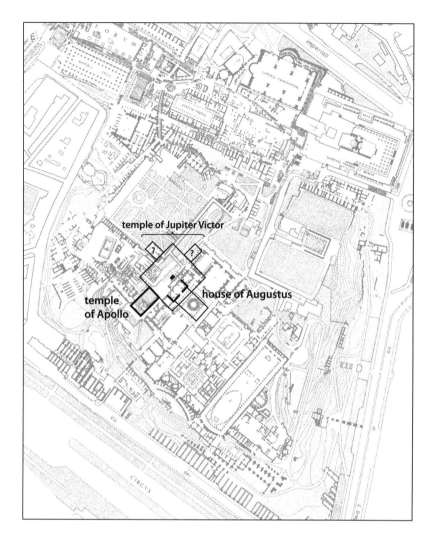

Horace *Epodes*
7.17–20

That's how it is. What hounds the Romans is bitter fate and the crime of a brother's murder, ever since the blood of innocent Remus flowed into the earth, a curse to his descendants.

In his time, as we know from Livy, the prevailing version was that Romulus killed Remus with his own hand.

Not everyone accepted it, however. Varro, who cared deeply about civic concord, insisted on the traditional view of the twins as joint founders, allowing no hint of conflict. In a famous passage of the *Georgics* Virgil cited 'Remus and his brother' as examples of honest rural simplicity, and Jupiter's great prophecy in the first book of the *Aeneid* used both of them to symbolise the return of good government under Caesar Augustus:

Then wars will be laid aside and the harsh ages will grow mild: silver-haired Trust, and Vesta, and Quirinus [the deified Romulus] with his brother Remus, will dispense justice.

Virgil *Aeneid* 1.291–3

The young Caesar had associated himself with Romulus from the very beginning; in this scenario, Remus was his consular colleague, close friend, and exact contemporary, Marcus Agrippa.

Fratricide was not the inevitable ending to this story. Poets from Catullus to Juvenal named Remus interchangeably with Romulus as the eponym of Rome. One historian, ignored or dismissed by modern scholarship, said that he even outlived Romulus. Propertius, like Virgil, thought of him as sharing Romulus' rule, and evidently knew where he had lived:

Where that house stands on the steps, the house of Remus once stood; the brothers' greatest realm was a single hearth.

Propertius 4.1.9–10

We don't know what house and steps he meant, but Agrippa certainly lived on the Palatine.

Yet again, we see the absurdity of the archaeologists' belief in a single 'legend of Rome' reflecting real events. Roman myths are indeed important for the historian, but as evidence for the times when the various stories were created and exploited, not for the times when the supposed events supposedly happened. They never happened at all in historical time. What makes the stories important is their variety.

One item in the mix that seems to have puzzled our ancient sources as much as it puzzles us is the phrase 'square Rome', describing either Romulus' new city or an earlier foundation by both twins together, as found respectively in the Solinus and Tzetzes passages we looked at in the previous section. The idea goes back at least as far as Ennius, who was cited by the learned Pompeius Festus in the second century AD. The text is corrupt, but the essentials are clear enough:

'Square Rome' is the name of [a place] on the Palatine in front of the temple of Apollo. It is where those things have been stored which are customarily used for the sake of a good omen in founding a city. [It is so called] because it was originally defined[?] in stone in a square shape. Ennius refers to this place when he says 'And [. . .] to rule over square Rome'.

Festus 310-12L (Ennius *Annales* 150 Sk)

Ennius' phrase 'to rule over' suggests that his 'square Rome' was in some sense the city itself; not surprisingly, therefore, some historians took it as a description of Romulus' city wall.

Dionysius conflated it with the ploughed-furrow ritual for marking the line of the wall, implausibly requiring the ploughman to make right-angle turns. Appian even gave the dimensions of the square city, each side four *stadia* (about 740 metres) in length, exactly the size of the Roman fortified colonies at Turin and Aosta (*Augusta Taurinorum* and *Augusta Praetoria*); those cities were veteran settlements founded in the twenties BC, a fact that offers an excellent context for this interpretation of the phrase. A third author—anonymous, known only from a scrap of papyrus—mentioned the wall and 'square Rome' in the context of Servius Tullius' division of the city into four districts for the purpose of military enrolment. But none of this is compatible with what Festus says about 'a place in front of the temple of Apollo'.

For that we must come back one more time to Julius Solinus. His definition of 'square Rome', that 'it begins from the grove which is in the precinct of Apollo, and has its end at the brow of the stairs of Cacus', was interpolated into a narrative taken from Varro, so it seems likely that both he and Festus were using an author of Augustan date who adapted Varro's classic treatment to the Palatine as it now was, after the completion of the Apollo temple and its porticos in 28 BC. We even know who that author was, since Festus tells us that he was using the work of Verrius Flaccus, the great antiquarian and lexicographer who taught Augustus' grandsons in one of the *princeps'* properties on the Palatine.

So what did Varro think 'square Rome' meant? He himself indicates the answer in his book on agriculture. One of the participants is discussing land measurements:

Varro *Res rusticae* 1.10.2

'A *iugerum* contains two square *actūs*; a square *actus* is one that is 120 feet wide and the same long. . . . They called two *iugera* together a *heredium*, because it was said that that amount was first allotted individually by Romulus as property that could pass to an heir.'

Romulus divided up the land into equal lots, and Varro's explanation shows that they were square. In fact a *heredium* plot, 240 feet each way, was known as a 'square field' (*ager quadratus*). Here is a later land-surveyor's definition, using the term *fundus* for Varro's 'square *actus*':

'Julius Frontinus' in Campbell 2000.10–11

Two of these *fundi* joined define a *iugerum*, and then two of these *iugera* joined together make a 'square field', because it is two *actūs* [2 x 120 feet] in each direction.

In Roman land settlements stone markers (*termini* or *cippi*) were used to define the main boundaries. If the text of Festus—or Verrius Flaccus—did indeed say that 'square Rome . . . was originally defined in stone in a square shape', that is probably what it meant.

Fig. 43

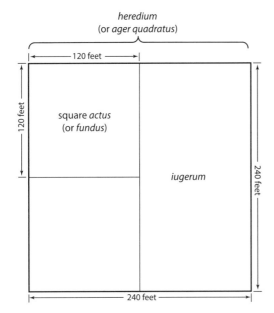

FIGURE 43. *fundus* (square *actus*) x 2 = *iugerum*; *iugerum* x 2 = *heredium* or *ager quadratus*. So a 'square field' measured 240 x 240 Roman feet, about 71 x 71 metres.

In the middle republic, at least, the standard unit for land distribution was seven *iugera*, not two. Two hundred and forty feet each way is less than the size of a soccer pitch, a very small plot to cultivate. But perhaps that was Varro's point. Romulus' citizens were poor shepherds: 'Their way of life was that of herdsmen, living by their own labour on the hills, mainly in roofed huts built from wood and reeds.' A hard and simple life was a sign of moral excellence.

I suggest Varro's account of the foundation went something like this. When the gods endorsed Romulus' choice of site, the twins laid out their settlement on the summit of the Palatine, carefully marking out square fields of a standard size. They began this process at Faustulus' hut, where they had been brought up, and the first field to be marked out was centred on the hut and called 'square Rome'. Subsequently, Romulus used the hut to confirm by augury the gods' approval of his rule as king. His augural staff (*lituus*) was kept in the hut, even surviving its destruction when the Gauls burned the city, and for that reason 'square Rome' was said to keep 'the things customarily used for the sake of a good omen in founding a city'.

'Centred on the hut' is an important detail. Roman land surveyors took their position looking notionally west, and defined the four quarters of each plot as 'right' (north) or 'left' (south), and '*in front*' (west) or '*behind*' (east). If the hut was the surveyor's seat looking west, in the centre of the square, and then the augur's station looking east for the gods' sign at dawn, it is easy to see why Varro placed the foundation 'at the balancing-point', on the summit of the hill. And if

FIGURE 44. A possible position for Varro's *Roma quadrata*. The alignment on the cardinal points is merely *exempli gratia*: Varro's conception of the original layout was probably influenced by the Palatine townscape of his own time, about which, unfortunately, we know very little. It seems likely (Coarelli 2012.112–18) that no fewer than fourteen of the twenty streets of the pre-Neronian Palatine, along with all the buildings on them, disappeared completely in the palatial redevelopment after the fire of AD 64.

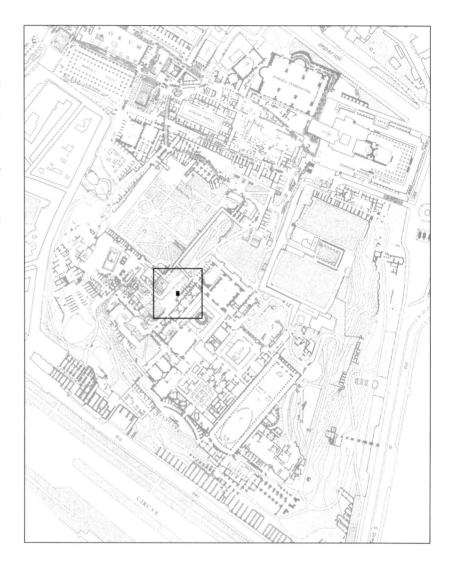

we are right to identify Faustulus' hut as 'the hut just in front of the residence' in Josephus' assassination narrative, then we can even try to map Varro's idea of 'square Rome' on to the plan of the Palatine.

Fig. 44

   As always, legends spoke to the present day. Land distribution was a central issue in the violent ideological conflicts of the late republic (**1.1** above). In 133 BC, the tribune Tiberius Gracchus brought in legislation to reverse the illegal privatisation of public land and redistribute it in equal lots to poor citizens; a group of senators beat him to death at a public assembly. In 59 BC, Caesar as consul forced through two land-distribution laws; thereafter his life was constantly under threat, and in 44 BC he was murdered at a meeting of the Senate. At about the time he was composing his *Antiquities*, Marcus Varro served on the

Figure 45. The young Caesar as founder of colonial settlements: *denarius* of 29–28 BC. The obverse shows a bust of Apollo, whose temple on the Palatine was dedicated in 28 BC; on the reverse, 'Commander Caesar' (IMP. CAESAR in the exergue) ploughs a furrow with a yoke of oxen, just as Romulus had done at the foundation (Varro *De lingua Latina* 5.143, Plutarch *Romulus* 11.2–3). British Museum, *RIC* I² Augustus 272: Sutherland 1984.60. © The Trustees of the British Museum. All rights reserved.

commission that administered Caesar's land laws. It is not surprising that his version of the foundation story made the equal distribution of land a defining quality of Rome itself.

The young Caesar avenged his adoptive father (**1.2** above) and carried on his work. In particular, he had tens of thousands of citizen soldiers, veterans of the civil wars, to find land for in 41, 36, and 30 BC. Confiscated estates had to be surveyed and divided up; the old Gracchan and Caesarian allotments had to be restored with new boundary stones; new colonies had to be founded, and their territories defined. Varro had noted a scandalous paradox: Romulus' citizens were shepherds who taught themselves agriculture, but the great landowners of his own time had turned tilled fields back into pasture. Now, however, that trend would be reversed.

Fig. 45

The Caesars, father and son, broke the power of the 'optimate' oligarchy that had dominated the republic for three generations. The oligarchs' great estates were divided up for citizens' farms. In Rome too, their sumptuous properties could be repossessed and redeveloped for public benefit (**2.2** above). That was already on the agenda in 44 BC, when a surveying expert, used by Caesar for the veteran settlement programme, was one of the tribunes; as Cicero told the Senate, he had brought his measuring-pole into the city and was sizing up the *optimates*' town houses for confiscation. In fact the confiscations came the following year, with the People's vengeance on Caesar's murderers.

Where better to begin the process than the Palatine, where the founders had first laid out equal plots for equal citizens? We don't know the layout of the late-republican Palatine, but we do know that space was at a premium. The grand houses were tightly packed together, and the only ways to expand were to excavate basement rooms, or buy out your neighbour, or encroach on any available public space (like the precinct of Jupiter Victor). Caesar Augustus always took pride in rescuing public space from private use, and he started on the Palatine, using agents to buy up confiscated houses during the war years from 42 to 36 BC (**2.2** above).

Figure 46. 'Square Rome' in the Augustan context: a preliminary hypothesis. The plan is based on the following assumptions: (1) that 'square Rome' was 240 Roman feet in each direction, as implied by Varro; (2) that it was centred on the 'hut of Faustulus', identified as 'the hut just in front of the residence' in Josephus' narrative; (3) that the entrance to 'the residence' in Josephus' time corresponded to the upper entrance of the post-Neronian *domus Augustana*; (4) that the Augustan 'square Rome' presupposed the temple of Apollo, as implied by Festus and Solinus; and (5) that the temple dictated its orientation.

The suggested positions for the Jupiter Victor temple are no more than guesswork (as in Fig. 42 above). All we have to go on is Conon's indication that before Augustus' time Faustulus' hut was 'in the precinct of Jupiter'; the precinct was presumably a clear space in front of the temple, but we have no idea of its size or shape, and the position of the hut is itself hypothetical.

Similarly *exempli gratia* is the outline of Augustus' house. It should be a comparatively modest dwelling (Suetonius *Diuus Augustus* 72.1) behind a substantial public forecourt (Fig. 39 above); but the details of its size and shape are unknown.

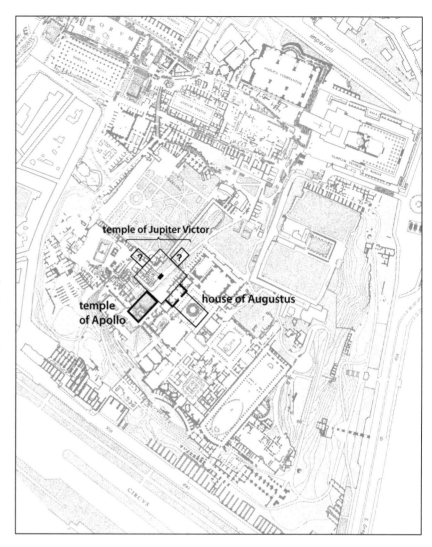

Varro's great work provided him with a template. Once those symbols of divisive luxury were cleared away, 'square Rome' could be recreated. Where Faustulus' historic hut was hemmed in by the oligarchs' private mansions, there could be a spacious public piazza—and it would be a precinct not just for Jupiter Victor, but for Apollo too. 'Square Rome' in Augustus' time, as Verrius Flaccus (via Festus) tells us, was 'a place in front of the temple of Apollo'.

Fig. 46

7

COMMANDER CAESAR AND HIS GODS

Augustus was born Gaius Octavius. He became 'Caesar' at the end of March 44 BC, at Brundisium (modern Brindisi). The historian Appian, who used Augustus' memoirs among his sources, records the moment:

> His relatives warned him still more solemnly to beware of Caesar's enemies, because he was Caesar's son and heir, and advised him to renounce both the inheritance and the adoption. But as he thought that this course, along with failure on his part to avenge Caesar, would be disgraceful, he made his way to Brundisium, after first sending ahead to find out if the murderers had laid any trap for him.
>
> When the troops there came to meet him and greeted him as Caesar's son, he took heart and sacrificed and immediately assumed the name 'Caesar', because the Romans have a custom whereby adoptive children take the names of those who have adopted them. He did not, however, simply add it [as 'Octavius Caesar'], but changed both his own name and his patronymic completely, so that he became 'Caesar, son of Caesar', instead of 'Octavius, son of Octavius', and continued to use these names.

Appian *Civil Wars* 3.11.36–8 (trans. John Carter)

To call him 'Octavian', as modern historians do, is to miss the point entirely, or (worse) to side with the assassins and their friends.

Note: the first thing he did was sacrifice. Whether or not this narrative came from Augustus' memoirs, it certainly picked out two essential elements in the story of his life: first, the devotion of Rome's citizen soldiers to the memory of Caesar, their great commander; and second, his own constant determination to ensure the gods' approval. (They sent him their sign three months later; it is, I think, impossible to overestimate the effect the comet of July 44 BC had on the young Caesar's confidence in his project of vengeance.) In this chapter, building on what can be inferred from the 'Romulus paradigm', we shall see how those two elements helped to shape the Augustan Palatine.

Fig. 46

7.1 *IMPERATOR CAESAR*

At first the enthusiastic veterans could be no more than a private army. It took a lot of political manoeuvring (**1.2** above) to get legal command of them. When Augustus summed up his extraordinary career more than half a century later (**1.3** above), the details could be omitted and the essential fact emphasised:

> At the age of nineteen, on my own initiative and at my own expense, I raised an army with which I brought about the freedom of the republic from oppression by a dominant faction. On that account, the Senate . . . granted me command [*imperium*].

Augustus *Res gestae* 1.1–2

That grant was made on 7 January 43 BC, 'on which day', as the loyal citizens of one veteran settlement put it, 'his command of the whole world was inaugurated'.

One of the many honours voted to Caesar in 45 BC had been the right to use 'Commander' (*Imperator*) not as a title but as part of his name. So far as we know, he never used that right, but his adopted son certainly did. The earliest certain evidence is the legend *Imp. Caesar diui Iuli f.* on a *denarius* issue struck in 38 BC by Marcus Agrippa, Remus to the young Caesar's Romulus. From now on the young man's name was *Imperator Caesar diui filius*, 'Commander Caesar, son of the deified [Julius]'. The command bestowed on him at the age of nineteen was what defined his identity.

When he reclaimed the Palatine for public use in 36 BC he was a military leader, Caesar's son and heir, who had just defeated the Roman People's enemies in war. Any citizen who had served in the legions would have recognised the new layout immediately: it was the commander's *praetorium* with a parade ground in front of it.

When a Roman army was on the march, its encampments were constructed on a standard rectangular plan that resembled a fortified town. Polybius explained the details to his Greek readers, and what he said to them he also says to us:

> There is surely nobody so indifferent to excellence in performance as to refuse to take a little extra trouble to understand matters of this kind; if once he has read of these technicalities, he will be well-informed on a subject which certainly deserves his attention.
>
> The Roman method of laying out a camp is as follows. Once the site has been chosen, the position which affords the best view of the whole area, and is most convenient for giving out orders, is reserved for the general's tent [*praetorium*]. They plant a standard on the spot where they intend to pitch the tent, and measure off round this a square plot of ground, each side of the square being 100 feet distant from the standard, so that the whole area of the square is four *plethra* [200 feet each way].

Polybius 6.26.12–27.2 (trans. Ian Scott-Kilvert)

The same pattern was used for permanent forts, except that the commander's quarters were placed to the side of the square, or behind it.

Two or three centuries after Polybius, a Roman military surveyor's handbook provides precious information. By this time the *praetorium* area was not square but oblong, between 160 and 220 feet wide and up to 720 feet in length. This is how the anonymous surveyor describes it:

Fig. 47

> When the altars have been set up according to the plan below [which unfortunately does not survive], we shall place the *auguratorium* at the right side of the *praetorium* on the *uia principalis*, so that the commander can use it to take the augury in the proper manner. On the left side a tribunal is set up, so that when the augury has been taken he may go up on to it and address the army under favourable auspices.
>
> The place at the entrance to the *praetorium* at the central point on the *uia principalis* is called the 'the *groma* place', either because it is where the force assembles [*congruat*] or because in the survey instruction an iron rod is to be planted at that point and a *groma* placed on top of it, so that the gates of the camp make a [four-pointed] star for direction-finding. For that reason experts in the art [of surveying] are called *gromatici*.

'Hyginus' *De munitionibus castrorum* 11–12

The second paragraph is best explained by illustrating a *groma* that happens to survive, found in Pompeii in 1912.

Fig. 48

The surveyor's art was also vital in the founding of cities, including colonies of veterans. As another professional text puts it, 'the *groma* is put in place under favourable auspices, perhaps in the presence of the founder himself'. It must have been one of those 'things customarily used for the sake of a good omen in founding a city' which according to Verrius Flaccus (via Festus, **6.3** above) were kept at 'square Rome' in the time of Augustus.

The Augustan Palatine evidently replicated the features of the military *praetorium* as described in the surveyor's text. The *auguratorium*, first used by Romulus at the foundation of Rome (**6.2** above), is securely attested on the regionary gazetteer's Palatine list. The tribunal is shown on a coin issue of 16 BC, and also mentioned by the historian Dio Cassius in his account of Augustus' later years:

Fig. 49

> Even when old age and bodily weakness tired him . . . he still heard judicial cases in person, with his advisers, and gave judgement seated on a tribunal on the Palatine.

Dio Cassius 55.33.5

Confirmation is provided by Ovid's account of the assumption of Romulus to heaven. Mars has received Jupiter's permission to bring his son to Olympus:

> Fearless Gradivus mounted his chariot, lashed his horses with a crack of the whip and plunged headlong through the sky. He halted on the summit of the

FIGURE 47. Diagram of a Roman fortress laid out as instructed in the *De munitionibus castrorum* handbook (based on Lenoir 1979 fig. 13). + marks 'the *groma* place', from which the gates of the fortress were sited.

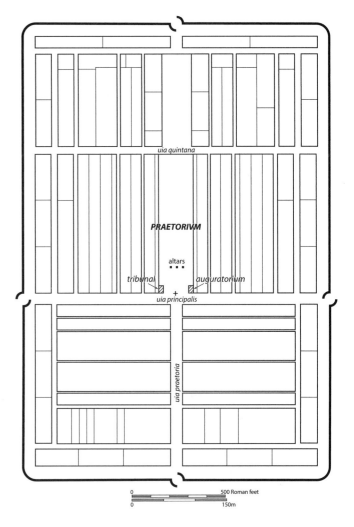

FIGURE 48. Reconstruction of the *groma* found at Pompeii (Dilke 1971.16 fig. 1). The bracket distancing the centre of the four-pointed 'star' from the metal rod is to prevent the latter impeding the surveyor's line of sight from each plumb-bob to its opposite equivalent.

FIGURE 49. *Aureus* of L. Mescinius, dated 16 BC, reverse showing Augustus seated on a tribunal marked LVD S, *lud(is) s(aecularibus)*, 'at the Secular Games' (**1.3** above). The legend in the exergue reads AVG SVF P, *Aug(ustus) suf(fiit) p(opulo)*, or *Aug(ustus) suf(fimenta dat) p(opulo)*, 'Augustus gives purification materials to the People'. *RIC* I² Augustus 350: Sutherland 1984.67. © The Trustees of the British Museum. All rights reserved.

The 'Secular Games' inscription (*CIL* 6.32323.29–32) specifies that these materials were given out at different places: on the Capitol in front of the temples of Jupiter Optimus Maximus and Jupiter Tonans, and on the Palatine in front of the temple of Apollo and in its portico. No doubt there were *tribunalia* at each site, as there certainly were when the same ritual was carried out in AD 204 (*CIL* 6.32327.II.7, *quibus locis in tribunalibus su[ffimenta populo distribuere deberent]*, and II.12, *[in tribunali quod es]t ad Romam quadratam*).

leafy Palatine, where Ilia's son was giving untyrannical judgements to his own Quirites—and he carried him off.

Ovid
Metamorphoses
14.820–4

In every other version of the story Romulus had been addressing his citizens (or organising his soldiers) in the Campus Martius. Only now—in the real time of 'Commander Caesar' and the legendary time of Romulus—was there space on the Palatine for public business.

Neither tribunal nor *auguratorium* was the military surveyor's first priority. Before all else there must be altars for sacrifice to the gods—and here too there is a precise Palatine parallel. It is found in the most quintessentially Augustan of all Latin texts, Horace's hymn for the 'Secular Games' that marked a new era for Rome:

If Phoebus the augur, glorious with his shining bow and dear to the nine Camenae, who lightens the body's weary limbs with his health-giving art, looks with favour on the Palatine altars . . .

Horace *Carmen*
saeculare 61–5

The hymn was sung, as we shall see, on 3 June 17 BC at the new temple of Apollo, and the Palatine altars on which the god looked out were another result of Commander Caesar's determination to turn the oligarchs' residential area into a public space (**2.2** above).

But which gods were they for? To which divine helpers did the young Caesar owe his success? To answer that, we must go back more than thirty years from Horace's hymn. Once again, our main witness will be Marcus Varro.

7.2 APOLLO AND THE SIBYL

Sixteen of the forty-one volumes of Varro's *Antiquities* were devoted to the history of Roman religion, and dedicated to Julius Caesar as *pontifex maximus*. At the time they were published, probably in 46 BC, Caesar's victory over the oligarchs had offered the chance of a new start for Rome. The oligarchs' chosen values—avarice and extravagance—had encouraged the neglect of religion, and now the best thing Varro could do for his misguided fellow-citizens was reconnect them with their gods.

Varro regarded the corruption of the republic as a plague or pestilence, and as with any plague or pestilence divine remedy must be sought. That had always been done by consulting the Sibyl's books in Jupiter's temple on the Capitol. Having explained at length the origin of this treasured resource, Varro reported a previous consultation at a time when neglect of religion had led to disaster. That was in 249 BC, and on the Sibyl's advice the Romans had instituted 'Secular Games' to be held every hundred years. Since he also reported the next games in 149 BC, it is clear that Varro regarded the failure to hold them in 49 BC as a cause of divine displeasure.

The books were evidently consulted, and their response, very unusually, was made public. It began as follows:

> Whenever the longest time of life for humans passes,
> making its journey as a cycle of a hundred and ten years,
> remember, Roman, even if you are unaware of it,
> remember all these things: to sacrifice to the immortal gods
> in the plain by the boundless waters of Thybris,
> at the narrowest point, when night comes upon earth
> while the sun hides his light.

Phlegon of
Tralles *FGrH* 257
F 37.5.4, lines 1–7

The Sibyl had changed the rules: not 100 years but 110. She went on to specify which divinities should receive sacrifice: the Fates (*Moirai*), the goddesses of childbirth (*Eleithyiai*), Earth (*Gaia*), Jupiter and Juno, and finally 'Apollo whose name is also *Helios* [the Sun]'.

Caesar was murdered, and the gods sent their sign—the 'star of Caesar' that so encouraged his son and heir. It was said to mark the start of a new era (*saeculum*), ruled by the sun-god Apollo. Meanwhile, on the Sibyl's revised timetable the 'Secular Games' were due in five years' time (39 BC).

Or perhaps four years' time, according to a poet whose patron would be consul in 40 BC. Our evidence now comes from one of the most famous poems in the whole of Latin literature:

> Now has come the last age of the Cumaean [Sibyl's] song. The great sequence of the
> *saecula* is born anew. Now the virgin [Justice] returns, the realms of Saturn return,

now a new lineage is sent down from high heaven. To the child's birth, in which at last the age of iron will cease and a race of gold arise in all the world, give your blessing, chaste Lucina. Now your [brother] Apollo reigns. And you, you will be consul, Pollio, when this time's glory comes.

Virgil Eclogues
4.4–12

Who was the saviour child? In a dangerous time, the poet gave no name. What matters more for our enquiry is that he made the goddess of childbirth Diana, Apollo's sister and the moon to his sun.

Once again, it was all a false hope. The oligarchs still fought on with Sextus Pompey in Sicily, and the Sibyl's 'Secular Games' would have to wait. Not until four years after Pollio's consulship did Commander Caesar, now twenty-seven years old, return to Rome after a desperate war. He entered the city not in a formal triumphal procession (the enemy was too contemptible for that), but with the less spectacular celebration that the Romans called *ouatio*.

It was 13 November 36 BC, the main festival day of the Plebeian Games in honour of Jupiter, and the crowds escorted him to the house he had bought near Jupiter Victor's temple on the Palatine. He too was a victor, but Apollo, not Jupiter, was the god he chose to honour:

Fig. 46

> On his return to the city victorious Caesar announced that he was marking out for public use several houses which he had brought together by purchase through agents in order to give his own more space; and he promised to build a temple of Apollo and porticoes round it, a work that was constructed by him with remarkable munificence.

Velleius
Paterculus 2.81.3

The new public piazza on the site of those private mansions would be not just a military commander's space (**7.1** above), and not just Romulus' 'square Rome' symbolizing equal shares for equal citizens (**6.3** above); the *area Palatina* would also be the *area Apollinis*, a precinct for Apollo the sun-god.

Peace in Italy allowed time to build. Meanwhile, Commander Caesar and his triumviral colleague and brother-in-law Marcus Antonius resumed the elder Caesar's programme of conquest, respectively in Illyria and against the Parthians. Here was another short-lived moment of hope and confidence, marked as such by the new Palatine buildings, on which (perhaps) the two men were honoured in conspicuous symmetry.

Fig. 50

It was not just a question of macho militarism. In the absence of her menfolk, attention in Rome was centred on Antony's wife Octavia, who ran his household and looked after his interests as a great patrician lady would. It would be good to know Octavia better than we do. We can only trust Plutarch's description of her as 'a marvel of a woman, in whom dignity and intelligence were added to beauty'. Her brother was devoted to her, and she was conspicuously loyal to her husband, despite the stories about the queen of Egypt. The siblings were the children of Gaius Octavius, a middle-ranking senator who had died in his forties and was

FIGURE 50. Terracotta 'Campana' plaque for architectural decoration, showing Apollo and Hercules with the Delphic tripod; found in 1968 during Carettoni's excavation. Rome: Museo Palatino inv. no. 379983. The strict symmetry of the design gives the two gods equal prominence and dignity; the young Caesar associated himself with Apollo (Suetonius *Diuus Augustus* 70.1–2), while Antony claimed descent from Hercules (Plutarch *Antonius* 4.1, Appian *Civil Wars* 3.19.72).

The old view that these plaques were used to decorate the Apollo temple or its portico is now known to be mistaken; they were found, already forcibly detached (Tomei 2014d.150), in the remains of the 'palatial' house that the young Caesar's architects exploited in order to construct the new platform on which the temple and portico stood (**2.3** above).

now given a spectacular memorial in the Palatine redevelopment. We know of it only by chance, from the elder Pliny's catalogue of Greek sculpture in Rome:

> It is clear from its reputation that a work of Lysias was considered a masterpiece—I mean the four-horse chariot with Apollo and Diana, made from a single block of marble. The Deified Augustus dedicated it in honour of his father Octavius on the Palatine, on top of an arch in a shrine ornamented with columns.

Pliny *Natural History* 36.36

Rome's citizens could be in no doubt about what it meant. Diana and Apollo were the divine equivalents of Octavia and her brother, Commander Caesar.

In 32 BC Antony divorced Octavia. In 31 BC he and the queen were defeated in the naval battle at Actium, off the Adriatic coast of northern Greece. In 30 BC Alexandria was taken and the Ptolemaic kingdom of Egypt was brought under the control of the Roman People.

Surprisingly, it was not the fall of Alexandria and the deaths of Cleopatra and Antony that came to mark an epochal date in the history of Rome, but the battle of Actium the year before, which in military terms was only the first part of Commander Caesar's campaign. That was the result of deliberate policy. Alexandria was where Antony killed himself, and victorious Caesar had no wish to remind Rome's citizens of that sad story. At Actium, on the other hand, there was a famous temple of Apollo, and the god himself could be credited with the outcome of the war. The poets would tell the tale, and the great new temple, now nearing completion on the Palatine, would be dedicated to *Actian* Apollo, 'Apollo of the ships'.

After so many false dawns, at last Rome was at peace. Actian Apollo had thwarted Antony's invasion plans, and the defeat of the queen and her renegade lover had also completed the avenging of Caesar's murder. The last of the assassins was Cassius of Parma, who had fought and lost with Brutus, with Sextus Pompey, and finally with Antony. After Actium he fled to Athens, but was found and executed by Commander Caesar in the name of the Roman People. Rome's civil wars were now officially at an end.

There was still a debt owed to the gods. The 'Secular Games' should have been held in 49 BC; but the elder Caesar's war against Pompey and the oligarchs made that impossible. Even when the Sibyl changed '*saeculum*' to mean 110 years, they should have been held in 39 BC; but the younger Caesar's war against Sextus Pompey and the assassins made that impossible too. Virgil's great poem had been premature. Pollio's consulship had come and gone, and only now, ten years later, with the victory of Commander Caesar, was there a chance that the new age of peace and plenty, the reign of Apollo, might come to pass.

The original Sibylline books had been destroyed in a previous civil war (83 BC). The priesthood responsible, the *quindecimuiri sacris faciundis*, had sought out other prophecies as replacements and put them in the rebuilt temple of Jupiter Optimus Maximus on the Capitol. But how scrupulously had the *quindecimuiri* done their work? In his capacity as senior member of the college, Commander Caesar now carried out a thorough review to weed out supposedly inauthentic items, and placed the remainder, now two volumes instead of the original three, in the new temple of Apollo on the Palatine.

At some point (we don't know exactly when) the *quindecimuiri* published their historical commentary on the 'Secular Games'. They registered earlier celebrations in 456, 346, 236 and 126 BC, occasions unknown to any previous historian. The learned author who tells us this is too polite to say it was invention, but of course it must have been. The priestly college had done its duty, reassuring the Roman People: the debt to the gods was not yet due after all, and would be paid in due course.

Meanwhile, in 29 BC victorious Caesar returned to Rome. On 13–15 August he held three successive triumphal processions, for the Illyrian, Actian, and Alexandrian campaigns. The following year he undertook the restoration of all the city's temples that needed repair, and in the autumn held the first of a new series of quadrennial games to celebrate the victory at Actium. That led straight to the dedication, on 9 October 28 BC, of the temple of Apollo.

Virgil presented a composite tableau of all these events as the prophetic culmination of the scenes on the shield of Aeneas:

> But Caesar, who had entered the walls of Rome in a triple triumph, was consecrating an everlasting vow to the gods of Italy—three hundred great shrines throughout the whole city. The streets were loud with gladness and games and applause; at all the temples there were matrons dancing, and altars, and before the altars slain bullocks strewed the ground. He himself, seated in the snow-white threshold of gleaming Phoebus, is reviewing the gifts of nations and fixing them to the proud doors. The conquered peoples process in a long line, as varied in language as they are in costume and arms.

Virgil *Aeneid* 8.714–23

The 'gifts' of conquered peoples were of course the spoils of war. Paraded on wagons in the triumphal processions, they were now, at the end of the long sequence of celebrations, brought to the Palatine for dedication to the god and display at his temple. This too was a parade, and Commander Caesar had provided the space to accommodate it.

Fig. 51

Fig. 46

7.3 APOLLO'S MOTHER AND SISTER

Gold and silver from the Ptolemies' treasury was melted down and re-minted as Roman currency. A magnificent series of coin issues, inscribed *Caesar Diui f.* or *Imp. Caesar*, was used in 29 BC for cash donations to the legionary veterans (1000 sesterces each) and to the long-suffering citizens of Rome (400 sesterces each). Those grants were given in silver *denarii* (each worth four sesterces), one issue of which we have already used to illustrate Commander Caesar's commitment to veteran settlement and devotion to Apollo. Senior figures, however, would get their reward in gold, and two of the *aureus* issues of this time are of particular interest for the theme of this chapter.

Fig. 45

The winged goddess Victoria was honoured on 28 August 29 BC, when Commander Caesar dedicated a shrine for her in the newly completed Senate-house (*curia Iulia*): it consisted of an altar and a famous Greek statue of the goddess,

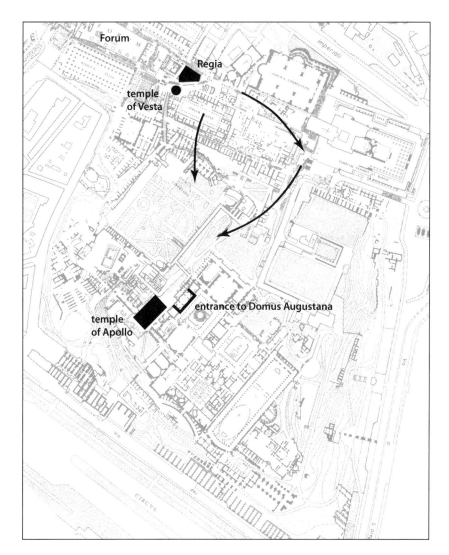

FIGURE 51. Access routes to the Palatine from the Forum area. The direct route, up the primeval 'landslide site' (**4.1** above), is that described by Ovid as leading from the Sacra Via, the Vesta temple and the Regia (*Tristia* 3.1.29–32); it was destroyed by Nero's engineers to create space for the extended 'house of the Vestals'. The longer and more circuitous route, used by modern tourists, offered a gentler slope suitable for wheeled vehicles. The procession to the temple of Apollo that Virgil describes must have used the latter. As in Fig. 46 above, the upper entrance to the post-Neronian *domus Augustana* is taken as indicating the site of the fore-court of Augustus' house.

now adorned with the spoils of Egypt. That must be the statue portrayed on one of the *aureus* issues, carrying a legionary flag (*uexillum*) on her shoulder. Another *aureus* issue shows Diana on the obverse, and on the reverse a temple containing a naval trophy. Although the front columns are 'opened up' to show the trophy, the temple was evidently tetrastyle, with a porch four columns wide.

Fig. 52

Fig. 53

Both goddesses had old cult sites on the Palatine. That of Victoria was a temple founded in mythological time by Evander's Arcadians (**5.1** above), in historical time by one of the consuls of 294 BC. There was also a shrine of Noctiluca, 'she who shines by night', an archaic divinity identified as Diana, goddess of the moon. Now Commander Caesar, soon to be Augustus, brought them together in a new mythic and iconographic context.

FIGURE 52. The goddess Victoria: *aureus* of 29–28 BC. As with most of the issues of these years, the obverse shows Commander Caesar himself; the only exceptions in the IMP. CAESAR sequence show Apollo (Fig. 45 above), Diana (Fig. 53 below), and Mars. *RIC* I² Augustus 268: Sutherland 1984.60. © The Trustees of the British Museum. All rights reserved.

FIGURE 53. Diana and a tetrastyle temple: *aureus* of 29–28 BC. Obverse: the goddess is identified by her quiver. Reverse: the symbol in the pediment is a *triskeles*, the three legs evidently signifying the triangular island of Sicily (cf. Fig. 56 below), and the trophy inside the temple stands on the stern of a ship (*aplustre*). *RIC* I² Augustus 273: Sutherland 1984.61. © The Trustees of the British Museum. All rights reserved.

Fig. 54

Victoria receives a stately procession of newly enshrined divinities. Leading the way is Apollo, wearing the long robe of a *citharoedus* and carrying a large cithara strapped to his left arm. The god of music is ready to play, and sing, a victory ode. Behind him, and holding on to his robe, walks his sister Diana; she holds the lighted torch that identifies her as Noctiluca, the night-shining moon. The last of the three is Latona, mother of the siblings, carrying the sceptre of

Fig. 53

authority. Their temple—tetrastyle, as on the coin—is visible in the background, behind the wall that defined their precinct.

Also behind the wall was the famous portico that surrounded the new temple on three sides. It is described in an exactly contemporary poem of Propertius:

> You ask why I'm rather late coming to you? The golden portico of Phoebus has been opened by great Caesar. It had all been laid out for a promenade, with Punic columns and old Danaus' crowd of daughters between them. Here the marble Phoebus seemed to me more handsome than the god himself, his mouth open to sing to the silent lyre, and around the altar stood four oxen of Myron the sculptor, statues that seemed alive.
>
> Then there was the temple of shining marble rising up in the middle, dearer to Phoebus than his native Ortygia [Delos], on which was the chariot of the Sun above

FIGURE 54. Greeting the new neighbours: early-Augustan marble relief from Rome (Villa Albani 1014, Alinari Archives, Florence). From right to left: the winged goddess Victoria, pouring a libation by a round altar; Apollo in a long robe, carrying a cithara; Diana, her quiver slung over her shoulder, carrying a lighted torch; Latona, carrying a long sceptre. The divine siblings and their mother have evidently come to visit Victoria, whose stance implies that the altar is her own, not theirs.

The tetrastyle temple in the background is separated from the scene by a wall, at the left end of which Apollo's Delphic tripod marks the entrance to the precinct; the pediment of the temple is decorated with Tritons flanking a Gorgon head, clearly alluding to a naval victory. The obvious identification is with the new Apollo temple, established immediately south-east of the existing temple of Victoria, but it is not an exact representation, since the columns on the real temple were further apart (Vitruvius *De architectura* 3.3.4).

> the pediment, and doors, a masterpiece of Libyan ivory: one of them [showed] the Gauls hurled down from the height of Parnassus, the other mourned the bereavements of Tantalus' daughter [Niobe]. Then the Pythian god himself, between his mother and his sister, plays and sings in his long robe.
>
> Propertius 2.31

The ivory doors of the temple showed not only Apollo's power, warding off the Gallic attack on his temple at Delphi in 279 BC, but also his and Diana's ruthless punishment of Niobe for insulting their mother Latona. It may be relevant that Cassius of Parma, last survivor of the assassins, had insulted the young Caesar's mother, and that the design of the temple complex was presumably

FIGURE 55. Diana, Apollo, and Latona on the 'Sorrento base' (cf. Fig. 39 above for two of its other sides). Although the style is quite different from the archaizing Victoria relief (Fig. 54), the iconography is the same: Diana's burning torch, Apollo's long robe, Latona's sceptre, even the Delphic tripod in the background. Slumped in front of Latona sits the Sibyl, with her left hand (extreme bottom right) holding the urn that contains the scrolls of her prophecies. Sorrento, Museo Correale: neg. D-DAI-ROM-2004.0607.

completed not long after his execution in 31 BC. But even without such specific motivation, the prominence of Apollo's mother and sister at the new temple must have made people think of Atia and Octavia, mother and sister of Commander Caesar.

The divine triad also appears on a slightly later relief sculpture, the 'Sorrento base'. Here we find another iconographic innovation, the representation of the Sibyl herself.

Fig. 55

Thanks to Virgil, creating his great Augustan narrative in the twenties BC, the Sibyl was now part of an epic story. At the beginning of the sixth book of the *Aeneid*, the hero has at last reached Italy and beached his ships at Cumae (Greek Kyme):

Fig. 29

The devout Aeneas made for the citadel where Apollo sits throned on high and for the vast cave standing there apart, the retreat of the awesome Sibyl, into whom Delian Apollo, the God of Prophecy, breathes mind and spirit as he reveals to her the future.

Virgil *Aeneid* 6.9–12 (trans. David West)

He now approached 'the groves and golden roofs of *Triuia*'. That name—'she of the three ways'—was a Roman title of Diana, especially in her capacities as goddess of childbirth and goddess of the moon.

Virgil's Aeneas comes to the temple of Apollo on the edge of the Cumae acropolis, and there meets the Sibyl, 'priestess of Apollo and of *Triuia*', who leads him down to her cave. He sees her overcome by the god's inspiration (hence her exhaustion on the Sorrento base), and prays for her help in finding a home in Latium for the Trojans and their exiled gods:

'Then I shall found for Phoebus and for *Triuia* a temple of solid marble and festal days in Phoebus' name. For you too in our kingdom a great inner shrine awaits: here I shall place your oracles and the secret prophecies made to my people, and I shall consecrate chosen men [as your priesthood], gracious one.'

Virgil *Aeneid* 6.69–74

The vow would be paid, of course, by Aeneas' descendant. The Palatine temple was for both Apollo and Diana, the newly edited Sibylline books were kept there, and the *quindecimuiri sacris faciundis* were responsible for them.

It was not only the poets who responded to Commander Caesar's magnificent gift to the Roman People. The architect Vitruvius, also writing in the twenties BC, took a professional interest in the temple's design. In the third chapter of his third book he listed the five different types of temple, as defined by the respective distances between the columns. The third of those types was called *diastylos*, and he described it like this:

The *diastylos* arrangement will be when we can insert the thickness of three columns in the intercolumniation, as in the temple of Apollo and Diana.

Vitruvius *De architectura* 3.3.4

That wide spacing makes perfect sense for a building that served as a victory monument, displaying trophies and the spoils of war. Since the width of the temple is known (from the surviving concrete core of its podium) and the diameter of its columns can be accurately calculated (from fragments of Corinthian capitals found at the site), Vitruvius' description confirms that it was tetrastyle, with only four columns across the front.

The young Caesar had vowed the Apollo temple in 36 BC, after winning the hard-fought Sicilian war in a naval battle at Naulochus. Five years later, at Actium, the god gave him victory in the decisive sea-battle of another war. The gift of gratitude had to be adjusted, and the way it was done can be seen on the

FIGURE 56. Apollo and Actium, Diana and Sicily: *aureus* and *denarius* of 15–14 BC. Obverses: head of Augustus with the legend AVGVSTVS DIVI F. Reverses: Apollo in long robe holding cithara, ACT(*ium*) in the exergue; Diana in short tunic with bow and hunting-dog, SICIL(*ia*) in the exergue. The legend IMP(*erator*) X refers to Augustus' tenth imperatorial salutation, granted in 15 BC for the victories of his stepsons Drusus and Tiberius in Raetia (Cooley 2009.121–2); since there was a large-scale programme of veteran settlement in 14 BC (Augustus *Res gestae* 16.1), it seems likely that these issues were used to pay the last of the legionaries who had fought at Naulochus and Actium (Brunt 1971.333–4). *RIC* I² Augustus 170, 173a: Sutherland 1984.52–3. © The Trustees of the British Museum. All rights reserved.

Fig. 53   *aureus* issue that featured Diana: a tetrastyle temple, a naval trophy, and the symbol of Sicily on the pediment. Later coin-types are more explicit, showing Apollo

Fig. 56   as *citharoedus* with the legend *Act*(*ium*), and Diana as huntress with the legend *Sicil*(*ia*). Thanks to the evidence of Virgil and Vitruvius, we know that the temple of 'Actian Apollo' was finally dedicated to both the divine siblings, with Diana now given retrospective credit for the Sicilian victory.

That double homage is conspicuously displayed on the most iconic of all

Fig. 57   Augustan artworks, the statue from Prima Porta. The scene on the cuirass presents the military achievements of Caesar Augustus in a symmetrical frame of

Fig. 58   divine powers—on one side the Sun-god and Apollo, on the other the night-shining moon and Diana. These are not four gods but two, each presented in two iconographic forms. The Sibyl had specified (**7.2** above) that the 'Secular Games' should honour 'Apollo whose name is also Helios [the Sun]'; now equal honour is offered to Diana, represented with a lighted torch as Noctiluca, goddess of the moon.

The time for the long-delayed celebration of the *saeculum* was coming due. The *quindecimuiri* had made their case for holding the Games in what we call 16 BC, but it evidently suited Caesar Augustus to bring them one year forward, to the start of the second period of military authority (*imperium*) granted him by the Senate and People of Rome. So on 3 June 17 BC, Augustus and Agrippa made sacrifice on the Palatine to Apollo and Diana, with exactly the same prayer formula for each, and a choir of twenty-seven boys and twenty-seven girls sang the hymn composed for the occasion by Quintus Horatius Flaccus. By great good fortune we have the text, not only of the hymn itself but also of the poet's preliminary address to the choir.

FIGURE 57. Augustus as commander: the Prima Porta statue. It was found in 1863 in the ruins of the villa called 'The Hens' (*ad Gallinas*) belonging to Augustus' wife Livia Drusilla, nine miles north of Rome on the Via Flaminia (Pliny *Natural History* 15.136–7); it probably stood in the *atrium* of the villa (Klyne and Liljenstolpe 2000). It commemorates an event of 20 BC, the culminating achievement of Augustus' first ten-year grant of *imperium*: 'I compelled the Parthians to give back to me spoils and standards of three Roman armies and humbly to request the friendship of the Roman People' (Augustus *Res gestae* 19.2, trans. Alison Cooley). Vatican Museums, Braccio Nuovo; this lithograph formed the frontispiece of Burn 1871.

FIGURE 58. Detail of the cuirass on the Prima Porta Augustus (Studniczka 1910.31 fig.1). At the top, under the spread mantle of Caelus (Heaven), the chariot of the Sun is preceded by Aurora (Dawn) and a goddess with a lighted torch, evidently Noctiluca, her duty now finished with the coming of day. The central scene of the surrender of the standards is flanked by the personifications of defeated nations, probably Spain and Gaul, which were finally subdued by Augustus in 26–24 BC. At the bottom is Tellus (Earth), with a cornucopia and infant children; above her to the left is Apollo riding a griffin, to the right Diana riding a stag. Like the goddess in the upper register, Diana carries a lighted torch.

What we call 'Horace *Odes* 4.6' is a hymn to Apollo that starts with the avenging of Latona's honour—the story on the door of the new temple—and ends
with Jupiter's promise to Aeneas of 'walls marked out with a better augury'—the
augury of Romulus at this very spot (**6.2** above). Then the poet turns to the waiting choristers:

> Phoebus has given me inspiration, Phoebus has given me the art of song and the
>   name of poet. First of maidens and boys born of famous fathers,
> You the wards of the Delian goddess who checks running lynxes and stags with
>   her bow, keep the metre of Lesbos and the beat of my thumb
> When you sing, as is proper, Latona's boy and Noctiluca, the waxing moon with
>   her torch, favouring the crops and swift to roll the headlong months.

Horace *Odes*
4.6.29–40

One day the girls will be married women, recalling with pride that they learned
the measures of 'Horace the bard' and sang the hymn for the *saeculum*.

The hymn itself was structured in nineteen stanzas, six sequences of three and
a single-stanza conclusion. Here is the first sequence:

> Phoebus, and Diana who rules the forests, bright glory of the heaven, always
>   worshipped and always to be worshipped, grant what we pray for at this
>   sacred time,
> When the Sibylline verses have instructed chosen maidens and chaste boys to
>   sing the hymn to the gods who are pleased with the seven hills.
> Nourishing Sun, who in your shining chariot bring forth the day and then
>   conceal it, who are born another and yet the same, may you be able to look on
>   nothing greater than the city of Rome!

Horace *Carmen
saeculare* 1–12

The Sun's chariot was there in bronze above them, set on the pediment of the
temple, literally looking out on the seven hills of Rome. At the middle point of
the hymn, in the ninth stanza they repeat the prayer:

> Mild and peaceful, your weapon put away, listen to the suppliant boys, Apollo.
>   Two-horned queen of the stars, Moon, listen to the girls.

If Rome is your business, they sing, then bless the descendants of Aeneas and the
race of Romulus! The hymn ends with these four stanzas:

> If Phoebus the augur, glorious with his shining bow and dear to the nine
>   Camenae, who lightens the body's weary limbs with his health-giving art,
> Looks with favour on the Palatine altars and prolongs the prosperity of Rome
>   and fortunate Latium into another five-year cycle and an age ever better,

> And if Diana, who holds the Aventine and Algidus, takes note of the prayers of
>   the *quindecimuiri* and lends friendly ears to the children's vows,
> Then I, the chorus trained to speak the praises of Phoebus and Diana, bring
>   home the good and certain hope that this is the will of Jupiter and all the gods.

Horace Carmen
saeculare 61–76

As an augur, like Romulus, Apollo looked eastwards. Under his gaze were 'the Palatine altars', in the public piazza which was also the *praetorium* of Caesar Augustus (**7.1** above), his command prolonged into 'another five-year cycle'.

For Augustus, military command was the necessary means to an end. Much had happened since 40 BC, when the young Virgil prematurely announced the reign of Apollo in a time of civil war. Commander Caesar had purged the republic of a murderous oligarchy; he had conquered Egypt, pacified western Europe and neutralised Parthia. Now at last there was a new *saeculum*, a golden age of peace and plenty. In 18 BC Augustus sponsored legislation to improve the moral behaviour of the Roman aristocracy (and did his best to present his own family life as exemplary). Those fifty-four boys and girls assembled in the piazza, singing their hymn in front of the marble temple, were a sign of hope and confidence for the future.

Close by in the piazza were the temple of Jupiter Victor and Romulus' *auguratorium*, which no doubt account for Horace's repeated references to Jupiter, Romulus, and augury. Also close by was the forecourt of the house of Augustus, and among those who passed through that famous door was his sister Octavia, now a dignified widow. (At twenty-two and nineteen years of age, her daughters by Antony were already too grown-up to be choristers; one day far in the future, their respective grandsons would be the emperors Gaius 'Caligula' and Nero.) It is not hard to see why Augustus honoured Apollo not just as the avenging archer but as one of a close-knit family with his mother and sister.

Fig. 39

Figs. 54, 55

8

THE TEMPLE AND THE PORTICO

Throughout this enquiry we have tried to privilege eye-witness accounts, the evidence of people who were there at the time. That is particularly important for the Augustan Palatine, which was destroyed by the great fire of AD 64 (**3.1** above). Horace, Virgil, Propertius, and Vitruvius were all writing in the twenties BC, just when the Apollo temple and its portico were completed. We are very fortunate to have those texts, and what they tell us is uniquely authoritative evidence.

Propertius tells us that the temple stood high in the centre of the portico; Horace tells us that Apollo looked out over the city and 'the altars of the Palatine'; Virgil presents us with Augustus seated at the front of the temple inspecting a parade of tribute that can only have been marshalled in an open space. That all fits very well with what we have inferred about the *area Palatina*, the piazza on the summit of the hill (**6.2** above) that could be thought of as the first plot marked out by Romulus (**6.3** above) or as Commander Caesar's parade ground (**7.1** above).

How then can we account for the practically universal assumption that the Apollo temple faced south-west, away from the city and the Palatine summit, and that the portico was in front of the temple and not around it?

8.1 THE ROSA FALLACY

Fig. 59

The story begins in 1865, the fifth season of Pietro Rosa's excavations on the Palatine for the Emperor Napoleon III (**3.3** above).

Rosa had no gift for writing, and only ever published one short report of the discovery of the temple. He began by quoting three ancient texts: Livy's account of the battle of Sentinum (295 BC), in which the consul Fabius Rullianus vowed a temple to Jupiter Victor; Ovid's report of 13 April as the dedication date of the Jupiter Victor temple; and the Palatine list in the fourth-century regionary gazetteer (**6.2** above), which places that temple on the Palatine. Though its exact site was not known, Rosa believed that his own topographical investigations had now provided the necessary knowledge. What his belief was based on is not

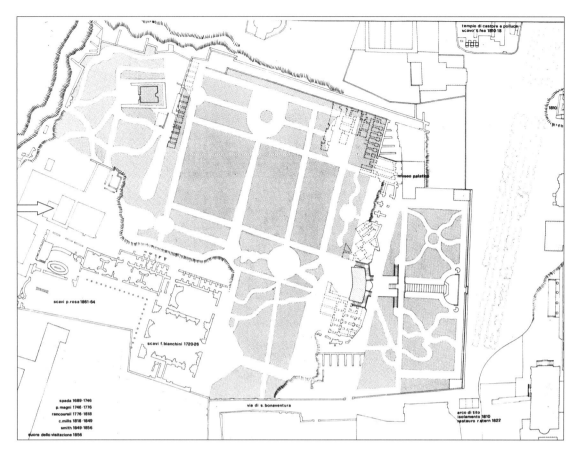

FIGURE 59. The Farnese gardens, with Rosa's excavations (Cosmo 1990.837 fig. 8). North is to the right; the building at the bottom left-hand corner is the convent of the Villa Mills (Fig. 18 above). The arrow indicates the temple podium excavated by Rosa and identified by him as 'the temple of Jupiter Victor'.

made clear, but it was enough to convince him that the 'monument' he uncovered in 1865 was the very temple founded by Fabius Rullianus.

It was not, of course, an actual temple; it was not even a platform on which a temple had stood. It was the remains of the concrete core of a platform on which a temple had stood. Even so, Rosa was sure which way the temple had faced: it looked south, he said, towards the Circus Maximus and the Aventine. That was because of its position on the edge of the hill, which reminded him of temples of the republican period at Tibur, Tusculum, and Praeneste:

Fig. 7

> Just as to those temples, so to our Palatine temple one ascended by means of imposing ramps of steps, symmetrically arranged and alternating with equally symmetrical terraces or level areas, from the road at the foot of the Palatine that ran past the buildings adjacent to those on this side of the Circus Maximus.

Rosa 1865.363

He did not explain why such a monumental access system should begin from a comparatively minor road.

It seems clear that these ramps and terraces up the side of the hill existed only in Rosa's mind's eye. His account continued:

> The largest of those level areas is visible today, largely preserved; it may be regarded as the sacred precinct around the temple, while the temple itself, rising high from the said level, still contains, though shapeless, the remains of the steps, which are divided by means of another, more elevated flat level into two large ramps.

Rosa 1865.363

Fig. 60

The shapeless 'remains of steps' were probably just the randomly sloping top surface of the surviving masses of concrete. But Rosa immediately created steps of his own, and the way he left the site may be better evidence for what he meant

Fig. 61

than his attempt to explain it in print.

However interpreted, these remains are at the top of the hill, not on the steep slope down to the Circus Maximus. For that, the key point of his reconstruction, Rosa had nothing to offer. Having noted the construction of the temple platform in tuff blocks of *opus quadratum*, he went on with this puzzling observation:

> . . . and the substructions that on the Palatine slope support the great piazza are constructed in the same way with similar material in *reticolato incerto*.

Rosa 1865.364

But *opus quadratum*, *opus reticulatum*, and *opus incertum* are quite different types of construction. And what exactly was that 'great piazza'?

Rosa's most expert interpreter, Maria Antonietta Tomei, warns that this passage is no longer intelligible, since Carettoni's excavations (**2.3** above) 'have fundamentally changed the aspect of the area'. In his rough notes and draft letters, painstakingly deciphered by Tomei, Rosa admitted that the topography of the area could not be fully explained, and that his supposed ramps and steps on the slope had disappeared 'almost totally'. But at least the notes explain the 'great piazza': Rosa used the phrase to mean the sacred precinct, now described as 'in front of' the temple rather than 'around' it, and evidently identified as the open

Fig. 62

area between the site and the top of the hillside.

So what does it all add up to? Rosa's dating and naming of the temple were soon refuted: the correct identification, as the Augustan temple of Apollo, was made by Giovanni Pinza in 1910 and confirmed beyond dispute in 1966, when further exploration recovered part of one of the marble doorposts, decorated with a low-relief sculpture of the Delphic tripod guarded by griffins. Rosa's argument for the orientation of the temple was now invalid. If it was not a mid-republican building, then the analogy with the supposedly mid-republican temple complexes at Tibur, Tusculum, and Praeneste no longer applied. But that

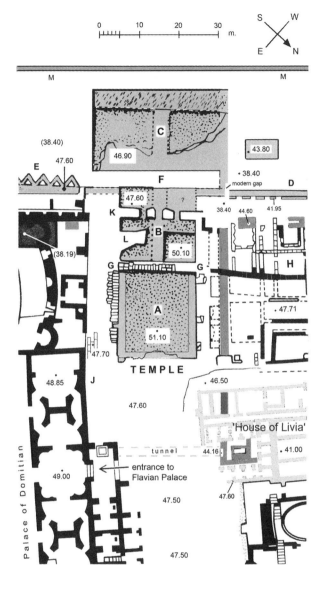

FIGURE 60. Plan of the temple site (Claridge 2014.149 fig. 4); for the section, see Fig. 7. A, B, and C indicate the masses of concrete on which Rosa reconstructed his steps (Fig. 61); K marks the supposed foundations of the frontal columns of the *pronaos*.

consequence was never admitted. On the contrary, every subsequent account of the temple accepted its south-west orientation as an axiomatic truth.

The power of this preconception was demonstrated in 1950, when Giuseppe Lugli carried out a new survey of the site. He drew attention to four deep holes in the concrete, two rectangular and two square, which he interpreted as the robbed-out foundations of the six frontal columns of the *pronaos*. But that was inconsistent with the contemporary evidence of Vitruvius (**7.3** above) that the temple design was *diastylos*, with intercolumniations of three columns' width.

Fig. 60

FIGURE 61. The temple site as tidied up by Rosa, with modern steps to facilitate tourist access (compare Fig. 5): lithograph by Amedeo Terzi (Schoener 1898.65). The visitors are at the level of Rosa's 'sacred precinct' (Fig. 60, C); from there, steps lead up to his 'more elevated flat level' (Fig. 60, B), and at the top, marked by column drums of unattested provenance, is the level of the temple itself on its platform (Fig. 60, A). It is not clear how Rosa imagined the sacred precinct as 'around' the temple, as the ancient sources require, nor how the steps were 'divided' or 'symmetrically arranged'.

The flat surrounding area must be what Rosa called the 'great piazza'; a century later it was all excavated away in Carettoni's investigation of the remains of the house beneath (**2.3** above). See Fig. 8, where the bottom right-hand corner of 'Peristyle B' was about 6 m directly below Terzi's viewpoint for this scene.

The *pronaos* of the Apollo temple could only have had four frontal columns, not six.

The archaeologists' reaction was to dismiss Vitruvius (perhaps he was referring to some other temple?) and accept Lugli's interpretation as if it were self-evidently true. And that is still the case today:

> Zink 2012.389
>
> The SW orientation of the Palatine temple of Apollo was never questioned over the last 150 years for a single, good reason: a series of enormous foundation holes indicates the location of the temple's columnar façade.

When Stephan Zink made that pronouncement, the south-west orientation had, in fact, already been questioned. In 1998 Amanda Claridge ventured to suggest that 'it is worth entertaining the contrary view', and in 2010 she repeated the suggestion with specific reference to Vitruvius. Her archaeological colleagues have ignored it completely. Perhaps they don't take textual evidence seriously, or perhaps they just overlooked her brief allusion to what the textual evidence says:

FIGURE 62. Detail of Fig. 12: the site is visible, complete with Rosa's steps still in place in the 1930s, to the left of the *casino del belvedere* (Fig. 18).

> Written sources suggest that the temple façade made a tremendous visual impact on those who approached it (as they seem invariably to have done) from the Palatine side, passing the house of Augustus on the way.
>
> Claridge 2010.143

We may gain their attention if we proceed more formally. Let's call one of our contemporary witnesses and see what he has to say.

He is Ovid, in exile in AD 10, sending his loyal readers in Rome the third book of his *Tristia*. In the first poem the book itself is speaking, as it tries to find its way from the Forum to the library in the portico of the Apollo temple. Directed by a friendly guide, it turns right just beyond the temple of Vesta, goes up to the Palatine by the old direct route (**4.3** above), and finds itself at the forecourt of Augustus' house. After a few lines on Augustus as Jupiter and the poet's hope for mercy, the book moves on:

Ovid *Tristia*
3.1.59–62

From there, in the same direction, I am led to the white temple of the unshorn god towering high on its lofty steps, where there are statues alternating with columns of foreign marble, the grand-daughters of Belus and their barbarous father with his sword drawn.

We shall see below who the grand-daughters of Belus were; for now, what matters is 'in the same direction' (*tenore pari*). The book is coming from the Forum across the Palatine summit, and the temple steps and portico are straight ahead. So anyone who still believes the temple faced south-west must explain how Ovid, who knew the Augustan Palatine all his adult life, could possibly have got it wrong.

8.2 MAKING SPACE

Ovid remembered that the portico columns were of 'foreign marble'. In fact they were Numidian, *giallo antico* from the old Carthaginian territory in north Africa, which in the deplorable days of the late republic had been a favourite status symbol for the extravagant rich. The whole purpose of Commander Caesar's Palatine project was to confiscate the lavish houses of the oligarchs and use the space for the benefit of the Roman People (**2.2** above). Those Numidian columns were probably rescued from some grandee's palatial residence, perhaps even from the two peristyles of the house Carettoni explored and wrongly labelled 'the house of Augustus'.

Fig. 8

The remains of that house were used to support the platform that extended the summit level of the hill to make space for the temple and its surroundings. The 'precinct around the temple' attested by Dio Cassius must have been on this artificial extension:

Claridge 2014.143

Embracing the temple from the rear but leaving it free at the front, . . . the precinct had porticoes on three sides and is an obvious candidate for the Porticus of the Danaids, which was built by Octavian at the same time as the temple.

The central part of it rested on the great mass of concrete that converted the rooms of the house between the peristyles into 'a subterranean buttress designed to anchor the south-west end of the temple'. Beyond that, it was supported on vaulted substructures datable by tiles stamped 'from the kilns of Asinius Pollio'. It is appropriate that the man who was to have presided over the coming reign of Apollo (**7.2** above) should now provide the materials for its creation.

At the summit level too, houses were demolished to make space. Once again, to understand the archaeology we must go back to Pietro Rosa in the 1860s.

Just north-west of the Apollo temple, then believed to be the temple of Jupiter Victor, Rosa discovered a building which he decided was some sort of priestly college (*schola*) associated with the temple. We have no idea what led him to

FIGURE 63. View north-west from the 'casino del belvedere' (Lanciani 1888.108). In the foreground is the podium of the temple, with one of Rosa's identification notices on its metal pole. Immediately beyond is the so-called *schola*, and to the right of it the 'house of Livia' with its new protective cover. Behind, the row of vaulted rooms supports the south end of the Domus Tiberiana platform (Fig. 12).

this improbable idea. Then in 1869–70 (his last season of work for the ill-starred French emperor), he excavated a house immediately north-east of it, which turned out to contain magnificent wall-paintings and was immediately protected with modern reinforcement and roofed over as a tourist attraction. Attributed to various owners over the years, it is conventionally identified as 'the house of Livia'.

Fig. 63

The name derives from one of the stamped water-pipes found in a subterranean passage leading eastwards from the house under the paved area in front of the temple. It reads IVLIAE AVG., and Iulia Augusta became the name of Augustus' widow when she was adopted into the house of the Caesars in AD 14; however, the house evidently dates from the early first century BC, and the passage was a later addition. The Livia connection was encouraged by Carettoni's excavations (**2.3** above), because he treated Rosa's 'schola' site as the upper level of his 'house of Augustus'. That in turn has led to Carandini's elaborate reconstruction of a 'house of Augustus' that actually incorporated the 'house of Livia' itself. But these imaginative interpretations are just a distraction. We need to focus firmly on the archaeological data.

Fig. 9

FIGURE 64. The naked *Luperci*: fragment of a terracotta wall-plaque (von Rohden and Winnefeld 1911.262, Pensabene 2017.2.290–1). The standing figure, evidently older than the runners, wears a mask with long shaggy hair attached; none of them wears the goatskin loincloth (*cinctus* or *diazoma*) attributed to the *Luperci* by authors of Augustan date. Rome, Museo Nazionale Romano, Palazzo Massimo alle Terme, inv. 4359.

Credit is due again to Amanda Claridge, for insisting on the essential fact that all the surviving rooms of the 'house of Livia' are at basement level:

Claridge
2014.130–1

> The proximity of its S corner to the N corner of the [Apollo] temple ruin has often been remarked on (as yet another reason why the temple will not have faced inwards) but in reality there is no evidence that the two buildings ever co-existed in space or time.

Since nothing either of this house or of the neighbouring one (Rosa's '*schola*') has been found above the level of the Palatine summit plateau at about 47.60 metres above sea level, the simplest reading of the remains is that both buildings were demolished in the thirties BC in order to extend the paving at that level, not only in front of the temple for the *area Palatina*, but also at the side of it, for the portico and its appurtenances. Confirmation of the date can, I think, be found, and it comes from a very surprising source.

Fig. 60

Fig. 42

Fig. 64

Between the supposed *schola* and the 'house of Livia' Rosa uncovered the paving of a street, complete with kerb-stones. Either among the debris in the street or in the 'house of Livia' itself (he reported both), he found part of a terracotta plaque showing young men running naked as *Luperci* at the famous festival on 15 February. Since Greek authors had to explain to their readers what went on at the Lupercalia, we have good detailed descriptions from Dionysius of Halicarnassus, Nicolaus of Damascus, and later Plutarch; their accounts tally well with Ovid's long aetiological treatment of the festival in the second book of his *Fasti*. Not only that, but Dionysius, Nicolaus, and Ovid were contemporaries of Augustus, so the accuracy of their information can hardly be challenged. Yet all these authors state specifically that the *Luperci* wore goatskin loincloths, and none of them says they were masked.

The scene on the plaque is quite different, reflecting a time when the *Luperci* ran completely naked, smeared with mud and deliberately flouting civilised conventions. (They might wear a newly flayed goatskin knotted round the shoulders, but nothing so decorous as a loincloth.) They were masked like actors, as was appropriate for young men of good family impersonating savages. This traditional masquerade was still performed in the late republic, though sober citizens like Cicero deplored it. Caesar encouraged it, but after his murder there was a backlash, and public funding was evidently withdrawn early in 43 BC.

Suetonius includes the Lupercalia among the ancient ceremonies fallen into disuse that were revived by Augustus, noting that he forbade boys before the age of puberty to take part. Like the *ludi saeculares*, mentioned in the same passage, the restored Lupercalia were updated to suit the new times, and moral welfare was part of the motivation. So the inconsistency between the scene on the plaque and what the Augustan authors say is easily explicable. When the Lupercalia were reinstated, presumably in 28–27 BC, along with all the other elements of civic life that had fallen into abeyance (**1.2** above), the new rules may have included the wearing of loincloths, thus making masks unnecessary. Now the young men could show off their athleticism without hiding their faces.

If you look up the few places where Rosa's terracotta plaque was noticed in print, you will find its date given confidently as 'Augustan'. But that's just what it was not. It was evidently made no later than the 40s BC, as part of the decoration of one of the houses bought up and demolished by the young Caesar long before he ever became Augustus. When the '*schola*' house was razed to the ground, and the 'house of Livia' taken down to its basement level, the plaque was part of the debris left lying as Commander Caesar's builders covered the street between the houses with two metres of fill to support the paving of their extended piazza.

All this circumstantial evidence is consistent with our inferences about the 'precinct of Jupiter' and *area Palatina* (**6.2** above), the marked-out square called *Roma quadrata* (**6.3** above), and Commander Caesar's *praetorium*, laid out like a parade-ground (**7.1** above)— all of them different conceptions of the same open space, the new public area that replaced the houses of the defeated oligarchs.

Fig. 46

What the piazza was used for may be seen from two narratives, both by the Jewish historian Josephus, of an event in 4 BC. After the death of Herod the Great, a deputation came from Judaea to ask Augustus not to grant the kingdom to Herod's son Archelaus. The first account is in the *Jewish War*:

Josephus *Jewish War* 2.80–1 (trans. H. St J. Thackeray)

> Fifty deputies appeared, but more than eight thousand of the Jews in Rome espoused their cause. Caesar assembled a council, composed of the Roman magistrates and his friends, in the temple of the Palatine Apollo, a building erected by himself with astonishingly rich ornamentation. The Jewish crowd took up a position with the deputies; opposite them was Archelaus with his friends.

The second account is in the *Antiquities*:

Josephus *Jewish Antiquities* 17.300–1 (trans. Louis H. Feldman)

> The number of the envoys, who had been sent with the consent of the nation, was fifty, and they were joined by more than eight thousand of the Jews in Rome. When Caesar had assembled a council of his own friends and the leading Romans in the temple of Apollo, which had been built by him at great expense, the envoys presented themselves together with the crowd of local Jews, as did Archelaus and his friends.

Archelaus' advocate in the hearing was the historian Nicolaus of Damascus, and since he was probably Josephus' source, this effectively counts as eye-witness evidence.

As Fergus Millar pointed out long ago, 'in the temple of Apollo' must mean in the open space in front of it, where there was room for a crowd of eight thousand people. The piazza itself was the *area Apollinis*, Apollo's precinct; the hearing was held there not only to remind those present of the piety and munificence of Caesar Augustus (the temple built at such enormous expense), but also because public business must be transacted in a public space. Herod had been a 'Friend of the Roman People', and the question was whether the Roman People would bestow their friendship on his son. They had delegated the power of decision to Caesar, but it was still their right to witness what was done in their name. And they did so in the public space he had provided.

Pietro Rosa's idea of a great piazza in front of the Apollo temple was absolutely right, but unfortunately he put it in the wrong place. A century and a half later, having at last set aside his dogmatic belief in a south-west-facing temple, we are in a position to offer a better hypothesis.

Fig. 61

Fig. 46

8.3 SHADY WALKS AND SENATORS

Augustus' biographer naturally made much of his building projects. The Apollo temple was high on the list, and it wasn't just the temple building itself:

He added porticoes with a Latin and Greek library and, when he was old, he often used this location even for holding meetings of the Senate and revising the jury-panels.

Suetonius *Diuus Augustus* 29.3 (trans. D. Wardle)

The main purpose of the portico, which Suetonius did not need to mention, is made clear by the poets of the Augustan age:

You ask why I'm a bit late coming to you? The golden portico of Phoebus has been opened by great Caesar. It had all been marked out as a place to walk, with Punic columns and the female throng of ancient Danaus between them. Here it seemed to me that the marble Phoebus, silently singing to the silent lyre, was more handsome than the god himself, and around the altar Myron's cattle were standing, four oxen sculpted by an artist but full of life.

Propertius 2.31.1–8

Yesterday I saw a young lady walking in the portico that contains Danaus' troop of daughters. I was smitten, so straight away I sent a note asking her. With trembling hand she wrote back 'Not allowed!'.

Ovid *Amores* 2.2.3–6

Before everything else, the portico was a place for ordinary citizens to stroll for pleasure.

In the bad old days, colonnades of exotic marble and masterpieces of classic Greek sculpture had been strictly for private enjoyment, in the villas and gardens of the super-rich. The People's champions in the late republic had begun to change that, Pompey with the great portico he attached to his theatre, Caesar with the suburban gardens he bequeathed to the Roman People; but it was the young Caesar and his friend Marcus Agrippa who pursued most systematically the principle of public ownership. Already in 33 BC, Agrippa as aedile had decorated the city with three hundred bronze and marble statues; making them public property, he said, was preferable to having them banished in private villas. Books too were luxury goods, hand-written on imported papyrus, so the library in the portico was part of the same programme, making valuable cultural assets publicly accessible.

Augustus' wife and sister helped to carry out this policy. Octavia's portico was next to the great theatre built in the name of her son Marcellus; Livia's portico on the Esquiline replaced the luxurious town house of a particularly unpleasant grandee. Ironically, our best evidence for their contribution comes from a work of which Augustus deeply disapproved.

In the first book of Ovid's *Ars amatoria*, the poet tells his male readers where to go to pick up women:

When the sun approaches the back of Hercules' lion [the star-sign Leo], just stroll at leisure under Pompey's shade, or where a mother [Octavia] added her gifts to the gifts of her son, a rich work of foreign marble; and don't fail to visit the portico

Ovid *Ars*
amatoria 1.67–74

dotted with ancient pictures which has Livia as the name of its donor, and the one
where Belus' grand-daughters dare to plan their cousins' murder, and their father
stands fierce with his sword drawn.

Belus' grand-daughters were the fifty Danaids, whose statues stood between the
columns in the portico of Palatine Apollo. And where men can look for sex, so
too can women. Here's Ovid's advice to his female readers:

Ovid *Ars*
amatoria
3.387–92

> When your head burns under the heavenly horses of the virgin [the star-sign
> Virgo], you're entitled—and it's worth your while—to go beneath the Pompeian
> shade; or visit the Palatine, sacred to laurel-bearing Phoebus (he sank the Egyptian
> ships in the deep sea), and the monuments that our leader's sister and wife have
> provided, and his son-in-law [Agrippa] crowned with naval honour.

For present purposes we can ignore the impudence of these suggestions (no
wonder Augustus banished Ovid a few years later), and notice instead their as-
trological setting. The sun was in Leo and Virgo during August and September,
the hottest time of the Roman year, when people who could afford it were out
of town. Ordinary citizens didn't have villas in the hills or by the sea, but now,
thanks to Augustus and his family, they too could find shade to stroll in and
works of art to enjoy.

Some of the shade in the Palatine portico was under foliage, the 'gentle grove'
where Propertius and his fellow-poets dined and drank at Apollo's invitation.
The goddess of groves and woods was Diana, who in her capacity as Noctiluca
shared the whole complex with her brother (**7.3** above), and it seems likely—
though the evidence is very indirect—that the grove in the portico replaced
Noctiluca's ancient cult site.

It has recently been argued that the grand two-peristyle house on top of
which the platform for the portico was built—Carettoni's 'house of Augustus',
Carandini's 'palace of Octavian' (**2.3** above)— incorporated into its structure a
small pre-existing shrine that evidently dated back to the sixth or fifth century
BC. If Stephan Zink's proposal is right, then perhaps we have the archaic cult
site of Noctiluca, swallowed up into some oligarch's private property and then
restored by Commander Caesar in the great portico he created nine metres
directly above it.

We know from Varro that the ancient shrine of Noctiluca had torches burning
all night. The iconography of the Augustan Diana Noctiluca, identified by the
burning torch she carries, suggests that the same was true of the restored cult
site. Propertius tells us that he and the other poets will stay all night in the grove,
drinking and reciting 'until the day throws its rays on my wine', thus replicating
exactly the sequence of Diana Noctiluca and Phoebus Apollo on the breastplate
of the Prima Porta statue. In the great fire of AD 64, Apollo's temple survived

Figs. 54, 55

Fig. 58

on its high podium, but the portico was destroyed, and Diana Noctiluca with it. That is the implication of Nero's punishment of the Christians as scapegoats for the fire: he used them as burning torches, he said, 'to give light at night', like the goddess whose shrine they were supposed to have destroyed.

Other features of the portico are more easily documented. Late in AD 19, when the Senate was proposing elaborate honours for the recently deceased Germanicus Caesar, it took care that its proposals should be publicly recorded on bronze,

> and that that bronze should be fixed on the Palatine, in the portico which is by (the temple) of Apollo, in the *templum* in which meetings of the Senate were held.

Tabula Siarensis b.2.20–1 (trans. M.H. Crawford)

The consuls of the following year presided over a legislative assembly that voted the honours into law. That too was inscribed on bronze, and part of a copy survives. It included the provision

> that on the Palatine, in the portico which is by (the temple) of Apollo, in that *templum* in which meetings of the Senate are accustomed to be held, [among the likenesses] of men of distinguished talent, there be placed likenesses of Germanicus Caesar and of Drusus Germanicus, his natural father [and the brother] of Ti. Caesar Augustus, who himself also was of fertile talent, over the capitals of the columns of [that roof] by which the statue of Apollo is covered.

Tabula Hebana 1–4 (trans. M.H. Crawford)

The Latin word *templum*, necessarily untranslated here, meant an area marked out by an augur as sacred ground. The Senate could only meet in a *templum* (this information too comes from Varro), which might be a temple in the normal sense, but in this case clearly was not.

The records of two other Senate meetings in AD 19 happen to survive, and both use the same formula to describe the venue: *in Palatio in porticu quae est ad Apollinis*, 'on the Palatine, in the portico which is by (the temple) of Apollo'. The 'likenesses of men of distinguished talent', among whom those of Germanicus and his father were to be installed, show that the Senate met in the part of the portico that was used as a library; it was decorated with portraits of the authors whose books were stored there, not just poets and historians, but orators too, fellow-senators whose presence might inspire eloquence in debate.

Two further bits of documentary evidence can be added. The first, a scrap of papyrus from the rubbish tip of the Egyptian town of Oxyrhynchus, was part of the official report of an embassy to Rome in AD 12 or 13. After the archive file number and the date 'in the 42nd year of Caesar', it begins:

> At the ninth hour Augustus took his seat in the temple of Apollo in the Roman library and gave audience to the ambassadors from Alexandria.

Oxyrhynchus Papyri 2435.30–4

The second item is an inscription discovered in the 1960s, when construction of the Autostrada del Sole about 40 km north of Rome revealed the villa of the Volusii at Lucus Feroniae. As the career record of Lucius Volusius Saturninus, who died in AD 56 at the age of ninety-three, it listed not only the magistracies he held but also the public statues that were erected in his honour:

> Triumphal: one in bronze in the Forum of Augustus, two in marble at the new temple of Divus Augustus. Consular: one at the temple of Divus Iulius, a second on the Palatine inside the *tripylum*, a third in the *area Apollinis* within sight of the Senate-house (*curia*). Augural, at the Regia; equestrian, next to the Rostra; seated on a curule chair, at the Pompeian theatre in the portico of the Lentuli.

Année Épigraphique 1972.174.7–12

What concerns us here is the third consular statue. It may perhaps have been visible from the Senate-house in the Forum (*curia Iulia*), but in the context it is more probably identified by its proximity to where the Senate met on the Palatine; Tacitus refers to 'the threshold of the *curia*' when reporting a meeting in the Palatine portico library.

Some useful conclusions can be drawn from this body of evidence. The library, which was also the *curia*, the designated *templum* in which the Senate met, was an integral part of the portico; the formula for the venue in official records was not 'in the library' but 'in the portico'. What that meant can be seen by comparison with two of Rome's other grand public porticoes, those of Pompey and Livia. Each of them featured a substantial *exedra* opening off the back wall of one of the colonnades and forming a rectangular roofed hall with a floor space of about 480 square metres. In Pompey's portico, the *exedra* was the *curia* where the Senate met on the Ides of March 44 BC (and some of our sources for the murder of Caesar say that the meeting was 'in the portico'); the *exedra* in Livia's portico is less well attested, but we know Trajan used it for judicial hearings.

Comparative evidence for libraries is less direct, since the best examples are at Ephesus in the second century AD and Timgad (north Africa) probably in the third. By then there seems to have been a standard layout: a roofed hall provided space for readers (the Ephesus example has an area of 187 square metres), and around three sides of it a raised podium a metre or so deep supported a colonnade that masked the wooden cabinets, set into niches in the walls, from which the library staff would bring the volumes; in the centre of the back wall the podium and colonnade were interrupted by a chapel-like space for a presiding statue. It might be of Minerva, the goddess of wisdom—Juvenal's phrase for a library was 'books, cabinets, and Minerva in the middle'—but in the Palatine library it was evidently Apollo, set in a shrine under a *baldacchino* supported by the two projecting columns on to which the portraits of Germanicus and his father were to be attached.

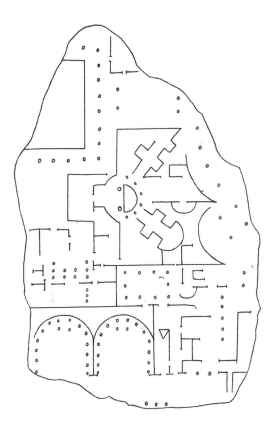

FIGURE 65. A lost fragment of the Severan marble plan of Rome, as recorded in a sixteenth-century manuscript (*Cod. Vat. Lat.* 3439 fol. 14r): Jordan 1874 Taf. XX frag. 163, now *FUR* fr. 20b. The twin halls (bottom left) are presented as an integral part of the Flavian *domus Augustana*, though in fact they are slightly differently oriented from the rest, on the same alignment as the temple of Apollo (cf. Fig. 40, right-hand side). They are very plausibly identified as libraries, and since one of them was built on top of substantial first-century BC substructures, it is assumed nowadays that they are the Flavian replacement for the Augustan library.

That layout is clearly visible in the two halls of Flavian date that were built about forty metres south-east of the Apollo temple, each of which evidently had a floor-space of about 341 square metres. It is natural to assume that they replaced the Augustan library, destroyed in the fire of AD 64, and that the two buildings respectively housed the new Latin and Greek collections. Augustus had evidently received the Alexandrian ambassadors in the Latin ('Roman') part of his library—no doubt to remind them that there was now a literature beyond what their own library held—but he did not have separate buildings for the two languages. Suetonius' singular noun, 'a Latin and Greek library', is decisive on that point, and the use of the building for Senate meetings implies an unusually large reading-room space. One would expect an area at least the size of the *exedrae* in the porticos of Pompey and Livia.

The two Flavian halls are on the same alignment as the Apollo temple and the palatial house that was destroyed to create the platform for the portico, and the one to the north-east was evidently built on Augustan foundations. Current archaeological orthodoxy identifies that hall as the Augustan library itself, rebuilt in the same form, and the other as a Flavian construction built to match it. Certainly the north-eastern hall would be intelligible as an *exedra* of Apollo's

Fig. 65

portico, but can we be sure it was the one originally used as a library and Senate chamber? If Domitian replaced the library *in situ*, it isn't obvious why he had to double the space. And remember the consular statue of Volusius Saturninus, 'in the *area Apollinis* within sight of the *curia*'. That would only be possible if the *area Apollinis* were identical with the portico, and situated paradoxically *behind* Apollo's temple.

Archaeologists are oddly reluctant to admit that the Augustan 'portico at the temple of Apollo' was destroyed in the Neronian fire. But the evidence is compelling. We know that the portico was 'around' the temple, which must mean along each side and across the back, whereas the substantial remains of the post-Neronian *domus Augustana* are only five metres distant from the side of the temple podium, obviously encroaching on where the portico had been. The fact is that practically all of the artificial platform created by Augustus' engineers, and everything that stood on it, has been lost for ever. Rather than leaping to conclusions from inadequate archaeological evidence, we should remember how little we know—and if that makes us 'pusillanimous empiricists' (**2.3** above), well, so be it.

There is enough surviving substructure to show that the platform extended about thirty metres beyond the back wall of the temple. Comparison with the porticos of Octavia and Livia makes it overwhelmingly likely that the architectural design was symmetrical, centred on the temple. The principle of symmetry is confirmed by the placing of the temple in relation to the two peristyles, thirty feet below, on top of which the platform was constructed. If the peristyles, and what was between them, indicate the full extent of the platform, then it extended about 40 metres beyond the temple on each side. Assuming a rectangle about 106 metres broad and about 76 metres deep, we would have an area very similar to that of the portico of Livia and more than half the size of the portico of Octavia, which surrounded two temples.

Fig. 8

Fig. 66

How the various features of the portico complex were arranged is anybody's guess. The colonnade itself probably consisted of fifty-one columns, with the fifty Danaids between them; the shady grove may have been behind the temple, if our suggestion about Diana Noctiluca happens to be right; and the library space, which was also a *templum* marked out for Senate meetings, may have been in one or the other of the lateral wings, offering a view into the *area Apollinis* in front of the temple, where the statue of Volusius Saturninus evidently stood.

The existence of those lateral wings, unrecognised in the current topographical literature, is a necessary corollary of the 'portico around the temple' securely attested in our sources. There is no reason to expect archaeological confirmation of it; we are dealing with a comparatively short phase of urban history, just the century from 36 BC, when the young Caesar implemented his policy of confiscation, demolition, and redevelopment, to AD 64, when the Augustan Palatine was reduced to smoking ruins, to be demolished and redeveloped in their turn.

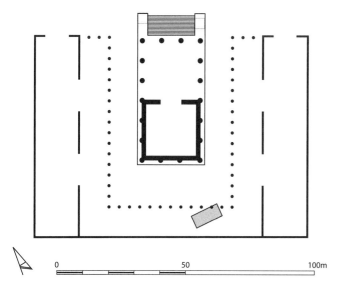

FIGURE 66. A possible layout for the Apollo temple and its portico. The temple plan is as suggested in Claridge 2014.152 fig. 11; the hypothesis for the portico, purely *exempli gratia*, assumes a total of 51 columns with extra space behind the temple that could have accommodated a shrine of Diana 'Noctiluca'; the shaded rectangle marks the position, 9m below, of the remains identified as an archaic cult site (Zink 2015). The purpose of this conjectural reconstruction is to show that even with a portico of generous proportions, there could still be plenty of room for a library and Senate-chamber; each of the two lateral areas offers a space of more than 1200 square metres.

0   50   100m

Archaeologists, and historians who believed them, have been culpably content with Rosa's unfounded assumption that the Apollo temple faced south-west, and culpably unwilling to recognise that there is no evidence above the basement level for the existence of the so-called 'house of Livia' after the thirties BC.

The argument matters historically, because 'the portico which is at the temple of Apollo', together with the *area Apollinis* piazza in front of the temple, was a symbolic gift to the Roman People. Elected consul at the age of nineteen, the young Caesar had had the murderers of his adoptive father tried and condemned by due process of law; as *triumuir* and military commander he had defeated them, and the rest of the oligarchy, in the civil wars of 42–36 BC. It was from their confiscated property that he had purchased the Palatine houses he needed for his project, to make over to the Roman People what he had taken from their enemies.

It was a space for the gods, a space for public business, a space for pleasure and entertainment, created at the site of Rome's foundation by Commander Caesar, soon to be Augustus, whose forecourt, decorated with laurels and the oak-wreath crown 'for the saving of citizens' looked out on it all.

Fig. 39

9

PALATINE POETS

Fig. 67

The marble steps of the Apollo temple and the lateral wings of the portico on either side, a total width of about 106 metres (358 Roman feet), must have occupied the whole south-west side of the Palatine piazza. For comparison, think of the National Gallery in London, of which the neo-classical façade, about 125 metres wide, forms the whole north side of Trafalgar Square. As the commander's Fig. 47 *praetorium* (**7.1** above), the piazza may have been oblong rather than square, but it was evidently broad enough to encompass 'square Rome', the space in front of the Apollo temple that we have identified as the first marked-out plot, 240 Roman feet each way, of Romulus' newly-founded settlement (**6.3** above).

In the same area was the *auguratorium*, the hut of Faustulus from which Romulus as augur obtained divine approval for his rule of Rome, on the occasion that provided Augustus with his honorific name. As we noted earlier (**6.2** above), in the pre-Augustan Palatine topography the hut was 'in the precinct of Jupiter', presumably Jupiter Victor, and in AD 41 it was 'just in front of the residence', used as part of the *ad hoc* theatre erected each year for the games in memory of Augustus. The men who killed Augustus' great-grandson Gaius 'Caligula' chose that time and place as their chance to strike, 'with so many thousands of people crowded in a narrow space'. It is a reminder of the use of the piazza as a place of entertainment.

We can be sure that the new *area Palatina* was used for festival occasions right from the start; obvious examples are the annual holiday for Augustus' birthday on 23 September, the dedication date of Apollo's temple on 9 October, and the games in honour of the Actium victory, first held in the autumn of 28 BC and repeated every four years after that. Traditionally, the steps of temples were used as vantage points for watching stage performances or other kinds of spectacle, so we may imagine the steps of the Apollo and Jupiter Victor temples serving as grandstands for the audience, supplemented by temporary wooden terraces of seats. But what was that audience watching and listening to?

Sometimes, as you would expect, it was actors and dancers on the stage. But the Augustan age was famous for its poets, and they too often performed in public. Perhaps, with careful enough reading, we may be able to guess which classic texts first found their audience on the Palatine.

9.1 HORACE

The best place to start is the third book of Horace's *Odes*, which opens with a sequence of six poems linked by metre, serious patriotic content, and the poet's self-presentation as a priest or prophet. They were addressed to the Roman People, and must therefore have been delivered on public occasions. This is how these 'Roman Odes' begin:

> I hate the profane mob and keep them at a distance. Maintain a holy silence. As priest of the Muses I sing for girls and boys songs never heard before.
> Dread kings hold sway over their flocks; over kings rules Jupiter resplendent in triumph over the Giants, moving all things with an eyebrow.

Horace *Odes* 3.1.1–8 (trans. David West)

The poet as priest of the Muses could be just a banal metaphor—'Horace's reference is entirely literary', says the standard commentary—but everyone knew that Apollo was the god who led the Muses' song, and a statue of Apollo singing to his lyre was a conspicuous feature of the Palatine temple. And then we have Jupiter's defeat of the Giants, the defining myth of Jupiter *Victor*. Why resist the conclusion that Horace composed this piece for performance where both divinities' temples were in full view?

The same combination is presented at greater length in the fourth poem of the sequence:

> Descend from the sky, Queen Calliope, come, utter a long melody on the pipe or with your piercing voice if you now prefer or on the lyre or cithara of Phoebus.
> Do you hear? Or does some pleasing madness mock me? I seem to hear and to be wandering through sacred groves visited by gracious winds and waters.

Horace *Odes* 3.4.1–8 (trans. David West)

This queen who may play on Apollo's strings is the Muse of epic, a narrative form normally beyond Horace's scope. He invokes her here, uniquely, because he is going to tell the story of Jupiter's victory, and the sacred groves that give him inspiration may be another Palatine allusion. Certainly he is addressing an audience: though undetectable in English, the 'you' of 'do you hear?' is plural.

After explaining his devotion to the Muses, who will protect him wherever he goes, the poet goes on to address them in person:

> As soon as high Caesar had hidden away his war-weary cohorts in the towns and was seeking to put an end to his labours, you renewed him in your Pierian cave.
> You, nurturing goddesses, give gentle counsel and rejoice in it when given. We know how the impious Titans and their monstrous crew were carried off by the falling thunderbolt

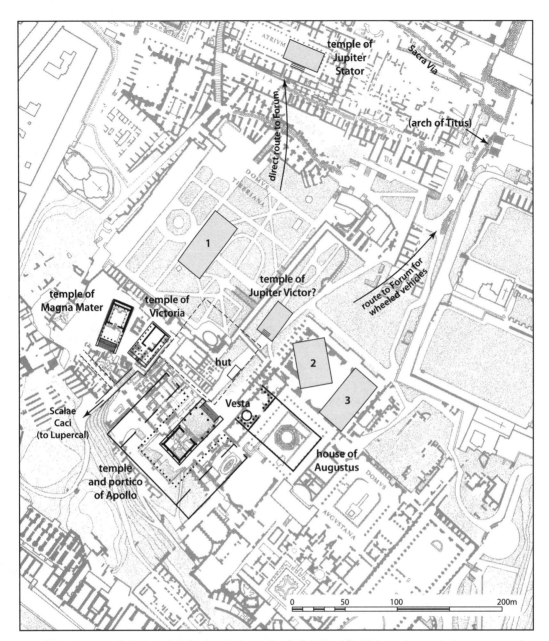

FIGURE 67. The Augustan Palatine: developing the hypothesis (cf. Fig. 46). This conjectural plan assumes the layout of the Apollo temple and portico suggested in Fig. 66; the square in dashed lines represents an *ager quadratus* (240 Roman feet each way), identifiable as *Roma quadrata*, 'square Rome', the place 'in front of the temple of Apollo' (Festus 310L) that extended as far as 'the brow of the Scalae Caci' (Solinus 1.18).

It is assumed that the great platform for the *domus Tiberiana* palace (Fig. 12) did not yet exist; there was therefore space available for the piazza in front of the Apollo temple (*area Apollinis*) from the forecourt of Augustus' house as far as the temple of Victoria; the plan of the Victoria temple is as suggested in Pensabene 1998.30 fig. 10. Since the position of the Jupiter Victor temple is wholly hypothetical, the width of the piazza can only be guesswork. *(Caption continues at foot of next page.)*

> Of him who governs dull earth and windy ocean, who rules alone with just
>   authority the gloomy cities and kingdom of the dead, the gods, and the armies
>   of men.

Horace Odes
3.4.37–48 (trans.
David West)

This passage dates the poem to 29 BC, when Commander Caesar completed the settlement of his veterans after the defeat of Cleopatra. As the audience would know, it was here on the Palatine that 'square Rome' housed the symbolic instruments for surveying and inaugurating those settlements (**6.3** above). They would naturally associate Jupiter's victory with Caesar's (he held his three-day triumph in August that year), and would find it easy to apply the phrase describing Jupiter, 'who rules alone with just authority', to the occupant of the house that looked on to the Palatine piazza.

Horace was not usually so formal and hieratic. A short poem in the first book—just four stanzas, of which I quote the first and last—is revealing because of the opening word:

> We are required. If ever I have played with you at leisure beneath the shade (and
>   sung) something that may live this year and more, then come, my lyre, and
>   sing a Latin song . . .
> Shell, glory of Phoebus and welcome at the feasts of supreme Jupiter, sweet easer
>   of labours and healer, be propitious when I duly call upon you!

Horace Odes
1.32.1–4, 13–16

The first word, *poscimur*, appears in some manuscripts as *poscimus*, 'we require' or 'we ask', but the unexpected passive verb is more likely to have been corrupted into an active one than vice versa. I think it implies a commissioned public performance, of which this short prayer to the lyre may have served as a preface. Once again, we note the juxtaposition of Apollo and Jupiter, the two main gods of the *area Palatina*.

The 'wooden hut in front of the residence' (Josephus *Jewish Antiquities* 19.75), used as part of the stage building for theatre performances (ibid. 19.90), is identified both as Romulus' *auguratorium* 'on the summit of the hill' (Dionysius of Halicarnassus *Roman Antiquities* 14.2.2) and as the 'hut of Faustulus in the precinct of Jupiter' (Conon *FGrH* 46 F1.48.8, referring to the pre-Augustan situation), but is no longer assumed to represent the surveyor's vantage-point at the centre of the *ager quadratus*.

The arrangement of the forecourt of the house of Augustus is based on the scene on the Sorrento base (Fig. 39). The shaded rectangles represent the approximate positions and alignments of houses for which pre-Neronian archaeological evidence (in the basement areas) happens to survive: (1) the nucleus of the *domus Tiberiana*, (2) the house that featured the *aula Isiaca*, (3) the 'House of the Griffins'. The dwellings excavated by Rosa and Carettoni (the '*schola*', the 'House of Livia', and the so-called 'House of Augustus') are of course not marked, because *ex hypothesi* they were demolished and/or covered over in the construction of the Augustan complex.

Immediately before this poem in book 1 is a piece evidently composed for the dedication of the Apollo temple in October 28 BC. Again, I quote the first and final stanzas:

Horace *Odes* 1.31.1–4, 17–20 (trans. David West)

> What does the bard ask for from Apollo whose temple is now dedicated? What does he pray for as he pours the new wine from the bowl? Not the fertile crops of wealthy Sardinia . . .
> Grant, son of Latona, that I may enjoy what I have with good health and, I pray, with sound mind, and that my old age may not be squalid and not without the lyre.

Figs. 54, 55

Latona reminds us that Apollo shared the temple with his mother and his sister, and another short item in book 1 is a hymn to all three:

Horace *Odes* 1.21.1–4, 13–16 (trans. David West)

> Sing, tender virgins, of Diana. Sing, boys, of unshorn Cynthius and of Latona, dear to the heart of supreme Jupiter. . . . (Apollo) will drive war with its tears and famine and pestilence with their misery, far from the people and from Caesar the *princeps*, to the Persians and Britons, moved by your prayer.

The prayer for the *populus* and *princeps Caesar* is appropriate to a public occasion, and once again the reference to Jupiter, with the same epithet as in the prayer to the lyre (1.32), may allude to Apollo's neighbour in the Palatine piazza.

We have already taken note of Horace's hymn to Apollo and Diana for the *ludi saeculares* of 17 BC (**7.3** above), so our survey here can conclude with the last poem in the whole *Odes* collection. Here are the first two stanzas:

Horace *Odes* 4.15.1–8

> I wanted to tell of battles and captured cities, but Phoebus with his lyre struck a warning note, to stop me setting my small sail across the Tyrrhenian ocean.
> Your age, Caesar,
> Has brought back rich crops to the fields, and restored to our own Jupiter the standards torn down from the Parthians' proud doors . . .

The Parthian standards were returned in 20 BC. That gives the approximate date of the poem, but it also raises a historical problem. According to Dio Cassius, Augustus arranged for a law to be passed authorising a temple of Mars Ultor on the Capitol for the dedication of the standards; but the great temple of Mars Ultor was in the Forum Augustum, and it was not completed until 2 BC.

It seems clear that Dio was mistaken, and that until the Mars temple was ready the standards were dedicated in another temple. Horace's statement makes it certain that a temple of Jupiter was used, and that of Jupiter Victor on the Palatine is an obvious candidate. Yet again, the proximity of Phoebus Apollo, Caesar

Augustus, and Jupiter in the same poetic text may be taken as reflecting the physical proximity of the two temples and the forecourt of the house, all looking out on to the piazza. It was Caesar's time (*tua, Caesar, aetas*, said Horace), and this was Caesar's place, hung with the spoils of his own triumphs.

9.2 TIBULLUS, PROPERTIUS, OVID

Inside the Apollo temple, each in a gilded case set into the base of the cult statue, were the two scrolls of the Sibyl's prophecies (**7.2** above). The original nine autograph volumes had all been burned to ashes: six of them by the Sibyl herself when king Tarquin declined to buy them, the other three in 83 BC, when the temple of Jupiter Optimus Maximus on the Capitol, which had kept them safe for centuries, was destroyed in a civil war. These two were the newly purged survivors, judged to be authentic, of the replacements gathered by the priesthood responsible, the *quindecimuiri sacris faciundis*.

Our next poetic Palatine occasion was the induction into the college of *quindecimuiri* of a young patrician, Messalla Messallinus, whose father Messalla Corvinus had fought for the oligarchs at Philippi but then changed sides. Corvinus was not only a military commander and a great orator, he was also a discerning literary critic and a patron of poets. The best known of his protégés was Albius Tibullus, who now presented a substantial celebration of young Messallinus' sacerdotal honour.

The opening lines identify the venue, the temple of Apollo where the books were kept:

> Favour us, Phoebus: a new priest is entering your temple, so come to us, with your cithara and songs! Now I pray you to strike with your thumb the speaking strings, and turn the words of your song to pious praise. Come in person, your brows bound with triumphal laurel; while they are heaping the altar, come to your own rites! But come shining and beautiful, put on now the robe you set aside, comb now your long hair—just as they say you were when you joined in singing the praises of victorious Jupiter after the expulsion of king Saturn. You see from afar the things to come; dedicated to you, the augur knows well what the bird that sees the future sings.
>
> Tibullus 2.5.1–12

It would be equally possible to translate line 10 as 'singing the praises of Jupiter Victor', so explicitly does Tibullus identify the god of the Palatine cult, Apollo's neighbour. Equally striking is the declaration at lines 11–12 that Apollo gives the *augur* his prophetic skill; that can hardly be irrelevant to the primal augury of Rome's foundation, which took place at the *auguratorium* hut immediately in front of Apollo's temple. Perhaps that was where Tibullus was on stage.

The narrative setting of the poem is the fall of Troy, where Aeneas hears the Sibyl's prophecy. At that time, says Tibullus,

> Romulus had not yet shaped the walls of the eternal city—not to be dwelt in by Remus as a partner—but at that time cattle cropped the grassy Palatine, and humble huts stood on Jupiter's citadel. Under the holm-oak's shade were Pan, drunk on milk, and a wooden Pales carved by a rustic knife.

Tibullus 2.5.23–8

This topographical excursus emphasises the Palatine in particular, with Romulus' walls and the eponymous shepherds' goddess Pales. Later in the poem the festival of Pales symbolises the peace brought by Apollo; although it is not known exactly where her cult-site was, it would not be surprising if hers were one of the 'Palatine altars' under Apollo's gaze. The poem ends with a prayer that associates the god with his sister Diana, as was right and proper at the temple they shared (**7.3** above).

Young Messallinus was born about 36 BC. Belonging to such an ancient family—it traced its line back to the time of Romulus, and provided one of the first consuls of the republic—he could have been granted membership of the *quindecimuiri* as soon as he was legally adult, which makes 21 BC a likely date for Tibullus' poem. The poet's untimely death came not long afterwards.

Propertius' fourth collection of elegiacs was published in or soon after 16 BC. Marking a conspicuous move away from love poetry to more public themes, it begins on the Palatine, with a contrast between then and now:

> Whatever you see here, stranger, where greatest Rome is, was hill and grass before Phrygian Aeneas; and where the Palatine stands, sacred to Phoebus of the Ships, the exiled cattle of Evander lay down. These golden temples have grown great for gods who were once made of clay, and a hut built artlessly was nothing to be ashamed of.

Propertius 4.1.1–6

The standard commentary on book 4 takes it for granted that 'poem 1' is the prologue of a book to be read. And in one sense, of course, it is. But 150 lines is long for a mere preface, and a dramatic format in which the poet addresses the citizens of Rome, and is then answered by the 'stranger' he was talking to, ought surely to be regarded in the first instance as a text composed for performance.

That inference is even more compelling when we turn to 'poem 6'. In the first ten lines the poet, inspired as a prophet (*uates*), acts as master of ceremonies for a sacrifice before the temple; in the final eighteen lines he manages the transition from solemn ceremony to festal banquet. What he offers in between is a long hymn in the form of a narrative:

> Muse, I shall tell of the temple of Palatine Apollo; it is a subject worthy of your favour, Calliope. My songs are drawn out for Caesar's name; while Caesar is sung,

> Jupiter, I ask even you to give way. There is a harbour of Phoebus, receding to the Athamanian shores, where a bay quells the sound of the Ionian Sea: Actian Leucas, monument to the Julian keels . . .

Propertius
4.6.11–17

Why 'Caesar's *name*'? Perhaps the occasion was the annual thanksgiving on 16 January that commemorated the conferral of the name 'Augustus'; certainly Propertius uses that name unusually often in this poem.

When the story is the battle of Actium, even his neighbour Jupiter Victor gives way to 'Apollo of the Ships'. And even in mid-narrative, as the god, with his quiver full of deadly arrows, stands over the future Augustus' ship, the audience are reminded of where they are. Apollo speaks to Rome's leader:

> 'Save your native land from fear; relying now on you as her champion, she has heaped public prayers upon your prow. If you do not defend her, it was in vain that Romulus, augur for his walls, saw the Palatine birds in flight.'

Propertius
4.6.40–4

By now it should be a familiar juxtaposition: Apollo, Augustus, and the Romulean augury that gave him his name. For the audience on the Palatine, the piazza they sat or stood in presented all those historic elements before their eyes.

The youngest and greatest of the elegiac poets was Ovid. He did not perform on such grand occasions (his Muse was not Calliope but Thalea, who looked after comedy and 'mime'), but he did 'read his poems to the People', evidently on public holidays and at the stage games. We know that in his time the regular *ludi scaenici* required stages in various parts of the city, and the Palatine piazza must have been a prime site.

If Ovid too sometimes performed on the Palatine, that would explain the unexpected prominence of Apollo in the second book of the *Ars amatoria*. As always, use of the second person plural presupposes an audience:

> Cry 'Io Paean!', and again cry 'Io Paean!' The prey I sought has fallen into my nets. . . . Just as I was singing this, Apollo, suddenly manifest, plucked with his thumb a string of his gilded lyre. The laurel was in his hands, the laurel was worn in his sacred hair; the divine bard approached in visible form. He said to me: 'Come, instructor of wanton Love, bring your pupils to my temple, where there is a text renowned in fame throughout all parts of the world, telling each person "know yourself"'. . . . So Phoebus advised; obey the advice of Phoebus; in the sacred mouth of this god is certain truth.

Ovid *Ars
amatoria* 2.1–2,
493–500, 509–10

The same device is used in the *Remedia amoris*, where Apollo is even referred to as the work's inspiration:

> Whatever I sing is good advice, so obey the singer—and do you, healing Phoebus, be present in my undertakings, as you always are. Phoebus is present—the lyres

Ovid *Remedia amoris* 703–6

have sounded, the quivers have sounded, I recognise the god through his own signs—Phoebus is present.

Presenting the god's epiphany in this way would be particularly appropriate in a poem delivered before his temple.

A stronger case can be made for the opening scenario of Ovid's epic master-piece, the *Metamorphoses*. After the creation of the world and the descent from the Age of Gold to the Age of Iron, the poet brings in the story that gave Jupiter Victor his honorific name:

Ovid *Metamorphoses* 1.151–5

That lofty heaven might be no safer than the earth, they say the Giants made an at-tempt on the celestial realm and built heaped-up mountains to the high stars. Then the almighty father sent his thunderbolt, shattered Olympus and shook Pelion down from its base on Ossa.

He then goes on with a scene placed explicitly on a heavenly Palatine:

Ovid *Metamorphoses* 1.168–75

There is a Way on high, visible in the clear (night) sky, called Milky, famed pre-cisely for its whiteness. This is the divinities' route to the great Thunderer's halls and the royal residence. To left and right the reception-rooms of the nobles are thronged through open doors. The common people live elsewhere; in this neigh-bourhood the powerful and famous heavenly ones have placed their dwellings. This is the place (if boldness be granted to my words) that I should not fear to call the Palatine of great heaven.

The gods take their seats in a marble chamber – clearly analogous to the hall for Senate meetings in the portico of the Apollo temple (**8.3** above)—where Jupi-ter reports on the wickedness of Lycaon and his punishment. Then follows the flood, with the embedded story of Pyrrha and Deucalion; then the emergence of Python, killed by Apollo, and the foundation of the Pythian games, where the victors' wreaths were of oak, not laurel.

There was of course an oak wreath above Augustus' door. The allusion is only latent at this point, but it is activated at the end of the story that follows, of Apollo and Daphne:

Ovid *Metamorphoses* 1.557–65

'Since you cannot be my wife,' the god said to her, 'at least you shall be my tree. My hair, my lyres, my quivers shall always have you, laurel. You shall be there for the Latian leaders when the joyful voice cries 'Triumph!' and the Capitol witnesses the long procession. Yes, and you shall stand before the entrance, most faithful guard of the Augustan doorposts, and protect the oak between. Just as the hair of my youthful head is never shorn, so may you too always bear evergreen the honours of your branch.'

The Palatine, victorious Jupiter, his oak, Apollo's laurel, Augustus' house: the only thing missing from the implied topography is Romulus' hut and the augury that gave Augustus his name. Romulus must wait until book 14, when Mars comes in his chariot to carry him back to heaven. We have already noted Ovid's unique location of this story—on the Palatine rather than at the 'Goat's Marsh' in the Campus Martius (**7.1** above). It seems a reasonable guess that he composed these episodes of the *Metamorphoses* in the hope that they would be delivered to an audience in the very piazza where he makes Romulus address his *Quirites*.

The same Palatine associations appear in the poet's loyal prayer after the final episode:

> I pray: you gods who came with Aeneas, you to whom sword and fire gave way [at Troy]; and you native gods, and Quirinus [Romulus] father of our city, and Gradivus [Mars] father of unconquered Quirinus, and Vesta, consecrated within Caesar's residence, and with Caesar's Vesta you, Phoebus of the household ...

Ovid
Metamorphoses
15.861–4

In *Fasti* too, Apollo and Vesta are described as inhabiting the residence itself. Of course that is not to be taken literally, though Vesta was at least in the forecourt. What Ovid's flattering conceit really attests is the first hint of a new and powerful idea, that the whole of the Palatine was the *princeps'* residence.

Fig. 39

In due course *Palatium*, the Palatine, really did become 'the palace'—but only after the fire of AD 64, when Nero could exploit the whole hill for a purpose-built imperial complex (**3.1** above). The Augustan poets knew nothing of that. They took for granted a redeveloped late-republican townscape, already associated with Romulus and with Jupiter Victor, into which the young Caesar had modestly inserted his own house and then magnificently created a whole new performance space for the god of music and poetry.

9.3 POETRY AND THE PUBLIC

> He encouraged the talents of his age in every way that he could. He listened courteously and patiently as they read not only poems and histories but also speeches and dialogues. But he was offended when anything was written about him that was not serious and by the most eminent, and he used to warn the praetors not to let his name become degraded in competitions.

Suetonius *Diuus
Augustus* 89.3
(trans. D. Wardle)

Consistently misinterpreted by commentators, the third sentence of this revealing passage offers important evidence about authors and their public in Augustan Rome.

The praetors were in charge of the regular annual *ludi*, from the *Megalenses* in April to the *plebeii* in November, adding up each year to 56 days of 'stage games' in the theatres and piazzas of Rome and 17 days of 'circus games' in the Circus Maximus. These were the times when a poet or prose author might hope to bring his work to the Roman People, taking his turn among all the varied types of instruction or amusement that were needed to fill those days from morning till night. But how did he get on the praetor's programme? If he was one of 'the most eminent', he might expect to be invited; failing that, he would have to enter one of those competitions.

We know about them indirectly, from poets who did *not* compete. Horace was content to perform to the small but distinguished private audience at Maecenas' house:

Horace *Satires* 1.10.37–9

These things I play about with aren't meant to resound in the temple, in a competition with Tarpa as judge, or to come back again and again as theatre shows.

Horace *Epistles* 1.19.39–44

As one who listens to noble authors and avenges attacks on them, I don't see fit to canvass literary constituencies and stages. *That*'s what causes the trouble. If I say 'I'm ashamed to recite my unworthy writings in crowded theatres and add weight to trifles', then someone replies: 'You're laughing—you keep your stuff for the ears of Jove.'

Propertius too claimed to write only for private approval:

Propertius 2.13.13–14

Once I achieve that, it's goodbye to the public's confused talk. I'll be safe with my mistress as judge.

Clearly it mattered who was doing the judging. A fragment of papyrus preserves part of a line of Cornelius Gallus, 'I'm afraid with you as judge, Cato', evidently addressing the Valerius Cato who was known as 'the one selector and maker of poets'. Like Maecius Tarpa, mentioned by Horace, Cato seems to have been a literary arbiter for the praetors, choosing the best for their programmes at the games.

There is much that we don't know, and it is important not to ignore evidence that opens up an unfamiliar perspective. One item that has not received the attention it deserves is the inscription from the tomb of Tiberius Claudius Tiberinus, found in the eighteenth century not far from the Baths of Caracalla.

Fig. 68

Tiberinus was an *Augustalis*, a member of the humble priesthood created by Augustus in 7 BC to look after the new cult of the *Lares Augusti* (and his own *Genius*) at the crossroads of each neighbourhood in the city. *Augustales* were usually freedmen, but Tiberinus was free-born and proud of it, pointedly spelling out in full (it was usually abbreviated) the voting district *Esquilina* in which he was enrolled. The distinctive forename suggests he was the son of a freedman of a patrician Tiberius Claudius—perhaps Livia's first husband, or his son who became Tiberius Caesar, or his grandson who became the emperor Claudius.

Figure 68. The 'Belvedere altar', left-hand side: Hölscher 1988.394–5, Galinsky 1996.319–21. Augustus presents cult-statues of the *Lares* to the Vestals, no doubt to inaugurate the new cult in 7 BC; 'the setting, festively adorned with garlands of fruits, may well be his house on the Palatine where Augustus, as *pontifex maximus*, set up an altar and image to Vesta in his own residence' (Galinsky 1996.319, cf. Ovid *Fasti* 4.949–54). Musei Vaticani, Museo Gregoriano Profano, inv. 1115: photo C. Rossa, neg. D-DAI-ROM-75.1290.

Tiberinus died in his late twenties, and his mother, who put up the tomb, arranged for him to tell his story with a fine epitaph in elegiac couplets:

You traveller, whoever you are who ride by the threshold of my tomb, please check your hurried journey. Read this through, and so may you never grieve for an untimely death.

You'll find my name attached to the inscription. Rome is my native city, my parents were true plebeians, my life was then spoiled by no ills. At one time I was well known as a favourite of the People; now I'm just a little ash from a wept-over pyre.

Who didn't see good parties with a laughing face, and (who didn't see) that my cheerfulness stayed up late with me? At one time I was skilled in reciting the works of bards with Pierian tunefulness in swan-like measures, skilled in speaking poems that breathed with Homeric verse, poems well known in Caesar's forum.

Figure 69. The 'Belvedere altar', front, right-hand side, back: Hölscher 1988.394–6 (see also Fig. 68). Musei Vaticani, Museo Gregoriano Profano, inv. 1115: photos C. Rossa, negs. D-DAI-ROM-75.1285 (*a*), 75.1286 (*b*), 75.1289 (*c*).

The respective scenes seem to be: (*a*) the goddess of victory carrying the shield, inscribed with Augustus' virtues, that was set up in the Julian Senate-house (Augustus *Res gestae* 34.2); (*b*) Aeneas' arrival in Italy, and the white sow that fulfilled the prophecies given to him (Virgil *Aeneid* 3.389–93, 8.42–9); (*c*) the apotheosis of Romulus, witnessed by the Sun-god (top left) and by mortal figures probably representing the Roman People.

All of these, including Augustus' victories (Propertius 2.1.25, 2.10.3–4, Ovid *Fasti* 1.13), were themes suitable for epic poetry, and all of them, in different ways, allude to the Palatine: (*a*) features Victoria, whose temple was near that of Apollo (Fig. 67 above), and the laurels that

Of all my body, which both my parents sadly strew with tears, love and a name are now what's left. They place garlands and fresh flowers for me to enjoy; that's how I remain, laid out in the vale of Elysium. My fates gave me as many birthdays as the stars that pass in (the signs of) the Dolphin and winged Pegasus.

CIL 6.10097

Although this professional entertainer was evidently available for private parties too, it must have been the public bookings that made him the People's favourite. The praetor could not always hire poets to perform in person, and in any case a professional performer might do a better job with the poet's text.

At this point we should think about the most iconic of all works of Augustan literature. Virgil was hugely popular in his lifetime, and everyone knew that his *Aeneid* would be a masterpiece. Although he himself was never satisfied with it, after his death Augustus made sure the text was preserved. But how did it reach the audience for which it was written? The answer must be through the work of people like Tiberinus, 'skilled in speaking poems that breathed Homeric verse'. And of course the audience loved them for it.

Such works were 'well known in Caesar's forum'—a very puzzling phrase. Was it a true toponym, referring to the Forum Iulium begun by Julius Caesar in 54 BC (**2.1** above)? Or was it a description, 'Caesar's public space', referring to the Palatine piazza? Either is possible, but since Tiberinus was an *Augustalis*, the attested association of the *Lares* cult with specifically Augustan themes and places may perhaps favour the latter.

Fig. 69

We don't know the date of Tiberinus' epitaph, but his pride in plebeian birth and free citizen status would fit well with the ethos of Augustus' time. The authority of the *princeps* was defined as the protection of the citizen body, using the traditional powers of the tribunes of the *plebs* (**1.2** above). His way of life was deliberately unpretentious, as his biographer makes clear:

When he was consul he walked about in public usually on foot, and when he was not consul often in an open litter. At his open audiences he admitted even the common people, accepting the requests of those who approached him with such affability that he jokingly reproved one man for hesitating as he held out his petition to him 'like a coin to an elephant'. . . .

---

flanked the doorway of Augustus' house (Fig. 3 above); in (*b*) the figure reading from the scroll could be the Sibyl, or Apollo himself as the god of prophecy; the solar chariot in (*c*) stood in bronze on the pediment of Apollo's temple (Propertius 2.31.11), and in one version of the story (Ovid *Metamorphoses* 14.820-4) the assumption of Romulus took place from the Palatine itself.

The altar was evidently found on the Palatine in the late fifteenth or early sixteenth century (La Rocca 2013.318), and three of the four scenes are set on conspicuously rocky ground, perhaps an indication of the *mons Palatinus*.

Suetonius *Diuus*
Augustus 53.2, 74
(trans. D. Wardle)

Sometimes he would arrive at dinner parties late and leave early, as his guests would start eating before he took his place and would continue after he had left. He used to serve dinners of three courses, or six at his most generous, without excessive expenditure but with utmost conviviality. For he would encourage the silent or those who talked quietly to share in the general conversation. He would intersperse entertainments and actors or even street-players from the Circus, and more frequently story-tellers.

'Entertainments' (*acroamata*) were often poetry readings, and it is easy to imagine performers like Tiberinus giving as much pleasure to the guests in Augustus' dining-room as they did to their fellow-citizens in the piazza when the games were on.

'He honoured with his attention,' says Suetonius, 'every category of those who offered their services in public shows.' A conspicuous example was the star dancer Pylades, famous for his bravura performance in *The Madness of Hercules*:

Macrobius
Saturnalia 2.7.17

In this play he even shot arrows into the public audience, and he drew his bow and shot his arrows when playing the same role by order in Augustus' dining-room. Caesar wasn't offended that for Pylades he and the Roman People occupied the same position.

Fig. 39

Of course he wasn't: why should he be? He was not an emperor in a palace. He was *Caesar*, who had freed the republic from the domination of an oligarchy. His house was respectable but not luxurious, appropriate for the first citizen (*princeps*). Only its forecourt made a big public statement, opening on to the piazza he had created from the confiscated town houses of the oligarchs. In that piazza, we have suggested, the poets who were the glory of his age might read or sing their works to the Roman People.

10

A MISCARRIAGE OF JUSTICE

As promised, we have followed where the evidence leads, and at last it has led us inside the house of Augustus. Despite what the guidebooks say, archaeology cannot take us there. What it can do—and has done, brilliantly—is reveal what Augustus buried out of sight when he built the Apollo temple and its portico for the citizens of Rome. Where he lived himself is no longer to be found. After the house was destroyed in Nero's fire, the great palace called *domus Augustana* covered the site and everything around it.

During the century between Commander Caesar's redevelopment of the Palatine and his great-great-grandson's creation of the imperial palace, the nature of Rome's government changed (**1.3** above), and the reputation of Caesar Augustus has suffered as a result.

·

10.1 DYNASTY

'While Caesar is the guardian of our affairs,' sang Horace, 'no civil madness or violence will drive out peace.' I don't think modern readers are entitled to dismiss this as a mere 'message of propaganda and cliché'. Horace and his audience had seen bad times, and didn't want to see them again. If Caesar Augustus prevented the free play of oligarchic politics, well and good—that was what the citizens of Rome wanted. But their very enthusiasm was a problem for him.

What characterised the oligarchs was their arrogance; Augustus by contrast behaved as a citizen among citizens, as the long section on his *ciuilitas* in Suetonius' biography amply attests. One of the examples is particularly revealing:

> He always recoiled from being addressed as 'Lord' [*dominus*] as insulting and disgraceful. When he was watching a show and in the course of a mime the words 'O just and good Lord' were delivered and the entire audience leapt to its feet and applauded as if they were spoken of him, immediately by gesture and expression he put an end to the inappropriate flattery and the following day rebuked them in a very severe edict.

Suetonius *Diuus Augustus* 53.1 (trans. D. Wardle)

Of course he didn't want to be called *dominus*: it was from *dominatio* (by the oligarchs) that he had rescued the republic in the first place. The scene of the story is also significant: he was there in the audience, sharing the entertainment with his fellow-citizens and annoyed at being thought of as their master. And the next day's edict was characteristic too: he was constantly in dialogue with the Roman People, rebuking them when he thought it necessary, but always making it clear what his policies were for.

The nuances of Augustus' unprecedented position can be sensed only from contemporary sources. Here for example is Horace, respectful but not sycophantic, showing how one addressed Caesar:

Horace Epistles
2.1.1–4

In view of all the great responsibilities you carry alone—defending Italy with arms, gracing her with good habits, correcting her with legislation—it would be a crime against the public good if I took up your time with a long conversation, Caesar.

'Alone' (*solus*) probably means that this was written after the death of Agrippa in 12 BC. Augustus' oldest friend and most dependable ally, his son-in-law and the father of his grandchildren (two of whom Augustus adopted as his own sons), Agrippa was very conspicuously a man of the people. There were some who objected to that, as we know from another eye-witness source. The elder Seneca's reminiscences, written years later, provide a valuable sense of perspective:

Seneca
Controuersiae
2.4.13

There was such freedom under the deified Augustus that for all his pre-eminence at that time Marcus Agrippa received plenty of criticism for his ignoble birth. . . . I think it is admirable of the deified Augustus that in his time so much was permitted.

Seneca knew that it was not like that in the time of Tiberius or Gaius 'Caligula'. Under Gaius, who refused to acknowledge that the ignoble Agrippa was his grandfather, a proper form of address was to kiss his jewelled slipper.

It is almost inevitable that the children of self-made men grow up taking privilege for granted. Augustus' daughter Julia was contemptuous of the suggestion that she should live as modestly as her father did. 'He forgets he is Caesar,' she said, 'but I remember I am Caesar's daughter.' If Gaius and Lucius, her sons by Agrippa (adopted as the sons of Augustus himself), grew up with the same attitude, that was partly the fault of the Roman People, who were already standing to applaud them in the theatre while they were still children. The problem came to a head in 6 BC, when Gaius was fourteen and Lucius ten:

Augustus was displeased to see that Gaius and Lucius, though being brought up to a life of public responsibility, did not at all emulate his own conduct. They not only lived too luxuriously but were presumptuous as well; once Lucius even went into the theatre unattended. Everyone in the city flattered them, either genuinely or to gain favour, and as a result they became more and more spoiled.

For instance, the People elected Gaius consul in advance, before he was even of military age. That made Augustus pray to the gods that no critical situation might arise, as once had happened in his own case, to require a man less than twenty years old to be consul.

Dio Cassius
55.9.1–3

The prayer was surely made in public—perhaps in one of those admonitory edicts—and its purpose is self-evident: to remind Rome of the murderous civil strife that was only kept at bay 'while Caesar is the guardian of our affairs'. For the two boys, however, that was just history, like Tarquin or Hannibal. Julia herself was only nine years old when the civil wars ended.

For the Roman People, the issue was simple. There had to be a Caesar, legally empowered by them, to prevent the republic falling once again into the selfish control of the rich and powerful. Augustus would not live for ever, and they understood very well that his two sons—by birth the sons of Agrippa, one of their own—were being brought up to fulfil that role. Naturally they were eager to confer authority on the elder boy as soon as possible; and they got their way. When Gaius came of age the following year (5 BC) he was designated as consul, to hold office five years later (AD 1); the same process followed for Lucius three years afterwards.

Fig. 70

It was during Gaius' consulship, when the young man was away on military and diplomatic duty in Syria, that Augustus completed his astrologically perilous sixty-third year. That very day he wrote to Gaius:

FIGURE 70. The start of the dynasty: *aureus* of 2 BC–AD 4. The obverse shows Augustus crowned with a laurel wreath, and the legend CAESAR AVGVSTVS DIVI F PATER PATRIAE, 'Caesar Augustus, son of the Deified (Caesar), *pater patriae*' (**1.3** above); on the reverse, Gaius and Lucius (C. L. CAESARES in the exergue), each with shield and spear and the symbols of their priesthoods, with the legend AVGVSTI F COS DESIG PRINC IVVENTVT, 'sons of Augustus, consuls designate, *principes* of the youth'. Addressing young Gaius, probably in the year of his consulship (AD 1), Ovid called him '*princeps* now of the young men, soon to be of the old' (*Ars amatoria* 1.194). *RIC* I[2] Augustus 209: Sutherland 1984.56. © The Trustees of the British Museum. All rights reserved.

Especially on days like today my eyes miss my dear Gaius. Wherever you have been today, I hope you've been happy and well, celebrating my sixty-fourth birthday—for as you see, I've got through the sixty-third year, the climacteric common to all elderly men! I pray the gods that I may pass whatever time is left to me in good health, with the republic in the happiest possible state, and with the two of you acting as good men should, ready to succeed to my station.

quoted in Aulus Gellius 15.7.3

The last phrase could equally mean 'to relieve me at my post', with *statio* in its military sense of guard-duty.

Lucius never made it to his consulship: on the way to a military command in Spain, he fell ill and died, aged eighteen. Gaius too died abroad, in Lycia on his way back to Italy: he was twenty-three. Augustus was sixty-six, and it was even more urgent to arrange for another Caesar to take over his guard-post. Addressing the Roman People at a public meeting in AD 4, he declared on oath that he was adopting Tiberius 'for the sake of the republic'. There is no reason to think they were happy with this outcome (**1.3** above). But were they right to distrust Tiberius? Would Gaius or Lucius have been any more successful in prolonging that 'happiest state of the republic' made possible by Augustus' unique personal authority? The very fact of a succession made it clear that the republic was becoming a dynastic monarchy.

The clearest indicator of the transition is the Praetorian Guard. Every commander of a Roman army had his own personal body of troops, separate from the legionary formations and known by the traditional title 'praetor's cohorts' (*cohortes praetoriae*). When Commander Caesar—soon to be Augustus—was granted military authority in 27 BC, his first act was to raise the pay of his praetorian cohorts to double that of legionary soldiers. He used them as protection for the city and himself, but he was careful to keep them inconspicuous:

He never allowed more than three [out of nine] cohorts to be in the city, and even they had no permanent barracks; the others he used to send away to winter or summer quarters around the nearby towns.

Suetonius *Diuus Augustus* 49.1

It is surely significant that we never hear of them in the contemporary sources on Augustus' principate. When he turned sixty he deputed command of the cohorts to two 'prefects', and even during the last decade of his life, so full of disasters and popular unrest, there is no record of the use of military force in the city.

That changed immediately under Tiberius, who had already—probably in AD 12—been given military authority (*imperium*) equal to that of Augustus:

Tiberius was beginning everything through the consuls, as if it were the old republic and he were hesitant about issuing commands. . . . But as soon as Augustus was dead he had given the praetorian cohorts their watchword as commander; there were armed guards and all the other features of a court; soldiers escorted him to the Forum, soldiers escorted him to the Senate-house.

Tacitus *Annals* 1.7.3 and 5

Six years later he brought together all nine of the cohorts, under a single Prefect (Sejanus), and housed them in purpose-built barracks just outside the Viminal Gate. When Tiberius retired to Capri in AD 26, Sejanus used them to control the city, and in particular to eliminate those whose popularity might be a threat either to Tiberius' position or his own.

This new Gestapo-like role continued after the fall of Sejanus and under Tiberius' successor Gaius 'Caligula', as a praetorian officer complained to his Prefect in AD 41:

> 'We aren't soldiers—we're bodyguards and executioners! We bear these arms not to defend the freedom and sovereignty of the Romans, but to protect the man who has enslaved their bodies and their minds. Every day we kill and torture them, polluting ourselves with blood until the time when someone else at Gaius' bidding will do the same to us.'

Josephus *Jewish Antiquities* 19.42

Cassius Chaerea killed Gaius, but it was the praetorian cohorts themselves who preserved the dynasty by finding a new Caesar. The grateful Claudius paid them a huge bonus of five thousand *denarii* per man, the equivalent of seven years' pay. He was the first of the Caesars, as Suetonius noted, to secure the loyalty of his soldiers by paying for it. A generation later, the praetorian cohorts ended the dynasty by withdrawing their loyalty from Augustus' great-great-grandson (there was no choice for Nero but suicide); and then they killed his successor, in the Forum in broad daylight, for failing to do what Claudius had done.

Fig. 71

FIGURE 71. The re-start of the dynasty: *aureus* of AD 41–2. The obverse shows Claudius crowned with a laurel wreath, and the legend TI(*berius*) CLAVD(*ius*) CAESAR AVG(*ustus*) P(*ontifex*) M(*aximus*) TR(*ibunicia*) P(*otestate*); unlike his brother Germanicus, Claudius had not been adopted into the Iulii Caesares, so the right to use the names 'Caesar' and 'Augustus' had to be granted to him after his *de facto* succession. The reverse shows the barracks of the praetorian cohorts, and on the battlement the legend IMPER(*ator*) RECEPT(*us*), 'the Commander (is) received'; the praetorians had found Claudius hiding in the Palatine house after the killing of Gaius, taken him to the barracks, and persuaded him to assume power. *RIC* I[2] Claudius 7: Sutherland 1984.122. © The Trustees of the British Museum. All rights reserved.

The scene of Galba's murder—and that of Vitellius, tortured to death in the Forum eleven months later—was where the Senate and People of Rome, in conspicuous harmony, had honoured Augustus as *pater patriae* seventy-one years before (**1.3** above). He had put an end to one sort of conflict, between the arrogant oligarchs and the *populares* who resisted them (**1.1** above); but the fact of his mortality, and the People's need for another Caesar to carry on his work, brought about conflict of a different sort, in a new world of dynastic politics where the only end in view was winning the position of supreme power.

The Augustan consensus was still taken for granted as late as AD 20, when the Senate put it on record that

Senatus consultum de Cn. Pisone patre 46–7 (trans. Cynthia Damon)

all the evils of civil war had long since been laid to rest by the divine will of the deified Augustus and the virtues of Tiberius Caesar Augustus.

But it was precisely the characteristics (let's not call them virtues) of Tiberius and his successors that brought 'civil madness and violence' back to the streets of Rome.

10.2 THE GREAT HISTORIANS

The arrogant *optimates* of the late republic (**1.1** above) took it for granted that any successful *popularis* politician was a tyrant who could be 'lawfully killed'. Above all, that was their view of Caesar, and the reason they gloried in his murder. To their successors three generations later, brought up on Cicero in the rhetorical schools and traumatised by their experience of Tiberius Caesar and Gaius Caesar, that opinion must have seemed self-evidently true.

There was a brief moment after the killing of Gaius when they thought their freedom of action had been restored. The consul Gnaeus Sentius Saturninus addressed the Senate:

Josephus *Jewish Antiquities* 19.172–3

'What happened in the old days I know only from report, but I have experienced myself and seen with my own eyes the evils with which tyrannies fill the state. They discourage all excellence, deprive generosity of its freedom, set up schools of flattery and fear—and all because they leave public affairs not to the wisdom of the laws but to the caprice of the rulers. Ever since Julius Caesar decided to destroy the republic and throw the state into confusion by doing violence to the rule of law, making himself the master of justice but the slave of whatever brought him personal satisfaction, there is no evil that the city has not suffered.'

As a description of what happened in 59 and 49 BC, that is a tendentious travesty; but dispassionate historical analysis was not what the situation required.

Similarly under Nero, Lucan's great epic on the civil war took as its premise the optimate view that Caesar's political alliance with Pompey and Crassus in the fifties BC was a tyranny (*regnum*). Lucan's pose of neutrality was undermined from the start:

> It is forbidden to know who took up arms more justly. Each defends himself with a powerful judgement: the gods favoured the winning side, but Cato the vanquished.

Lucan *Pharsalia*
1.126–8

With Sulla in Elysium and the *populares* in Tartarus, the whole poem brilliantly mythologises the optimate cause.

It is likely that this was the way most educated people thought about the end of the Roman republic at the time when Rome's greatest historian was growing up. If Tacitus was born in AD 58, as the evidence seems to suggest, he was probably old enough to have understood the fall of Nero and the terrifying civil wars of 'the year of the four emperors'. That was his chosen starting point when thirty years later he began writing the history of his own times, 'a work rich in disasters'.

After narrating the murder of Galba, Tacitus imagined the Roman People—the *uulgus*, as well as the senators and equestrians—anxiously harking back to the memory of earlier civil wars:

> They talked about the city, so often captured by its own armies, about the devastation of Italy and the plundering of provinces, about Pharsalia and Philippi and Perusia and Mutina, well-known names of public calamities.

Tacitus *Histories*
1.50.2

The reference is explicitly to the wars of the forties BC, but during those wars the city was never 'captured by its own armies'. The only time that had happened was in 88 BC, and the perpetrator was Sulla. In March 49 Caesar entered Rome unopposed, with huge popular support, and the same was true of his adopted son in July 43. The idea that Caesar oppressed Rome by force of arms was an optimate slander, but by Tacitus' time it was evidently believed. His summary of the People's anxieties continues:

> Even when the struggle for supremacy was between men of honour [unlike Otho and Vitellius] the world was almost overthrown, but there was still military command [*imperium*] after the victory of Gaius Julius and after the victory of Caesar Augustus; there would still have been the republic under Pompey and Brutus.

Tacitus *Histories*
1.50.2

Tacitus took it for granted that the wars of Pharsalus and Philippi were simply 'military command' overpowering 'the republic'.

In the second book of the *Histories* he returned to the subject with a more elaborate digression:

The old lust for power, innate in humans, increased and broke out along with the magnitude of empire. Equality is easy to keep when resources are limited; but when the world was conquered and all rival cities and kings destroyed, when there was leisure to covet wealth in safety, the first conflicts flared up between the Senate and the *plebs*. At one moment there were seditious tribunes, at another there were over-bearing consuls; trial runs for the civil wars took place in the city and the Forum.

Tacitus *Histories* 2.38.1

The corrupting effect of wealth is taken from Sallust, but Sallust also identified its consequence—an arrogant oligarchy whose crimes began the slide towards civil war. Tacitus ignores that; his schematic opposition of tribunes and consuls conflates the crisis of the second century BC with that of the early republic as reported by Livy. No mention, therefore, of the Gracchi and how they died.

Then Gaius Marius, from the lowest of the *plebs*, and Lucius Sulla, the most brutal of the *nobiles*, conquered freedom by force of arms and turned it into tyranny [*dominatio*]. After them Gnaeus Pompeius was no better, just less open, and from then on there was never any aim but supremacy.

Tacitus *Histories* 2.38.1

If it was just about supremacy (*principatus*), there was no need to distinguish between the oligarchy and the *populares*. They were all as bad as each other.

This evasive narrative, too generous to the oligarchs, condemns Augustus in advance as just the last in a sequence of power-hungry warlords. That becomes explicit in the first paragraph of the *Annals*:

The city of Rome was from the beginning held by kings. Lucius Brutus introduced freedom and the consulship. Dictatorships were assumed only for emergencies, the power of the Decemvirs was for only two years, and the consular authority of military tribunes did not last long either. Domination by Cinna and by Sulla was short-lived; the power of Pompey and Crassus quickly passed to Caesar, the armed forces of Lepidus and Antony to Augustus, who took everything, exhausted as it was by civil strife, under his command [*imperium*] with the designation 'first citizen' [*princeps*].

Tacitus *Annals* 1.1.1

After a brief aside on the historiography of the principate, Tacitus announces his theme and resumes his narrative:

I intend to relate a few things about Augustus and his last days, then the principate of Tiberius and what came after, without anger and partisanship, reasons for which I avoid.

When after the killing of Brutus and Cassius there were no more public forces, when [Sextus] Pompey had been overpowered [at sea] around Sicily, Lepidus got rid of and Antony killed, even the Julian party had no leader left but Caesar.

Tacitus *Annals* 1.1.3–2.1

That is, Commander Caesar in 30–28 BC, who then restored constitutional government and was granted the name Augustus (**1.2** above).

Tacitus' account is another tendentious travesty, even more shocking after that virtuous protestation of impartiality. It was Brutus and Cassius who did the killing; they ended their own lives as outlaws, condemned by due judicial process for the murder of Caesar, defeated in war by commanders elected and empowered for that very purpose by the Roman People. Far from being lost, the 'public forces' were the ones that won at Philippi. It's not that Tacitus didn't know. A few pages further on, reporting Augustus' funeral, he made it clear where his sympathies lay:

> On the day of the funeral soldiers were on duty, much mocked by those who had been eye-witnesses or heard from their parents of that day of still undeveloped slavery, and freedom unsuccessfully reclaimed, when the killing of Caesar the dictator seemed to some the worst, to others the finest of deeds.

Tacitus Annals
1.8.6

Well aware of the ideological polarity, Tacitus chose to align himself with those who called Caesar a tyrant and the assassins liberators. For him, Augustus' principate too was a tyranny (*dominatio*).

Tacitus' point of view is perfectly understandable. He was a distinguished senior senator. During the late years of Domitian he had seen the Senate terrorised and men like himself subjected to arbitrary arrest and execution. His whole subject was the origin and progress of the dynastic system that brought about such murderous abuse of power. As he saw it, the Roman People had no understanding of politics, so he was unwilling to accept that the first of the Caesars had been empowered by them to counter the equally murderous dominance of men like himself.

However understandable, Tacitus' view is patently prejudiced. If Augustus, as he sourly put it, 'won over the soldiers with bonuses, the People with a subsidised food supply, and everyone with the sweet taste of peace', that in itself hardly counts as *dominatio*. But the great historians are eloquent and persuasive. It is not easy to resist their influence, their powerful vision of how it must have been.

That is certainly true of Edward Gibbon—and he worked hard to make it so. In 1773 he began to write *The History of the Decline and Fall of the Roman Empire*:

> The style of an author should be the image of his mind; but the choice and command of language is the fruit of exercise. Many experiments were made before I could hit the middle tone between a dull chronicle and a rhetorical declamation; three times did I compose the first chapter, and twice the second and third, before I was tolerably satisfied with their effect.

Gibbon 1984.158

It was in the third chapter, composed after 'meditating Tacitus', that he delivered his verdict on Caesar Augustus:

The tender respect of Augustus for a free constitution which he had destroyed, can only be explained by an attentive consideration of the character of that subtle tyrant. A cool head, an unfeeling heart, and a cowardly disposition, prompted him, at the age of nineteen, to assume the mask of hypocrisy, which he never afterwards laid aside. . . . When he framed the artful system of the imperial authority, his moderation was inspired by his fears. He wished to deceive the people by an image of civil liberty, and the armies by an image of civil government.

Gibbon 2000.76

What reputation could survive that sort of treatment? And worse was to come in the twentieth century.

The bimillennium of Augustus' birth was celebrated in 1937 with a huge exhibition in Rome designed to present the Augustan age as a model for Fascist Italy. In fierce reaction to this panegyrical trend, the young Ronald Syme wrote his masterly account of Augustus' rise to power, *The Roman Revolution*, under the pressure of imminent war. Its tone, he warned, was 'pessimistic and truculent'. 'It was not composed in tranquillity . . . But the theme, I firmly believe, is of some importance.'

The introductory chapter, subtitled 'Augustus and History', displays the truculent tone in the very first sentences:

The greatest of the Roman historians began his *Annals* with the accession to the Principate of Tiberius, stepson and son by adoption of Augustus, consort in his powers. Not until that day was the funeral of the Free State consummated in solemn and legal ceremony. The corpse had long been dead.

Syme 1939.1

The homage to Tacitus (Gibbon is invoked a few pages later) was far from merely ornamental. Tacitus' whole neo-optimate scenario is taken as read, including the exculpation of Brutus and Cassius, whose 'noble deed' was 'to slay a tyrant'. In Syme's narrative the assassins are always 'the Liberators', their supporters 'the Republicans'. As for the Roman People, who demanded vengeance for the murder, they were just a 'motley and excitable rabble', 'debauched by demagogues and largess'.

One Tacitean phrase, 'the Julian party' (*Iulianae partes*), had a particular resonance at the time of writing. In the 1930s the word 'party' brought to mind the Communist Party, the Fascist Party, the National Socialist Party, disciplined organisations exploiting popular resentments to become, by violence, totalitarian regimes. That was precisely the theme of *The Roman Revolution*:

The present enquiry will attempt to discover the resources and devices by which a revolutionary leader arose in civil strife, usurped power for himself and his faction, transformed a faction into a national party, and a torn and distracted land into a nation, with a stable and enduring government.

Syme 1939.4

When that was written, the governments of the Soviet Union, Fascist Italy, and Nazi Germany seemed to be stable and enduring, however unwelcome that might be. It is not surprising that Syme's account of Augustus was 'unfriendly'. 'It all seems inevitable, as though destiny ordained the succession of military tyrants.'

The pejorative tone is unrelenting. 'The new dispensation . . . was the work of fraud and bloodshed'; the young Caesar 'perfected himself in the study of political cant and the practice of dissimulation'; 'the cause of Caesar's heir was purely revolutionary in origin, attracting all the enemies of society'; 'the young adventurer who made his way by treachery . . . represented Caesarism and the Revolution in all that was most brutal and odious'; 'in some way, by propaganda, by intimidation and by violence, Italy was forced into a struggle which in time she came to believe was a national war'; 'ostensible moderation was only a step to greater consolidation of power.' That takes us down to the moment in 27 BC when Commander Caesar became Caesar Augustus. But Syme allows no moral distinction between the triumvir and the *princeps*; Augustus remained what he had always been, 'the least honest and the least republican of men'.

Although it's easy to miss his acknowledgment of the fact, Syme knew perfectly well that this negative judgement is not found in the contemporary evidence. He also knew, and tacitly rejected, Sallust's account of popular resistance to a corrupt and murderous oligarchy. For him the *populares* were just cynical demagogues. Like Tacitus, he took an optimate view of the late republic, as legitimate aristocratic government undermined by unconstitutional attacks. Like Tacitus with a twentieth-century twist, he saw Caesar and Augustus not as champions of a necessary popular cause but as party leaders usurping unlimited personal power.

Syme's version of events was clear, consistent and powerfully expressed. 'The principate arose from usurpation.' 'The last of the dynasts prevailed in violence and bloodshed.' Of course no good could come of it: 'from first to last the dynasty of the Julii and the Claudii ran true to form, despotic and murderous.' As in Tacitus and Gibbon, Augustus is damned by the deeds of Tiberius, Caligula, and Nero. Syme could have argued it differently, by challenging what the *optimates* meant by 'freedom':

> *Libertas* was most commonly invoked in defence of the existing order by individuals or classes in enjoyment of power and wealth. The *libertas* of a Roman aristocrat meant the rule of a class and the perpetuation of privilege.

Syme 1939.155

Sallust would have given him a context, the *dominatio* of the oligarchy (**1.1** above). But the experience of modern totalitarian regimes outweighed all that. Only the sombre Tacitean reading could make sense of it.

The overwhelming influence of Syme's view may be illustrated by two conspicuous recent examples. A brilliant analysis of 'Roman power' by a distinguished senior historian states without argument that Augustus was a tyrant, his power usurped; and an author who even adapts Syme's own title casually describes Augustus' principate as an 'authoritarian regime' and a 'totalitarian state'. In my view, that judgement is a gross historical injustice.

10.3 EPILOGUE

On 21 January 2017, the day after President Trump was sworn into office, his Press Secretary Sean Spicer announced emphatically that 'this was the largest audience to ever witness an inauguration'. That seemed to be disproved by the TV footage, so next day, on NBC's 'Meet the Press', Chuck Todd asked Kellyanne Conway, a senior member of the White House staff, why the President had asked his spokesman 'to come out in front of the podium for the first time and utter a falsehood'. Her reply coined a phrase that became instantly proverbial:

http://www
.factcheck.org
/2017/01/the
-facts-on-crowd
-size

> Don't be so overly dramatic about it, Chuck. What – You're saying it's a falsehood.
> And they're giving – Sean Spicer, our Press Secretary, gave alternative facts to that.

Just twelve days earlier in his farewell address, the outgoing President had warned against the habit of 'accepting only information, whether it's true or not, that fits our opinions, instead of basing our opinions on the evidence that is out there'. He was very quickly proved right.

What happened at an event witnessed by all the world's media was up for anyone to decide (without getting overly dramatic about it) only two days later. In our 'post-truth' digital world we can instantly access a limitless supply of information from which to choose what we want to believe. There is never any shortage of 'alternative facts'; but President Obama, a Law School graduate, reminds us to think about *evidence*.

I have called this book a detective story, because the criminal justice system and the novels and screenplays that depend on it seem to me a helpful analogy for understanding the nature of history-writing. Like a detective or an investigating judge, the historian is always looking for reliable evidence, interrogating witnesses, trying to deduce what happened and why. A police investigation or judicial enquiry has to come to a conclusion—a case to send to the prosecutors, a verdict to deliver. Error is always possible, but the methodology allows correction; the case can be reopened, the verdict overturned. That applies to historical judgements too. Our enquiry has taken the form of a re-examination of the evidence, uninfluenced (I hope) by the authority of previous investigators.

The story begins with the suspicion that a major archaeological site in Rome, elaborately reconstructed as a tourist attraction, is wrongly identified as 'the house of Augustus'. The political and ideological background of Augustus' rise to power (ch. 1) suggests a radically different interpretation of the site (ch. 2). Since the Augustan Palatine was destroyed in AD 64 and replaced by the imperial palace complex (ch. 3), a proper understanding of the pre-Neronian topography requires a very long historical perspective (ch. 4). That in turn helps to illustrate the various legendary stories about the origin of Rome (ch. 5), and in particular Romulus' foundation and inauguration of the city on the summit of the Palatine, exactly where Augustus had his house (ch. 6). The years of crisis between 44 and 27 BC are explored against that background, using the literary, documentary, iconographic, and archaeological evidence together, in order to understand the new temple of Apollo and the piazza it overlooked (ch. 7), and the portico around and behind it, with its library used as a hall for Senate meetings (ch. 8). The results are tested against contemporary evidence provided by the Augustan poets (ch. 9). Finally, the premise of the whole argument—that Commander Caesar, who became Caesar Augustus, was the champion of the Roman People against an oppressive oligarchy—is defended against the contrary opinion of Tacitus, Gibbon, and Syme (ch. 10).

Part of me wants to present this book as an object lesson in historical method, an indignant rebuttal of unexamined assumptions parroted as facts. That is because scholars are always tempted to take themselves a bit too seriously. I do, in fact, think it's important to get it right as far as humanly possible, to question orthodox dogmas, even (if we can) to do justice to the dead. If visitors to the Palatine are being misled about the house of Augustus, that is something I would like to put right. But in the end, what has driven all this investigation is curiosity. If we take the trouble to listen to the sources, what they have to say is just so varied and so interesting.

If my readers ever think about Augustus in the future, I hope they will remember that he slept in the same bedroom for forty years, that he gestured angrily at the theatre audience when they applauded the word *dominus*, that he wept with emotion at the consensus of Senate and People. I hope they may also remember the Bronze Age prospectors, finding their way up to the hill by the river; Marcus Varro, noting the position of ancient gates and drawing his own conclusions; Claudius Tiberinus, proud to be plebeian, reciting epic verse in Caesar's piazza; Master Gregory, taking time off from church business to look at the 'palace of Augustus'; Pietro Rosa, reporting to Paris on what lay below His Majesty's Palatine gardens; Ronald Syme, in the shadow of war, writing Hitler and Mussolini into Roman history.

Syme's manner of scholarship has always been an inspiration to me (which is why I had to say where I think he was wrong); so I'm glad to give the final word to him. It was spoken about half a century ago at a meeting of the Oxford Philological Society. Syme had just given a paper on the *Historia Augusta*, the fourth-century collection of imperial biographies that purports to be the work of six separate (but invented) authors. Discussion naturally turned to the real composer of this elaborate farrago of history and fiction: what could have been his motive? Sir Ronald was sitting in an armchair, gently tapping his fingertips together. 'Perhaps,' he murmured, 'the mere fascination of the thing in itself.'

NOTES

PREFACE

xv Date of death: Suetonius *Diuus Augustus* 100.1, Dio Cassius 56.30.5; Degrassi 1947.184–5 (*Fasti Ostienses*), 1963.208 (*Fasti Antiates ministrorum*). Question: Suetonius *Diuus Augustus* 99.1 (*admissos amicos percontatus ecquid iis uideretur mimum uitae commode transegisse*).

Caesar empowered by the Roman People: I have tried to trace Caesar's *popularis* career in a separate book (Wiseman 2016).

Comet: Pliny *Natural History* 2.93–4, citing Augustus' own words; Dio Cassius 45.7.1, Obsequens 68; exhaustive source material (texts and translation) in Ramsey and Licht 1997.155–77. Northern sky: i.e., where the gods were believed to live (Festus 454L, quoting Varro); Linderski 2007.17–18.

Country estate (Nola in Campania): Velleius Paterculus 2.123.1, Suetonius *Diuus Augustus* 98.5, Dio Cassius 56.29.2. Solemn procession: Suetonius *Diuus Augustus* 100.2, Dio Cassius 56.31.2.

Forecourt (*uestibulum*): Suetonius *Diuus Augustus* 100.2; cf. Augustus *Res gestae* 35.1, Ovid *Tristia* 3.1.33–6; the colonnades are shown on the 'Sorrento Base' (Wiseman 2013a.103–5, and Fig. 39 above); for the architectural form of a *uestibulum*, see Aelius Gallus fr. 7 Funaioli (Aulus Gellius 16.5.2-3), with Wiseman 2008.282–4. Modest house: Suetonius *Diuus Augustus* 72.1 ('remarkable neither in size nor in elegance'). 'House of Augustus': Tomei 2014b (excavation), Iacopi 2007 (wall-paintings); full details in Pensabene 2017.2.43–111. Reopened in 2014: Tomei 2014c; Fraser 2008 and Bucci 2014 for the project costs.

1. UNDERSTANDING AUGUSTUS

1 Misunderstanding: for a typical example see Alston 2015.vii, who asserts that the actions of Caesar's assassins in 44 BC 'brought an end to the republic and ushered in a new political system, which we know as the Roman empire'.

1.1 The Oligarchs

Cicero *Pro Sestio* 96:

duo genera semper in hac ciuitate fuerunt eorum qui uersari in re publica atque in ea se excellentius gerere studuerunt; quibus ex generibus alteri se populares, alteri optimates et haberi et esse uoluerunt. qui ea quae faciebant quaeque dicebant multitudini iucunda uolebant esse, populares, qui autem ita se gerebant ut sua consilia optimo cuique probarent, optimates habebantur.

Modern historians' attempts to explain this passage away (e.g., Alston 2015.353, Mouritsen 2017.120–2) are a tacit admission that their preconceived ideas of what the republic was like are incompatible with the primary evidence.

2 Cicero *De republica* 3.23:

cum autem certi propter diuitias aut genus aut aliquas opes rem publicam tenent, est factio, sed uocantur illi optimates.

Climax in 52 BC: Asconius 31–33C; Dio Cassius 40.48.1–49.3.

Hirtius *De bello Gallico* 8.50.2:

contendebat enim gratia cum libenter pro homine sibi coniunctissimo, quem paulo ante praemiserat ad petitionem, tum acriter contra factionem et potentiam paucorum, qui M. Antoni repulsa Caesaris decedentis gratiam conuellere cupiebant.

Caesar *De bello ciuili* 1.22.5:

se non malefici causa ex prouincia egressum sed uti se a contumeliis inimicorum defenderet, ut tribunos plebis in ea re ex ciuitate expulsos in suam dignitatem restitueret, ut se et populum Romanum factione paucorum oppressum in libertatem uindicaret.

Law of the ten tribunes: Caesar *De bello ciuili* 1.32.3; Cicero *Ad Atticum* 7.3.4, 8.3.3. *Populi Romani benefi-cium*: Caesar *De bello ciuili* 1.9.2; Cicero *Ad Atticum* 9.11A.2 (to Caesar). Frustrated by oligarchs: Caesar *De bello ciuili* 1.1–5; Dio Cassius 41.1–3.

Support of the People: Cicero *Ad Atticum* 7.3.5 (*illa urbana ac perdita plebs*), 7.7.6 (*plebes urbana*), 8.3.4 (*multitudo et infimus quisque*), 10.4.8 (*populi studium*).

Sallust as tribune in 52: Asconius 37C, 49C. Truth over partisanship: Sallust *Bellum Catilinae* 4.2, *Historiae* 1.6M.

3   Sallust *Bellum Iugurthinum* 42.1:

postquam Ti. et C. Gracchus, quorum maiores Punico atque aliis bellis multum rei publicae addiderant, uindicare plebem in libertatem et paucorum scelera patefacere coepere, nobilitas noxia atque eo perculsa . . . Gracchorum actionibus obuiam ierat.

Sallust *Bellum Catilinae* 39.1:

postquam Cn. Pompeius ad bellum maritumum atque Mithridaticum missus est, plebis opes imminutae, paucorum potentia creuit.

Speeches of People's champions: Sallust *Bellum Iugurthinum* 31, 85, *Historiae* 3.48M, *Bellum Catilinae* 20. Sallust *Bellum Iugurthinum* 5.1:

bellum scripturus sum quod populus Romanus cum Iugurtha rege Numidarum gessit, . . . quia tunc primum superbiae nobilitatis obuiam itum est; quae contentio diuina et humana cuncta permiscuit eoque uecordiae processit ut studiis ciuilibus bellum atque uastitas Italiae finem faceret.

Sallust's analysis of the corruption of the republic and the origin of the civil wars is surprisingly ne-glected by students of ancient political thought. According to a recent study of ancient democracy (Car-tledge 2016.263), 'It is telling that no Roman Thucydides stepped forward to describe or analyse this classic case of *stasis*'. But that is quite untrue: as was obvious to his readers (Velleius Paterculus 2.36.2, Seneca *Controuersiae* 9.1.13, Quintilian 1.10.101), Sallust deliberately imitated Thucydides.

According to Henrik Mouritsen, Sallust 'presents a picture of Roman politics that is not easily recon-ciled to a binary, "Sestian", model' (Mouritsen 2017.123, referring to Cicero *Pro Sestio* 96 on *optimates* and *populares*). But that too is false: Sallust's narrative constantly pits the *pauci* or *nobilitas* against the *plebs* or *populus* (see for instance *Bellum Catilinae* 39.1, *Bellum Iugurthinum* 5.1, 27.2, 30.3, 31.2, 31.20, 40.3–5, 41.5–7, 42.1, *Historiae* 3.48.28).

Civil war of 41 BC: Propertius 1.22.3–4, Velleius Paterculus 2.74.4, Appian *Civil Wars* 5.49 (Perusia); Dio Cassius 48.13.6 (Sentinum, Nursia).

Scipio Nasica as national hero: e.g., Cicero *Pro Plancio* 88, *Tusculan Disputations* 4.51, *De officiis* 1.109, *Philippics* 8.13; Valerius Maximus 3.2.17.

4   [Cicero] *Ad familiares* 11.28.2–3:

nota enim mihi sunt quae in me post Caesaris mortem contulerint. uitio mihi dant quod mortem hominis necessari grauiter fero atque eum quem dilexi perisse indignor; aiunt enim patriam amicitiae praeponen-dam esse, proinde ac si iam uicerint obitum eius rei publicae fuisse utilem . . . 'plecteris ergo' inquiunt 'quo-niam factum nostrum improbare audes.' o superbiam inauditam!

Who should or should not be allowed to live: cf. Cicero *Philippics* 8.13–16.

Cicero *Pro Cluentio* 146:

hoc enim uinculum est huius dignitatis qua fruimur in re publica, hoc fundamentum libertatis, hic fons aequitatis: mens et animus et consilium et sententia ciuitatis posita est in legibus. ut corpora nostra sine mente, sic ciuitas sine lege suis partibus, ut neruis et sanguine et membris, uti non potest. legum ministri magistratus, legum interpretes iudices, legum denique idcirco omnes serui sumus ut liberi esse possimus.

Cicero *Ad familiares* 11.5.1, 11.7.2:

qua re hortatione tu quidem non eges, si ne in illa quidem re quae a te gesta est post hominum memoriam maxima hortatorem desiderasti. . . . nullo enim publico consilio rem publicam liberauisti, quo etiam est res illa maior et clarior.

Caesar assumed to be a tyrant: e.g., Cicero *Ad Atticum* 7.11.1, *De officiis* 3.82 (quoting Euripides *Phoenis-sae* 506 and 524–5 respectively); *Philippics* 2.117 ('it's a glorious thing to kill a tyrant').

Powers and honours voted to him: Dio Cassius 42.21.1, 43.14.7, 43.45.1, 44.1.1, 44.4.2, 44.5.3, 46.13.1.

What Cicero later claimed: *De officiis* 3.84 ('the man who used the Roman People's army to hold down the Roman People itself'). For more detail on Caesar's popularity (and optimate hypocrisy), see Wiseman 2016.81–105.

Cicero *Ad familiares* 6.6.10:

admirari soleo grauitatem et iustitiam et sapientiam Caesaris. numquam nisi honorificentissime Pompeium appellat. at in eius persona multa fecit asperius. armorum ista et uictoriae sunt facta, non Caesaris. at nos quem ad modum est complexus! Cassium sibi legauit, Brutum Galliae praefecit, Sulpicium Graeciae; Marcellum, cui maxime suscensebat, cum summa illius dignitate restituit.

5   *Sacrosanctitas*, making each murder a pollution (μύσος, ἄγος): Appian *Civil Wars* 1.2.5, 1.17.71 (Gracchus); 2.118.494, 2.124.520 (Caesar).

Optimates exultant: Cicero *Ad Atticum* 14.9.2 (*laetamur*); 14.12.1, 14.13.2, 14.14.4 (*laetitia*); 14.22.2 (*laetati sumus*). 'Fouler than Sulla's': Cicero *De officiis* 2.27 (*uictoria etiam foediore*).

1.2 The Young Caesar

Octavius and Atia: Nicolaus of Damascus *FGrH* 90 F127.5–7, 128.34; Suetonius *Diuus Augustus* 4.1, 8.1.

Games of 46 BC: Nicolaus of Damascus *FGrH* 90 F127.19. In Epirus: Nicolaus of Damascus *FGrH* 90 F130.37–45; Suetonius *Diuus Augustus* 8.2, 89.1.

6   Speech at the temple of Castor: Appian *Civil Wars* 3.41; Dio Cassius 45.12.4–5.

Cicero *Ad Atticum* 16.15.3:

quamquam enim in praesentia belle iste puer retundit Antonium, tamen exitum exspectare debemus. at quae contio! nam est missa mihi. iurat 'ita sibi parentis honores consequi liceat' et simul dextram intendit ad statuam. μηδὲ σωθείην ὑπό γε τοιούτου.

[Cicero] *Ad familiares* 11.20.1:

saepe enim mihi cum esset dictum neque a me contemptum, nouissime Labeo Segulius, homo sui simillimus, narrat mihi apud Caesarem se fuisse multumque sermonem de te habitum esse; ipsum Caesarem nihil sane de te questum nisi dictum, quod diceret te dixisse laudandum adulescentem ornandum tollendum; se non esse commissurum ut tolli posset.

Livy fr. 50 (Seneca *Suasoriae* 6.22):

. . . mortem, quae uere aestimanti minus indigna uideri potuit, quod a uictore inimico nihil crudelius passus erat quam quod eiusdem fortunae compos ipse fecisset.

Tribunician law: Appian *Civil Wars* 4.7.27; Dio Cassius 47.2.1–2.

7   Appian *Civil Wars* 4.8.31–2:

Μᾶρκος Λέπιδος, Μᾶρκος Ἀντώνιος, Ὀκτάουιος Καῖσαρ οἱ χειροτονηθέντες ἁρμόσαι καὶ διορθῶσαι τὰ κοινὰ οὕτως λέγουσιν· εἰ μὴ δι' ἀπιστίαν οἱ πονηροὶ δεόμενοι μὲν ἦσαν ἐλεεινοί, τυχόντες δὲ ἐγίγνοντο τῶν εὐεργετῶν ἐχθροί, εἶτα ἐπίβουλοι, οὔτ' ἂν Γάιον Καίσαρα ἀνῃρήκεσαν, οὓς ἐκεῖνος δορὶ λαβὼν ἐλέῳ καὶ φίλους θέμενος ἐπὶ ἀρχὰς καὶ τιμὰς καὶ δωρεὰς προήγαγεν ἀθρόως . . . .

Under the rule of law: e.g., Cicero *De republica* 1.49 ('Since law is the bond of the citizens' community, and the justice of the law is equal, by what right can a community be held together if the citizens are not treated in the same way?')

'Commander Caesar': the name *Imperator Caesar* is first attested on a coin issue of 38 BC (Crawford 1974.535 no. 534); see Syme 1958 = 1979.361–77.

Oath of all Italy: Augustus *Res gestae* 25.2 ('The whole of Italy swore allegiance to me of its own accord, and demanded me as leader of the war in which I was victorious at Actium').

Law on the Prefecture of Egypt: Ulpian *Digest* 1.17.1 (*lege*); Millar 2000.25. Prohibition on senators: Tacitus *Annals* 2.59.3.

Sutherland 1984.79 (no. 476):

[obv.] *Imp. Caesar diui f. cos. VI libertatis p. R. uindex* [rev.] *Pax.*

For the phraseology (*populum Romanum uindicare in libertatem*), cf. Sallust *Bellum Iugurthinum* 42.1, Caesar *De bello ciuili* 1.22.

8   British Museum CM 1995-4-1-1:

[obv.] *Imp. Caesar diui f. cos. VI* [rev.] *leges et iura p. R. restituit.*

For the historical significance of the issue, see Rich and Williams 1999.

New name: Augustus *Res gestae* 34.1–2; Ovid *Fasti* 1.587–616, Velleius Paterculus 2.91.1, Degrassi 1963.114–5 and 279 (*Fasti Praenestini* and *Feriale* Cumanum, 16 Jan.), Suetonius *Diuus Augustus* 7.2.

Degrassi 1963.112–3 (*Fasti Praenestini*, 13 Jan.):

corona querc[ea, uti super ianuam domus imp. Caesaris] Augusti poner[etur senatus decreuit quod rem publicam] p. R. rest[it]u[it].

See also Augustus *Res gestae* 34.2, where the Greek text explains that the crown 'is given for saving fellow-citizens'; Ovid *Fasti* 1.614, *Tristia* 3.1.36.

Long but limited period: Dio Cassius 53.12.1–2, 53.13.1.Horace *Odes* 3.1.10–14:

. . . hic generosior | descendat in Campum petitor, | moribus hic meliorque fama | contendat, illi turba clientium | sit maior.

Horace *Epistles* 1.6.49–54:

si fortunatum species et gratia praestat, | mercemur seruum qui dictet nomina, laeuum | qui fodicet latus et cogat trans pondera dextram | porrigere: 'hic multum in Fabia ualet, ille Velina; | cui libet hic fasces dabit eripietque curule | cui uolet importunus ebur.'

Indignation at Augustus' refusal to stand for the consulship: Dio Cassius 54.6.1–3, 54.10.1–2.

9   Greek observer: Polybius 6.14.9 (καὶ μὴν τὰς ἀρχὰς ὁ δῆμος δίδωσι τοῖς ἀξίοις).

Livy fr. 55 (Apponius *In Canticum canticorum* 12.53, CCL 19.291–2):

Caesar Augustus in spectaculis, sicut Liuius narrat, Romano populo nuntiat regressus a Britannia insula totum orbem terrarum tam bello quam amicitiis Romano imperio pacis abundantia subditum.

Tribute from Britain re-established: Dio Cassius 53.22.5, Strabo 4.5.3 (C200).

Tribunician power granted by law: Augustus *Res gestae* 10.1 (*lege*). To protect the common people: Tacitus *Annals* 1.2.1 (*ad tuendam plebem*).

Horace *Odes* 4.15.17–20:

custode rerum Caesare non furor | ciuilis aut uis exiget otium, | non ira quae procudit enses | et miseras inimicat urbes.

1.3 The Augustan Age

10   New *saeculum*: Censorinus *De die natali* 17; Augustus *Res gestae* 22.2, Horace *Carmen saeculare* and *Odes* 4.6.31–44; CIL 6.32323 (lines 90–152 = *ILS* 5050 = Thomas 2011.274–6, translated in Beard, North, and Price 1998.2.140–4); Phlegon of Tralles *FGrH* 257 F 37.5.4 (= Thomas 2011.277–8); see in general Beard, North, and Price 1998.1.201–6, Malloch 2013.176–8 and 181-2. 'Age of Caesar': Horace *Odes* 4.15.4 (*tua, Caesar, aetas*).

Suetonius *Diuus Augustus* 58.2:

'senatus te consentiens cum populo Romano consalutat patriae patrem.' cui lacrimans respondit Augustus his uerbis (ipsa enim, sicut Messallae, posui): 'compos factus uotorum meorum, patres conscripti, quid habeo aliud deos immortales precari quam ut hunc consensum uestrum ad ultimum finem uitae mihi perferre liceat?'

Modern scholars have to put their own spin on this scene: 'Augustus had the senate, which he had "packed" with his own supporters, confer upon him the name "father of the fatherland"' (Atkins 2018.30); 'as the colourless Senatorial stooge who formally proposed the award obsequiously stated . . . .' (Cartledge 2016.269). Contrast Tacitus *Annals* 4.34.4 on Messalla Corvinus, who made no secret of the fact that he had served under the command of Cassius at Philippi. As for the Roman People, who had initiated the proposal, they were a mere mob, living in 'grindingly horrible conditions' and politically relevant only through 'organised mass violence' (Cartledge 2016.261).

Suetonius *Diuus Augustus* 31.5:

. . . statuas omnium triumphali effigie in utraque fori sui porticu dedicauit, professus et edicto commentum id se ut ad illorum ˹normam˺ uelut ad exemplar et ipse, dum uiueret, et insequentium aetatium principes exigerentur a ciuibus.

11   Cicero *De oratore* 1.226:

quae uero addidisti, non modo senatum seruire posse populo sed etiam debere, quis hoc philosophus tam mollis, tam languidus, tam eneruatus, tam omnia ad uoluptatem corporis doloremque referens, probare posset senatum seruire populo, cui populus ipse moderandi et regendi sui potestatem quasi quasdam habenas tradidisset?

According to Atkins 2018.119, Crassus 'shamelessly pandered to the people'—a nice example of the way modern students of Roman political thought have internalised Cicero's optimate viewpoint.

Senator populi Romani: Cicero *In Verrem* 2.1.156–7, 3.93, 4.25, 4.42 (69 BC). *Senatus populi Romani*: Varro fr. 58 Funaioli (Aulus Gellius 17.21.48, on philosophers 'sent by the Athenians as ambassadors on public business to the Senate of the Roman People'); Sallust *Bellum Catilinae* 34.1 ('The Senate of the Roman People has always been of such forbearance and compassion that no-one ever sought help from it in vain').

12   *CIL* 11.1420.9–12 = *ILS* 139.9–12:

cum senatus populi Romani inter ceteros plurimos ac maximos honores L. Caesaris [sic], *Augusti Caesaris patris patriae pontificis maximi tribuniciae potestatis XXV filio, auguri consuli designato per consensum omnium ordinum studio* . . . .

Everything going wrong: Pliny *Natural History* 7.149; cf. Suetonius *Diuus Augustus* 65.1 ('Fortune deserted him'). 'The people's thing': Cicero *De republica* 1.39 (*res publica* as *res populi*).

Suetonius *Tiberius* 21.7:

teque oro ut parcas tibi, ne si te languere audierimus, et ego et mater tua exspiremus et summa imperi sui populus Romanus periclitetur. . . . deos obsecro ut te nobis conseruent et ualere nunc et semper patiantur, si non p. R. perosi sunt.

Tiberius' father in 44 BC: Suetonius *Tiberius* 4.1.

Suetonius *Tiberius* 21.3, 68.3:

. . . uitiis Tiberi uirtutibusque perpensis potiores duxisse uirtutes, praesertim cum et rei p. causa adoptare se eum pro contione iurauerit. . . . quae omnia ingrata atque arrogantiae plena et animaduertit Augustus in eo et excusare temptauit saepe apud senatum ac populum professus naturae uitia esse non animi.

Augustus on his *statio*: Aulus Gellius 15.7.3 (in a letter to his adopted son Gaius).

13   Augustus *Res gestae* 1.1–4:

annos undeuiginti natus exercitum priuato consilio et priuata impensa comparaui, per quem rem publicam a dominatione factionis oppressam in libertatem uindicaui. eo [nomi]*ne senatus decretis honorif*[i]*cis in ordinem suum m*[e adlegit C. Pansa et A. Hirti]*o consulibus con*[sula]*rem locum s*[ententiae dicendae simu]*l* [dans et i]*mperium mihi dedit. res publica n*[e quid detrimenti caperet] *me pro praetore simul cum consulibus pro*[uidere iussit. p]*opulus autem eodem anno me consulem, cum* [consul uterqu]*e in bel*[lo ceci]*disset, et triumuirum rei publicae constituend*[ae creauit.]

The domination of a faction: assumed by Wallace-Hadrill (2018.131), without argument, to be Augustus 'subtly, or simply outrageously, distort[ing] the truth'.

Idea of consensus: e.g., *Res gestae* 5.1–2, 6.1, 25.2, 34.1. *Pater patriae* title: *Res gestae* 35.1 (*populus Romanus uniuersus*).

'Poor Roman People!': Suetonius *Tiberius* 21.2 ('*miserum populum Romanum*'). Tiberius' contempt: Tacitus *Annals* 3.65.3 ('*o homines ad seruitutem paratos*').

Body of advisers: Dio Cassius 53.21.4. Tiberius' preferred system: Tacitus *Annals* 4.6.2 ('All public business, and the most important private business too, was handled by the Senate').

14   Late-republican conditions: Tacitus *Annals* 3.14.4 (AD 20), 5.4.2 (AD 29); Dio Cassius 58.12.1 (AD 31). Jubilant Roman People: Suetonius *Tiberius* 75.1 ('To the Tiber with Tiberius!'), *Gaius* 13.

Josephus *Jewish Antiquities* 19.227–8:

οἱ μὲν ἀξιώματος τε τοῦ προτέρου ὀρεγόμενοι καὶ δουλείαν ἔπακτον αὐτοῖς ὕβρει τῶν τυράννων γενομένην φιλοτιμούμενοι διαδιδράσκειν χρόνῳ παρασχόν, ὁ δὲ δῆμος φθόνῳ τε πρὸς ἐκείνην καθιστάμενος καὶ τῶν πλεονεξιῶν αὐτῆς ἐπιστόμισμα τοὺς αὐτοκράτορας εἰδὼς καὶ αὐτοῦ καταφυγὴν ἔχαιρεν Κλαυδίου τῇ ἁρπαγῇ στάσιν τε ἔμφυλον, ὁποία καὶ ἐπὶ Πομπηίου γένοιτο, ἀπαλλάξειν αὐτῶν ὑπελάμβανον τοῦτον αὐτοκράτορα καθισταμένου.

For Josephus' contemporary source(s), see Wiseman 2013a.xiv–xvii, 109–16.

All the Caesars had been tyrants: Josephus *Antiquitates* 19.172–4, 187, 227, 230.

Renewal of powers not automatic: still true in AD 34 (Dio Cassius 58.24.1).

2. HISTORY AND ARCHAEOLOGY

2.1 Public and Private

16   Private luxury and public magnificence: *odit populus Romanus priuatam luxuriam, publicam magnificentiam diligit* (Cicero *Pro Murena* 76); cf. Russell 2016.8–10.

Cicero as *popularis*: Cicero *De lege agraria* 2.6–10; Q. Cicero *Commentariolum petitionis* 51–3. Oligarchic corruption: Cicero *In Verrem*, esp. 1.34–52, 2.5.173–7. Reforming tribunes: Cicero *Pro Cornelio* (Crawford 1994.65–144), esp. frr. 1.47–52 (Asconius 76–8C), 2.5 (Asconius 80C).

Decisive step: Cicero *In Catilinam* 1.2–4 (optimate precedents), 4.9–11 (*popularis* opposition expected).

Expensive house: Cicero *Ad familiares* 5.6.2 (cost), *Ad Atticum* 1.13.6 (loans needed), 1.16.10 (Clodius' taunt); Aulus Gellius 12.12.2–4 (popular disapproval).

North slope: Cicero *Ad Atticum* 2.24.3, Suetonius *Diuus Iulius* 46 (near Caesar, who lived on the Sacra Via); *Ad Atticum* 2.4.7, 4.3.2 (above his brother Quintus); *De haruspicum responso* 33 (above Clodius); Velleius Paterculus 2.14.3 (could be looked into from above).

17   Cicero *Ad Atticum* 2.4.7:

his temporibus, tam dubia uita optimi cuiusque, magni aestimo unius aestatis fructum palaestrae Palatinae. *Palaestra* as scene of Socratic dialogues: e.g., Plato *Charmides* 153a, *Lysis* 204a; cf. [Longinus] *De sublimitate* 4.4 on Xenophon and Plato 'from the *palaistra* of Socrates'. Cicero's Palatine house featured a lawn with a portico (*xystum*) and a statue of Plato (Cicero *Brutus* 10, 24), and the equivalent feature at his country house at Tusculum was named after Plato's Academy: Cicero *Ad Atticum* 1.8.2 (*xystum*), 1.9.2 and 1.11.3 (*Academia*), 1.10.3 (*palaestra*).

Cicero's cultural interests unpopular: Plutarch *Cicero* 5.2; implied also by Cicero *Pro Archia* 1–3 (defending *studia humanitatis et litterarum*), 23–4 (defending Greek culture).

Law for Cicero's banishment and confiscation of his property: Livy *Epitome* 103, Asconius 10C; Cicero *Ad Atticum* 3.4, *De domo* 47–51, *In Pisonem* 30. Portico and shrine: Dio Cassius 38.17.6–7; Cicero *De domo* 100–3, 114–21, *Ad Atticum* 4.2.5; full discussion in Wiseman 2012b.658–60.

Equal citizens: Dionysius of Halicarnassus *Roman Antiquities* 2.7.4 (division of land provides τὴν κοινὴν καὶ μεγίστην ἰσότητα), 2.28.3 (ἐξ ἴσου); Livy 4.5.1 (*omnibus aequa libertas*), cf. Columella 1.3.10 (equal division of land after the expulsion). For 'equal liberty' see also Livy 34.54.5 (threatened by senatorial privilege), Florus 2.1.4 (protected by *popularis* legislation).

Manius Curius and Gaius Fabricius (censors respectively in 272 and 275 BC): Columella 1.pref.14, 1.3.10; Frontinus *Stratagems* 4.3.12; Pliny *Natural History* 18.18; Valerius Maximus 2.9.4, 4.3.5–6; *De uiris illustribus* 33.6–8; for the historical context, see Wiseman 2009a.42–4.

Marcus Cato: Plutarch *Cato maior* 16.5; detailed discussion in Astin 1978.91–103. For the continuity with Curius and Fabricius, see Cicero *De senectute* 15, 43; Plutarch *Cato maior* 2.1–2.

Influx of wealth: for 'the origins of luxury' see Livy 39.6.67 (187 BC), Pliny *Natural History* 33.148–50 (187 or 146 BC).

Public expenditure: e.g., Velleius Paterculus 1.11.5 (first marble temple, 146 BC), 2.1.1–2 ('private luxury followed public magnificence'); Fenestella *FRHist* 70 F12 = Frontinus *De aquis* 7.4 (180m sesterces spent on Aqua Marcia, 143 BC). Attempted regulation of private spending: Aulus Gellius 2.24.2–10, Macrobius *Saturnalia* 3.17.1–10 (successive 'sumptuary laws' in the second century BC).

Secret of Rome's success: Polybius 6.18.3 (cooperation κοινῇ καὶ κατ' ἰδίαν), 6.54.3–4 (enthusiasm and self-sacrifice 'for the common good'), 6.56.14–15 (honesty and integrity in public life).

Sallust *Bellum Catilinae* 10.3–5:

igitur primo pecuniae deinde imperi cupido creuit: ea quasi materies omnium malorum fuere. namque auaritia fidem probitatem ceterasque bonas artes subuortit; pro his superbiam crudelitatem, deos neglegere, omnia uenalia habere edocuit.

Appeal to traditional ideology: Appian *Civil Wars* 1.11.44 (διηρώτα δ' ἐπ' ἐκείνοις εἰ δίκαιον τὰ κοινὰ κοινῇ διανέμεσθαι); Siculus Flaccus *De condicionibus agrorum* 102.29–33 Campbell (*Gracchus . . . intellegebat . . . contrarium esse morem maiorem modum possidere quam qui ab ipso possidente coli possit*).

Brazen justification: detailed discussion in Wiseman 2009a.179–87.

Memory of Curius and Fabricius: e.g., Cicero *Pro Plancio* 60, *De amicitia* 28, *De senectute* 43, *Paradoxa Stoicorum* 12, 38, 48.

Cicero *Pro Flacco* 28:

haec etiam ratio ac magnitudo animorum in maioribus nostris fuit ut . . . in priuatis rebus suisque sumptibus minimo contenti tenuissimo cultu uiuerent.

18   Contemptuous comments: e.g., Cicero *Ad Atticum* 1.16.11 (*illa contionalis hirudo aerarii, misera ac ieiuna plebecula*), 1.19.4 ('the sewer of the city'), 2.1.8 ('the filth of Romulus'), 2.16.1 ('a shouting crowd of our own servants').

Political equality unjust: Cicero *De republica* 1.43 (*ipsa aequabilitas est iniqua, cum habet nullos gradus dignitatis*), cf. 1.53 on *aequabilitas iniquissima*.

A certain status: Cicero *Ad Atticum* 1.13.6 (*ad dignitatem aliquam peruenire*); cf. also 1.17.6, 1.19.6, 1.20.2 on Cicero's care for his *dignitas*.

What was at stake: Cicero *De domo* 100–1, cf. 147 (*meo dedecore*). 'Their own Liberty': Cicero *Ad Atticum* 4.2.3, cf. 4.3.2–3, Dio Cassius 39.20.3–21.4.

Status restored: Cicero *Ad Q. fratrem* 2.5.1 (*uiuo paulo liberalius quam solebam: opus erat*), *Ad familiares* 1.9.17 (*splendorem et speciem huius uitae*).

Political shift: Cicero *Ad Atticum* 4.5.1 (palinode), *Ad familiares* 1.9.4–22. Previously deplored: e.g., Cicero *Ad Atticum* 2.17.1 ('tyranny'), 2.18.1–2 ('slavery'), 2.19.2 (*isti populares*), 2.20.3–4 (*odium popularium*), 2.21.1 (*dominatio*).

Not on private luxury: Caesar's lack of personal excess is attested by a contemporary, Aurunculeius Cotta (quoted in Athenaeus 6.273b). Public magnificence: Cicero *Pro Flacco* 28 for the traditional combination of frugality and self-restraint in private life with splendour and magnificence in the public domain.

Cicero *Ad Atticum* 4.6.8:

Caesaris amici, me dico et Oppium dirumparis licet, <in> monumentum illud quod tu tollere laudibus solebas, ut forum laxaremus et usque ad atrium Libertatis explicaremus, contempsimus sescenties sestertium; cum priuatis non poterat transigi minore pecunia. efficiemus rem gloriosissimam. nam in campo Martio saepta tributis comitiis marmorea sumus et tecta facturi eaque cingemus excelsa porticu ut mille passuum conficiatur. simul adiungetur huic operi uilla etiam publica. dices 'quid mihi hoc monumentum proderit?', at quid id laboramus?

2.2 Material Evidence

19 Stepfather's house: Nicolaus of Damascus *FGrH* 90 F127.5; Servius on *Aeneid* 8.361, cf. Horace *Epistles* 1.7.46–8 (Philippus' house at 'Carinae').

House of his own: Nicolaus of Damascus *FGrH* 90 F128.34 (πλησίον); Suetonius *Diuus Augustus* 72.1 (*iuxta Romanum forum*). Despite what is regularly asserted (e.g., Papi 1999), the site of the house is unknown; but it is obvious from Suetonius' text that it was not on the Palatine (see Wiseman 2012b.661–2). Appropriate for a *popularis*: Gaius Gracchus moved from the Palatine to the Forum area, because 'it was more democratic to live where most of the lowly and poor were' (Plutarch *Gaius Gracchus* 12.1). Caesar's house: Suetonius *Diuus Iulius* 46 (*modicis aedibus*).

Suetonius *Diuus Augustus* 72.1:

habitauit primo iuxta Romanum forum supra scalas anularias in domo quae Calui oratoris fuerat; postea in Palatio, sed nihilo minus aedibus modicis Hortensianis, et neque laxitate neque cultu conspicuis, ut in quibus porticus breues essent Albanarum columnarum et sine marmore ullo aut insigni pauimento conclauia. ac per annos amplius quadraginta eodem cubiculo hieme et aestate mansit, quamuis parum salubrem ualitudini suae urbem hieme experiretur assidueque in urbe hiemaret.

Contemporary eye-witnesses: e.g., Sallust *Bellum Catilinae* 12.3 (built like cities), 20.11–12 (joined together, building and demolishing); Horace *Odes* 2.15.1 (palaces), 2.18.3–6 (African marble, like a king's palace), 3.1.41–6 (Phrygian marble, *atrium* columns), *Epistles* 1.1.100 (demolishing, building, changing). See also Strabo 5.2.5 (C223) on houses in Rome 'like Persian palaces', and 5.3.7 (C235) on constant buying and selling, with purchasers demolishing and rebuilding to suit their tastes.

Appropriate to public architecture: Vitruvius 6.5.2 (*non dissimili modo quam publicorum operum magnificentia*). Contrast with traditional values: cf. Varro *Res rusticae* 1.13.7 for the extravagant building of Lucullus and Metellus Scipio 'to great public detriment' (*pessimo publico*).

Horace *Odes* 2.15.10–20:

non ita Romuli | praescriptum et intonsi Catonis | auspiciis ueterumque norma. || priuatus illis census erat breuis, | commune magnum: nulla decempedis | metata priuatis opacum | porticus excipiebat Arcton, || nec fortuitum spernere caespitem | leges sinebant, oppida publico | sumptu iubentes et deorum | templa nouo decorare saxo.

'Augustus' and Romulus' auspices: Suetonius *Diuus Augustus* 7.2, Ennius *Annales* 155 Skutsch.

20 Triumvirs' auction: Dio Cassius 47.6.5, 47.14.5; Appian *Civil Wars* 4.5.19, 4.29.127, 4.31.133. Hortensius and Brutus: Cicero *Philippics* 10.13 and 24, Dio Cassius 47.21.4–5. Hortensius at Philippi: Livy *Epitome* 124, Velleius Paterculus 2.71.2, Plutarch *Brutus* 28.1, *Antony* 22.4.

Velleius Paterculus 2.81.3:

uictor deinde Caesar reuersus in urbem contractas emptionibus complures domos per procuratores, quo laxior fieret ipsius, publicis se usibus destinare professus est templumque Apollinis et circa porticus facturum promisit, quod ab eo singulari exstructum munificentia est.

Dio Cassius 49.15.5:

. . . τότε δὲ οἰκίαν τε αὐτῷ ἐκ τοῦ δημοσίου δοθῆναι ἔγνωσαν· τὸν γὰρ τόπον ὃν ἐν τῷ Παλατίῳ ὥστ' οἰκοδομῆσαι τινα ἐώνητο ἐδημοσίωσε καὶ τῷ Ἀπόλλωνι ἱέρωσεν, ἐπειδὴ κεραυνὸς ἐς αὐτὸν ἐγκατέσκηψε.

The subject of the verb is implied by the context, an assembly of the People outside the *pomerium* (49.15.3), and the subsequent vote (49.15.5 ἐψηφίσαντο).

Handed over to public ownership: cf. Russell 2016.191 ('a civic space on an even grander scale than the elite houses which prefigured it'), who however also claims (192) that under Augustus 'public space . . . was defined out of existence'.

21   Apollo temple excavation (by Pietro Rosa): Tomei 1999.67–79. Correct identification: Pinza 1910, cf. Claridge 2014.128–9.

Circular domed chamber: Iacopi 2007.8–9; Carandini and Bruno 2008.23–4 (fig. 9), 126–32 (figs. 56–7, 59), with very speculative interpretation; Coarelli 2012.132–9.

22   Intense archaeological investigation: e.g., Tomei 2014b.41–291 (Gianfilippo Carettoni, 1955–84), Iacopi and Tedone 2006, Pensabene and Gallocchio 2011 and 2013, Zink 2015; summary reconstruction at Carandini and Carafa 2012.tav. 69 = 2017.tab. 69. For varied interpretation of the results, see Carandini and Bruno 2008.30–50 and 138–79, Wiseman 2009b.557–9, Carandini 2010.162–210, Coarelli 2012.347–94, Wiseman 2012b.665–8, Hall 2014.167–85; the uncritical '*storia degli studi*' at Pensabene 2017.2.43–52 treats Carettoni's identification as axiomatic.

9m below: spot heights of 38.19–38.89 masl are given at Tomei 2014b.61, 107, 194, 243 (figs. 39, 101, 173, 231). Rooms with panoramic view: Pensabene and Gallocchio 2013.561.

'Palace': e.g., Iacopi and Tedone 2006.363; Carandini and Bruno 2008.43, 45, 168, 176-8; Gros 2009.170; Carandini 2010.174, cf. 176 ('un edificio regale'); Pensabene and Gallocchio 2011.477; Coarelli 2012.382; Hall 2014.177, 182; Carandini 2014.21 ('il sontuoso palazzo'); Pensabene 2017.2.96 ('una grandiosa casa'). Note also Gros 2001.240, already referring to 'le système palatial augustéen', and Tomei 2014a.38, who rejects the 'palace of Octavian' idea but still believes that Augustus created 'la prima reggia del Palatino'.

Il palazzo di Ottaviano: e.g., Carandini and Bruno 2008.168, Carandini 2010.174, 2016.46-8. Deliberate imitation: Carandini and Bruno 2008. 43 ('alla maniera delle grandi residenze ellenistiche'), 178 ('simile alla reggia di un sovrano ellenistico'); Carandini 2010.173 ('assunse la dimensione, la simmetria e l'armonia di un palazzo ellenistico'); Daniela Bruno in Carandini and Carafa 2012.228 ('una residenza dinastica di stampo ellenistico'), cf. 2017.228 ('manifesting clear Hellenistic influence'); Coarelli 2012.354 ('a imitazione di alcuni palazzi ellenistici') ; Carandini 2014.21 ('somigliava troppo a una reggia ellenistica'), 2016.46 ('una vera e propria reggia ellenistica').

Carandini 2010.176: 'Chi altri avrebbe potuto permettersi a Roma – in quel tempo e a quell'indirizzo – un edificio regale se non il quasi monarca Ottaviano?'

Coarelli 2012.378: 'Dal resto, chi altro, anche in via del tutto ipotetica, avrebbe potuto realizzare un intervento di tale portata in quest'area e in questi anni?'

So too Pensabene and Gallocchio 2013.563: '. . . un progetto unitario che forse solo il futuro imperatore, visto l'impatto urbanistico che una tale azione doveva comportare, poteva realizzare.'

23   Unlawful power: Carandini and Bruno 2008.42-3, Hall 2014.177. Megalomania: Carandini and Bruno 2008.40, Carandini 2010.171 and 174, 2016.46; cf. Carandini 2014.21 ('il triumviro Ottaviano, arrivista e crudele').

Powerful few (*pauci potentes*): Sallust *Bellum Catilinae* 20.7, 39.1, 58.11, *Bellum Iugurthinum* 3.4, 31.19, *Historiae* 1.12; cf. Hirtius *De bello Gallico* 8.50.2. Arrogant aristocrats: Sallust *Bellum Catilinae* 23.6, *Bellum Iugurthinum* 5.1, 31.2 and 12, 64.1, 85.19 and 38. Building and rebuilding: Sallust *Bellum Catilinae* 20.12; cf. Strabo 5.3.7 (C235).

Horace on regal houses and villas: *Odes* 2.15.1, 2.18.5–6; cf. Vitruvius 6.5.2 (*uestibula regalia*) on the houses of *nobiles*.

Biographer: Suetonius *Diuus Augustus* 72.3 (*ampla et operosa praetoria grauabatur*).

2.3 The Wrong Track

Gianfilippo Carettoni: Tomei 2014b.59–106 (Carettoni's own resumé, evidently written in 1984); Carettoni 1960.202, 1963.497. Layout of the house: best described in Claridge 2010.137–40.

Carettoni 1966–7.67: 'Il carattere singolare dell'edificio, il suo aspetto di sede ufficiale e insieme di abitazione privata, non possono non richiamare alla mente le caratteristiche dell'abitazione di Augusto.' Cf. Iacopi 1995.47 on the remains attesting 'la duplice funzione, ufficiale e privata insieme'.

24 Vitruvius 6.5.2:

nobilibus uero, qui honores magistratusque gerendo praestare debent officia ciuibus, faciunda sunt uestibula regalia alta atria et peristylia amplissima, siluae ambulationes laxiores ad decorum maiestatis perfectae; praeterea bibliothecas basilicas non dissimili modo quam publicorum operum magnificentia comparatas, quod in domibus eorum saepius et publica consilia et priuata iudicia arbitriaque conficiuntur.

25 Dio Cassius 54.27.3:

οὔτ' οἰκίαν τινὰ δημοσίαν ἔλαβεν, ἀλλὰ μέρος τι τῆς ἑαυτοῦ, ὅτι τὸν ἀρχιέρεων ἐν κοινῷ πάντως οἰκεῖν ἐχρῆν, ἐδημοσίωσεν.

Dio Cassius 55.12a.5:

ὁ δὲ Αὔγουστος τὴν οἰκίαν οἰκοδομήσας ἐδημόσιωσε πᾶσαν, εἴτε δὴ διὰ τὴν συντέλειαν τὴν παρὰ τοῦ δήμου οἱ γενομένην, εἴτε καὶ ὅτι ἀρχιέρεως ἦν, ἵν' ἐν τοῖς ἰδίοις ἅμα καὶ ἐν τοῖς κοινοῖς οἰκοίη.

Suetonius quotations: *Diuus Augustus* 72.1, 73. Special pleading: e.g., Carandini and Bruno 2008.83–4, Gros 2009.170–1, Hall 2014.182–3.

Momentous discovery: Carettoni in Tomei 2014b.131 (date), 173 ('una rampa di m. 4 di ampiezza, che saliva parallelamente alla fronte dell'area sacra verso il terrazzo del tempio, mettendolo in diretta comunicazione con l'abitazione e riservandone quindi l'uso agli abitanti della medesima'). Carettoni's plan is still reproduced as authoritative by Wallace-Hadrill 2018.45 (fig. 3.1).

Carettoni 1983.9: 'Aufgrund der besonderen Verehrung des Augustus für Apollo kann man verstehen, weshalb zuerst ein direkter Verbindungsgang zwischen dem Wohnsitz des Kaisers und der Tempelterrasse bestand.'

Cf. Carettoni 1983.8 (plan), 48 (reconstruction drawing), 51 ('[die] zum Tempel ansteigenden Rampe').

26 Short life: Carettoni in Tomei 2014b.173 ('la rampa venne in seguito modificata, tagliandone la parte media per creare un nuovo ingresso frontale'); the supposed frontal entrance could only have been an unfulfilled project (cf. Iacopi and Tedone 2006.366–7). According to Carettoni's editor (Tomei 2014b.151), the abolition of the ramp was post-Augustan; but the dating of the associated pottery evidently rules that out: 'any such arrangement [linking the house with the temple] must have been short-lived and one may doubt that it ever existed' (Claridge 2010.141).

Paul Zanker on the young Augustus: Zanker 1983.21–7, esp. 24 on 'Haus und Tempel als Einheit . . . [ein] Element eines umfassenden Konzeptes autokratischer Selbstdarstellung'.

Zanker 1983.23–4: 'Der Sieger von Actium wohnte also nicht nur neben, sondern bei und mit seinen Schutzgott . . . . Man hat dies bisher kaum reflektiert und auch nicht gefragt, welche Vorbilder hinter dieser Baukonzeption, die Tempel und *domus* verband, stehen könnten. Die Antwort liegt auf der Hand: Es sind hellenistische Königssitze.'

So too Zanker 1988.51: 'Recent excavations have shown that a ramp connected the house directly to the forecourt of the temple. The bond between the god and his protégé could not have been more explicitly conveyed. The house itself was relatively modest, but the temple area, because of its close proximity, became like a part of the whole complex. In this Octavian took his cue from the Hellenistic kings.'

Supporting examples: Zanker 1983.24–5. Exactly contemporary: Dio Cassius 51.22.2 (Divus Julius temple 29 BC), 53.1.3 (Apollo temple 28 BC); Suetonius *Diuus Augustus* 100.4 (Mausoleum 28 BC); *CIL* 6.896, Dio Cassius 53.27.2–3 (Pantheon 27–5 BC).

27 Modest private expenditure: Suetonius *Diuus Iulius* 46, *Diuus Augustus* 72.1 (houses); Athenaeus 6.273b (Caesar travelling with just three servants); Cicero *Ad Atticum* 13.7.1 (Caesar determined to enforce his sumptuary law).

Colossal public expenditure: Augustus *Res gestae* app.4 (*impensa innumerabilis*).

Suetonius *Diuus Augustus* 100.5:

id opus inter Flaminiam uiam ripamque Tiberis sexto suo consulatu exstruxerat circumiectasque siluas et ambulationes in usum populi iam tum publicarat.

Strabo 5.3.8 (C236):

ἐπὶ κρηπῖδος ὑψηλῆς λευκολίθου πρὸς τῷ ποταμῷ χῶμα μέγα, ἄχρι κορυφῆς τοῖς ἀειθαλέσι τῶν δένδρων συνηρεφές· ἐπ' ἄκρῳ μὲν οὖν εἰκών ἐστι χαλκῆ τοῦ Σεβαστοῦ Καίσαρος, ὑπὸ δὲ τῷ χώματι θῆκαί εἰσιν αὐτοῦ καὶ τῶν συγγενῶν καὶ οἰκείων, ὄπισθεν δὲ μέγα ἄλσος περιπάτους θαυμαστοὺς ἔχον.

'Groves and covered walks': cf. Vitruvius 6.5.2.

'Relatively modest': Zanker 1988.51.

Iacopi 1995.48: 'La connessione tra la domus e l'edificio templare, peculiarità del complesso palatino nonostante se ne siano volute vedere i presupposti nelle regge pergamene degli Attalidi collegate al temenos del tempio di Athena (Zanker), evidenzia la contestualità costruttiva dei due edifice, sulla cui contemporaneità danno, per altro, chiara notizia anche gli autori antichi.'

See Tomei 2014b.201 for Carettoni's resumé, and Iacopi 1995.47 on the 'rampa che permetteva il collegamento diretto tra la casa e il luogo di culto'.

28   Iacopi and Tedone 2006.366–7: 'Non si ritiene, infatti, che tale accesso potesse essere funzionale al tempio, vuoi per mancanza dello spazio necessario alla realizzazione di una scala o di una rampa verso di esso, considerato il notevole dislivello esistente, vuoi per l'inevitabile interferenza che si sarebbe determinate tra le parti riservate alla frequentazione degli occupanti la *domus* e quelle templari destinate al pubblico, vuoi in fine perché, sempre per mancanza di spazio, sarebbe venuto meno un elemento importante del complesso cultuale, il *temenos*'.

See also Iacopi and Tedone 2006.365: the ramp 'doveva mettere in comunicazione il terrazzo inferiore della casa coi livelli superiori, ma non con il tempio che, come vedremo, non era stato ancora progettata'. *Contra* Tomei 2014a.28, who remains faithful to Carettoni's hypothesis.

Inherently improbable: cf. Gros 2009.171 ('cette démarche un peu étrange'), Carandini 2016.47 ('accade qualcosa che definire bizzarro è poco e che ricorda l'arbitrio dei despoti').

Chimerical idea: Wiseman 2009b (on Carandini and Bruno 2008), 2012b.665–8 (on Carandini 2010.165–225); the criticisms are ignored by Pensabene 2017.2.50, who seems to know Wiseman 2009b only at second hand, and Wiseman 2012b not at all. Subsequently enshrined: Carandini and Carafa 2012, ill.9, tavole 64, 69 (unchanged in Carandini and Carafa 2017), Carandini 2016.46–8; see also Bruno in Carandini 2014.362–8, esp. 366 for an attempt to explain the absence of any evidence for the identification.

Cautious and scrupulous: Tomei 2014b.326–7.

Carandini 2008.148: 'Le realtà antiche ci vengono trasmesse generalmente . . . in modo parziale e discontinuo, ma proprio per questa ragione le ricostruzioni devono mirare a ritrovare la totalità perduta, evitando gli scetticismi degli ipercritici, che nulla vorrebbero ricostruire, per un voto di castità fatto al "Dato". Le integrazioni delle lacune non vanno mascherate, anzi, devono figurare, manifestando con espedienti grafici il giudizio di probabilità che l'editore ha loro attribuito. Non esiste un arte del "sapere" e una del "non sapere" —come ritengono empiristi e pusillanimi'.

29   Contemptuous of empirical method: e.g., Carandini 2000.29, 39–40, 98; discussion and further bibliography in Wiseman 2012b.669–70. Nobody's house ('la casa di nessuno'): Carandini 2010.187, cf. 176.

Literary sources: Carandini 2010.151 ('sono scarse e rivelano momenti scelti di una storia molto più articolata e sorprendente, che solo un'archeologia professionale è in grado di svelare').

Classicists: Carandini 2008.7 ('classicisti tradizionalisti, chiusi in un insopportabile scetticismo snobistico').

Free thinking: Carandini 2007, 2008.44, 107. See now Carandini 2017.165: 'Il patto dell'indagatore con l'evidenza è di reciproca donazione di valore, la quale implica un fare oltre l'accadere, nel quale il frammento del passato genera l'interpretazione e al tempo stesso ne è generato, completato e integrato. Dato e archeologo sono per un verso distinti e per l'altro un tutt'uno—questo non intende l'antichista più normale—, ché la ragione non soltanto distingue ma anche relaziona: quel capitello a quali altri elementi architettonici si congiungeva e per significare che cosa? A ciò si aggiunga l'elemento emozionale entusiasmante di veder risorgere un morto'.

3. THE PALACE

30   For 'the development of the Palatine as the Imperial Palace', see above all Claridge 2018.122–8.

Divus Iulius temple *in foro*: Frontinus *Aqueducts* 129.1, *Fasti Allifani* and *Amiternini* on 18 August (Degrassi 1963.180–1, 190–1); Appian *Civil Wars* 1.4.17, 2.148.616, Dio Cassius 47.18.4. Looking over Forum to Capitol: Ovid *Metamorphoses* 15.841–2.

Regia: Servius on *Aeneid* 8.363 (*in radicibus Palati finibusque Romani fori*); Dio Cassius 48.42.4–6 (rebuilt 36 BC).

31 Vesta temple: Livy 26.27.1–4 (*circa forum*); Dionysius of Halicarnassus *Roman Antiquities* 6.13.1-2, Ovid *Fasti* 6.401–4 (close to Forum); Orosius 4.11.9 (*in circuitu fori*). Associated with *regia*: e.g., Ovid *Fasti* 6.263-4, *Tristia* 3.1.29-30, Plutarch *Romulus* 18.7, Tacitus *Annals* 15.41.1.

3.1 Nero's Urban Landscape

Tacitus *Annals* 15.38.2–3:

initium in ea parte circi ortum quae Palatino Caelioque montibus contigua est, ubi per tabernas, quibus id mercimonium inerat quo flamma alitur, simul coeptus ignis et statim ualidus ac uento citus longitudinem circi corripuit. neque enim domus munimentis saeptae uel templa muris cincta aut quid aliud morae interiacebat. impetu peruagatum incendium plana primum, deinde in edita adsurgens et rursus inferiora populando, antiit remedia uelocitate mali et obnoxia urbe artis itineribus hucque et illuc flexis atque enormibus uicis, qualis uetus Roma fuit. 'The heights' here may refer to the Aventine, where we know the temple of Luna was destroyed (Tacitus *Annals* 15.41.1, cf. Livy 40.2.2).

Tacitus *Annals* 15.39.1:

eo in tempore Nero Antii agens non ante in urbem regressus est quam domui eius, qua Palatium et Maecenatis hortos continuauerat, ignis propinquaret. neque tamen sisti potuit quin et Palatium et domus et cuncta circum haurirentur.

Maecenas' gardens on the Esquiline: Donatus *Vita Vergilii* 6 (Virgil's house *Esquiliis iuxta hortos Maecenatianos*).{ditto}

Use of *continuare*: Cicero *De lege agraria* 3.14, Sallust *Bellum Catilinae* 20.11, Livy 34.4.9; cf. Cicero *De domo* 115 (*coniungere*).

32 Suetonius *Nero* 31.1:

domum a Palatio Esquilias usque fecit, quam primo transitoriam, mox incendio absumptam restitutamque auream nominauit.

Josephus *Jewish Antiquitites* 19.117:

. . . ὁδούς τε ἑτέρας χωροῦντες παρῆσαν εἰς τὴν Γερμανικοῦ μὲν οἰκίαν τοῦ Γαΐου πατρός ὃν τότε ἀνηρήκεσαν, συνημμένη δὲ ἐκείνῃ, διὰ τὸ ἕν τὸ βασίλειον ὃν ἐπ' οἰκοδομίαις ἑκάστου τῶν ἐν τῇ ἡγεμονίᾳ γεγονότων ἀσκηθὲν ἀπὸ μέρους ὀνόματι τῶν οἰκοδομησαμένων ἢ καί τι τῶν μερῶν οἰκήσεις ἀρξάντων τὴν ἐπωνυμίαν παρασχέσθαι.

For Josephus' use of *basileion* ('ruler's residence') interchangeably with *oikos* or *oikia* ('house'), see *Antiquitates* 19.75, 122, 126, 162, 195, 212.

Extravagant developers: Suetonius *Gaius* 22.2-4, 37.3–4 (cf. Josephus *Antiquitates* 19.207), *Nero* 31.1–2, 39.2 (cf. Martial *De spectaculis* 2.1–8). Eye-witness: Pliny *Natural History* 36.111 (*bis uidimus urbem totam cingi domibus principum Gai et Neronis*).

Palatine destroyed: Dio Cassius 62.18.2 (τὸ Παλάτιον τὸ ὄρος σύμπαν τὸ Παλάτιον τὸ ὄρος σύμπαν).

Nero's architects: Tacitus *Annals* 15.43.1 (*dimensis uicorum ordinibus et latis uiarum spatiis cohibitaque aedificiorum altitudine ac patefactis areis additisque porticibus quae frontem insularum protegerent*).

Narrow streets on Palatine: Josephus *Antiquitates* 19.116 (στενῶν οὐσων τῶν ὁδῶν), cf. 104 (κατὰ στενωπὸν), 212 (ἔν τινι στενωπῷ).

Roman senators: e.g., Velleius Paterculus 2.14.3 (Sisenna Statilius Taurus, consul AD 16); Asconius 27C, Pliny *Natural History* 17.5 (C. Caecina Largus, consul AD 42). For what happened to their properties, cf. Eck 1997.180: 'Only the disastrous fire of 64 and Nero's maniacal construction of the *domus aurea* caused the last senatorial families owning *domus* on the Palatine to "emigrate" into other *regiones*. They were probably encouraged to do so by liberal financial compensation for their property.'

On a grand scale: Claridge 2018.126–7 attributes it all to Domitian, but the design at least must be Nero's; it is inconceivable that the Palatine, of all places, was omitted from his reconstruction plans (Tacitus *Annals* 15.43.1–4).

Suetonius *Nero* 31.1:

de cuius spatio atque cultu suffecerit haec rettulisse: uestibulum eius fuit in quo colossus CXX pedum staret ipsius effigie.

On Sacra Via: Dio Cassius 65.15.1. Forum to Esquiline: Varro *De lingua Latina* 5.47 (Forum to *Carinae*), Dionysius of Halicarnassus *Roman Antiquities* 3.22.8 (*Carinae* near *uicus Cuprius*), Livy 1.48.6 (*uicus Cuprius* on Esquiline). Cf. Martial *De spectaculis* 2.1–2 for the site of the colossus—and therefore of the forecourt too—as *media uia*, meaning not 'in the middle of the street' but 'at the mid point of the [Sacra] Via'; detailed discussion in Coleman 2006.22–7.

Sacra Via realigned: Van Deman 1923 (esp. 403–11) and 1925. Dominating the view: Martial 1.70.5–8; cf. Dio Cassius 69.4.3 on the temple that replaced the forecourt (ἵν᾽ ἔς τε τὴν ἱερὰν ὁδὸν ἐκφανέστερος ἐξ ὑψηλοτέρου εἴη).

On the north side: despite the conventional belief (e.g., Richardson 1992.30, 339–40), there is *no* reason to associate the Arch of Titus with the Sacra Via, which led north-eastwards from the ridge to the *Carinae* on the Esquiline (Varro *De lingua Latina* 5.47) and must therefore have turned left at the Neronian platform.

34   Ornamental lake and gardens: Suetonius *Nero* 31.1, Tacitus *Annals* 15.42.1, Martial *De spectaculis* 2.5–10. Sacra Via from Forum to Palatine: e.g., Martial 1.70.3–6, Tacitus *Histories* 3.68.3, Dio Cassius 65.20.2–3, 77.4.3; cf. Plutarch *Publicola* 19.5, *Cicero* 16.3, 22.1, where the topography is evidently that of the author's time. Before Nero one had to turn off the Sacra Via to get to the Palatine (Ovid *Tristia* 3.1.32, Dionysius of Halicarnassus *Roman Antiquities* 2.50.3).

Rebuilt by Domitian: Martial 7.56, 8.36; Statius *Siluae* 1.1.32–5, 3.4.47–9, 4.1.6–10, 4.2.18–31; Plutarch *Publicola* 15.5. More secure: Suetonius *Domitian* 14.4. '*Domus Flavia*': e.g., Gros 2001.252–3, Zanker 2004.88, cf. Torelli 2014.57; rightly dismissed by Coarelli 2012.494.

Domus Augustana: AE 2007.252 (found *in situ*); CIL 6.2271, 6.8651, 15.7246; sometimes spelled *Augustiana* (CIL 6.8640, 6.8647–9, 6.33736, 15.1860) or abbreviated as *domus Aug.* (CIL 6.8641–5, 10.8650); full analysis in Panciera 2007.

Gros 2001.252: 'L'entité juridique et spatiale du palais, considéré dans sa function officielle et de représentation, ne peut être que la *domus August(i)ana*, puisque c'est sous ce nom qu'elle a traversé les siècles: quelle que soit la dynastie, elle restait le siège des *Augusti*.' Misreading: as already pointed out by Castagnoli 1964.186–7.

35   Common Latin idiom: e.g., Nepos *Atticus* 13.2 (*domus Tamphiliana*); Cicero *Ad Atticum* 1.6.1 (*domus Rabiriana*), 1.13.6 (*Autroniana domus*), 1.14.7 (*Paciliana domus*), 4.3.3 (*Anniana domus*), *Ad familiares* 7.20.1 (*Papiriana domus*), *Ad Q. fratrem* 2.3.7 (*domus †Luciniana†*); Ovid *Tristia* 1.1.70 (*Caesarea domus*); Suetonius *De grammaticis* 17.2 (*Catulina domus*), *Diuus Augustus* 72.1 (*aedes Hortensianae*), *Tiberius* 15.1 (*Pompeiana domus*).

Domus Tiberiana: Tacitus *Histories* 1.27.2–3, Suetonius *Vitellius* 15.3, Plutarch *Galba* 24.4, Aulus Gellius 13.20.1, Galen *De indolentia* 18, Dio Cassius 71.35.4, Historia Augusta *Antoninus Pius* 10.4, *Marcus Aurelius* 6.3, *Verus* 2.4, 6.4, *Probus* 2.1; CIL 6.8653–5.

Huge structure: 'le mastodontiche strutture in laterizi che definiscono una gigantesca piattaforma rettangolare' (Daniela Bruno in Carandini 2010.281); full details in Tomei and Filetici 2011. Sometimes attributed to Tiberius himself (e.g., Torelli 2014.56), but that cannot be right: Tiberius followed Augustus' precedent 'as if by a law', and was 'moderate in private building' (Tacitus *Annals* 4.37.3, 6.45.1).

Fourth rectangle: Villedieu 1997, 2007; Coarelli 2012.497–538. 'Court of Adonis', flower-garden: Philostratus *Vita Apollonii* 7.32.1. Apartments: Plutarch *Publicola* 15.5, with Coarelli 2012.523. Offices: Dio Cassius 72.24.1–3 (imperial record office), with Villedieu 2007.261–3, Coarelli 2012.533–8.

End of Nero: Suetonius *Nero* 31.2 (*quasi hominem tandem habitare coepisse*), 55 (*destinauerat et Romam Neropolim nuncupare*).

3.2 The Emperor and Rome

Vespasian's frugality: Tacitus *Annals* 3.55.4, Suetonius *Diuus Vespasianus* 12, Dio Cassius 66.10.3–11.1.
Amphitheatre and baths: CIL 6.40454, Martial *De spectaculis* 1; Suetonius *Diuus Vespasianus* 9.1, *Diuus Titus* 7.3, 8.2; Dio Cassius 66.25.1, Aurelius Victor *De Caesaribus* 9.7, 10.5.
Martial *De spectaculis* 2.5-8, 11–12:
hic ubi conspicui uenerabilis amphitheatri | erigitur moles, stagna Neronis erant; | hic ubi miramur uelocia munera thermas, | abstulerat miseris tecta superbus ager. . . . | reddita Roma sibi est et sunt te praeside, Caesar, | deliciae populi, quae fuerant domini.
    Detailed commentary in Coleman 2006, 14–36.

36   Colossal statue remodelled: Pliny *Natural History* 34.45; cf. Dio Cassius 65.15.1.

Hadrian: Historia Augusta *Hadrian* 19.12 (Decrianus and the elephants); Dio Cassius 69.4.3–5 (his own design); Jerome *Chronica* Ol. 227.3 (date). Venus and Rome temple: Boatwright 1987.119–33, Cassatella 1999. Coin issues: Mattingly and Sydenham 1926.370 nos. 263 and 265 (*Roma Aeterna*), 372 no. 280 (*Venus Felix*).

Two temples, Roma facing the Sacra Via: Prudentius *Contra Symmachum* 1.218–22; Galen *De methodo medendi* 10 (13.942 Kühn). Venus: *Homeric Hymn to Aphrodite* 58–69, 255–8 (Aeneas conceived and born on Mt Ida); Lucretius 1.1, Virgil *Aeneid* 8.648, Ovid *Fasti* 1.717, 4.161, *Metamorphoses* 15.682 (Romans as *Aeneadae*).

'Temple of the City': Aurelius Victor *De Caesaribus* 40.26, Historia Augusta *Hadrian* 19.12, Ammianus Marcellinus 16.10.14, Prudentius *Contra Symmachum* 1.221, Cassiodorus *Chronica* 142M.

Romulus the Founder: Mattingly and Sydenham 1926.371 no. 266, 382 no. 370, 383 no. 376, 425 no. 653 (*Romulo conditori*). Palatine as site of foundation: Ovid *Tristia* 3.1.31–2, Josephus *Antiquitates* 19.223.

Foundation date: Degrassi 1963.9, 66 (*Fasti Antiates* and *Caeretani*); Cicero *De diuinatione* 2.98; Dionysius of Halicarnassus *Roman Antiquities* 1.88.2–3; Ovid *Fasti* 4.807–8, *Metamorphoses* 14.774–5; Velleius Paterculus 1.8.4; Plutarch *Romulus* 12.1; Festus 248L. *Parilia* and Pales: Varro *De lingua Latina* 6.15, Ovid *Fasti* 4.721–4. Palatine named from Pales: Solinus 1.15.

Athenaeus *Deipnosophistae* 8.361e-f:

κατὰ πᾶσαν τὴν πόλιν αὐλῶν τε βόμβος καὶ κυμβάλων ἦχος ἔτι τε τυμπάνων κτύπος μετὰ ᾠδῆς γινόμενος. ἔτυχεν δὲ οὖσα ἑορτὴ τὰ Παρίλια μὲν πάλαι καλουμένη, νῦν δὲ Ῥωμαῖα, τῇ τῆς πόλεως Τύχῃ ναοῦ καθιδρυμένου ὑπὸ τοῦ πάντα ἀρίστου καὶ μουσικωτάτου βασιλέως Ἀδριανοῦ ἐκείνην τὴν ἡμέραν κατ' ἐνιαυτὸν ἐπίσημον ἄγουσι πάντες οἱ τὴν Ῥώμην κατοικοῦντες καὶ οἱ ἐνεπιδημοῦντες τῇ πόλει.

For the historical context, and Larensis in particular, see Braund 2000. 'Having a ball' (βαλλίζουσιν): Ulpianus prefers 'revelling' (κωμάζουσιν) or 'dancing' (χορεύουσιν).

37   Tyrant's hall: Martial *De spectaculis* 2.3 (*inuidiosa feri . . . atria regis*).

Dio Cassius 53.16.5–6 (trans. Millar 1977.20):

καλεῖται δὲ τὰ βασίλεια Παλάτιον, οὐχ ὅτι καὶ οὕτως αὐτὰ ὀνομάζεσθαι, ἀλλ' ὅτι ἔν τε τῷ Παλατίῳ ὁ Καῖσαρ ᾤκει καὶ ἐκεῖ τὸ στρατήγιον εἶχε . . . καὶ διὰ τοῦτο κἂν ἀλλοθί που ὁ αὐτοκράτωρ καταλύῃ, τὴν τοῦ παλατίου ἐπίκλησιν ἡ καταγωγὴ αὐτοῦ ἴσχει.

Origin of 'palace': Claudian *De sexto consulatu* 409 (*quae cunctis tribuere Palatia nomen*).

Extension of *domus Tiberiana* platform: Boatwright 1987.111–19, Krause 2004.58, Tomei and Filetici 2011.39–85.

Military headquarters (στρατήγιον translating *praetorium*): Dio Cassius 53.16.5; cf. Polybius 6.31.1–7, Josephus *Jewish War* 3.82. Cohort on duty: Tacitus *Annals* 1.7.5, 12.69.1, *Histories* 1.24.2, 1.29.2; Suetonius *Nero* 21.1, *Otho* 6.1; see in general Millar 1977.61–6.

Intimidating: Martial 9.79 (to Domitian), Pliny *Panegyricus* 47–9 (to Trajan), Ausonius *Gratiarum actio* 3 (to Gratian). 'Uneasy': Ausonius 11.5.23–4 OCT (*inquieto . . . Palatio*).

Domitian's *domus Augustana* (Gros 2001.252–60, Claridge 2010.145–52): Martial 8.36.7–10, Statius *Siluae* 4.2.18–20; Historia Augusta *Pertinax* 11.6 (*cenatio Iouis*). The emperor as Jupiter: a commonplace in Martial, from 4.8.12 to 9.24.3 (AD 88–94).

38   Honorius, Alaric, Ravenna: Jordanes *Getica* 146–54. Claudian and Rome: Cameron 1970.349–89, esp. 382–6 on *De sexto consulatu*.

Claudian *De sexto consulatu* pref.11–16, 21–6:

namque poli media stellantis in arce uidebar | ante pedes summi carmina ferre Iouis; | utque fauet somnus, plaudebant numina dictis | et circumfusi sacra corona chori. | [. . .] additur ecce fides, nec me mea lusit imago, | irrita nec falsum somnia misit ebur. | en princeps, en orbis apex aequatus Olympo! | en quales memini, turba uerenda, deos! | fingere nil maius potuit sopor, altaque uati | conuentum caelo praebuit aula parem.

Cf. Virgil *Aeneid* 3.578–82, 9.716 (Enceladus and Typhoeus); 6.893–6 (false gate of dreams).

Scene of delivery: Claudian *De sexto consulatu* 8 (*natiua Palatia*), 11 (*mons Euandrius*), 35 (*Palatino . . . monti*), 409 (*mea . . . Palatia*), 543 (*Palatino . . . colle*), 644 (*Pallanteus apex*).

39   Star of power: Claudian *De sexto consulatu* 22–3 (*haud aliter Latiae sublimis signifer aulae | imperii sidus propria cum sede locauit . . .*).

Claudian *De sexto consulatu* 35–44 (cf. 587–8 for the *rostra*):

ecce Palatino creuit reuerentia monti | exultatque habitante deo potioraque Delphis | supplicibus late populis oracula pandit | atque suas ad signa iubet reuiuescere laurus. | non alium certe decuit rectoribus orbis | esse larem, nulloque magis se colle potestas | aestimat et summi sentit fastigia iuris; | attollens apicem subiectis regia rostris | tot circum delubra uidet tantisque deorum | cingitur excubiis!

Goddess Roma: Claudian *De sexto consulatu* 358–9 (*penetralibus altis | prosiluit*), 420–1 (Hadrian and other emperors). Innocentius: *Liber pontificalis* 42.

3.3 Decay and Rediscovery

Procopius *Wars* 8.22.5–6:

καίτοι ἀνθρώπων μάλιστα πάντων ὧν ἡμεῖς ἴσμεν φιλοπόλιδες Ῥωμαῖοι τυγχάνουσιν ὄντες, περιστέλλειν τε τὰ πάτρια πάντα καὶ διασῴζεσθαι ἐν σπουδῇ ἔχουσιν, ὅπως δὴ μηδὲν ἀφανίζηται Ῥώμῃ τοῦ παλαιοῦ κόσμου. οἵ γε καὶ πολύν τινα βεβαρβαρωμένοι αἰῶνα τάς τε πόλεως διεσώσαντο οἰκοδομίας καὶ τῶν ἐγκαλλωπισμάτων τὰ πλεῖστα, ὅσα οἷόν τε ἦν χρόνῳ τε τοσούτῳ τὸ μῆκος καὶ τῷ ἀπαμελεῖσθαι δι' ἀρετὴν τῶν πεποιημένων ἀντέχειν.

Not all the great buildings could be preserved: see Santangeli Valenzani 2017.117–9 for the archaeological evidence.

40 Imperial headquarters: Procopius *Wars* 6.8.10 (Belisarius in 538), Agnellus *Liber pontificalis* 95 (Narses in 571), Martinus *Epistulae* 15 = *Patrologia Latina* 18.199–202 (Theodorus Calliopas in 651). Symbol of sovereignty: Llewellyn 1970.170.

Chapel and images: Gregorius Magnus *Epistulae* 13.1 MGH (Martyn 2004.886), 25 April 603; cf. *Liber pontificalis* 86 (AD 687).

Derelict: Augenti 1996.22–37, 2000.46–8. Heraclius' permission: *Liber pontificalis* 72; the same pope (Honorius) converted the Senate-house into the church of S. Adriano.

Otto III: Brühl 1954.15–29; Augenti 1996.74–5.

Master Gregory: Osborne 1987, esp. 14–15 for the likely date. Remains of the ancient city: Magister Gregorius *Narratio* 1 (*quae uel arte magica uel humano labore sunt condita*).

Magister Gregorius *Narratio* 17:

palatium autem diui Augusti non praetereo. haec quidem amplissima domus admodum excellebat, iuxta excellentiam conditoris Augusti. haec autem domus tota marmorea pretiosam materiam et copiosam aedificandis ecclesiis quae Romae sunt praebuit. de qua quoniam parum restat pauca dixisse sufficiat.

Aqueduct arches: ibid. 18 (*iuxta hoc palatium*).

Magister Gregorius *Narratio* 20:

palatium etiam LX imperatorum describere quis poterit? quod cum ex maiore parte lapsum sit, fertur tamen omnes Romanos huius temporis quod inde adhuc superest pro tota substantia sua posse dissoluere.

Romans of his own time: ibid. 4 on their absurd stories (*uanae fabulae*), 21 on their greed for gold (*inexplebilis cupiditas*). Use as a quarry: see for instance Lanciani 1901.180–252, Weiss 1969.98–101.

Petrarch: *Res familiares* 6.2.14 (*nusquam minus Roma cognoscitur quam Romae*), in a letter to Giovanni Colonna.

41 Part of the *disabitato*: subsequent research has modified Krautheimer's position (see Wickham 2015.112–20 for a nuanced account), but it remains valid for the Palatine.

Tunnels dug horizontally: Mocchegiani Carpano 1984.188–90.

Overgrown wilderness: see Werner 2004.144–9 for a good selection of sixteenth-century images.

Byron: *Childe Harold's Pilgrimage* 4.78.3 (mother of dead empires), 4.106.4 (fading light); note to 4.107 (scholarly ignorance); 4.109.9 (golden roofs).

42 Napoleon III and Roman history: Nicolet 1999. Rosa's excavations: Tomei 1999. Signage: Tomei 1999.505–14 and 535 tav. 9.

Boissier 1880.47 (trans. Boissier 1905.67): 'Cette colline, autrefois occupée par des villas de grands seigneurs et des jardins de monastères où l'on ne pénétrait pas, est devenue l'une des promenades les plus intéressantes de Rome. Je ne crois pas qu'il y ait un lieu où les souvenirs du passé se present plus à la mémoire et où l'on vive davantage en plein antiquité. Il faut pourtant reconnaître que cette antiquité ne nous a été rendue qu'en fort mauvais état; les gens qui se laissent tromper par l'écriteau qu'on a mis au dessus

de l'entrance des jardins Farnèse, et qui croient qu'on a vraiment retrouvé "le palais des Césars", risquent d'être fort surpris en voyant ce qui en reste; on n'en a plus que quelques décombres, et, pour le revoir tel qu'il était, il faut faire un grand effort d'imagination.'
Sacra Via: Lanciani 1897.190 ('queen of streets'), 208–9; Buranelli 1989. Controversy: Lanciani 1988.296 ('narrow, crooked lane'), 298–303; Ashby 1900.239–40.

45 Villa Mills: Bartoli 1929.3–8; cf. Morton 1957.417–20 on Charles Mills. Supposed site of Augustus' house: Tomei 1999.97 (letter of Rosa, 5 September 1864), 528–9 and 533 (Rosa's site plans of 1865, 1868 and 1870); Lanciani 1893.71, 1897.139–45 and figs. 40–1; cf. also Marucchi 1906.303–9, Bartoli 1929.26–7.

47 The very beginning of Rome: for the physical site of the city, Claridge 2018.94–100 is fundamental.

4. PALATINE PREHISTORY

48 Flood-plain and crossing place: Le Gall 1953.36–43. Bronze Age pottery: Fulminante 2014.67–71, cf. Hopkins 2016.20–1.

4.1 Geomorphology

49 Two separate summits: e.g., Platner and Ashby 1929.375, based on the erroneous belief that the toponym *Cermalus* referred to a summit of the hill; in fact, it was the slope at the foot of the hill closest to the river (Varro *De lingua Latina* 5.54, Plutarch *Romulus* 3.5); see Castagnoli 1964.173–7 and Castagnoli 1977. Recent landscape: Ammerman 1996.132 n. 77, 2009.160 n. 28.

50 'Elevated shoulder areas': Ammerman 1990.634–5, 1999.102, 2009.154 and 161, 2016.306–7; Virgili 1999.169, Hopkins 2016.34. Vicus Iugarius: Festus 370–2L. Vicus Tuscus: Dionysius of Halicarnassus *Roman Antiquities* 5.36.4, Livy 27.37.14–15, Porphyrio on Horace *Satires* 2.3.228, Plutarch *Romulus* 5.5. Ammerman 1992.103: '. . . le pendici del Campidoglio e del Palatino, i quali alla sommità arrivano ad altezze dell'ordine di m 40 s.l.m. Questi versanti, che nei tempi successivi sono stati regolarizzati e in alcuni punti fortemente modificati, originariamente dovevano essere piuttosto ripidi, irregolari e disseminati di rocce cadute lungo il pendio.'

51 *Cappellaccio*: Ammerman 1992.110, 1995.87, 1996.130.
Ammerman 1992.110: 'Il tufo litoide in sito deve essere stato utilizzato in un'epoca arcaica per tagliare blocchi per la costruzione di muri e pavimenti; il suo sfruttamento deve aver portato complessivamente ad una profonda modificazione del pendio stesso. In origine infatti l'andamento di questa unità doveva essere molto più irregolare e vi dovevano essere massi distaccati da questi e dagli strati tufacei superiori, così da creare una fascia alla base del pendio di aspetto decisamente caottico. Si può supporre che fra i primi interventi umani nell'area si sia cercato di sfruttare questi massi caduti e di regolarizzare la zona.'
Deep excavations: Arvanitis 2010.31, 32, 39 (fig. 15), 47–8.
Gully (*fossato*): Ammerman 1990.636, 644; 1992.110 (natural boundary); 2009.154–6.
Atrium Vestae (Ovid *Fasti* 6.263, Pliny *Letters* 7.19.2, Aulus Gellius 1.12.9): Lanciani 1883 and 1897.228–34; Middleton 1885.188–206 = 1892.307–29. Heights above sea level: Lanciani 1883.469 (ground floor); Tomei and Filetici 2011.72–3 (street), 75 (cross-section).
Cappellaccio outcrop: Ammerman 2009.159–60 (core nos. 61–3); Filippi 2004.103–4 (excavation).

52 Similar phenomenon: Ammerman 1996.123, 129, 131–2 (heights), 134–6; 2009.160; 2010.220 (noting that each site was also close to a natural spring). Comitium: Carafa 1998.91–2 ('una sorta di monumentale gradinata di tufo'), 93 fig. 73.

53 Exploited as a significant site: Filippi 2004, Carandini 2011.67–75, Carandini and Carafa 2012 tavv. 2–6 = 2017.tabs. 2–6, 277–8, Fulminante 2014.90–2. Formal public purpose: the site later became the house of the *rex sacrorum* (Dio Cassius 54.27.3, Festus 372L, Servius *auctus* on Virgil *Aeneid* 8.363).
Carcer: Livy 1.33.8, Valerius Maximus 6.9.13 (on the slope above the Forum). *Lautumiae*: Varro *De lingua Latina* 5.151, Livy 32.26.17, 37.3.8 (cf. 37.46.5). *Scalae Gemoniae*: Valerius Maximus 6.3.3a, Suetonius *Tiberius* 61.4, Pliny *Natural History* 8.145, Dio Cassius 58.1.3, 58.5.6, 60.16.1. See Coarelli 1985.59–87 for details of the *carcer–lautumiae–scalae Gemoniae* nexus.

At 20m contour: Carafa 1998.94 fig. 74, 115 fig. 79; cf. Ammerman 1996.131–2 for the *in situ* level of *cappellaccio* at the temple of Concordia, which was close to the *carcer* (Dio Cassius 58.11.4–5).

Direct stepped route: Dio Cassius 58.5.6.

River level not known: in the first or second century BC (Bauer 1993.289 for the date), the outflow of the *cloaca maxima*, the culverted form of the stream down the valley between the Capitol and Palatine, was at 4.7m above the present sea level (Ammerman 1990.638 n. 66), implying a normal river level below that. But how much had it risen in the previous 1300 years?

4.2 Learned Guesswork

Augustus and Roman history: Augustus *Res gestae* 8.5, 13; Suetonius *Diuus Augustus* 31.4–5, 43.2. Varro's *Antiquitates*: the surviving fragments are collected in Mirsch 1882.

54   Cicero *Academica* 1.9, as quoted by Augustine *City of God* 6.2.3 (Walsh 2010.23):

nos in nostra urbe peregrinantes errantesque tamquam hospites tui libri quasi domum reduxerunt, ut possemus aliquando qui et ubi essemus agnoscere. tu aetatem patriae, tu descriptiones temporum, tu sacrorum iura, tu sacerdotum, tu domesticam, tu publicam disciplinam, tu sedem regionum locorum, tu omnium diuinarum humanarumque rerum nomina genera officia causas aperuisti.

Four categories: Augustine *City of God* 6.31 (*qui agant, ubi agant, quando agant, quod agant*); Varro *De lingua Latina* 5.11–12.

55   Varro *De lingua Latina* 5.41, 6.24:

ubi nunc est Roma, Septimontium nominatum ab tot montibus quos postea urbs muris comprehendit.

dies Septimontium nominatus ab his septem montibus in quis sita urbs est; feriae non populi sed montanorum modo.

Hills called *montes*: Varro *De lingua Latina* 5.41 (*Capitolinus*), 43 (*Auentinus*), 46 (*Caelius*), 50 (*Oppius, Cispius*); cf. 5.51–2 for the *colles*. The Palatine was normally called just *Palatium*, but *mons Palatinus* at Tacitus *Annals* 12.24.1 evidently comes from an official source (the *publica acta* of Claudius' censorship, AD 48).

Already controversial: Antistius Labeo in Festus 476L (cf. also 458–9L), Servius on Virgil *Aeneid* 6.783 (*grandis dubitatio*); details in Fraschetti 1996.

'Proto-urban Rome': good up-to-date synthesis in Fulminante 2014.72–9 (cf. also Hopkins 2016.24–7).

Foundation story 'proved true': Carandini 1997, 2006a, 2006b, 2011, etc; cf. Grandazzi 1997.149–52, cf. 165 ('The foundation of Rome is now archaeologically perceptible'); for criticism of Carandini's methodology, see Poucet 2000.22–3 and 165–8, Wiseman 2004–6, Testa 2012, Ampolo 2013.

More ancient memory: e.g., Carandini 1997.385 ('risalire alla memoria più antica che avesse lasciato tracce sufficienti e concrete di sé'), cf. 270 ('in base ad una antica tradizione').

Historians unaware: e.g., Carandini 2006b.100 ('notizie . . . scartate dagli annalisti'), cf. 131 ('una Roma nata da nulla—come pretendono gli annalisti, ma non le fonti antiquarie che trasmettono il ricordo del *Septimontium*').

Roman cultural memory: e.g., Carandini 2006b.100 ('nella ricca riserva della memoria culturale dei Romani'), cf. 2006a.xlvii ('il mare fluttuante del patrimonio culturale collettivo').

Pre-urban organisation: e.g., Carandini 2006b.100 ('una organizzazione ch'essi ritenevano anteriore alla città—il *Septimontium*'), cf. 2006a.xliii ('antiquari romani come Varrone conoscevano un'organizzazione che avrebbe addirittura preceduto Roma, chiamata *Septimontium*').

56   Some archaeologists: e.g., Fulminante 2014.75–7, who is unduly impressed by Carandini's 'critical reading of literary accounts' (2014.72, cf. 75, 79, 342 n.2).

Festival at Alban Mount: Pliny *Natural History* 3.69, with Grandazzi 2008.676–727 (esp. 699–700 and 705–7 on *Querquetulani* and *Velienses*) and Wiseman 2010.435–6.

Varro *De lingua Latina* 5.5:

uetustas pauca non deprauat, multa tollit . . . illa quae iam maioribus nostris ademit obliuio, fugitiua secuta sedulitas Muci et Bruti retrahere nequit.

For P. Mucius Scaevola and M. Iunius Brutus, see Pomponius in *Digest* 1.2.2.39.

Knowledge and opinion: Varro *De lingua Latina* 5.8 (*si non perueniam ad scientiam, at opinionem aucupabor*).

Varro *De lingua Latina* 5.42:

hunc antea montem Saturnium appellatum prodiderunt et ab eo Latium Saturniam terram, ut etiam En-
nius appellat. antiquum oppidum in hoc fuisse Saturniam scribitur. eius uestigia etiam nunc manent tria,
quod Saturni fanum in faucibus, quod Saturnia porta quam Iunius scribit ibi, quam nunc uocant Panda-
nam, quod post aedem Saturni in aedificiorum legibus priuatis parietes postici muri <Saturnii> sunt scripti.

For *oppidum* as 'fortified settlement', see Varro *De lingua Latina* 5.141 (*quod munitur opis causa*),
Servius *auctus* on Virgil *Aeneid* 9.605 (*locum muro fossaue aliaue qua munitione conclusum*); for the *porta*
Pandana, which had always to be kept open, see Festus (Paulus) 246L, Polyaenus 8.25.1; for the conjec-
tural added word in the final phrase, see ten Brink 1855.8.

Saturn story: Virgil *Aeneid* 8.314–25 and 355–8, Ovid *Fasti* 1.233–40, Augustine *City of God* 7.4.2. Rejected by Varro: cf. *Antiquitates diuinae* fr. 241 Cardauns (Augustine *City of God* 7.18.2) for his preferred
allegorical explanation. Note that two authors whose prehistories of Rome were probably based on Varro
(Dionysius of Halicarnassus *Roman Antiquities* 1.34.1 and 2.1.4, Solinus 1.12) both refer to the Capitol as
mons Saturnius without telling the story that accounted for the name.

'Tales unworthy of the gods' (Wiseman 1998.17–24): Varro *Antiquitates diuinae* fr. 7 Cardauns (Augustine *City of God* 4.27.1–3, 6.5.2 and 5, 6.10.6, Tertullian *Ad nationes* 2.1.9 and 13).

57 Varro *De lingua Latina* 6.34:

ego magis arbitror Februarium a die februato, quod tum februatur populus, id est Lupercis nudis lustratur
antiquum oppidum Palatinum gregibus humanis cinctum.

For the meaning of *lustratur* (not implying a circuit), see Ziółkowski 2016.33–4 and 37–9; for the
Luperci and the *dies februatus*, see Varro *De lingua Latina* 6.13, Ovid *Fasti* 2.31–2, Plutarch *Moralia* 280b
and *Romulus* 21.3, Censorinus *De die natali* 24.14–15, Festus (Paulus) 75L.

Varro *De lingua Latina* 5.164:

praeterea intra muros uideo portas dici in Palatio Mucionis a mugitu, quod ea pecus in buceta tum <ante>
antiquum oppidum exigebant; alteram Romanulam ab Roma dictam, quae habet gradus in †noualia† ad
Volupiae sacellum.

For the spelling *Mugionis*, see Varro *De uita populi Romani* fr. 22 Pittà (Nonius 852L); *noualia* was
emended to *noua uia* by Joseph Scaliger in 1565.

Varro *De lingua Latina* 6.24:

hoc sacrificium fit in Velabro, qua in nouam uiam exitur, ut aiunt quidam ad sepulcrum Accae, ut quod ibi
prope faciunt diis manibus seruilibus sacerdotes; qui uterque locus extra urbem antiquam fuit non longe a
porta Romanula, de qua in priore libro dixi.

Velabrum not outside the city: Macrobius *Saturnalia* 1.10.15 (*locus celeberrimus urbis*).

Didn't see a wall: on the north side of the Palatine, at least, the Palatine walls of the eighth and seventh
centuries BC were destroyed in the sixth century (Carandini and Carafa 1995).

58 Gates of Roman London: for the essentials, see Marsden 1980.118 and 123–5, Barker and Jackson 1990.70.
Myth-historical accounts: e.g., Solinus 1.1, Servius on Virgil *Aeneid* 8.51 (attributed to Aborigines or
iuuentus Latina before the arrival of Evender's Arcadians); Solinus 1.14 (attributed to Evander); Tacitus
Annals 12.24.1 (attributed to Romulus?).

Famous story: Livy 1.12.3–7 (*ad ueterem portam Palati*), Dionysius of Halicarnassus *Roman Antiquities*
2.50.3 (ταῖς καλουμέναις Μουγωνίσι πύλαις), Plutarch *Romulus* 18.6–7.

Temple by the gate: Ovid *Tristia* 3.1.31–2, cf. *Fasti* 6.793–4 (in front of the 'ridge' of the Palatine); Livy
1.41.4 and Solinus 1.24 (near the house of Tarquinius Priscus, who lived *ad Mugoniam portam*).

Jupiter Stator temple: Livy 10.36.11, 10.37.14–16 (vowed in 294 BC); Tacitus *Annals* 15.41.1 (destroyed
in fire); Plutarch *Cicero* 16.3 (Senate meeting); Appian *Civil Wars* 2.11.38–40 (close to Forum), ps.Cicero
Priusquam in exsilium iret 24 (*in Palati radice*), Dionysius of Halicarnassus *Roman Antiquities* 2.43.4
(elevated position), Cicero *In Catilinam* 1.1 (*munitissimus locus*), Ovid *Tristia* 3.1.28–32 (right turn). For
the full argument, see Wiseman 2017.

4.3 Reconstructing the Topography

Tiber as *rumon*: Servius on Virgil *Aeneid* 8.90 and 8.343. Possible meaning of *porta Romanula*: Richter
1901.34–5.

Varro seems to say: *De lingua Latina* 5.164 (*quae habet gradus in †noualia†*), where Scaliger's emendation *in noua uia* would mean 'steps *on* the Nova Via'; but since 'on to' makes better sense, *in nouam uiam* may be a preferable reading.

He certainly says: *De lingua Latina* 6.24 (*in Velabro qua in nouam uiam exitur . . . non longe a porta Romanula*).

59   Velabrum: Tibullus 2.5.33 (open space); Plautus *Curculio* 483, *Captiui* 489, Horace *Satires* 2.3.229 (market); Livy 27.37.15, Dionysius of Halicarnassus *Roman Antiquities* 5.36.4, Suetonius *Nero* 25.2, Plutarch *Romulus* 5, Porphyrio on Horace *Satires* 2.3.228 (Vicus Tuscus and Circus Maximus).

Varro *De lingua Latina* 5.43–4:

ego maxime puto, quod ab aduectu: nam olim paludibus mons erat ab reliquis disclusus, itaque eo ex urbe aduehebantur ratibus, cuius uestigia, quod ea tum < . . . > dicitur Velabrum, et unde escendebant ad <in>fimam nouam uiam locus sacellum <ve>labrum. Velabrum a uehendo. uelaturam facere etiam nunc dicuntur qui id mercede faciunt. merces (dicitur a merendo et aere) huic uecturae qui ratibus transibant quadrans. ab eo Lucilius scripsit 'quadrantis ratiti'.

   (For clarity, I have omitted from the translation in the text Varro's parenthetical etymology of *merces*, 'fare', from *merere*, 'to earn', and *aes*, 'copper coin'.) Referring back to this passage at *De lingua Latina* 5.156, Varro imagined the ferries as rowing-boats (*lintres*), not rafts.

Nodal point: Plutarch *Romulus* 5.5 (routes north and south), Varro *De lingua Latina* 5.43 (down to river), 6.24 (exit on to Nova Via, close to the *porta Romanula*), 5.164 (steps); the church of S. Giorgio in Velabro is roughly on the 10m contour.

Steps up the hill to the gate: cf. Pensabene 2017.1.95 and 98–100 for a possible gate at the top of the hill at this point (just south-west of the temple of Magna Mater).

Route of the Nova Via: for the controversy, see Coarelli 1983.227–55, Ziółkowski 2004.31–4 and 41–6, Wiseman 2004b, Coarelli 2012.35–64. 'Branched off': Platner and Ashby 1929.361; cf. Coarelli 2013.41 (Sacra Via and Nova Via originating 'dallo stesso punto', at the *porta Mugonia*). Evidence illusory: Ziółkowski 2015.573–4 on Pliny *Natural History* 34.28–9.

60   Toponyms: Varro *De lingua Latina* 5.43 (*escendebant ad infimam nouam uiam*); Solinus 1.24 (Tarquinius Priscus lived *ad Mugoniam portam supra summam nouam uiam*), cf. Livy 1.41.4 (Tarquinius' house *ad Iouis Statoris*, with windows opening *in nouam uiam*). Solinus and Varro: Wiseman 2015a.95–100.

An absurdity: *pace* Carandini, and the contributors to Carandini and Carafa 2012, on whose assumptions see Wiseman 2013b.237–9. Oral tradition: Henige 2009, esp. 201, 232.

61   Surrounded by marshes: Varro *De lingua Latina* 5.43 and 156, Solinus 1.1; the idea was taken up by the poets of the Augustan age (Tibullus 2.5.33–4), Propertius 4.9.5–6, Ovid *Fasti* 6.401–8). But see Ammerman 1998 and 1999 for the geological reality.

62   Varro on Romulus (Wiseman 2015a): Solinus 1.32, Arnobius 3.8 = Varro *De gente populi Romani* fr. 20 Fraccaro (foundation date); Varro *De lingua Latina* 5.41, 6.24 (*Septimontium*); Varro *De lingua Latina* 5.152, Servius on Virgil *Aeneid* 7.657 = Varro *De gente populi Romani* fr. 35 Fraccaro (Aventine); Varro *De lingua Latina* 5.46, cf. Dionysius of Halicarnassus *Roman Antiquities* 2.36.2 (Caelian); control of the Capitol is presupposed by Varro's assertion that Romulus was buried at the *rostra*, i.e., on the Comitium (Porphyrio and ps.Acro on Horace *Epodes* 16.13).

Major public works project: Ammerman 1990.641–2, 644–5; the consequences are worked out in detail in Hopkins 2016.27–34. For still unanswered questions, including precise dating, see Ammerman 2016.308–10.

63   Circuit wall: Gabriele Cifani in Carandini and Carafa 2012.81–4 = 2017.81–4 (his sixth-century date depends wholly on literary sources that were in no position to have accurate information); for doubts, see Bernard 2012.

Greek speakers in Latium: see for instance Ridgway 1996 (Gabii, ninth century BC), Solin 1983 (Rome, seventh century BC). Art and architecture: see for instance Winter 2009, Hopkins 2016.

Roma as ῥώμη: Plutarch *Romulus* 1.1, Festus 326L ('Cephalon of Gergis' *FGrH* 45 F10). Some authors supposed it was translated from an earlier Latin *Valentia*: Solinus 1.1, Festus 328L (Hyperochus of Cumae *FGrH* 576 F3), Servius on Virgil *Aeneid* 1.273 (Ateius Praetextatus fr. 14 Funaioli).

Route of the Sacra Via: Varro *De lingua Latina* 5.47, Festus 372L.

Dionysius of Halicarnassus *Roman Antiquities* 2.50.3:

Ῥωμύλος μὲν Ὀρθωσίῳ Διὶ ταῖς καλουμέναις Μουγωνίσι πύλαις, αἳ φέρουσιν εἰς τὸ Παλάτιον ἐκ τῆς ἱερᾶς ὁδοῦ.

64   Ovid *Tristia* 3.1.28–32:

'haec est a sacris quae uia nomen habet, | hic locus est Vestae, qui Pallada seruat et ignem, | haec fuit antiqui regia parua Numae.' | inde petens dextram 'porta est' ait 'ista Palati, | hic Stator . . .'.

5. PALATINE LEGENDS

65   Romulus had lived there: Dio Cassius 53.16.5. Thought about using name: Dio Cassius 53.16.7–8, cf. Suetonius *Diuus Augustus* 7.2, Florus 2.34.66, Lydus *De mensibus* 4.111.

Romulus grandson of Aeneas: Servius *auctus* on Virgil *Aeneid* 1.273. Half-sister: Ennius *Annales* 36 Sk (Ilia's speech), implying Ilia was not the daughter of Eurydice (i.e., Creusa, Pausanias 10.26.1). Iulus: Cato *FRHist* 5 F6 (Servius on Virgil *Aeneid* 1.267), Livy 1.3.1–2.

Allusion to legend: Suetonius *Diuus Augustus* 7.2, citing Ennius *Annales* 155 Sk (*augusto augurio postquam incluta condita Roma est*). Two augury occasions: Ennius *Annales* 72–8 Sk (Aventine); Dionysius of Halicarnassus *Roman Antiquities* 2.4–6 (Palatine); Solinus 1.16 (*augurio*), 1.18 (*auspicato*); Wiseman 2015a.101–12.

Augustus and augury: Koortbojian 2006.207–10, Hofter 1988.311 (ring with *lituus*); Suetonius *Diuus Augustus* 95, Obsequens 69, Appian *Civil Wars* 3.94.388, Dio Cassius 46.46.2 (same augural sign as for Romulus, 43 BC).

Recent books: e.g., Grandazzi 1997 (1991), Fraschetti 2005 (2002), Carandini 2011 (2007); cf. Coarelli 2012.127–89 ('la città di Romolo'), Carandini and Carafa 2012.79–80 (Daniela Bruno on 'le mura di Romolo'), Fulminante 2014.96 ('Romulean buildings'), 112 fig. 32 ('pre-Romulean' and 'post-Romulean' phases'), 340 n. 115 ('monuments reviving memories of Romulus'), Pensabene 2017.1.7, 404 ('le mura di Romolo').

Other origin legends: e.g., Dionysius of Halicarnassus *Roman Antiquities* 1.72–3, Plutarch *Romulus* 1–2, Festus 326–9L, Servius *auctus* on Virgil *Aeneid* 1.273; sources collected and translated in Wiseman 1995.160–8. The oxymoronic concept of 'authentic myth' (Carandini 2006a.xx, xxviii, xlvii, etc.) appears already in Alföldi 1965.278 (cf. 115, 188, 239 for 'genuine legend').

5.1 Pallantion

Part of the Greek world: see in general Ridgway 1992.121–44, Wiseman 2004a.13–36, Coarelli 2011.29–42. *Kleiklos/Ktektos*: SEG 31.875; Solin 1983. Minotaur and panthers (from the Regia, third phase): Cristofani 1990.61, Holloway 1994.60–4, Winter 2009.144–8, Coarelli 2011.61–4; cf. Hopkins 2016.43–6 for the significance of the iconography.

66   Cult site of Vulcan (*Volcanal*): Coarelli 1983.172–3, Cristofani 1990.56.

Circe's island: Theophrastus *Historia plantarum* 5.8.3; cf. Hesiod fr. 150.25–6 M-W (scholiast on Apollonius Rhodius 3.311; Strabo 1.2.14, 232). Hesiod, *Telegony* etc: details in Wiseman 1995.45–50; for the *Telegony*, see West 2013.288–315.

Peoples of Latium: Hesiod *Theogony* 1011–17 (Circe's son Latinus as 'ruler of the famed Etruscans'); Dionysius of Halicarnassus *Roman Antiquities* 1.72.5 = Xenagoras *FGrH* 240 F29 (Circe's sons as eponyms of Rome, Ardea and Antium); Servius *auctus* on Virgil *Aeneid* 1.273 = anon. *FGrH* 819 F1 (Circe's daughter as eponym of Rome); Plutarch *Romulus* 2.1 = anon. *FGrH* 840 F40.e.2 (Circe's son as eponym and founder of Rome); Horace *Epodes* 1.29–30, *Odes* 3.29.8, Propertius 2.32.4, Festus 116L (Circe's son Telegonus as founder of Tusculum); Solinus 2.9 = Zenodotus *FGrH* 821 F1 (Circe's grandson as eponym and founder of Praeneste); Livy 1.49.9, Dionysius of Halicarnassus *Roman Antiquities* 4.45.2 (Mamilius of Tusculum descended from Circe and Odysseus).

Circus from Circe: Tertullian *De spectaculis* 8.2, Lydus *De mensibus* 1.12. The Circus Maximus was attributed to the Tarquins (Livy 1.35.8, 1.56.2, Dionysius of Halicarnassus *Roman Antiquities* 3.68.1,

4.44.1), who were descended from the Corinthian aristocrat Demaratus (Polybius 6.2.10. Cicero *De republica* 2.34, *Tusculan Disputations* 5.109, Livy 1.34.2, Dionysius of Halicarnassus *Roman Antiquities* 3.46.3–5, Strabo 5.2.2 C219–20). The god honoured at the earliest *ludi circenses* was the same as at the Isthmian Games in Corinth: Poseidon Hippios, Latinised as Neptunus Equester (Livy 1.9.6, Dionysius of Halicarnassus *Roman Antiquities* 1.33.2, 2.31.3, Plutarch *Romulus* 14.3); see Zevi 1995 for full discussion.

67   Stesichorus of Himera: Curtis 2011.1–9, Davies and Finglass 2014.1–23; for his 'Homeric', manner see especially Quintilian 10.1.62, 'Longinus' 13.3, Dio Chrysostom 55.7, *Anthologia Palatina* 7.75 and 9.184.3. I think Curtis (2011.23–37) and Davies and Finglass (2014.23–32) are wrong to insist that Stesichorus composed for choral singing; see West 2015, who more convincingly argues that he sang himself.

Prosperous enough: as shown by its ambitious architecture (Hopkins 2016.39–125) and the high-quality terracotta decoration of the buildings (Winter 2009.143–395).

Stesichorus on Hercules in Italy: details and discussion in Leigh 2000. Flattering connections: e.g., Hercules dedicated the *ara maxima* at Rome (Livy 9.34.18, Ovid *Fasti* 1.579–82, Festus 270L, Solinus 1.10) and the altar of Iuppiter Praestes at Tibur (*CIL* 14.3555), made the plain of Cumae cultivable (Diodorus Siculus 4.22.6), and founded the cities of Naples (Tzetzes on Lycophron 717), Herculaneum (Dionysius of Halicarnassus *Roman Antiquities* 1.44.1) and Pompeii (Servius on Virgil *Aeneid* 8.662).

The story he told: Stesichorus' treatment of Hercules and Evander is inferred from Pausanias 8.3.2 and Suda Σ 1095 = 4.433 Adler, as explained by Usener 1912.330 and Davies and Finglass 2014.290. Knowledge of it in Rome by c. 530 BC is implied by the *akroterion* statue-group of Athene and Hercules at the S. Omobono temple (Cristofani 1990.115–20, Holloway 1994.68–80, Wiseman 2004a.26–32, Winter 2009.316–8, and 377–80); Hercules is portrayed as wearing the lionskin, an innovation certainly followed by Stesichorus, if not invented by him (Athenaeus 12.512f–513a, with Davies and Finglass 2014.368–70). Rich grass: Livy 1.7.4, Dionysius of Halicarnassus *Roman Antiquities* 1.39.2, 2.2.1, *Origo gentis Romanae* 7.1. Small settlement: Diodorus Siculus 4.21.1 (μικρὰν πόλιν), Virgil *Aeneid* 8.554 (*paruam urbem*), Dionysius of Halicarnassus *Roman Antiquities* 1.31.3 (κώμην βραχεῖαν), Servius on Virgil *Aeneid* 8.51 (*modicum oppidum*). Fortified: Virgil *Aeneid* 8.98 (walls and citadel), 8.313 (citadel), 8.583 and 592 (gates and walls).

68   Pallantion political strife: Dionysius of Halicarnassus *Roman Antiquities* 1.31.2, cf. Virgil *Aeneid* 8.333, Ovid *Fasti* 1.471–84; for other accounts of why Evander left, see Pausanias 8.43.2 (leader of colonial expedition), Servius on Virgil *Aeneid* 8.333 (banished for murder). Two ships: Dionysius of Halicarnassus *Roman Antiquities* 1.31.3.

Themis: Dionysius of Halicarnassus *Roman Antiquities* 1.31.1, cf. Strabo 5.3.3 C230, Pausanias 8.43.2 (prophetic nymph, daughter of the river-god Ladon); other sources call her Nikostrate, and her Roman name was Carmenta or Carmentis (*Origo gentis Romanae* 5.2). Sibyl: Eratosthenes, quoted in scholiast to Plato *Phaedrus* 244b, Clement of Alexandria *Stromateis* 1.108.3 (Wiseman 2008.55–6). Prophetess: Virgil *Aeneid* 8.335–41; Ovid *Fasti* 1.473–538, 5.96, 6.531–48.

Pallantion becomes *Palatium*: Livy 1.5.1, Dionysius of Halicarnassus *Roman Antiquities* 1.31.4, Justin 43.1.6, Pausanias 8.43.2. Local dialect: i.e., Latin as the version of Aeolic Greek supposedly introduced by Evander (Cato *FRHist* 5 F3 = Lydus *De magistratibus* 1.5; Dionysius of Halicarnassus *Roman Antiquities* 1.90.1, 4.26.5; Hyginus *Fabulae* 277, Marius Victorinus in *Grammatici Latini* 6.23 Keil); see Gabba 1963 = 2000.159–64.

Earliest of the foundation stories: for Evander as a founder of Rome, see Virgil *Aeneid* 8.313 (*Romanae conditor arcis*), Strabo 5.3.3 C230 (Acilius *FRHist* 7 F7), Servius on *Aeneid* 7.678; cf. Festus 328L and Solinus 1.1 for Evander first *naming* Rome.

Themis' prophecy: implied in Dionysius of Halicarnassus *Roman Antiquities* 1.31.3; cf. Ovid *Fasti* 1.499–538 (Carmentis), Tibullus 2.5.15–66 (Sibyl).

69   Ancient cult sites: Dionysius of Halicarnassus *Roman Antiquities* 1.32.3 (Pan Lykaios, at the Lupercal 'as instructed by Themis'), 1.32.5 (Nike, on the crest of the Palatine), 1.33.2 (Poseidon Hippios and the games); Ovid *Fasti* 5.85–104 (Hermes and Pan); Strabo 5.3.3 C230, Tacitus *Annals* 15.41.1 (Hercules, at the *ara maxima*); see also Eratosthenes, as quoted by the scholiast on Plato *Phaedrus* 244b and Clement of Alexandria *Stromateis* 1.108.3, on Pan at the *Karmalon* (i.e., Cermalus, Wiseman 1995.77–8).

The altar of Poseidon Hippios, also identified as that of Consus, was close to 'the base of the Palatine hill' (Tacitus *Annals* 12.24.1), 'at the first turning-post of the Circus Maximus' (Tertullian *De spectaculis* 5.7); the temple of Demeter (Latin Ceres) was 'at the end of the Circus Maximus, just above the starting-gates' (Dionysius of Halicarnassus *Roman Antiquities* 6.94.3); the temple of Hermes (Latin Mercurius) 'looked out on the Circus' not far from the Porta Capena (Ovid *Fasti* 5.669, 673), 'behind the Murcian turning-posts' (Apuleius *Metamorphoses* 6.8).

Like other poets: e.g., *Homeric Hymns* 3.166–76 (Delos, for Apollo), *Oxyrhynchus Papyri* 2735.1.15–41 (Sparta, for the Dioscuri); the latter poet, plausibly identified as Stesichorus himself (West 2015.70–4), refers at line 41 to Themis.

70   Nike (Hesiod *Theogony* 383–4) as an Arcadian goddess: she was the daughter of Styx, a river in Arcadia (Pausanias 8.17.6), and Pallas, founder of Pallantion (Pausanias 8.3.1), who was either one of the Titans (Hesiod *Theogony* 375–6, cf. 237–9) or a son of the Arcadian king Lykaon (Apollodorus 3.8.1, Pausanias 8.44.6) and grandfather of Evander (Servius on Virgil *Aeneid* 8.51, 54).

Competing performers: Plato *Laws* 659c; cf. Aristophanes Frogs 391–3 on the dancers at Eleusis (τῆς σῆς ἑορτῆς ἀξίως παίσαντα καὶ σκώψαντα νικήσαντα ταινιοῦσθαι).

The critical battle (Sentinum, 295 BC): Zonaras 8.1, with Wiseman 1995.117–20; Livy 10.33.9 (Victoria temple dedicated 294 BC). Conquest of Germany: inferred from the epithet 'Victoria *Germaniciana*' in the Constantinian regionary catalogues (*Notitia* on *regio X*, with Wiseman 2013b.249–50); for Nero Drusus 'Germanicus', see *Consolatio ad Liuiam* 269, 337, 457; *ILS* 107.10, 147, 148, 198; Ovid *Fasti* 1.597, Suetonius *Diuus Claudius* 1.3, Dio Cassius 55.2.3, Florus 2.30.28.

Very thoroughly explored: for details see Battistelli 2001.80–94, Pensabene 2002 and 2017. 1907 excavation: Vaglieri 1907.187–91; up to date interpretation in Angelelli and Falzone 1999 and 2001. Level 7m below: Angelelli and Falzone 2001.66 fig. 24 (spot-heights from 38.28 to 39.06 masl); the summit level is about 45 masl. Identification of *skyphos*: Santoro 1989.964. Monteverde tuff: Hopkins (2016.148) gives the *terminus post quem* as early fourth century BC; other authors (e.g., Coarelli 2007.534) put it even later. Necropolis: Vaglieri's hypothesis is cautiously accepted by Angelelli and Falzone 2001.73–7. Archaeological dates: see for instance Bettelli 1997.191–8; cf. Nijboer at al. 1999–2000 for the 'high' chronology. Development around 500 BC: Battistelli 2001.94–117, Pensabene 2002.66–75, 94–5. Temple: Cristofani 1990.91–5 (plaques and antefixes), Coarelli 2012.222–5.

Redeveloped again: Battistelli 2001.117-44. Victoria temple: Livy 10.33.9. Monument: reconstructed as an altar (with very adventurous interpretation) by Paolo Brocato in Carandini and Cappelli 2000.262–3. Same axis as the grave: Pensabene 2017.1.5, 19–20, 24. Magna Mater temple: Livy 29.37.2 (contract), 36.36.3–4 (dedication); Valerius Maximus 1.8.11, Obsequens 39 (fire of 111 BC). Reconstruction in front of it: Pensabene and D'Alessio 2006.30–42.

71   Descent of Fabii from Hercules: Silius Italicus 6.6227–36 (by Evander's daughter), Plutarch *Fabius Maximus* 1.1 ('by one of the nymphs or an indigenous woman'); Ovid *Fasti* 2.237, *Ex Ponto* 3.3.100, Juvenal 8.14. Beginning of Pictor's narrative: *SEG* 26.1123.iii.A (*FRHist* 1 T7).

Pallantia daughter of Evander: Varro fr. 398 Funaioli (Servius on Virgil *Aeneid* 8.51). Hyperborean Palantho: Dionysius of Halicarnassus *Roman Antiquities* 1.43.1; cf. Silenus of Caleacte *FGrH* 175 F8 (Solinus 1.15), Festus 245L (a local inhabitant); according to Varro (*De lingua Latina* 5.53) Palantho was Latinus' wife, not his mother.

72   Cacus: Gellius *FRHist* 14 F17 (Solinus 1.8); Virgil *Aeneid* 8.184-305, Ovid *Fasti* 1.543-82, 5.643-50, 6.81-2; Dionysius of Halicarnassus *Roman Antiquities* 1.39.2-4.

Ignoring the Arcadians: e.g., Dionysius of Halicarnassus *Roman Antiquities* 1.39.2 ('Pallantion in the territory of the Aborigines'), cf. 1.6.2, 1.79.4, 7.71.1 for his use of Fabius; a composite version (Festus 328L, Solinus 1.14) had the Aborigines on the Palatine before the Arcadians arrived.

Diodorus Siculus 4.21.1–2 (cf. 7.5.4 for his use of Fabius):
Ἡρακλῆς δὲ διελθὼν τήν τε τῶν Λιγύων καὶ τὴν τῶν Τυρρηνῶν χώραν, καταντήσας πρὸς τὸν Τίβεριν ποταμὸν κατεστρατοπέδευσεν οὗ νῦν ἡ Ῥώμη ἐστίν. ἀλλ' αὕτη μὲν πολλαῖς γενεαῖς ὕστερον ὑπὸ Ῥωμύλου τοῦ Ἄρεος ἐκτίσθη, τότε δέ τινες τῶν ἐγχωρίων κατῴκουν ἐν τῷ νῦν καλουμένῳ Παλατίῳ, μικρὰν παντελῶς πόλιν οἰκοῦντες. ἐν ταύτῃ δὲ τῶν ἐπιφανῶν ὄντες ἀνδρῶν Κάκιος καὶ Πινάριος ἐδέξαντο τὸν Ἡρακλέα ξενίοις ἀξιολόγοις καὶ δωρεαῖς κεχαρισμέναις ἐτίμησαν· καὶ τούτων τῶν ἀνδρῶν

ὑπομνήματα μέχρι τῶνδε καιρῶν διαμένει κατὰ τὴν Ῥώμην. τῶν γὰρ νῦν εὐγενῶν ἀνδρῶν τὸ τῶν Πιναρίων ὀνομαζομένων γένος διαμένει παρὰ τοῖς Ῥωμαίοις, ὡς ὑπάρχον ἀρχαιότατον, τοῦ δὲ Κακίου ἐν τῷ Παλατίῳ κατάβασίς ἐστιν ἔχουσα λιθίνην κλίμακα τὴν ὀνομαζομένην ἀπ' ἐκείνου Κακίαν, οὐσανησίον τῆς τότε γενομένης οἰκίας τοῦ Κακίου.

'The indigenous people' (οἱ ἐγχώριοι) may be Diodorus' or Fabius' translation of *Aborigines*; cf. Plutarch *Fabius Maximus* 1.1 (γυναικὸς ἐπιχωρίας) on the ancestress of the Fabii.

Descent into the valley of the Circus: Plutarch *Romulus* 20.4, where βαθμοὺς καλῆς ἀκτῆς is evidently a textual corruption; Plutarch's site for Romulus' house corresponds to the *supercilium scalarum Caci . . . ubi tugurium fuit Faustuli* (Solinus 1.18). Arcadian cult-sites: Dionysius of Halicarnassus *Roman Antiquities* 1.32.3 and 5 (Lupercal ὑπὸ τῷ λόφῳ, Nike temple ἐπὶ τῇ κορυφῇ τοῦ λόφου). Discovered by Rosa: Tomei 1999.114–21.

5.2 The Troy Connection

73   Aeneas as future ruler: Homer *Iliad* 20.302–8 (line 308 trans. Martin Hammond); Stesichorus, as illustrated on the *tabula Iliaca Capitolina* (Squire 2011.34–9, Davies and Finglass 2014.428–36).

Aeneas and Odysseus together: Hellanicus *FGrH* 4 F84 (Dionysius of Halicarnassus *Roman Antiquities* 1.72.2), followed by Lycophron *Alexandra* 1233–45 (third century BC); commentary in Fowler 2013.564–7 (cf. 95: 'Hellanikos seems to have thought harder about the big picture and tried to account for everything, reconciling competing traditions by various ingenious conjectures').

Rome as a Greek city: still accepted by Aristotle and Heraclides Ponticus in the fourth century BC (quoted respectively by Dionysius of Halicarnassus *Roman Antiquities* 1.72.3–4 and Plutarch *Camillus* 22.2–3).

Ruling family (the Tarquins): Cicero *De republica* 2.34–6 (Corinthian), Polybius 3.22.1 (date of expulsion); full details in Zevi 1995. Alliance with Carthage: Polybius 3.21.9–26.1, Diodorus Siculus 16.69.1 and 22.7.5, Livy 7.27.2 and *Epitome* 13 (treaties in 507, 348, and 279/8 BC).

Pausanias 1.12.1:

ταῦτα λεγόντων τῶν πρέσβεων μνήμη τὸν Πύρρον τῆς ἁλώσεως ἐσῆλθε τῆς Ἰλίου, καί οἱ κατὰ ταὐτὰ ἤλπιζε χωρήσειν πολεμοῦντι· στρατεύειν γὰρ ἐπὶ Τρώων ἀποίκους Ἀχιλλέως ὢν ἀπόγονος.

Descent from Achilles: Plutarch *Pyrrhus* 1.2, 7.4, 13.1.

Polybius 12.4b.1 (Timaeus *FGrH* 566 F36):

καὶ μὴν ἐν τοῖς περὶ Πύρρου πάλιν φησὶ τοὺς Ῥωμαίους ἔτι νῦν ὑπόμνημα ποιουμένους τῆς κατὰ τὸ Ἴλιον ἀπωλείας, ἐν ἡμέρᾳ τινὶ κατακοντίζειν ἵππον πολεμιστὴν πρὸ τῆς πόλεως ἐν τῷ Κάμπῳ καλουμένῳ, διὰ τὸ τῆς Τροίας τὴν ἅλωσιν διὰ τὸν ἵππον γενέσθαι τὸν δούριον προσαγορευόμενον.

One particular day (15 October): Plutarch *Roman Questions* 97 (*Moralia* 287a), Festus 190L, Festus (Paulus) 246L.

Timaeus in Latium: Dionysius of Halicarnassus *Roman Antiquities* 1.67.4 (*FGrH* 566 F59). Timaeus' interest in Rome: Dionysius of Halicarnassus *Roman Antiquities* 1.6.1, Aulus Gellius 11.1.1; Baron 2013.43–52.

No trace at all: I do not count 'the ship of Aeneas', first mentioned in the sixth century AD (Procopius *Gothic Wars* 4.22.7–8).

One of his companions: 'Cephalon of Gergis' *FGrH* 45 F10 (Festus 326L), cf. Sallust *Catiline* 6.1. His wife Rhome: Clinias *FGrH* 819 F1 (Servius *auctus* on Virgil *Aeneid* 1.273: daughter of Odysseus' son Telemachus); Plutarch *Romulus* 2.1 (daughter of Hercules' son Telephus). Rhome as Ascanius' daughter: Agathocles *FGrH* 472 F5 (Festus 328L), Plutarch *Romulus* 2.1.

Alcimus: *FGrH* 560 F4 (Festus 326L), a complex genealogy in which the founder of Rome is Romulus' grandson 'Rhodius'; cf. Wiseman 1995.52–3 for the likely historical context.

Latin eponym (*Roma* derived from *Romulus*): e.g., Ennius *Annales* 72–7 Sk (Cicero *De diuinatione* 1.107), Varro *De lingua Latina* 8.18, Livy 1.7.3, Dionysius of Halicarnassus *Roman Antiquities* 1.9.4, Plutarch *Romulus* 19.7.

75   Livy 10.23.11–12:

eodem anno Cn. et Q. Ogulnii aediles curules aliquot faeneratoribus diem dixerunt; quorum bonis multatis ex eo quod in publicum redactum est . . . ad ficum Ruminalem simulacra infantium conditorum urbis sub uberibus lupae posuereunt.

For Romulus and Remus as joint founders, see also Diodorus Siculus 37.11.1, Varro *Res rusticae* 2.pref.4 and 2.1.9, Conon *FGrH* 26.F1.48,7, Strabo 5.3.2 C229, Pliny *Natural History* 15.77, Justin 43.3.1, Servius on Virgil *Aeneid* 6.777, *CIL* 6.33856, Lydus *De magistratibus* 1.3.

Ficus Ruminalis at Lupercal: Pliny *Natural History* 15.77, Servius on Virgil *Aeneid* 8.90; cf. Varro *De lingua Latina* 5.54, Festus (Paulus) 333L, Plutarch *Romulus* 4.1.

Philargyrius on Virgil *Eclogues* 1.19 (Courtney 1993.405):

Roma et ante Romulum fuit et ab ea sibi nomen acquisisse Marianus Lupercorum poeta sic ostendit: Sed diua flaua et candida | Roma, Aesculapi filia, | nomen nouum Latio facit, | quod conditoris nomine | Romam sub ipso omnes uocant.

Aesculapius and the Lupercal cult: see Wiseman 2008.75–8 for the historical context.

Poet or hymnodist: examples in Dionysius of Halicarnassus *Roman Antiquities* 1.31.2, 1.79.10, 8.62.3; cf. Wiseman 2014a.53–6. There were normally *ludi scaenici* at the dedication of temples (e.g., Livy 36.36.4 and 7, 40.52.1–3, 42.10.5), and Ovid *Fasti* 4.247–348 ('attested by the stage', 326) gives an idea of the kind of story that might be presented.

Jupiter Victor temple: Livy 10.29.14 and 18 (battle of Sentinum), Conon *FGrH* 26 F1.48.8 (hut in precinct); it is named in the Constantinian *Notitia* under *regio X* (*Palatium*); for the controversy over its position see Coarelli 2012.234–49, Wiseman 2013b.251–4.

Festus 328L (Antigonus *FGrH* 816 F1):

Antigonus Italicae historiae scriptor ait Rhomum quendam nomine Ioue conceptum urbem condidisse in Palatio Romaeque ei dedisse nomen.

For Antigonus' approximate date, cf. Dionysius of Halicarnassus *Roman Antiquities* 1.6.1 (named after Timaeus but before Silenus and Polybius).

Rhomus featured in the Sibylline books: Servius *auctus* on Virgil *Aeneid* 1.273 (*Sibylla ita dicit,* Ῥωμαῖοι Ῥώμου παῖδες); the books were consulted in 292 BC (Livy 10.47.7), about the time the Jupiter Victor temple was dedicated.

Development of twins story: Wiseman 1995.126–8, 2004a.119–26 and 138–48.

76 Dionysius of Halicarnassus *Roman Antiquities* 1.73.5–74.1 (Timaeus *FGrH* 566 F60):

περὶ μὲν οὖν τῶν παλαιῶν κτίσεων ἱκανὰ ἡγοῦμαι τὰ προειρημένα. τὸν δὲ τελευταῖον γενόμενον τῆς Ῥώμης οἰκισμὸν ἢ κτίσιν ἢ ὅ τι δήποτε χρὴ καλεῖν Τίμαιος μὲν ὁ Σικελιώτης οὐκ οἶδ' ὅτῳ κανόνι χρησάμενος ἅμα Καρχηδόνι κτιζομένῃ γενέσθαι φησὶν ὀγδόῳ καὶ τριακοστῷ πρότερον ἔτει τῆς πρώτης ὀλυμπιάδος.

Timaeus and chronology (Baron 2013.23–8): Polybius 2.10.4, 2.11.1–2. Use of Tyrian records (Baron 2013.223–4): Polybius 12.28a.3; cf. Josephus *Against Apion* 1.107-27 (Menander of Ephesus *FGrH* 783 F1) for the Tyrians' record of their kings down to the foundation of Carthage. Date for the fall of Troy: Censorinus *De die natali* 21.2–3 (Timaeus *FGrH* 566 F125).

Eratosthenes as chronographical authority: Clarke 2008.64–70.

Servius *auctus* on Virgil *Aeneid* 1.273 (Eratosthenes *FGrH* 241 F45):

Eratosthenes Ascanii Aeneae filii <filium> Romulum parentem urbis refert. Naeuius et Ennius Aeneae ex filia nepotem Romulum conditorem urbis tradunt.

Naevius and Ennius on the twins story: Nonius 167L (Naevius on Amulius), Cicero *De diuinatione* 1.107 (Ennius *Annales* 72–7 Sk), Ilia: Nonius 317L, Festus 364L (Ennius *Annales* 60 Sk); cf. Horace *Odes* 1.2.17. Other Roman authors: Dionysius of Halicarnassus *Roman Antiquities* 1.73.1–2 ('not specifying who the father was'), Diodorus Siculus 7.5.1; Dionysius also reports that some made the twins the sons of Aeneas himself.

Naevius and Ennius as classics: see for instance Cicero *Brutus* 75 (Naevius' epic *quasi Myronis opus*), *De oratore* 1.198 (Ennius *summus poeta*), *Tusculan Disputations* 3.45 (Ennius *poeta egregius*). Listened to for centuries: Aulus Gellius 18.5.2–4, describing an Ennius recital in the second century AD.

Eratosthenes' dates (*FGrH* 241 F1): Censorinus *De die natali* 21.3, Clement of Alexandria *Stromateis* 1.138.1–3. Date of Tarquin's expulsion: Polybius 3.22.1. Creative reconstruction: see Wiseman 2008.314–6 on the canon of 'seven kings', and the possibility that Ancus Marcius and Tullus Hostilius were creations of the fourth and third centuries BC.

77 Lavinium: Castagnoli et al. 1981. Alba Longa: Grandazzi 2008. Silvius: Cato *FRHist* 5 F8 (Servius on Virgil *Aeneid* 6.760), Livy 1.3.6–7, Virgil *Aeneid* 6.760–70, Dionysius of Halicarnassus *Roman Antiquities* 1.70.1–3.

Royal dynasty: Diodorus Siculus 7.5.7–12, Livy 1.3.6–11, Dionysius of Halicarnassus *Roman Antiquities* 1.71.1–4, Ovid *Fasti* 4.39–56 and *Metamorphoses* 14.609–21; Forsythe 1994.113–23, Grandazzi 2008.731–890 (and pl. 22), Wiseman 2010.437–8.

Fifteen generations later: Dionysius of Halicarnassus *Roman Antiquities* 1.73.3, cf. 1.45.3, 2.2.1. Rhea Silvia: Castor of Rhodes *FGrH* 250 F5, Varro *De lingua Latina* 5.144, Dionysius of Halicarnassus *Roman Antiquities* 1.76.3, Plutarch *Romulus* 3.3.

First exploited: *SEG* 26.1123.iii.A (Fabius *FRHist* 1 T7), Romulus 'long after' Aeneas. Foundation dates: Dionysius of Halicarnassus *Roman Antiquities* 1.74.1 (Fabius Pictor *FRHist* 1 F5, Cincius Alimentus *FRHist* 2 F2a).

Great Mother: details and discussion in Gruen 1990.5–33. Full Roman title: e.g., *CIL* 6.499, 6.2183, 14.41. *Mater* (or *parens*) *Idaea*: Livy 29.10.5, 29.14.5, Virgil *Aeneid* 9.619–20, 10.252, Ovid *Fasti* 4.182; cf. Dionysius of Halicarnassus *Roman Antiquities* 2.19.3 ('the goddess of Ida').

Aeneas' birthplace: Hesiod *Theogony* 1010. Surviving Trojans: *Ilioupersis* arg.1d (West 2013.232, cf. Fowler 2013.563); Virgil *Aeneid* 2.696, 2.801, 3.112, 10.158; Dionysius of Halicarnassus *Roman Antiquities* 1.46.3, 1.48.2. Ships: Virgil *Aeneid* 3.5–6.

Traditional Greek theology: e.g., Hesiod *Theogony* 453–8, 630–4, Plato *Timaeus* 41a. Temple on Palatine: Cicero *De haruspicum responso* 24, Livy 29.37.2, 36.36.3–4; at *CIL* 12.405 the goddess is named as *Mater Deum Magna Idaea Palatina*.

5.3 Alba Longa and the Iulii

Imaginary mother-city: Grandazzi 2008.179–514, cf. Wiseman 2010.433–5; *contra* Carandini 1997.533–5 (cf. 104 fig. 11). Imaginary dynasty: Wiseman 2010.436–8; *contra* Grandazzi 2008.731–890.

Family cult site: Tacitus *Annals* 2.41.1, 15.23.2; cf. Suetonius *Diuus Augustus* 100.2; details and discussion in Weinstock 1971.5–12. Young (or little) Jupiter: Ovid *Fasti* 3.437 (*Iuppiter est iuuenis*), 3.448 (*non magni Iouis*); Festus 519L (*paruum Iouem*).

Magistrates called Iulius Iul(l)us: Dionysius of Halicarnassus *Roman Antiquities* 8.1.1, 8.90.5 (489 and 482 BC); *Fasti Capitolini*, Degrassi 1947.24–9 (473, 451, 408, 403, and 401 BC); Livy 5.16.1, 6.4.7 (397 and 388 BC).

79   *Origo gentis Romanae* 15.4–5 (Postumius *FRHist* 4 F4, Cato *FRHist* 5.F11):
is postea per legatos amicitiam societatemque Latinorum impetrauit, ut docet Lucius Caesar libro primo itemque Aulus Postumius in eo uolumine quod de aduentu Aeneae conscripsit atque < . . . > dedit. igitur Latini Ascanium ob insignem uirtutem non solum Ioue ortum crediderunt sed etiam, per diminutionem declinato paululum nomine, primo Iolum dein postea Iulum appellarunt. a quo Iulia familia manauit, ut scribunt Caesar libro secundo et Cato in Originibus.

The missing word in the text must have been the name of the person to whom Postumius dedicated his book on Aeneas.

According to Servius on Virgil *Aeneid* 1.267, L. Caesar also reported two other derivations of *Iulus*, from ἰοβόλος ('archer') or ἴουλος ('boy's first beard').

Other citations: *Origo gentis Romanae* 9.6 (Aeneas' trumpeter Misenus), 10.4 (Caieta leading the women to burn the ships), 11.3 (the white sow and the foundation of Lavinium), 16.4 (Lavinia and Silvius), 18.5 (king Silvius Aventinus), 20.3 (the exposure and rescue of the twins). See Smith and Cornell 2013 for full discussion of *OGR* and the sources it cites; for a stemma showing the various Lucii Caesares, see Sumner 1971.343.

Funeral of Iulia: Suetonius *Diuus Iulius* 6.1 (*genus . . . paternum diis immortalibus coniunctum est. nam . . . a Venere Iulii, cuius gentis familia est nostra*). Caesar and Venus: details and discussion in Weinstock 1971.15–18.

80   Dio Cassius 44.37.3–4 (from Antony's funeral speech):
. . . τῆς πόλεως ἡμῶν ὅλης συγγενής ἐστιν . . . ὥστ' εἰ καί τις ἠμφεσβήτει μήποτ' ἂν ἐκ τῆς Ἀφροδίτης τὸν Αἰνείαν γενέσθαι, νῦν δὴ πιστευσάτω.

Dio Cassius 43.43.2 (45 BC):
καὶ τῇ ὑποδέσει καὶ μετὰ ταῦτα ἐνίοτε καί ὑψηλῇ καὶ ἐρυθροχρόῳ κατὰ τοὺς βασιλέας τοὺς ἐν τῇ Ἄλβῃ ποτὲ γενομένους, ὡς προσήκων σφίσι διὰ τὸν Ἴουλον.

Part of Augustus' ancestry: Virgil *Aeneid* 6.789–90, Propertius 4.6.37–8, Ovid *Fasti* 4.39–40. Some classicists nowadays: e.g., Heyworth and Morwood 2011.115–6, who quote with approval the dogmatic assertion that 'no one ever seriously projected an epic on the kings of Alba, a dim line of shadows invented to fill a chronological gap' (Hubbard 1974.79 n.1).

Virgil *Eclogues* 6.3–4, with Servius' commentary:

cum canerem reges et proelia, Cynthius aurem | uellit et admonuit . . .

significat aut Aeneidem aut gesta regum Albanorum, quae coepta amisit nominum asperitate deterritus.

Servius' first alternative was an easy guess for a late commentator (as if Apollo had said 'Don't try it *yet*'), but there is not the slightest probability that Virgil had already conceived the *Aeneid* in the late forties BC. What is significant is the existence of the other tradition; why should anyone have invented it?

Propertius 3.3.1–4:

uisus eram molli recubans Heliconis in umbra | Bellerophontei qua fluit umor equi, | reges, Alba, tuos et regum facta tuorum, | tantum operis, neruis hiscere posse meis.

Apollo warned him off: Propertius 3.3.13–24.

Virgil *Aeneid* 1.1–3 and 6–7:

arma uirumque cano, Troiae qui primus ab oris | Italiam fato profugus Lauiniaque uenit | litora . . . | genus unde Latinum | Albanique patres atque altae moenia Romae.

What the Fates had in store: Virgil *Aeneid* 1.257–77.

81 Virgil *Aeneid* 1.286–8:

nascetur pulchra Troianus origine Caesar, | imperium Oceano, famam qui terminet astris, | Iulius, a magno demissum nomen Iulo.

Silvius and his Alban dynasty: Virgil *Aeneid* 6.760–76.

Pallanteum: Virgil *Aeneid* 8.54, 8.341, 9.196, 9.241; so too Livy 1.5.1, Justin 43.1.6, Solinus 1.14.

Cow pasture: Virgil *Aeneid* 360–1 (*passimque armenta uidebant | Romanoque foro et lautis mugire Carinis*); *mugire* is a clear allusion to the Porta Mugionis (Varro *De lingua Latina* 5.164).

Virgil *Aeneid* 8.362–7:

ut uentum ad sedes, 'haec' inquit 'limina uictor | Alcides subiit, haec illum regia cepit. | aude, hospes, contemnere opes et te quoque dignum | finge deo, rebusque ueni non asper egenis.' | dixit, et angusti subter fastigia tecti | ingentem Aenean duxit.

6. THE ROMULUS PARADIGM

82 Ovid *Fasti* 3.183–6:

quae fuerit nostri si quaeris regia nati, | aspice de canna straminibusque domum. | in stipula placidi capiebat munera somni, | et tamen ex illo uenit in astra toro.

See also Valerius Maximus 2.8.pref. and 4.4.11, Seneca *Ad Heluiam de consolatione* 9.3 (*Romuli casa* as an example of virtuous frugality).

Seventeenth generation: Dionysius of Halicarnassus *Roman Antiquities* 1.45.3, cf. 1.73.3, 2.2.1. Many variants: summarised in Wiseman 1995.1–17.

Flood-waters: Livy 1.4.4 (*super ripas Tiberis effusus*), Dionysius of Halicarnassus *Roman Antiquities* 1.79.5 (τοῦ γνησίου ῥείθρου τὸν Τέβεριν . . . ἐκτετραμμένον), Ovid *Fasti* 2.390 (*hibernis forte tumebat aquis*), Plutarch *Romulus* 3.5 (τοῦ δὲ ποταμοῦ κατακλύζοντος ἡ πλήμμυρα), *Origo gentis Romanae* 20.3 (*in Tiberim qui tum magnis imbribus stagnauerat*).

Foot of the Palatine: Dionysius of Halicarnassus *Roman Antiquities* 1.79.5 (ἔνθα πρῶτον ἡ τοῦ ποταμοῦ πλήμη τῆς ὑπωρείας ἥπτετο), *Origo gentis Romanae* 20.3 (*circa radices montis Palatii*); cf. Justin 43.1.6–7 (*Lupercal in huius* [*Palatii*] *radicibus*), Servius on Virgil *Aeneid* 8.343 (*Lupercal sub monte Palatino*).

Ancient fig-tree (*ficus Ruminalis*): Varro *De lingua Latina* 5.54, Livy 1.4.5, Ovid *Fasti* 2.411-12, Plutarch *Romulus* 4.1, Festus (Paulus) 333L, *Origo gentis Romanae* 20.4. Lupercal: Ovid *Fasti* 2.421-2, Pliny *Natural History* 15.77, Servius on Virgil *Aeneid* 8.90.

Deserted place: Livy 1.4.6 (*uastae tum in his locis solitudines erant*); cf. Tibullus 2.5.25–6 (*herbosa Palatia*), Ovid *Fasti* 3.71 (*siluae pecorumque recessus*).

Faustulus: he is described variously as a *pastor* or ποιμήν (Cicero *De republica* 2.4, Varro *De re rustica* 2.1.9, Florus 1.1.3, Justin 43.2.6, Conon *FGrH* 26 F1.43.5), or as a swineherd (Dionysius of Halicarnassus *Roman Antiquities* 1.79.9, Strabo 5.3.2 C229, Plutarch *Romulus* 6.1, *Origo gentis Romanae* 20.3), or as 'in charge of the [Alban] king's flocks' (Livy 1.4.6, *Origo gentis Romanae* 19.7). Humble hut: Florus 1.1.3; cf. Ovid *Fasti* 3.56 (*Faustule pauper*).

Grew up among shepherds: Cicero *De republica* 2.4, Virgil *Georgics* 2.532–3; Livy 1.4.7–9, 1.5.7; Dionysius of Halicarnassus *Roman Antiquities* 1.79.7 (τοῦ ποιμενικοῦ ὁμίλου), 1.79.9–14. 1.80.2–3, 1.84.6–8, 2.2.1; Ovid *Fasti* 2.369–72, 3.61–4 (specifying cattle, not sheep); Plutarch *Romulus* 6.2–7.2, 8.3; Justin 43.2.8–9; *Origo gentis Romanae* 21.4, 22.2.Shepherds' huts in the Roman *campagna*: Cervesato 1913.159–205, Bartolini 1994.196–9.

'Where they were brought up': Livy 1.6.3, Dionysius of Halicarnassus *Roman Antiquities* 1.85.2 and 6, Valerius Maximus 2.2.9, Plutarch *Romulus* 9.1, Florus 1.1.5. At Faustulus' hut: Zonaras 7.3, Tzetzes on Lycophron *Alexandra* 1232. Faustulus lived on the Palatine: Dionysius of Halicarnassus *Roman Antiquities* 1.84.3 (cf. 1.79.9), *Origo gentis Romanae* 20.3 (*eius regionis*).

Shepherds as first citizens: Cassius Hemina *FRHist* 6 F14 = Diomedes *Grammatici Latini* 1.384K (*pastorum uulgus*), Varro *De re rustica* 2.1.9 (*Romanorum uero populum a pastoribus esse ortum quis non dicit?*), Ovid *Fasti* 4.810 (*pastorum uulgus*), Juvenal 2.126–7 (*Latii pastores*); Varro and Ovid both emphasise the foundation of the city on the Parilia, the shepherds' festival.

Rationalising historians (Livy 1.6.3, Dionysius of Halicarnassus *Roman Antiquities* 1.85.3–4, Velleius Paterculus 1.8.5, Florus 1.1.9) made the shepherds only a minor part of the new citizen body, outnumbered by Latin colonists from Alba; that expedient postdates the invention of the Alban dynasty.

Romulus' asylum: Livy 1.8.5 (*obscuram atque humilem multitudinem*), Dionysius of Halicarnassus *Roman Antiquities* 2.15.3–4 (free-born refugees only), Strabo 5.3.2 C230 (σύγκλυδας), Florus 1.1.9 (*Latini Tuscique pastores*), Plutarch *Romulus* 9.3 (runaway slaves, debtors, criminals), Justin 38.7.1 (*conluuies conuenarum*).

Livy 1.8.6:

eo ex finitimis populis turba omnis, sine discrimine liber an seruus esset, auida nouarum rerum perfugit.

Ovid *Fasti* 3.432–5:

'quilibet huc' dixit 'confuge: tutus eris.' | o quam de tenui Romanus origine creuit, | turba uetus quam non inuidiosa fuit!

84 Shepherds and brigands: e.g., Livy 39.29.8–9, Cicero *Pro Sestio* 12, Caesar *De bello ciuili* 3.21.2. Enemies despised them: Dionysius of Halicarnassus *Roman Antiquities* 2.8.3 (διαβάλλοντες εἰς δυσγένειαν τὴν πόλιν), cf. 1.4.2, 1.89.1, 7.70.1 ('homeless vagabonds and fugitives').

Justin 28.2.8:

quos autem homines Romanos esse? nempe pastores, qui latrocinio iustis dominis ademptum solum teneant.
Justin was excerpting Pompeius Trogus, who wrote under Augustus (Justin 43.5.12, cf. 42.5.11, 44.5.8) and found his material in earlier Greek authors (Justin pref. 3).

Formal colony: Dionysius of Halicarnassus *Roman Antiquities* 1.85.2–3 (including aristocrats of Trojan birth). Dionysius constantly refers to Rome as a colonial foundation: e.g., 1.31.1, 2.1.3 (Evander); 1.72.1 (Rhomus son of Aeneas); 1.71.5, 1.75.4, 1.86.1, 2.2.3–4 (Romulus and Remus together); 1.45.3, 1.87.3 (Romulus alone).

Juvenal 8.272–5:

et tamen, ut longe repetas longeque reuoluas | nomen, ab infami gentem deducis asylo; | maiorum primus, quisquis fuit ille, tuorum | aut pastor fuit aut illud quod dicere nolo.

6.1 Huts

Latest thinking: Cicero *Academica* 1.9 (46 BC), on Varro's *Antiquities*.
Varro *Res rusticae* 2.1.9, 2 pref.4:

Romanorum uero populum a pastoribus esse ortum quis non dicit? quis Faustulum nescit pastorem fuisse nutricium qui Romulum et Remum educauit? non ipsos quoque fuisse pastores obtinebit, quod Parilibus potissimum condidere urbem? . . . itaque in qua terra culturam agri docuerunt pastores progeniem suam qui condiderunt urbem, ibi contra progenies eorum propter auaritiam contra leges ex segetibus fecit prata.

Cf. *Res rusticae* 1.13.7 on the country houses of Varro's contemporaries Metellus and Lucullus, built 'to great public detriment' (*pessimo publico*).

Vitruvius *De architectura* 2.1.5:

item in Capitolio commonefacere potest et significare mores uetustatis Romuli casa et in arce sacrorum stramenta tecta.

Anxiously awaiting: Donatus *Vita Vergili* 31 (Augustus' letter to Virgil from Spain).

85   Virgil *Aeneid* 8.652–6:

in summo custos Tarpeiae Manlius arcis | stabat pro templo et Capitolia celsa tenebat, | Romuleoque recens horrebat regia culmo. | atque hic auratis uolitans argenteus anser | porticibus Gallos in limine adesse canebat.

Gilded roof-tiles: Pliny *Natural History* 33.57 (an innovation by Q. Catulus of which not everyone approved), Virgil *Aeneid* 8.347–8 (*hinc ad Tarpeiam sedem et Capitolia ducit | aurea nunc, olim siluestribus horrida dumis*); cf. Propertius 4.1.5 (*aurea templa*).

Roman moralists: Livy 5.53.8, Valerius Maximus 2.8.pref., 4.4.11, Seneca *Controuersiae* 1.6.4, 2.1.5, Seneca *Consolatio ad Heluiam* 9.3; Tibullus 2.5.26, Ovid *Fasti* 1.199, 3.183–4, Martial 8.80.6, Silius Italicus 13.814.

Romulus living on Palatine: Dionysius of Halicarnassus *Roman Antiquities* 1.79.11, Plutarch *Romulus* 20.4; Dio Cassius 53.16.5 for the relevance to Augustus' house. For Varro's likely view, cf. Wiseman 2015a.106–8.

Casa Romuli in gazetteer: Valentini and Zucchetti 1940.128 (*Curiosum*), 177 (*Notitia*). Augustan original: Coarelli 2012.112–15, Wiseman 2013b.249–53. Creation in 8 BC: Suetonius *Diuus Augustus* 30.1, Dio Cassius 55.8.6–7; for the date, see Augustus *Res gestae* 8.3, with Lott 2004.84–9.

Anthologia Palatina 7.222.1–4 (Gow and Page 1968.1.366–7, 2.296–8; Sider 1997.178–87):

ἐνθάδε τῆς τρυφερῆς μαλακὸν ῥέθος, ἐνθάδε κεῖται | Τρυγόνιον, σαβακῶν ἄνθεμα σαλμακίδων, | ἣ καλύβη καὶ δοῦμος ἐνέπρεπεν, ἣ φιλοπαίγμων | στωμυλίη, μήτηρ ἣν ἐφίλησε θεῶν . . .

Magna Mater temple: Livy 36.36.3–4 (dedication); Valerius Maximus 1.8.11, Obsequens 39 (fire); it was burned again in AD 3, and rebuilt again by Augustus (Ovid *Fasti* 4.348, Augustus *Res gestae* 19.2).

86   'Holy assembly': Sider 1997.182–3. Within her sight: as the *ludi Megalenses* were held *in ipso Matris Magnae conspectu* (Cicero *De haruspicum responso* 24).

Varro *De lingua Latina* 5.54:

huic Cermalum et Velias coniunxerunt, quod in hac regione scriptum est 'Germalense: quinticeps apud aedem Romuli. Germalum a germanis Romulo et Remo, quod ad ficum ruminalem, et ii ibi inuenti, quo aqua hiberna Tiberis eos detulerat in alueolo expositos.

Liturgical document: Varro *De lingua Latina* 5.50 (*in sacris Argeorum scriptum est*), 5.52 (*apparet ex Argeorum sacrificiis*). *Germalus* from *germani*: Plutarch *Romulus* 3.5, cf. 4.1 for the 'nearby' *ficus Ruminalis*.

Ficus Ruminalis at Lupercal: Pliny *Natural History* 15.77 (*in Lupercali*), Servius on *Aeneid* 8.90 (*ubi nunc est Lupercal in circo*); cf. Justin 43.1.7 (Lupercal *in [Palati] radicibus*). Associated with the suckling of the twins: Livy 1.4.5, Ovid *Fasti* 2.411-12, Conon *FGrH* 26 F1.48.4, Festus 332-3L, Florus 1.1.3. Precinct (τέμενος) and statue-group: Dionysius of Halicarnassus *Roman Antiquities* 1.79.8 (cf. 1.32.3, Lupercal), Livy 10.23.12 (296 BC).

Cermalus as Palatine summit: Carandini and Carafa 2017.50 and tables 61–2, 64, 70. *Aedes* and *casa* identical: e.g., Ampolo and Manfredini 1988.324, Coarelli 1993a.241, Pensabene 1998.59–70 and 2017.1.19–23, Coarelli 2012.130 and 132, Carandini and Carafa 2017.219, 222, and tables 61C, 64A, 65 (no. 17), 70, 71, 273 (no. 21).

At a low level: Varro *De lingua Latina* 5.54 (above), cf. Livy 33.26.9 (on the route from Vicus Tuscus to Porta Capena); Castagnoli 1964.173–7 and 1977, Coarelli 2012.127–32.

87   Dionysius of Halicarnassus *Roman Antiquities* 1.79.11:

βίος δ' αὐτοῖς ἦν βουκολικὸς καὶ δίαιτα αὐτουργὸς ἐν ὄρεσι τὰ πολλὰ πηξαμένοις διὰ ξύλων καὶ καλάμων σκηνὰς αὐτορόφους· ὧν ἔτι καὶ εἰς ἐμὲ ἦν τις τοῦ Παλλαντίου ἐπὶ τῆς πρὸς τὸν ἱππόδρομον στρεφούσης λαγόνος Ῥωμύλου λεγομένη, ἣν φυλάττουσιν ἱερὰν οἷς τούτων ἐπιμελὲς οὐδὲν ἐπὶ τὸ σεμνότερον ἐξάγοντες, εἰ δέ τι πονήσειεν ὑπὸ χειμῶνος ἢ χρόνου τὸ λεῖπον ἐξακούμενοι καὶ τῷ πρόσθεν ἐξομοιοῦντες εἰς δύναμιν.

Plutarch *Romulus* 20.4:

ᾤκει δὲ Τάτιος μὲν ὅπου νῦν ὁ τῆς Μονήτης ναός ἐστι, Ῥωμύλος δὲ παρὰ τοὺς λεγομένους βαθμοὺς σκάλας Κακίας. οὗτοι δὲ εἰσὶ περὶ τὴν εἰς τὸν ἱππόδρομον τὸν μέγαν ἐκ Παλατίου κατάβασιν.

σκάλας Κακίας: text as in Ampolo and Manfredini 1988.140 (the MSS reading is καλῆς ἀκτῆς).

Solinus 1.17–18 (see Walter 1969.73–4 for the date):

nam, ut adfirmat Varro auctor diligentissimus, Romam condidit Romulus, Marte genitus et Rea Siluia, uel ut nonnulli Marte et Ilia: dictaque primum est Roma quadrata, quod ad aequilibrium foret posita. ea incipit a silua quae est in area Apollinis, et ad supercilium scalarum Caci habet terminum, ubi tugurium fuit Faustuli.

'August augury': Suetonius *Diuus Augustus* 7.2, citing Ennius *Annales* 155 Sk.

6.2 Faustulus and the *auguratorium*

88 Augurs faced east: Livy 1.18.7, Servius *auctus* on *Aeneid* 2.693 (north to the left); Linderski 1986.2280–3. Dionysius of Halicarnassus *Roman Antiquities* 2.5.1–2:

ὡς δὲ κἀκείνοις ἦν βουλομένοις προειπὼν ἡμέραν, ἐν ᾗ διαμαντεύσασθαι περὶ τῆς ἀρχῆς ἔμελλεν, ἐπειδὴ καθῆκεν ὁ χρόνος ἄναστας περὶ τὸν ὄρθρον ἐκ τῆς σκηνῆς προῆλθεν· στὰς δὲ ὑπαίθριος ἐν καθαρῷ χωρίῳ καὶ προθύσας ἃ νόμος ἦν εὔχετο Διί τε βασιλεῖ καὶ τοῖς ἀλλοῖς θεοῖς, οὓς ἐποιήσατο τῆς ἀποικίας ἡγεμόνας, εἰ βουλομένοις αὐτοῖς ἐστι βασιλεύεσθαι τὴν πόλιν ὑφ' ἑαυτοῦ, σημεῖα οὐράνια φανῆναι καλά. (2) μετὰ δὲ τὴν εὐχὴν ἀστραπὴ διῆλθεν ἐκ τῶν ἀριστερῶν ἐπὶ τὰ δεξιά. τίθενται δὲ Ῥωμαῖοι τὰς ἐκ τῶν ἀριστερῶν ἐπὶ τὰ δεξιὰ ἀτραπὰς αἰσίους, εἴτε παρὰ Τυρρηνῶν διδαχθέντες εἴτε πατέρων καθηγησαμένων, κατὰ τοιόνδε τινά, ὡς ἐγὼ πείθομαι, λογισμόν, ὅτι καθέδρα μέν ἐστι καὶ στάσις ἀρίστη τῶν οἰωνοῖς μαντευομένων ἡ βλέπουσα πρὸς ἀνατολάς, ὅθεν ἡλίου τε ἀναφοραὶ γίνονται καὶ σελήνης καὶ ἀστέρων πλανήτων τε καὶ ἀπλανῶν . . .

For σκηνή as 'hut', cf. Dio Cassius 48.43.4, 54.29.8.

Dionysius of Halicarnassus *Roman Antiquities* 14.2.2:

ἐν δὲ τῇ Ῥώμῃ καλιάς τις Ἄρεος ἱερὰ περὶ τὴν κορυφὴν ἱδρυμένη τοῦ Παλατίου συγκαταφλεγεῖσα ταῖς πέριξ οἰκίαις ἕως ἐδάφους, ἀνακαθαιρομένων τῶν οἰκοπέδων ἕνεκα τῆς ἐπισκευῆς, ἐν μέσῃ τῇ περικαύστῳ σποδῷ τὸ σύμβολον τοῦ συνοικισμοῦ τῆς πόλεως διέσωσεν ἀπαθές, ῥόπαλον ἐκ θατέρου τῶν ἄκρων ἐπικάμπιον, οἷα φέρουσι βουκόλοι καὶ νομεῖς, οἱ μὲν καλαύροπας οἱ δὲ λαγωβόλα καλοῦντες, ᾧ Ῥωμύλος ὀρνιθευόμενος διέγραφε τῶν οἰωνῶν τὰς χώρας ὅτε τὴν πόλιν οἰκίζειν ἔμελλεν.

The same story, with the same details, is told by Plutarch (*Romulus* 22.1–2, *Camillus* 32.4–5); cf. *Romulus* 12.3–4 for Plutarch's use of Varro.

Cicero *De diuinatione* 1.30:

quid? lituus iste uester quod clarissimum est insigne auguratus [cf. σύμβολον in Dionysius]*, unde uobis est traditus? nempe eo Romulus regiones direxit tum cum urbem condidit. qui quidem Romuli lituus, id est incuruum et leuiter a summo inflexum bacillum, quod ab eius litui quo canitur similitudine nomen inuenit, cum situs esset in curia Saliorum quae est in Palatio, eaque deflagrauisset, inuentus est integer* [cf. ἀπαθές in Dionysius]*.*

89 Ancient priesthood of Mars: Livy 1.20.4, Ovid *Fasti* 3.259–60 and 387–8, Plutarch *Numa* 13. Varro's *Antiquities*: cf. Cicero *Academica* 1.9; Dionysius of Halicarnassus *Roman Antiquities* 1.14.1, 2.21.2, 2.47.4, 2.48.4; Wiseman 2009a .81–98.

Solinus 1.17–18:

nam, ut adfirmat Varro auctor diligentissimus, Romam condidit Romulus, Marte genitus et Rea Siluia, uel ut nonnulli Marte et Ilia: dictaque primum est Roma quadrata, quod ad aequilibrium foret posita. ea incipit a silua quae est in area Apollinis, et ad supercilium scalarum Caci habet terminum, ubi tugurium fuit Faustuli. ibi Romulus mansitauit, qui auspicato murorum fundamenta iecit duodeuiginti natus annos.

Based on Varro: cf. Solinus 1.32, the same chronological terminus (43 BC, the consulship of Hirtius and Pansa) that Varro used in his *De gente populi Romani* fr. 20 Fraccaro (Arnobius 5.8); see Wiseman 2015a.95–100.

'At the balancing-point': perhaps an allusion to Rome's star-sign, Libra (Manilius 4.773–4); see Wiseman 2015a.117–18. The enigmatic phrase has given rise to various implausible explanations: my own earlier guess, that it was a chronological metaphor (Wiseman 2004-6.115–18), was rightly dismissed by

Daniela Bruno, but her suggestion, that it somehow referred to the Pythagorean 'perfect square' (Bruno 2010.295), is equally unsatisfactory.

'Stayed overnight': the perfect tense shows that the phrase cannot mean 'that was where Romulus lived'. The correct meaning was detected more than a century ago (Richmond 1914.223, 'there was Romulus' augural *mansio*'), and then forgotten again; see Wiseman 2015a.102–3, Claridge 2018.120.

'After receiving good auspices': *Thesaurus linguae Latinae* 2.1552.16–53; see Wiseman 2015a.101–2. Texts written after Varro: Cicero *De republica* 2.5, 2.16, 2.51 (51 BC); *De legibus* 2.33 (c. 50 BC); *De diuinatione* 1.3, 2.70 (44 BC); also Livy 5.52.2, 28.28.11.

Comet of July 44 BC: Pliny *Natural History* 2.93–4 (Augustus *FRHist* 60 F1); full details in Ramsey and Licht 1997. Romulus had lived there too: Dio Cassius 53.16.5 (πρὸς τὴν τοῦ Ῥωμύλου προενοίκησιν).

Where Romulus and Remus grew up: Varro *Res rusticae* 2.1.9, Livy 1.4.7, Dionysius of Halicarnassus *Roman Antiquities* 1.79.9–10, Conon *FGrH* 26 F1.48.5, Valerius Maximus 2.2.9, Plutarch *Romulus* 6.1, Florus 1.1.3, *Origo gentis Romanae* 20.3, 21.4, *De uiris illustribus* 1.3.

Zonaras 7.3:

ὀκτωκαίδεκα δ' εἶναι ὁ Ῥωμύλος ἀναγέγραπται ὅτε τὴν Ῥώμην συνῴκισεν. ἔκτισε δὲ αὐτὴν περὶ τὴν τοῦ Φαυστούλου οἴκησιν, ὠνόμαστο δ' ὁ χῶρος Παλάτιον.

90 Tzetzes on Lycophron *Alexandra* 1232:

τῷ δὲ Νεμέτωρι πάππῳ αὐτῶν τὴν βασιλείαν τῆς Ἄλβης παρασχόντες αὐτοὶ τὴν Ῥώμην κτίζειν ἀπήρξαντο ἰῇ ἔτει τῆς Ῥωμύλου ἡλικίας. πρὸ δὲ τῆς μεγάλης ταύτης Ῥώμης, ἣν ἔκτισε Ῥωμύλος περὶ τὴν Φαιστύλου οἰκίαν ἐν ὄρει Παλατίῳ, καὶ τετράγωνος ἐκτίσθη Ῥώμη παρὰ Ῥώμου ἢ Ῥωμύλου παλαιοτέρα τούτων.

Roman land-surveyors took their observations from the centre of the area to be divided up (Varro, quoted by Julius Frontinus): Campbell 2000.8 (lines 23–9), cf. Wiseman 2015a.116–17.

The hut was on the summit of the hill: see now Claridge 2018.120–1.

King of Cappadocia: Conon *FGrH* 26 T1 (Photius 186.130b5).

Conon *FGrH* 26 F1.48.7–8:

δείκνυται δὲ μαρτύρια τῶν τότε παρὰ Ῥωμαίοις ἐπὶ τῆς ἀγορᾶς ἐρινεὸς ἱερά, τοῦ βουλευτηρίου κιγκλίσι χαλκαῖς περιειργομένη· καὶ καλύβη τις ἐν τῷ τοῦ Διὸς ἱερῷ γνώρισμα τῆς Φαιστύλου διαίτης, ἣν ἐκ φορυτῶν καὶ νέων φραγάνων συνιστῶντες διασῴζουσιν.

Sources cited but not reproduced: Photius 186.130b25 (*FGrH* 26 T1); Cameron 2004.72–3.

Notitia (Valentini and Zucchetti 1940.177–8, cf. 128–32 for the *Curiosum* version):

regio X Palatium continet casam Romuli, aedem Matris deum et Apollinis Ramnusii, pentapylum, domum Augustianam et Tiberianam, auguratorium, aream Palatinam, aedem Iouis Victoris, domum Dionis, curiam ueterem, Fortunam respicientem, Septizonium diui Seueri, Victoriam Germanicianam, Lupercam.

For Apollo 'Ramnusius' and Victoria 'Germaniciana' as probable Augustan titles, see Wiseman 2013b.249–50; for *curia uetus* (Tacitus *Annals* 12.24.1) and Fortuna Respiciens, see Coarelli 2012.87–93, 200–19.

92 Romulus' prayer to Jupiter: Dionysius of Halicarnassus *Roman Antiquities* 2.5.1–2.

Areae in front of temples: e.g., Varro in Aulus Gellius 2.10.2 (*area Capitolina*), Ovid *Fasti* 6.205 (Hercules Custos), Livy 2.41.11 (*area ante Telluris aedem*), *CIL* 10.1781.5–6 (*area quae est ante aedem*). Assemblies in *area Capitolina*: Livy 25.3.14, Velleius Paterculus 2.3.2. Named after divinity: e.g., *area Apollinis* (*Année épigraphique* 1972.174, Solinus 1.18), *area Volcani et Concordiae* (Livy 40.19.2).

Long digression: Josephus *Jewish Antiquities* 19.1–273. Complex of imperial properties: Josephus *Jewish Antiquities* 19.117; Wiseman 2013a.56, 100–8. Josephus' sources: Wiseman 2013a.xiv–xvi, 109–16.

Josephus *Jewish Antiquities* 19.223:

ἐν εὐρυχωρίᾳ δὲ τοῦ Παλατίου γενομένοις (πρῶτον δὲ οἰκηθῆναι τῆς Ῥωμαίων πόλεως τοῦτο παραδίδωσιν ὁ περὶ αὐτῆς λόγος) καὶ ἤδη τοῦ δημοσίου ἀντιλαμβανομένοις πολὺ πλείων ἢ ἐπιφοίτησις ἦν τῶν στρατιωτῶν χαρᾷ τὴν ὄψιν δεχομένοις τοῦ Κλαυδίου . . .

Ludi Palatini: Tacitus *Annals* 1.73.3, Dio Cassius 56.46.5; cf. *Année Épigraphique* 1956.67.1–4 (a *pantomimus* competing *in Palatio*).

93 Josephus *Jewish Antiquities* 19.75–6 and 90:

. . . μικρόν τε πρὸ τοῦ βασιλείου καλύβης πηκτοῦ γενομένης, καὶ Ῥωμαίων τε οἱ εὐπατρίδαι θεωροῦσι ὁμοῦ παισὶν καὶ γυναιξὶν καὶ ὁ Καῖσαρ· ῥᾳστώνην τε αὐτοῖς ἔσεσθαι πολλῶν μυριάδων ἀνθρώπων εἰς ὀλίγον χωρίον καθειργνυμένων . . . κατεσκεύαστο δὲ τὸ θέατρον, πηκτὸν δὲ ἐγίνετο κατὰ ἕκαστον ἐνιαυτόν, τοιόνδε τρόπον· θύρας ἔχει δύο φερούσας τὴν μὲν εἰς αἴθριον, τὴν δ' εἰς στοὰν εἰσόδοις καὶ ἀποχωρήσεσιν, ὅπως μὴ ταράσσοιντο οἱ ἔνδον ἀπειλημμένοι, ἐκ δ' αὐτῆς τῆς καλύβης ἐνδοτέρω διαφράγμασιν ἑτέραν ἀπειληφυίας ἐπ' ἀναστροφῇ τοῖς ἀνταγωνισταῖς καὶ ὁπόσα ἀκροάματα.

Ionic colonnade: as illustrated on the 'Sorrento base' (see for instance Guarducci 1971 Tafeln 64-9, Hölscher 1988.376). Famous space: Augustus *Res gestae* 34.2–35.1; Ovid *Fasti* 1.614, 4.953–4, *Metamorphoses* 1.562–3, *Tristia* 3.1.33–6; Dio Cassius 53.16.4. Vesta 'at the threshold': Ovid *Fasti* 4.949–50 (*limine*), cf. Degrassi 1963.66 (*fasti Caeretani*), 132–3 (*fasti Praenestini*); Wiseman 2011.

Real house of Augustus: as pointed out long ago (Castagnoli 1964.186–7), and wrongly denied on the strength of Carettoni's excavations (Sasso D'Elia 1995.41).

94   *Area Palatina* relocated: Aulus Gellius 20.1.1 (cf. 4.1.1, *in uestibulo aedium Palatinarum*) for the place where people waited for admission to the palace. Rosa's concrete podium (Tomei 1999.67–79) was wrongly identified as the temple of Jupiter Stator, which was near the Forum (Appian *Civil Wars* 2.11.40); cf. Torelli 1987.578–81 for the suggestion that it was Jupiter Victor.

Third century BC: cf. Livy 10.29.14, 10.42.7 (temple to Jupiter Victor vowed in 295 BC); *CIL* 6.438, 475, 30767a, with Coarelli 2012.239–41 (temple to Jupiter Victor on the Quirinal, evidently dedicated in 236 BC and restored in 212 BC after a fire). There was also a temple to Jupiter Victor on the Capitol (Josephus *Jewish Antiquities* 19.248, Dio Cassius 45.17.3, *Acta fratrum Arualium* 40.I.86–8 and 40.II.4–5, with Vella 2010–11 and Coarelli 2012.243–6), which may be the one reported by Livy and referred to by Ovid (*Fasti* 4.621–2) and in the pre-Julian *fasti Antiates* (Degrassi 1963.8); on the other hand, Livy's temple of 295 BC could be the Palatine temple itself, with the Capitoline temple remaining unattributed.

I am not convinced by Coarelli 2012.247–8, who suggests that the Palatine temple listed in the regionary gazetteer was really Jupiter *Vltor*, and that the hut 'in the precinct of Jupiter' referred to by Conon was 'on the Cermalus'.

6.3 Remus and 'Square Rome'

95   Founded by both twins: Livy 10.23.12 (296 BC); Cassius Hemina *FRHist* 6 F14 (mid-second century BC), quoted in *Grammatici Latini* 1.384 Keil; Diodorus Siculus 37.11.1 (91 BC); plural founders also in Pompeius Trogus (Justin 43.3.1), Varro *Res rusticae* 2.pref.4, 2.1.9, Conon *FGrH* 26 F1.48.7, Strabo 5.3.2 C229, Valerius Maximus 2.2.9, Pliny *Natural History* 15.77, *CIL* 6.33856, *De uiris illustribus* 1.4, Orosius 2.4.1, Lydus *De magistratibus* 1.3. Amicably decided: Ovid *Fasti* 4.811–18, Florus 1.1.6–7; Wiseman 1995.4–6. Turned murderous: details in Wiseman 2009a.176–210.

Late-republican historian: Licinius Macer *FRHist* 27 F3 (*Origo gentis Romanae* 23.5); cf. Livy 1.6.4 (*regni cupido . . . foedum certamen*), 1.7.2 (*in turba ictus*), Plutarch *Romulus* 10.1–2 (ἐν τῇ μάχῃ), Servius on *Aeneid* 1.273 (*bellum*), 6.779 (*a Romuli militibus occisus*), Zonaras 7.3 (διὰ μάχης); for details of the various versions see Wiseman 1995.6–17.

96   Horace *Epodes* 7.17–20:
sic est: acerba fata Romanos agunt | scelusque fraternae necis, | ut inmerentis fluxit in terra Remi | sacer nepotibus cruor.

Prevailing version: Livy 1.7.2 (*uolgatior fama*); assumed as fact by Cicero (*De officiis* 3.40–1), Pompeius Trogus (Justin 28.2.10), Lucan (1.95) etc.

Varro on civic concord: e.g., *De uita populi Romani* frr. 65, 66, 106, 108 Pittà (Nonius 443L, 771L, 438L, 728L) = frr. 66, 67, 124, 114 Riposati; cf. Dionysius of Halicarnassus *Roman Antiquities* 2.11.2–3, where the reference to C. Gracchus (as in *De uita p.R.* fr. 108 = 114) suggests Varro as a source. Varro on joint founders: *Res rusticae* 2.pref.4, 2.1.9; Wiseman 2015a.93.

Famous passage: Virgil *Georgics* 2.533 (*Remus et frater*).

97   Virgil *Aeneid* 1.291–3:
aspera tum positis mitescunt saecula bellis: | cana Fides et Vesta, Remo cum fratre Quirinus | iura dabunt.
From the very beginning (19 August 43 BC): Suetonius *Diuus Augustus* 95, Appian *Civil Wars* 3.94.388, Dio Cassius 46.46.2.

Remus as Agrippa (consular colleague in 28 and 27 BC): Servius on *Aeneid* 1.292; cf. Pliny *Nat. Hist.* 35.26 (Agrippa's *rusticitas*), Nicolaus of Damascus *FGrH* 90 F127.7.16 (friend and schoolfellow).

Poets: Catullus 58.5 (*Remi nepotes*), Diodorus *Anthologia Palatina* 9.219.3 = Gow and Page 1968.1.232 (ἄστυ Ῥέμοιο, 24 BC), Propertius 4.6.80 (*signa Remi*), Martial 10.76.4 (*de plebe Remi*), 12.2.16 (Palatine as *domus alta Remi*), Juvenal 10.73 (*turba Remi*). Historian: Egnatius *FRHist* 105 F1 (*Origo gentis Romanae* 23.6).
Sharing Romulus' rule: Propertius 2.1.23 (*regna prima Remi* as a possible subject for epic).
Propertius 4.1.9–10:
qua gradibus domus ista, Remi se sustulit olim: | *unus erat fratrum maxima regna focus.*
Agrippa on the Palatine: Dio Cassius 53.27.5.
'Legend of Rome': Carandini 2006a, cf. 2006b for Remus in particular. Rational argument is useless against this belief: 'si apre a questo punto un dissenso epistemologico insanabile che rende inutile ogni confronto' (Carandini 2007.15).
'Square Rome' (*Roma quadrata*) founded by Romulus: Dionysius of Halicarnassus *Roman Antiquities* 1.88.2, Plutarch *Romulus* 9.4, Solinus 1.17. By both twins: Appian *Wars of the Kings* fr. 1a.9 (*codex Paris. Suppl. Gr.* 607A), Tztezes on Lycophron *Alexandra* 1232.
Festus 310–12L:
quadrata Roma in Palatio <locus> ante templum Apollinis dicitur, ubi reposita sunt quae solent boni ominis gratia in urbe condenda adhiberi, quia saxo †minitus† est initio in speciem quadratam. eius loci Ennius meminit cum ait 'et †quis est erat† Romae regnare quadratae'.

The missing noun has to be masculine in order to agree with the (corrupt) participle *minitus*. That word is normally read as *munitus*, 'constructed', referring to a building (Richardson 1992.333, 'shrine'; Coarelli 1999.208, *ricettacolo*). But why should a building be called 'Rome', and why make a point of it being square and built of stone?

An equally easy emendation (accepted by Goldberg and Manuwald 2018.187) is *finitus*, 'bounded', referring more naturally to an open area. A land-surveyor was a *finitor* (Plautus *Poenulus* 48–9), and though one might expect *lapidibus, cippis*, or *terminis* rather than *saxo*, Juvenal 16.38 offers a parallel for *saxum* in the context of land boundaries.
Some historians: Dionysius of Halicarnassus *Roman Antiquities* 1.88.2, 2.65.3; Wiseman 2013b.242–3. Appian *Wars of the Kings* fr. 1a.9 (*codex Paris. Suppl. Gr.* 607A), giving dimensions; for Turin and Aosta, see Conventi 2004.144–9, cf. also 110–12 on Pavia (*Ticinum*). Anon. *FRHist* 109 F1 (*Oxyrhynchus Papyri* 2088).

98   Solinus 1.18: *ea incipit a silua quae est in area Apollinis, et ad supercilium scalarum Caci habet terminum.* Apollo temple and porticos: Dio Cassius 49.15.5 (begun 36 BC), 53.1.3 (dedicated 28 BC); cf. Propertius 2.31.1–16, Velleius Paterculus 2.81.3.
Verrius Flaccus (Kaster 1995.190–1): Festus 242L, cf. 228L, 292L, 378L, 438L, 460L, 476L. Augustus' grandsons: Suetonius *De grammaticis* 17.2 (*in atrio Catulinae domus, quae pars Palati tunc erat*).
Varro *Res rusticae* 1.10.2:
iugerum, quod quadratos duos actus habeat. actus quadratus, qui et latus est pedes CXX et longus totidem. . . . bina iugera quod a Romulo primum diuisa dicebantur uiritim, quae heredem sequerentur, heredium appellarunt.

The relevance of this passage to the Palatine was pointed out long ago (Richmond 1914.224), and subsequently ignored.
Romulus' equal lots: Dionysius of Halicarnassus *Roman Antiquities* 2.7.4, 2.28.3; see Wiseman 2009a.81–98 for the argument that the whole passage on Romulus' institutions (*Roman Antiquities* 2.7.2–29.2) was based on Varro's *Antiquities*.
'Julius Frontinus' in Campbell 2000.10 lines 10–12:
hi duo fundi iuncti iugerum definiunt. deinde haec duo iugera iuncta in unum quadratum agrum efficiunt, quod sint in omnes partes actus bini.

We know that 'Julius Frontinus' used Varro: see Campbell 2000.8 line 23 (*sicut Varro descripsit*), Wiseman 2015a.116–7, Gargola 2017.175–6.
Stone markers: details in Campbell 2000.452–67 (surviving examples), 468–71 (general discussion).

99   Middle republic: Livy 5.30.8 (387 BC); Valerius Maximus 4.3.5b, Columella 1.pref.14, Pliny *Natural History* 18.18 (290 and 278 BC); cf. Columella 1.3.10 (*post reges exactos*).
'Their way of life . . .': Dionysius of Halicarnassus *Roman Antiquities* 1.79.11 (βίος δ' αὐτοῖς ἦν βουκολικὸς καὶ δίαιτα αὐτουργὸς ἐν ὄρεσι τὰ πολλὰ πηξαμένοις διὰ ξύλων καὶ καλάμων σκηνὰς αὐτορόφους); perhaps from Varro, who is cited at 1.14.1, 2.21.2, 2.47.4, 2.48.4.

Romulus' choice of site: Ennius *Annales* 77 Sk (Cicero *De diuinatione* 1.107), Dionysius of Halicarnassus *Roman Antiquities* 1.85.6 and 86.2, Plutarch *Romulus* 9.4, *Origo gentis Romanae* 23.1. Summit of Palatine: Dionysius of Halicarnassus *Roman Antiquities* 14.2.2. Standard size: Varro *Res rusticae* 1.10.2. Centred on the hut: Zonaras 7.3, Tzetzes on Lycophron *Alexandra* 1232. 'Things customarily used': Festus 310–12L (Coarelli 1999.208–9).

Land surveyors: 'Julius Frontinus' (following Varro) in Campbell 2000.8 lines 23–9, Hyginus in Campbell 2000.134 lines 7–13; Wiseman 2015a.116–7.

At the balancing-point: Solinus 1.17 (*ut adfirmat Varro . . . ad aequilibrium*). In front of the residence: Josephus *Jewish Antiquities* 19.75 (μικρόν τε πρὸ τοῦ βασιλέιου).

100 Tiberius Gracchus: see especially Appian *Civil Wars* 1.11.44 ('public property should be for the benefit of all'), Florus 2.1.2 ('it is right for the *plebs* to have what is its own'), Siculus Flaccus in Campbell 2000.102 lines 29–33 ('it is a bad custom that anyone should own more than he can farm himself'). His murder as the origin of political violence at Rome: Velleius Paterculus 2.3.3, Appian *Civil Wars* 1.2.4–8.

Caesar in 59: see especially Dio Cassius 38.1.3 (encouragement of agriculture). His life under threat: Caesar *Gallic War* 1.44.12 (58 BC), Caelius in Cicero *Ad familiares* 8.14.2 (51 BC).

101 Varro on Caesar's land commission: Varro *Res rusticae* 1.2.10, Pliny *Natural History* 7.176; Caesar's instructions evidently began with the origin of land-surveying (*Demonstratio artis geometricae* 395–6 Lachmann).

Land for veterans: details and discussion in Keppie 1983.58–82; cf. Gurval 1995.58–9 on the *denarius* illustrated at Fig. 45 above. Old Gracchan and Caesarian allotments: *Liber coloniarum* in Campbell 2000.190 lines 5–11; cf. *ILLRP* 482 (Campanian boundary stones set up *iussu imp. Caesaris qua aratrum ductum est*).

On the agenda in 44 BC: Cicero *Philippics* 8.9 (houses), 11.12 (*castrorum metator*), 14.10 (measuring-pole); for the tribune, L. Decidius Saxa, see Syme 1937 = 1979.31–41. The context was probably Caesar's legislation against conspicuous consumption, which he was particularly keen to enforce (Cicero *Ad Atticum* 13.7.1).

Tightly packed together: Cicero *Pro Caelio* 69 (Q. Metellus and Q. Catulus share a party wall), *Ad Atticum* 4.3.5 (Cicero hears his neighbour snoring). Excavate basement rooms: see Daniela Bruno in Carandini 2010.113–28 (the best example is the so-called House of Livia). Buy out your neighbour: Cicero *De domo* 115 (*duas . . . domos coniungere*), Sallust *Bellum Catilinae* 20.11 (*binas aut amplius domos continuare*).

Rescuing public space: e.g., *CIL* 6.874, 40882 (*cippi* with the standard formula *Caesar August. redemptum a priuato publicauit*); cf. 6.1262 (*[imp. C]aesar Augustu[s] ex priuato in publicum restituit*).

7. COMMANDER CAESAR AND HIS GODS

103 Appian using Augustus' memoirs: *Civil Wars* 4.110.463, 5.45.191, *Illyrian Wars* 15.43 (*FRHist* 60 F 7c, 8, 9).

Appian *Civil Wars* 3.11.36–8 (Carter 1996.159):

οἱ μὲν ἔτι μᾶλλον αὐτὸν ἠξίουν τοὺς ἐχθροὺς Καίσαρος δεδιέναι, υἱόν τε αὐτοῦ καὶ κληρονόμον ὄντα, καὶ παρήνουν ἅμα τῷ κλήρῳ τὴν θέσιν ἀπείπασθαι· ὁ δὲ καὶ ταῦτά οἱ καὶ τὸ μὴ τιμωρεῖν αὐτὸν Καίσαρι αἰσχρὸν ἡγούμενος ἐς τὸ Βρεντέσιον ᾔει, προπέμψας καὶ διερευνησάμενος, μή τις ἐκ τῶν φονέων ἐγκαθέζοιτο ἐνέδρα. ὡς δὲ αὐτῷ καὶ ὁ ἐνθάδε στρατὸς οἷα Καίσαρος υἱὸν δεξιούμενος ἀπήντα, θαρρήσας ἔθυε καὶ εὐθὺς ὠνομάζετο Καῖσαρ. ἔθος γάρ τι Ῥωμαίοις τοὺς θετοὺς τὰ τῶν θεμένων ὀνόματα ἐπιλαμβάνειν. ὁ δὲ οὐκ ἐπέλαβεν, ἀλλὰ καὶ τὸ αὐτοῦ καὶ τὸ πατρῷον ὅλως ἐνήλλαξεν, ἀντὶ Ὀκταουίου παιδὸς Ὀκταουίου Καῖσαρ εἶναι καὶ Καίσαρος υἱός, καὶ διετέλεσεν οὕτω χρώμενος.

In fact, he may have been using 'Octavius Caesar' in November 43 BC, if Appian (*Civil Wars* 4.8.31) correctly translates the opening of the triumvirs' edict.

The assassins and their friends: Cicero uses the name 'Octavianus' only when writing to Brutus (*Ad M. Brutum* 5.2), Cornificius (*Ad familiares* 12.23.2, 12.25.4) or Atticus (*Ad Atticum* 15.12.2, 16.8.1, 16.9, 16.11.6, 16.14.1).

Ensure the gods' approval: unlike the elder Caesar, Augustus took omens, portents, and other signs of the divine will very seriously (Suetonius *Diuus Augustus* 90–3, contrast *Diuus Iulius* 59). Comet of July 44 BC: details in Ramsey and Licht 1997.

7.1 *Imperator Caesar*

104 Augustus *Res gestae* 1.1–2:
annos undeuiginti natus exercitum priuato consilio et priuata impensa comparaui, per quem rem publicam a dominatione factionis oppressam in libertatem uindicaui. eo [nomi]ne senatus . . . [i]mperium mihi dedit.

Loyal citizens (at *colonia Iulia Paterna Narbonis Martii*, *CIL* 12.4333.23–5): *qua die primum orbis terrarum auspicatus est.*

There were annual thanksgivings elsewhere too, for instance at Cumae (Degrassi 1963.279, *feriale Cumanum*): *[eo die Caesar] primum fasces sumpsit: supplicatio Ioui Sempi[terni].*

Imperator as a name: Suetonius *Diuus Iulius* 76.1 (*praenomen Imperatoris*), Dio Cassius 43.44.2–3 (τὸ τοῦ αὐτοκράτορος ὄνομα, applicable also to his son); Degrassi 1947.273–4 (*Fasti Colotiani* on 43 BC: *Imp. Caesar IIIuir r.p.c.*); Syme 1958a = 1979.361–77. Agrippa's coin legend: Crawford 1974.535 no. 534.3

Praetorium (Greek στρατήγιον): Polybius 6.32.8; 'Hyginus' *De munitionibus castrorum* 3–14 passim; *Roman Inscriptions of Britain* 1912, 1685–6; Johnson 1983.132–42. Used of Augustus' Palatine quarters: Dio Cassius 53.16.5; cf. Suetonius *Diuus Augustus* 72.3 (Augustus disliked 'large and sumptuous *praetoria*'), *Gaius* 37.2 (Caligula's extravagance 'in building *praetoria* and villas').

Standard rectangular plan: Polybius 6.27–32, esp. 6.31.10 (πόλει παραπλησίαν ἔχει τὴν διάθεσιν); see now Gargola 2017.178–81.

Polybius 6.26.12–27.2 (Scott-Kilvert 1979.324):
τίς γὰρ οὕτως ἐστὶν ἀπεοικὼς πρὸς τὰ καλὰ καὶ σπουδαῖα τῶν ἔργων, ὃς οὐκ ἂν βουληθείη μικρὸν ἐπιμελέστερον ἐπιστῆσαι περὶ τῶν τοιούτων, ὑπὲρ ὧν ἅπαξ ἀκούσας, ἐπιστήμων ἔσται πράγματος ἑνὸς τῶν ἀξίων λόγου καὶ γνώσεως;

ἔτι δὲ τὸ γένος αὐτῶν τῆς στρατοπεδείας τοιόνδε. τοῦ κριθέντος ἀεὶ τόπου πρὸς στρατοπεδείαν, τούτου τὸν ἐπιτηδειότατον εἰς σύνοψιν ἅμα καὶ παραγγελίαν ἡ τοῦ στρατηγοῦ σκηνὴ καταλαμβάνει. τεθείσης δὲ τῆς σημαίας, οὗ μέλλουσι πηγνύναι ταύτην, ἀπομετρεῖται πέριξ τῆς σημαίας τετράγωνος τόπος, ὥστε πάσας τὰς πλευρὰς ἑκατὸν ἀπέχειν πόδας τῆς σημαίας, τὸ δ' ἐμβαδὸν γίγνεσθαι τετράπλεθρον.

105 Two or three centuries after: see Lenoir 1979.111–44 for the probable date of 'Hyginus'. Oblong *praetorium*: dimensions given in 'Hyginus' *De munitionibus castrorum* 9.

'Hyginus' *De munitionibus castrorum* 11–12 (text as in Lenoir 1979.6):
aris institutis in formam partis imae, auguratorium parte dextra praetorii ad uiam principalem adsignabimus, ut dux in eo augurium recte capere posit; parte laeua tribunal statuitur, ut augurio accepto insuper ascendat et exercitum felici auspicio adloquatur.

in introitu praetorii partis mediae ad uiam principalem gromae locus appellatur quod turba ibi congruat siue in dictatione metationis posito in eodem loco ferramento groma superponatur, ut portae castrorum in conspectu rigoris stellam efficiant. et professores eius artis causa supra scripta gromatici sunt cognominati.

For a detailed description of the *groma* see Dilke 1971.66–70.

Another professional text: 'Hyginus' *Constitutio <limitum>* in Campbell 2000.136 lines 19–20 (*posita auspicaliter groma, ipso forte conditore praesente*). Verrius Flaccus: as the source of Festus 310–12L.

Regionary gazetteer: Valentini and Zucchetti 1940.128–32 (*Curiosum*), 177–8 (*Notitia*).

Dio Cassius 55.33.3:
καὶ ἐπειδὴ καὶ τῷ γήρᾳ καὶ τῇ τοῦ σώματος ἀσθενείᾳ ἔκαμνεν . . . αὐτὸς μετὰ τῶν συνέδρων καὶ διεσκόπει καὶ ἐδίκαζεν, ἐν τῷ Παλατίῳ ἐπὶ βήματος προκαθήμενος.

106 Ovid *Metamorphoses* 14.820–4:
impauidus conscendit equos Gradiuus et ictu | uerberis increpuit pronusque per aera lapsus | constitit in summo nemorosi colle Palati, | reddentemque suo non regia iura Quiriti | abstulit Iliaden.

Every other version: Ovid *Fasti* 2.491–2, Plutarch *Romulus* 27.6, *Camillus* 23.7 (addressing the People); Livy 1.16.1, Florus 1.1.17, *De uiris illustribus* 2.11 (conducting an army census); Plutarch *Numa* 2.1

(conducting a public sacrifice); Solinus 1.20. The revisionist account of his disappearance had him addressing the senators 'in the temple of Vulcan' (i.e., at the Volcanal) or 'in the Senate-house': Plutarch *Romulus* 27.5, Dionysius of Halicarnassus *Roman Antiquities* 2.56.4, Appian *Civil Wars* 2.114.476–7 (a precedent for the murder of Caesar).

107 Horace *Carmen saeculare* 61–5:

augur et fulgente decorus arcu | Phoebus acceptusque nouem Camenis, | qui salutari leuat arte fessos | corporis artus, | si Palatinas uidet aequus aras.

See Thomas 2011.82 on *Palatinas . . . aras* at line 65, where some manuscripts have *arces*. 3 June 17 BC: *CIL* 6.32323.139–49 (Thomas 2011.276). One of the 'Palatine altars' formed part of the temporary theatre in January AD 41 (Josephus *Jewish Antiquities* 19.87 and 142).

7.2 Apollo and the Sibyl

108 Varro's 16 books of *Antiquitates diuinae*: Augustine *City of God* 6.3.1. Dedicated to Caesar as *pontifex maximus*: Lactantius *Divine Institutions* 1.6.7, Augustine *City of God* 7.35.2; see Horsfall 1972.120–2 for the date and context. Chance of a new start: Cicero *Pro Marcello* 23–9, [Sallust] *Epistulae ad Caesarem* 1.5–7.

Avarice and extravagance: Sallust *Bellum Catilinae* 10.4 (*auaritia . . . deos neglegere, omnia uenalia habere edocuit*), 12.2 (*diuina atque humana promiscua*); [Sallust] *Epistulae ad Caesarem* 1.5.4 (*sumptuum et rapinarum licentiam*), 1.7.3 (*pecuniae . . . usum atque decus*). His misguided fellow-citizens: Varro *Divine Antiquities* fr. 2a Cardauns (Augustine *City of God* 6.2.5).

Plague or pestilence: Varro *De uita populi Romani* frr. 65, 117 Pittà (*aegrotare, gangraenam sanguinolentam*); cf. Sallust *Bellum Catilinae* 10.6 (*quasi pestilentia*), 36.5 (*uis morbi . . . uti tabes*), *Historiae* 4.46M (*ut tabes*).

Divine remedy: Varro *Divine Antiquities* fr. 56 Cardauns = Servius on Virgil *Aeneid* 6.72 (*libros in quibus erant fata et remedia Romana*), fr. 60 Cardauns = Dionysius of Halicarnassus *Roman Antiquities* 4.62.5 (στάσεως καταλαμβανούσης τὴν πόλιν); for the Sibyl's *remedia* cf. Livy 10.47.6, Pliny *Natural History* 7.105, Augustine *City of God* 3.17.2.

Sibylline books: details in Orlin 1997.76–97. Consulted in time of plague: Livy 4.25.3, 7.27.1, 10.31.8, 10.47.6, 40.37.1–2, 41.21.10, Obsequens 13; see Orlin 1997.203–7 for a full list of consultations. Varro on Sibyls and the origin of the books: *Divine Antiquities* frr. 56–9 Cardauns (Lactantius *Divine Institutions* 1.6.7–12, Servius on Virgil *Aeneid* 3.444–5, 6.36, Dionysius of Halicarnassus *Roman Antiquities* 4.62).

249 BC: Cicero *De natura deorum* 2.7, *De diuinatione* 1.29, 2.71 (two fleets lost by sailing *contra auspicia*); Augustine *City of God* 3.17.2 (*magno metu perturbata . . . ciuitas*); Varro fr. 70 Funaioli = Censorinus *De die natali* 17.8 (*utique ludi centesimo quoque anno fierent*).

149 BC: Varro cited in Censorinus *De die natali* 17.11 (also Valerius Antias *FRHist* 25 F64, Livy *Epitome* 49). In fact those games were held in 146 BC, as attested by the contemporary historians Cassius Hemina, L. Piso, and Cn. Gellius (*FRHist* 6 F40, 9 F41, 14 F30); the 149 BC date probably originated in Valerius Antias' revisionist history, which evidently attributed the games to P. Valerius Publicola in the first year of the republic and other Valerii thereafter (Censorinus *De die natali* 17.10, with Wiseman 1998.82–3 and 65–7).

Reponse made public: cf. Caesar's insistence on publication of the Senate's proceedings (Suetonius *Diuus Iulius* 20.1, *primus omnium instituit*).

Phlegon of Tralles *FGrH* 257 F 37.5.4 lines 1–7 (= Zosimus 2.6.1–7):

ἀλλ' ὁπότ' ἂν μήκιστος ἴῃ χρόνος ἀνθρώποισιν | ζωῆς, εἰς ἐτέων ἑκατὸν δέκα κύκλον ὁδεύσας, | μεμνῆσθαι, Ῥωμαῖε, καὶ εἰ μάλα λήσει ἑαυτόν, | μεμνῆσθαι τάδε πάντα, θεοῖσι μὲν ἀθανάτοισι | ῥέζειν ἐν πεδίῳ παρὰ Θύβριδος ἄπλετον ὕδωρ, | ὅππῃ στεινότατον, νὺξ ἡνίκα γαῖαν ἐπέλθῃ | ἠελίου κρύψαντος ἑὸν φάος·

The divinities are specified in lines 7–18.

It is usually assumed (e.g., Hansen 1996.187, Thomas 2011.56, Wiseman 2015b.153) that the response was created for the Secular Games of 17 BC; but the differences of detail between what it prescribes and what happened then (Thomas 2011.56–7), above all the absence of Diana, makes that unlikely.

Star of Caesar: Virgil *Eclogues* 9.47 (*Caesaris astrum*), Horace *Odes* 1.12.47 (*Iulium sidus*), Virgil *Aeneid* 8.681, Propertius 4.6.59, Ovid *Metamorphoses* 14.845–50. Encouraged his son: Augustus *FRHist* 60 F2 (Servius on Virgil *Eclogues* 9.46–7).

New era (the tenth *saeculum*): Servius on Virgil *Eclogues* 4.4 ([*Sibylla*] *dixit etiam quis quo saeculo imperaret, et Solem ultimum, id est decimum, uoluit*) and 4.10 (*ultimum saeculum ostendit, quod Sibylla Solis esse memorauit*); Servius quotes Nigidius Figulus' *De diis* (fr. lxvii Swoboda) for the *Apollinis regnum*.

109   Virgil *Eclogues* 4.4–12:

ultima Cumaei uenit iam carminis aetas; | *magnus ab integro saeclorum nascitur ordo.* | *iam redit et uirgo, redeunt Saturnia regna,* | *iam noua progenies caelo demittitur alto.* | *tu modo nascenti puero, quo ferrea primum* | *desinet ac toto surget gens aurea mundo,* | *casta faue Lucina: tuus iam regnat Apollo.* | *teque adeo decus hoc aeui, te consule, inibit,* | *Pollio . . .*

For the historical context of *Eclogue* 4, see above all Du Quesnay 1977.26–43 and Powell 2008.207–16. Lucina as Diana: Catullus 34.13–14, Cicero *De natura deorum* 2.68; cf. Horace *Odes* 3.22.1–2. Moon to his sun: Varro *Divine Antiquities* frr. 251, 276 Cardauns (Augustine *City of God* 7.16.1); cf. Catullus 34.15–16, Cicero *De natura deorum* 2.68.

Four years after: the Sicilian war was won on 3 September 36 BC (Degrassi 1963.32–3, 192-3: *Fasti fratrum Arualium* and *Amiternini*). Enemy too contemptible: Augustus *Res gestae* 25.1 ('pirates'), cf. Aulus Gellius 5.6.21 (*hostium nomen humile et non idoneum*). *Ouatio*: Augustus *Res gestae* 4.1, Suetonius *Diuus Augustus* 22.1; cf. Dionysius of Halicarnassus *Roman Antiquities* 5.47.2–3, 8.67.10, Plutarch *Marcellus* 22.1–2 (*ouatio* as 'lesser triumph').

13 November: Degrassi 1947.86–7 (*Fasti Capitolini*), 342–3 (*Fasti Barberiniani*). Escorted him to the house: Appian *Civil Wars* 5.130.538 (ἐς τὴν οἰκίαν . . . παρέπεμπον). Chose to honour: cf. Suetonius *Diuus Augustus* 70.1–2 (impersonating Apollo, c. 39–37 BC); Suetonius *Diuus Augustus* 94.4, Dio Cassius 45.1.2 ('son of Apollo').

Velleius Paterculus 2.81.3:

uictor deinde Caesar reuersus in urbem contractas emptionibus complures domos per procuratores, quo laxior fieret ipsius, publicis se usibus destinare professus est templumque Apollinis et circa porticus facturum promisit, quod ab eo singulari exstructum munificentia est.

Area Apollinis: Solinus 1.18, *Année Épigraphique* 1972.174.9–10, *CIL* 6.32327.23, *Forma urbis Romae* frr. 468–9.

Elder Caesar's programme: Cicero *Ad Atticum* 13.27.1, 13.31.3 (Parthia); Strabo 7.3.5 C298, 7.3.11 C304 (Danube); Velleius Paterculus 2.59.4, Suetonius *Diuus Iulius* 44.3, *Diuus Augustus* 8.2, Appian *Civil Wars* 3.25.93 (Dacians and Parthians).

Conspicuous symmetry: Tortorella 2013.227, Tomei 2014d.152, Pensabene 2017.2.138–9. The full catalogue of the 'Campana' plaques is Pensabene 2017.2.113–385; for the provenance and date (before 36 BC) of the 'Apollo and Hercules' examples, see Pensabene 2017.2.53, 118–9, 133–4, 138–9.

Octavia: Plutarch *Antonius* 31.1–2 (χρῆμα θαυμαστόν, ὡς λέγεται, γυναικὸς . . . ἐπὶ κάλλει τοσούτῳ σεμνότητα καὶ ωοῦν ἔχουσαν), 54.1–2 (ᾤκει τὴν οἰκίαν . . . καλῶς καὶ μεγαλοπρεπῶς). Patrician: Suetonius *Diuus Augustus* 2.1, Dio Cassius 45.2.7.

Died in his forties: Cicero *Philippics* 3.15, Suetonius *Diuus Augustus* 3.

110   Pliny *Natural History* 36.36:

ex honore apparet in magna auctoritate habitum Lysiae opus quod in Palatio super arcum diuus Augustus honori Octaui patris sui dicauit in aedicula columnis adornata, id est quadriga currusque et Apollo ac Diana ex uno lapide.

It is obvious from Pliny's language that the work no longer existed in his time; the identification of surviving blocks as part of the arch, and the consequent dating of it to c. 25 BC (Tomei 2000, Carandini and Bruno 2008. 62–3 and 185–8, Carandini and Carafa 2017 table 71), is therefore erroneous (Coarelli 2012.491). It is easy to guess why Nero's architects did not restore the arch after the fire of AD 64: it was a reminder of his late empress Octavia, divorced and executed two years earlier.

111   Divorce: Livy *Epitome* 132, Plutarch *Antonius* 57.2–3, Dio Cassius 50.3.2. Actium, 2 September 31 BC: Degrassi 1963.32–3, 192–3 (*Fasti Arualium* and *Amiternini*). Alexandria, 1 August 30 BC: Degrassi 1963.208 (*Fasti Antiates ministrorum*). Brought under the control of the Roman People (*in potestatem* *populi Romani redacta*): *CIL* 6.701–2, Macrobius *Saturnalia* 1.12.35 (senatorial decree, 8 BC), Degrassi 1963.134–5 (*Fasti Praenestini*).

Epochal date: e.g., Velleius Paterculus 2.86.1, Tacitus *Histories* 1.1.2, Dio Cassius 51.1.1–2, *De uiris illustribus* 79.3.

Actium temple: Strabo 7.7.6 C325, Suetonius *Diuus Augustus* 18.2, Dio Cassius 51.1.2. The poets: Virgil *Aeneid* 8.704–6; Propertius 2.34.61–2, 3.11.69–70, 4.6.27–58; Miller 2009.54–94. Actian Apollo: Virgil *Aeneid* 8.704, Propertius 4.6.67, *Elegiae in Maecenatem* 1.51, Ovid *Metamorphoses* 13.715; cf. Propertius 4.1.3 (*naualis*).

Rome at peace: the 'gate of Janus' was closed on 11 January 29 BC (*Fasti Praenestini*, Degrassi 1963.112–13; cf. Virgil *Aeneid* 1.293–6, Augustus *Res gestae* 13). Invasion plans: Livy *Epitome* 132, Velleius Paterculus 2.82.4, Florus 2.21.1–3, Dio Cassius 50.3.2; the end of the war 'saved the *res publica* from a most dreadful danger' (*Fasti fratrum Arualium* and *Amiternini*, Degrassi 1963.30–1 and 190–1).

Cassius of Parma: Appian *Civil Wars* 5.2.4–9, 5.139.579 (Brutus, Sextus Pompey); Valerius Maximus 1.7.7 (after Actium), cf. Velleius Paterculus 2.87.3, Orosius 6.19.20 (30 BC). In the name of the Roman People: by the law of 43 BC and the subsequent trial and condemnation of the assassins in absence (Augustus *Res gestae* 2.1, Appian *Civil Wars* 3.95.392–3, Dio Cassius 46.48.2–3).

Officially at an end: Macrobius *Saturnalia* 1.12.35, quoting a *senatus consultum* of 8 BC (*finisque hoc mense* [August 30 BC] *bellis ciuilibus impositus*); cf. Velleius Paterculus 2.87.1 (*ultimam bellis ciuilibus imposuit manum*, 30 BC).

Sibylline books destroyed and replaced: Varro *Divine Antiquities* frr. 56, 60 Cardauns, Fenestella *FRHist* 70 F19 (Lactantius *Divine Institutions* 1.6.11–14, Dionysius of Halicarnassus *Roman Antiquities* 4.62.6); Tacitus *Annals* 6.12.3.

Senior member: *CIL* 6.32323.150. Review: Suetonius *Diuus Augustus* 31.1. Placed in the Apollo temple: Tibullus 2.5.11–18; cf. Suetonius *Diuus Augustus* 31.1 (erroneously dated after 12 BC).

Historical commentary: Censorinus *De die natali* 17.10–11; Wiseman 1998.165–6.

112   Three triumphs: Degrassi 1947.344–5 (*Fasti Barberiniani*), Livy *Epitome* 133, Macrobius *Saturnalia* 1.12.35 (*senatus consultum* of 8 BC). Temples: Augustus *Res gestae* 20.4; cf. Livy 4.20.7, Ovid *Fasti* 2.59–66, Dio Cassius 53.2.4–5. Quadrennial games: Dio Cassius 51.19.2, 53.1.3–6.

Apollo temple (Miller 2009.185–252): Degrassi 1963.36–7, 194–5, 209 (*Fasti fratrum Arualium, Amiternini* and *Antiates*); Propertius 2.31.1–16, Ovid *Tristia* 3.1.59–64, Velleius Paterculus 2.81.3, Asconius 90C, Josephus *Jewish War* 2.81, *Jewish Antiquities* 17.301, Suetonius *Diuus Augustus* 29.3, Dio Cassius 49.15.5, 53.1.3.

Virgil *Aeneid* 8.714–23:

at Caesar, triplici inuectus Romana triumpho | moenia, dis Italis uotum immortale sacrabat, | maxima ter centum totam delubra per urbem. | laetitia ludisque uiae plausuque fremebant; | omnibus in templis matrum chorus, omnibus arae; | ante aras terram caesi strauere iuuenci. | ipse sedens niueo candentis limine Phoebi | dona recognoscit populorum aptatque superbis | postibus; incedunt uictae longo ordine gentes | quam uariae linguis, habitu tam uestis et armis.

Paraded on wagons: Plutarch *Aemilius Paullus* 32.5–8, Appian *Punic Wars* 66 (ἅμαξαι); cf. Livy 26.21.7–8, 34.52.4–8, Plutarch *Titus Flamininus* 14.1.

7.3 Apollo's Mother and Sister

Series of coin issues: Sutherland 1984.59–61; good discussion in Gurval 1995.47–65, emphasising the uncertainty of exact dating. Cash grants: Augustus *Res gestae* 15.1 (*ex bellorum manibiis*), 15.3 (*ex manibiis*); the regular pay of a legionary soldier was the equivalent of 225 *sesterces* per year (Tacitus *Annals* 1.17.4). Altar and statue of Victoria: Degrassi 1963.79, 174–5 (*Fasti Maffeiani* and *Vaticani*), Suetonius *Diuus Augustus* 100.2 (*Victoria quae est in curia*), Dio Cassius 51.22.1–2 (Αἰγυπτίοις λαφύροις ἐκοσμήθη).

113   Temple of Victoria: Dionysius of Halicarnassus *Roman Antiquities* 1.32.5 (Arcadians), Livy 10.33.9 (L. Postumius Megellus). Diana Noctiluca: Varro *De lingua Latina* 5.68, Horace *Odes* 4.6.38; cf. Varro *Menippean Satires* 292 Astbury = Nonius 348L (*noctiluca* evidently meaning 'lighted torch'), *De lingua Latina* 6.79. New iconographic context (the so-called *Kitharödenreliefs*): Simon 1984.412–3, Berger-Doer 1992.269–70.

114 Apollo's long robe: full iconographic analysis in Roccos 1989. Victory ode: Tibullus 2.5.9–10 (for Jupiter Victor), cf. Seneca *Agamemnon* 338–41. Famous portico: *CIL* 6.32323.31–2 (17 BC), Augustus *Res gestae* 19.1, Ovid *Tristia* 3.1.61–2, Crawford 1996.518.19–20 and 519.1 (AD 19), *Année Épigraphique* 1978.145.1–2 (AD 19), Velleius Paterculus 2.81.3, Suetonius *Diuus Augustus* 29.3.

115 Propertius 2.31 (28 BC):

quaeris cur ueniam tibi tardior? aurea Phoebi | porticus a magno Caesare aperta fuit. | tota erat in spatium Poenis digesta columnis, | inter quas Danai femina turba senis. | hic equidem Phoebus uisus mihi pulchrior ipso | marmoreus tacita carmen hiare lyra; | atque aram circum steterant armenta Myronis | quattuor artifices, uiuida signa, boues. | tum medium claro surgebat marmore templum, | et patria Phoebo carius Ortygia: | in quo Solis erat supra fastigia currus, | et ualuae, Libyci nobile dentis opus; | altera deiectos Parnasi uertice Gallos, | altera maerebat funera Tantalidos. | deinde inter matrem deus ipse interque sororem | Pythius in longa carmina ueste sonat.

Propertius' reference to Delos (*Ortygia*, line 10) is particularly significant:

(*a*) It seems likely that the archaic Greek sculpture that was set into the pediment of the Palatine temple (Pliny *Natural History* 36.13) was brought from Delos itself (Coarelli 2016.84–96); cf. also Coarelli 2016.109–11 for the possibility that the cult statues of Latona, Diana, and Apollo (Pliny *Nat. Hist.* 36.24. 36.25 and 36.32) are to be identified with the τρία ἀγάλματα τὰ ἐν τῷ Πυθίῳ mentioned in a Delian inscription of the third century BC (*Inscr. de Délos* 290.7.229).

(*b*) The sacred island, with its hill, Mount Cynthus, was where Leto (Latona) gave birth to Artemis (Diana) and Apollo (Strabo 10.5.2 C485), a mythic analogy for the young Caesar, his mother Atia, and his sister Octavia; for Virgil (*Georgics* 3.6) *Latonia Delos* was a well-known poetic theme.

(*c*) It was precisely in the thirties and twenties BC that Roman poets began describing Apollo and Diana as *Delius* and *Delia* (Virgil *Eclogues* 3.67, 7.29, *Aeneid* 3.162, 6.12, Horace *Odes* 3.4.64) or *Cynthius* and *Cynthia* (Virgil *Eclogues* 6.3, *Georgics* 3.36, Horace *Odes* 1.21.2, 3.28.12).

(*d*) In Virgil's *Aeneid* (3.73–101), Delos is where Aeneas and his refugees from Troy receive their first friendly welcome and their first (though riddling) divine guidance; cf. also *Aeneid* 1.498–502 (Dido like Diana at Delos with Latona), 4.143–9 (Aeneas like Apollo visiting *Delum maternam*).

Gallic attack: Pausanias 10.23.1–10, Justin 24.6–8. Ruthless punishment: Homer *Iliad* 24.602–17, Ovid *Metamorphoses* 6.146–313; cf. Horace *Odes* 3.28.12, 4.6.1–2. Cassius of Parma: Velleius Paterculus 2.87.3, Valerius Maximus 1.7.7 (executed in 31 BC); Suetonius *Diuus Augustus* 4.2 (offensive reference to Atia).

116 Prominence of Apollo's mother Latona: Pliny *Natural History* 36.24 (*Latona in Palatii delubro* by Praxiteles' son Cephisodotus, late fourth century BC); cf. Horace *Odes* 1.21.3–4, 1.31.18, 3.28.11–12, 4.6.37, Virgil *Aeneid* 12.198.

Part of an epic story: see Miller 2009.133–49 for full discussion and analysis.

117 Virgil *Aeneid* 6.9–12:

at pius Aeneas arces quibus altus Apollo | praesidet horrendaeque procul secreta Sibyllae, | antrum immane, petit, magnam cui mentem animumque | Delius inspirat uates aperitque futura.

Triuia: Virgil *Aeneid* 6.13 (*Triuiae lucos atque aurea tecta*). Roman name for Diana (Artemis): e.g., Lucretius 1.84, Propertius 2.32.10, Virgil *Aeneid* 7.516, 774. Childbirth and moon: Ennius fr. 191 Jocelyn (Varro *De lingua Latina* 7.16), Catullus 34.13–16, 66.5.

Aeneas meets the Sibyl: Virgil *Aeneid* 6.35 (*Phoebi Triuiaeque sacerdos*). Temple and cave: Austin 1977.48–58. Overcome by the god: Virgil *Aeneid* 6.45–51, cf. 77–82.

Virgil *Aeneid* 6.69–74:

tum Phoebo et Triuiae solido de marmore templum | instituam festosque dies de nomine Phoebi. | te quoque magna manent regnis penetralia nostris: | hic ego namque tuas sortis arcanaque fata | dicta meae genti ponam, lectosque sacrabo, | alma, uiros.

Writing in the twenties: Vitruvius' preface is dedicated to Imperator Caesar, therefore before 16 January 27 BC (contrast *Augusti* at 5.1.7); book 3 predates the construction of the *porticus Octauiae* in 23 BC (Vitruvius 3.2.5, *in porticu Metelli*); Wiseman 2014b.328.

Vitruvius *De architectura* 3.3.4:

diastyli autem haec erit conpositio, cum trium columnarum crassitudinem intercolumnio interponere possumus, tamquam est Apollinis et Dianae aedis.

Confirmed tetrastyle: Claridge 2014.136–43, Wiseman 2014b.327–31.

Gift adjusted: Wiseman 2014b.330–1; cf. Sutherland 1984.52–5, nos. 170–3, 175, 179–83, 190–7 (gold and silver issues of 15–10 BC).

118   Prima Porta statue: see for instance Hölscher 1988.386–7, Zanker 1988.186–92. Apollo as the Sun: Phlegon of Tralles *FGrH* 257 F 37.5.4 lines 16–18. Diana as Noctiluca: Horace *Odes* 4.6.38–40.

Quindecimuiri: Censorinus *De die natali* 17.10–11. Second period of *imperium*: Dio Cassius 53.16.2, 54.12.4–5 (five years in the first instance); cf. Horace *Carmen saeculare* 67 (*alterum in lustrum*). 3 June 17 BC: *CIL* 6.32323.139–49 (*eisdem uerbis Dianam*, 146).

120   Hymn to Apollo: Horace *Odes* 4.6.1–2 (Niobe), 23–4 (*potiore ductos alite muros*).

Horace *Odes* 4.6.29–40:

spiritum Phoebum mihi, Phoebus artem | carminis nomenque dedit poetae. | uirginum primae puerique claris | patribus orti, || Deliae tutela deae, fugacis | lyncas et ceruos cohibentis arcu, | Lesbium seruate pedem meique | pollicis ictum, || rite Latonae puerum canentes, | rite crescentem face Noctilucam | prosperam frugum celeremque pronos | uoluere menses.

One day: Horace *Odes* 4.6.41–4.

Structured in nineteen stanzas: details in Thomas 2011.60–1.

Horace *Carmen saeculare* 1–12:

Phoebe siluarumque potens Diana, | lucidum caeli decus, o colendi | semper et culti, date quae precamur | tempore sacro, || quo Sibyllini monuere uersus | uirgines lectas puerosque castos | dis quibus septem placuere colles | dicere carmen. || alme Sol, curru nitido diem qui | promis et celas aliusque et idem | nasceris, possis nihil urbe Roma | uisere maius!

Chariot on the pediment: Propertius 2.31.11.

Horace *Carmen saeculare* 33–6:

condito mitis placidusque telo | supplices audi pueros, Apollo; | siderum regina bicornis, audi, | Luna, puellas.

If Rome is your business: Horace *Carmen saeculare* 37 (*Roma si uestrum est opus*).

121   Horace *Carmen saeculare* 61–76:

augur et fulgente decorus arcu | Phoebus acceptusque nouem Camenis, | qui salutari leuat arte fessos | corporis artus, || si Palatinas uidet aequus aras, | remque Romanam Latiumque felix | alterum in lustrum meliusque semper | prorogat aeuum, || quaeque Auentinum tenet Algidumque, | quindecim Diana preces uirorum | curat et uotis puerorum amicas | applicat aures, || haec Iouem sentire deosque cunctos | spem bonam certamque domum reporto | doctus et Phoebi chorus et Dianae | dicere laudes.

As an augur: cf. Horace *Odes* 1.2.32, Virgil *Aeneid* 4.376 (*augur Apollo*); Tibullus 2.5.11 (*tibi deditus augur*). Golden Age: Virgil *Aeneid* 6.791–2 (*aurea . . . saecula*), Seneca *Controuersiae* 2.7.7 (*aureo, quod aiunt, saeculo*). 18 BC legislation: *CIL* 6.32323.57, Horace *Carmen saeculare* 17–20, Suetonius *Diuus Augustus* 34.1, Dio Cassius 54.16.1–2; Galinsky 1981. Family life exemplary: e.g., Suetonius *Diuus Augustus* 73, Dio Cassius 54.16.3–5, Macrobius *Saturnalia* 2.5.3–6.

Daughters by Antony: Plutarch *Antonius* 33.3 (elder born 39 BC), 35.2 (younger born 36 BC), 87.3–4 (grandsons).

8. THE TEMPLE AND THE PORTICO

122   Eye-witness accounts: Propertius 2.31.9 (*medium claro surgebat marmore templum*); Horace *Carmen saeculare* 11–12 (*urbs Roma*), 65 (*Palatinas aras*); Virgil *Aeneid* 8.720 (*niueo . . . limine*).

Universal assumption: see most recently Carandini 2014.17–19, 166–71 (D. Bruno); Carandini and Carafa 2017 ill.10–11, tables 70–2.

8.1 The Rosa Fallacy

No gift for writing: Tomei 1999.xxvi on his poor spelling and grammar. One short report: Rosa 1865.359–64; cf. Tomei 1999.141–56.

Three ancient texts: Livy 10.29.12–14, Ovid *Fasti* 4.621–2, *Notitia* (Valentini and Zucchetti 1940.177–8). Rosa believed: 'a quella mancanza credo di aver potuto supplire colle investigazioni topografiche da me dirette' (1865.360).

123 Rosa was sure: 'La fronte . . . era rivolta al mezzo giorno, ossia verso il Circo Massimo ed al monte Aventino' (1865.363). He made the same assumption, rightly in this case, about the building he identified as the *Auguratorium* (in fact the temple of Magna Mater).

Temples of the republican period: Rosa 1865.363 ('le sue disposizioni rassomigliano a quelle usate in alcuni dei principali templi tuttora visibili nell'antico Lazio, come p.e. a quelle del tempio di Ercole vincitore a Tibur, oppure di quello di Castore e Polluce a Tusculum'), repeated in Burn 1871.178 (cf. viii for Burn's direct information from Rosa); Tomei 1999.141, quoting Rosa's notes ('nelle disposizioni approssimative a quelle del tempio di Ercole Vincitore a Tivoli, di Castore e Polluce a Tuscolo e della Fortuna Prenestina'). The argument is still used by Iacopi and Tedone 2006.370 n. 43.

Rosa 1865.363: 'Come a questi tempj, così salivasi al nostro tempio palatino col mezzo di imponenti rampe di scale simmetricamente disposte ed alternate a terrazze o ripiani, parimente simmetrici, dalla via che alle radici del Palatino percorreva gli edificj contigui a quelli di questo lato del Circo massimo.'

So too in Rosa's manuscript notes: 'il tempio si vede situato nell'alto, ed accessibile col mezzo di alternate e simmetriche rampe di scale, con successive ed intermedi ripiani' (Tomei 1999.141 = 152); 'con un sistema di variati ripiani i quali, sostenendo il tempio nell'alto, erano accessibili con vaste e simmetriche scale, in modo che in questo del Palatino, dal livello della valle del Circo Massimo, montavano al pronao del tempio, situato nell'alto del Palatino, elevando con tali disposizioni il tempio al di sopra del med.ma valle m.30, fino al piano della cella tuttora visibile' (Tomei 1999.153).

See Royo 1985.348 fig. 170 for a reconstruction of Rosa's idea by the French architect Henri-Adolphe Deglane in 1887.

124 Rosa 1865.363: 'Di quei ripiani si vede oggi conservato in gran parte quello maggiore che potrebbe ritenersi per l'area sacra intorno al tempio, mentre questo elevandosi molto dal piano ridetto contiene ancora, sebbene informi, i resti delle scale, le quali per mezzo d'un altro più elevato ripiano vengono divise in due grandi rampe.'

Cf. also Tomei 1999.152–3 (extracts from Rosa's notes). The 'sacred precinct around the temple' is attested at Dio Cassius 53.1.3 (τὸ τεμένισμα τὸ περὶ αὐτό). For the 'remains of steps' see Claridge 2014.134 ('the product of natural or man-made erosion').

Tuff blocks of *opus quadratum*: Rosa 1865.363–4, referring back to 361, where he used this type of construction as evidence for a mid-republican date.

Rosa 1865.364: '. . . e le sostruzioni che nella pendice del Palatino sostengono la grande piazza, sono costruite parimenti con simile materiale in reticolato incerto.'

Different types of construction: see Coarelli 2007.536–8 for a convenient summary.

No longer intelligible: Tomei 1999.144 n.49 ('La situazione descritta da Rosa non è più verificabile, dopo che gli scavi del complesso augusteo . . . hanno cambiato profondamente l'aspetto della zona'). For the detail of Carettoni's excavations at this point, see Tomei 2014b.193–291; they revealed among other things 'i pesanti interventi di restauro e di ricostruzione realizzati da Rosa' (Tomei 2014b.202, cf. 204–5, 217, 219, 223).

Rough notes and draft letters: quoted in Tomei 1999.152 ('I molteplici differenti livelli di questi ripiani a terrazze . . . rendono impossibile lo stabilire la completa topografia'), 153 ('La parte inferiore di queste grandi scale è quasi tutto sparita').

The 'great piazza': Tomei 1999.152, from Rosa's notes ('il grande ripiano riferibile alla vasta area sacra situata avanti al tempio . . . Da questa grande piazza una prima vasta scalinata . . .').

Soon refuted: Pinza 1910, cf. Claridge 2014.128–9; for the doorpost fragment, see Carettoni 1966–7.71, Zanker 1988.87–8, Gros 2003.64–5.

125 Axiomatic truth: e.g., Platner and Ashby 1929.18 ('What remains of the temple is a podium of concrete of the Augustan period, with a long flight of steps, facing south-west').

Four deep holes: Lugli 1965.276, cf. Claridge 2014.134–5. Contemporary evidence: Vitruvius 3.3.5; Claridge 2014.138–40. Referring to some other temple: e.g., Castagnoli 1951–2.54, Zink 2012.402; but no other temple is available (Wiseman 2014b.327–30).

126 Ventured to suggest: Claridge 1998.131, 2010.142; followed by Wiseman 2012a. Overlooked her brief allusion: the full argument is in Claridge 2014, cf. 2018.123.

127 Tries to find its way: Ovid *Tristia* 3.1.27–32 (Forum to Palatine), 33–58 (Augustus' house).

128 Ovid *Tristia* 3.1.59–62:

inde tenore pari gradibus sublimia celsis | ducor ad intonsi candida templa dei, | signa peregrinis ubi sunt alterna columnis,| Belides et stricto barbarus ense pater.

8.2 Making Space

Numidian columns (Ward Perkins 1951.96–7): Propertius 2.31.3 (*Poenis . . . columnis*). Status symbol: Horace *Odes* 2.18.4–5 (*columnas ultima recisas | Africa*), cf. 3.1.45 (*inuidendis postibus*); Pliny *Natural History* 36.48–9 (citing Cornelius Nepos).

Precinct around the temple: Dio Cassius 53.1.3 (τὸ τεμένισμα τὸ περὶ αὐτό); cf. Velleius Paterculus 1.81.3 (*templum Apollinis et circa porticus*), Propertius 2.31.9 (*medium . . . templum*). Subterranean buttress: Claridge 2014.132 (C at 149 figs. 4 and 5 = our Figs. 7 and 60).

Tiles stamped (cf. *CIL* 15.2232–4): Pensabene and Gallocchio 2013, Claridge 2014.143, Pensabene 2017.2.64–7; Rosa had misdated them to the Claudian period (Tomei 1999.154).

Priestly college: 'potrebbe giudicarsi riferibile ad una Schola, per uso di uno di quei Collegi menzionatici sul Palatino, e spettante all'uso di esso tempio' (Tomei 1999.159, from Rosa's notes). Cf. Lanciani 1888.106–7, plan no. 36: 'remains of a building not yet identified.'

129   Wall-paintings: details in Tomei 1999.376–411. Attributed to various owners: e.g., Claudius Nero, Livia's first husband (Rosa, in Tomei 1999.420), or Germanicus (Lanciani 1888.106–7, plan no. 34), or Hortensius and then Augustus (Platner and Ashby 1929.156, Lugli 1970.167–8), or Catulus and then Augustus (Carandini 2010.120–8, Carandini and Carafa 2017 table 68); for the supposed evidence, see respectively Suetonius *Tiberius* 5, Josephus *Jewish Antiquities* 19.117, Suetonius *Diuus Augustus* 72.1, Suetonius *De grammaticis* 17.2.

Water-pipe: *CIL* 15.7264; details in Tomei 1999.424–8. Livia's adoption: Tacitus *Annals* 1.8.1.

Carettoni's excavations: Tomei 2014b.58. Elaborate reconstruction: Carandini 2014.369–73, Carandini and Carafa 2017 tables 69–72.

130   Demolished in the thirties BC: 'Carettoni's excavations in and around the house in 1949–53 . . . indicated that its drains went out of operation in the 40s or 30s BC, that is, as the temple was being built' (Claridge 2014.131).

Kerb-stones: see for instance Tomei 2014b.55 fig. 36. Plaque find-spot: Tomei 1999.438 (in the house), 440 (debris in the street), both from Rosa's letter of 24 November 1869 to Léon Renier, his opposite number in Paris.

131   Terracotta plaque: von Rohden and Winnefeld 1911.262; Tortorella 2000.251; Paris, Bruni, and Roghi 2014.100–1; Pensabene 2017.2.290–1. Lupercalia: see in general Wiseman 1995.77–88, 2008.52–83; Tortorella 2000; North 2008, North and McLynn 2008.

Greek authors: Dionysius of Halicarnassus *Roman Antiquities* 1.80.1 (γυμνοὺς ὑπεζωσμένους τὴν αἰδῶ ταῖς δοραῖς τῶν νεοθύτων), Nicolaus of Damascus *FGrH* 90 F130.21.71 (γυμνοί, ἀληλιμμένοι τε καὶ διεζωσμένοι), Plutarch *Romulus* 21.5 (ἐν περιζώμασι γυμνοί). Aetiological account: Ovid *Fasti* 2.267–452, 5.101 (*cinctuti*); cf. Valerius Maximus 2.2.9 (*cincti*).

Ran completely naked: Justin 43.1.7 (also for the goatskin cape), as illustrated on a mirror of the fourth century BC (Wiseman 1995.65–71, 2004a.79–80 and 114–5, North 2008.148–9). Smeared with mud, masked: Lactantius *Divine Institutions* 1.21.46 (*qui nudi uncti coronati aut personati aut luto obliti currunt*), probably based on Varro, Gavius Bassus, or Sextus Clodius, late-republican sources cited at 1.22.9–11 on the god Faunus. Flouting civilised conventions: Cicero *Pro Caelio* 26 (*fera quaedam sodalitas . . . ante est instituta quam humanitas et leges*).

Like actors: Varro fr. 435 Funaioli (Tertullian *De spectaculis* 5.3) on *Luperci* as *ludii*. Good family: e.g., L. Herennius Balbus, M. Caelius Rufus, Q. Tullius Cicero (Cicero *Pro Caelio* 26, *Ad Atticum* 12.5.1); the mask may have been less necessary for *Luperci* like Clesipus Geganius (*ILLRP* 696, Pliny *Natural History* 34.11).

The synchronic account at North 2008.147–55, assuming that 'the whole ritual is certainly together in its familiar form' by 44 BC, fails to make the necessary distinction between the republican and Augustan evidence. Hence North and McLynn 2008.178: 'The republican runners, it is universally believed, ran dressed only in a loin-cloth . . .' (the authors were unaware of Rosa's terracotta plaque).

Sober citizens: Cicero *Ad Atticum* 12.5.1 (disapproval of his nephew's participation), *Philippics* 2.84 (*turpitudo*). Caesar: Dio Cassius 44.6.2, 45.30.2 (*Luperci Iuliani*). Backlash: inferred from Cicero *Philippics* 7.1, 13.31.

Revived by Augustus: Suetonius *Diuus Augustus* 31.4 (*nonnulla ex antiquis caerimoniis paulatim abolita restituit . . . Lupercalibus uetuit currere imberbes*); cf. North and McLynn 2008.177, who assert without argument that the Augustan restoration 'seems to be virtually fiction'.

Could show off: Valerius Maximus 2.2.9 (*spectaculo sui*).

Date given as Augustan: von Rohden and Winnefeld 1911.262; Tortorella 2000.251; Paris, Bruni and Roghi 2014.100; Pensabene 2017.2.176; *contra* Pensabene 2017.2.291 ('alla metà circa del I sec. a.C. o un decennio oltre'). Two metres of fill: the street level descends east to west from 46.50 to 45.44 masl (Tomei 2014b.45 fig. 25); the ground-level in front of the temple is 47.60 masl.

132   Josephus *Jewish War* 2.80–1:

ἦσαν δὲ πεντήκοντα μὲν οἱ παρόντες, συμπαρίσταντο δ' αὐτοῖς τῶν ἐπὶ Ῥώμης Ἰουδαίων ὑπὲρ ὀκτακισχιλίους. ἀθροίσαντος δὲ Καίσαρος συνέδριον τῶν ἐν τέλει Ῥωμαίων καὶ τῶν φίλων ἐν τῷ κατὰ τὸ Παλάτιον Ἀπόλλωνος ἱερῷ, κτίσμα δ' ἦν ἴδιον αὐτοῦ, θαυμασίῳ πολυτελείᾳ κεκοσμημένον, μετὰ μὲν τῶν πρεσβευτῶν τὸ Ἰουδαικὸν πλῆθος ἔστη, σὺν δὲ τοῖς φίλοις ἄντικρυς Ἀρχέλαος.

Josephus *Jewish Antiquities* 17.300–1:

καὶ ἦσαν οἱ μὲν πρέσβεις οἱ ἀποσταλέντες γνώμῃ τοῦ ἔθνους πεντήκοντα, συνίσταντο δὲ αὐτοῖς τῶν ἐπὶ Ῥώμης Ἰουδαίων ὑπὲρ ὀκτακισχίλιοι. Καίσαρός τε συνέδριον φίλων τε τῶν αὐτοῦ καὶ Ῥωμαίων τῶν πρώτων συνάγοντος ἐν ἱερῷ Ἀπόλλωνος μεγάλοις τέλεσιν ὑπ' αὐτοῦ ἱδρυμένῳ, οἱ μὲν πρέσβεις μετὰ τοῦ πλήθους τῶν αὐτόθι Ἰουδαίων ἀφικνοῦνται, Ἀρχέλαος δὲ μετὰ τῶν φίλων.

Advocate at the hearing: Nicolaus of Damascus *FGrH* 90 F 136(9). Cf. Schürer 1973.28–9: 'No writer was used so fully by Josephus for the post-biblical period as Nicolaus of Damascus.'

In the open space: Millar 1977.19–20, 120; see now De Angelis 2010.145. *Area Apollinis*: *Année Épigraphique* 1972.174.10, Solinus 1.18.

'Friend of the Roman People': for the formula *amicus populi Romani*, see for instance Cicero *In Verrem* 2.4.67, *Pro rege Deiotaro* 40; Caesar *De bello Gallico* 1.3.4, 1.35.2; Sallust *Bellum Iugurthinum* 14.2; for Herod, cf. Josephus *Jewish Antiquities* 15.196 (δόσει Καίσαρος καὶ δόγματι Ῥωμαίων), with Schürer 1973.316–7.

8.3 Shady Walks and Senators

Building projects (*publica opera*): Suetonius *Diuus Augustus* 29–30; cf. Augustus' own list at *Res gestae* 19–21.

133   Suetonius *Diuus Augustus* 29.3:

addidit porticus cum bibliotheca Latina Graecaque, quo loco iam senior saepe etiam senatum habuit decuriasque iudicum recognouit.

Cf. Dio Cassius 53.1.3 ('the temple and the precinct around it and the book stores'); for the library, see also Horace *Epistles* 1.3.17 and 2.1.216–7, Ovid *Tristia* 3.1.63–4; for the staff *a bybliotheca Latina* or *Graeca*, see *CIL* 6.5188–91 and 5884 (Houston 2014.220–2).

Propertius 2.31.1–8:

quaeris cur ueniam tibi tardior? aurea Phoebi | porticus a magno Caesare aperta fuit. | tota erat in spatium Poenis digesta columnis, | inter quas Danai femina turba senis. | hic equidem Phoebus uisus mihi pulchrior ipso | marmoreus tacita carmen hiare lyra; | atque aram circum steterant armenta Myronis, | quattuor artificis, uiuida signa, boues.

Ovid *Amores* 2.2.3–6:

hesterna uidi spatiantem luce puellam | illa quae Danai porticus agmen habet. | protinus, ut placuit, misi scriptoque rogaui; | rescripsit trepida 'non licet' illa manu.

Pompey's portico: Catullus 55.6 (*in Magni . . . ambulatione*), Cicero *De fato* 8 (*in porticu Pompei . . . ambulemus*), Propertius 4.8.75 (*Pompei spatiabere . . . in umbra*). Caesar's gardens: Cicero *Philippics* 2.109 (paintings and statues), Valerius Maximus 9.15.1 (colonnade); Suetonius *Diuus Iulius* 83.2, Appian *Civil Wars* 2.143.596. Agrippa: Pliny *Natural History* 35.26 and 121.

Library as public asset (Nicholls 2013): cf. Suetonius *Diuus Iulius* 44.2 (*publicare*), Pliny *Natural History* 35.10 (*bibliothecam . . . rem publicam*); for libraries normally in rich men's villas, cf. Cicero *De finibus* 3.7–8 and 10 (Lucullus and Cicero at Tusculum), *Ad Atticum* 4.4a.1 and 8.2 (Cicero at Antium), 4.10.1 (Faustus Sulla at Cumae).

Portico of Octavia (Viscogliosi 1999): Velleius Paterculus 1.11.3, Festus 188L, Suetonius *Diuus Augustus* 29.4; cf. Dio Cassius 49.43.8 (misdated); it too had a library (Ovid *Tristia* 3.1.69–70, Suetonius *De grammaticis* 21.3, Plutarch *Marcellus* 30.6). Portico of Livia (Panella 1999): Ovid *Fasti* 6.637–48, Strabo 5.3.8 C236, Suetonius *Diuus Augustus* 29.4, Dio Cassius 54.23.1–6, 55.8.2.

134 Ovid *Ars amatoria* 1.67–74:

tu modo Pompeia lentus spatiare sub umbra, | cum sol Herculei terga leonis adit, | aut ubi muneribus nati sua munera mater | addidit, externo marmore diues opus; | nec tibi uitetur quae priscis sparsa tabellis | porticus auctoris Liuia nomen habet, | quaque parare necem miseris patruelibus ausae | Belides et stricto stat ferus ense pater.

Fifty Danaids: Apollodorus 2.1.4.

Ovid *Ars amatoria* 3.387–92:

at licet et prodest Pompeias ire per umbras, | Virginis aetheriis cum caput ardet equis; | uisite laurigero sacrata Palatia Phoebo | (ille Paraetonias mersit in alta rates) | quaeque soror coniunxque ducis monimenta pararunt | naualique gener cinctus honore caput.

For Agrippa's portico, which had a maritime theme, see Dio Cassius 53.27.1.

Augustus banished Ovid (AD 8): Ovid *Tristia* 2.207–12 (*Ars amatoria* one of the reasons). Out of town: e.g., Horace *Epistles* 1.7.1–9 (August), 1.16.15–16, Juvenal 6.517–8 (September).

Gentle grove: Propertius 4.6.69–86, esp. 71 (*candida nunc molli subeant conuiuia luco*); cf. Solinus 1.18 (*silua quae est in area Apollinis*), though it is not clear whether the *area* included the portico. For trees in porticos, see for instance Propertius 2.32.13 (Pompey's), Pliny *Natural History* 14.11 (Livia's); Gros 2003 emphasises the *bois sacré* aspect of Apollo's grove.

Goddess of groves and woods: Catullus 34.9–10 (*domina . . . siluarum uirentium*); Horace *Odes* 1.21.5 (*laetam . . . nemorum coma*), 3.22.1 (*custos nemorum*), *Carmen saeculare* 1 (*siluarum potens*); Virgil *Aeneid* 9.405 *nemorum Latonia custos*, 11.557 (*nemorum cultrix*); according to Servius (on *Georgics* 3.332) every *lucus* was sacred to Diana.

Incorporated pre-existing shrine: Zink 2015; cf. also Pensabene and Gallocchio 2013.565–7. For other examples of the same phenomenon, see Cicero *De haruspicum responso* 30–2.

Restored by Commander Caesar: probably in the programme of 28 BC (Augustus *Res gestae* 20.4, Virgil *Aeneid* 8.715–6, Livy 4.20.7, Ovid *Fasti* 2.59–66, Dio Cassius 53.2.4).

Torches burning all night: Varro *De lingua Latina* 5.68 (*in Palatio . . . noctu lucet templum*), cf. 6.79 (cult instituted *propter lucem amissam*—an eclipse?). All night in the grove: Propertius 4.6.85–6 (*donec | iniciat radios in mea uina dies*). Replicating exactly: both scenes celebrate the Parthians' surrender of the standards (Propertius 4.6.79–84).

135 Temple survived the fire: Pliny *Natural History* 36.13 and 32 (referring to its art-works in the present tense), Tacitus *Histories* 1.27.1, 3.65.2. Portico destroyed: it is never mentioned after the fire, and part of the Flavian palace occupied what must have been the eastern part of it.

Nero's punishment: Tacitus *Annals* 15.44.4 (*ut . . . in usum nocturni luminis urerentur*); the allusion was detected by Palmer 1978.1109, cf. Champlin 2003.112–3.

Tabula Siarensis b.2.20–1 (Crawford 1996.518, translation 529):

idque aes in Palatio in porticu quae est ad Apollinis in templo quo senatus haberetur figeretur.

Tabula Hebana 1–4 (Crawford 1996.519, translation 530):

utique in Palatio in porticu quae est ad Apollinis, in eo templo in quo senatus haberi solet, [inter ima]gines uirorum in<l>us<t>ris ingeni Germanici Caesaris et Drusi Germanici, patris eius naturali[s fratrisque] Ti. Caesaris Augusti, qui ipse quoq(ue) fecundi ingeni fuit, imagines ponantur supra capita columna[rum eius fas]tigi quo simulacrum Apollinis tegitur.

Templum: Varro *De lingua Latina* 7.8 (*dictum templum locus augurii aut auspicii causa quibusdam conceptis uerbis finitus*), Servius *auctus* on Virgil *Aeneid* 1.446, 4.200; for Senate meetings, see Varro Εἰσαγωγικός, cited by Aulus Gellius 14.7.7 (*in loco per augurem constituto, quo templum appellaretur*).

Same formula: *Année Épigraphique* 1978.145.2, *SC de Cn. Pisone patre* 1 (Damon and Takács 1999.14).

Decorated with portraits (Houston 2014.209–14): Suetonius *Tiberius* 70.2 (poets), *Gaius* 34.2 (Virgil and Livy); Tacitus *Annals* 2.37.2 (Q. Hortensius), 2.83.3 (*auctores eloquentiae*); scholiast on Horace *Satires* 1.4.21, Botschuyver 1935.281 (poets).

Oxyrhynchus Papyri 2435.30–4:

ὥρας θ’ ἐκάθισεν ὁ Σεβαστὸς ἐν τῷ τοῦ Ἀπόλλωνος ἱερῷ [ἐν τῇ Ῥ]ωμαικῇ βυβλιοθήκῃ καὶ δι[ήκουσ]εν τῶν πρεσβευτῶν <τῶν> Ἀλεξαν[δρέων] . . . .

The text went on to name the members of Augustus’ advisory panel who were present at the hearing.

136   L. Volusius Saturninus (consul in AD 3): Tacitus *Annals* 13.30.2.

Année Épigraphique 1972.174.7–12 (Panciera 2006.1075–7):

item statuas ei [ponend]as: tr[ium]fales in foro Augusti aeneam, in templo nouo diu[i Au]gusti [m]armoreas [du]as; consulares unam in templo diui Iuli, alteram [i]n [P]alatio intra tripylum, tertiam in aria Apolinis in conspectum curiae; auguralem in regia; equestrem proxime rostra; sella curuli residentem at theatrum Pompeianum in porticu Lentulorum.

Visible from *curia Iulia*: as argued, wrongly I now think, at Wiseman 2012a.377. Threshold of the *curia*: Tacitus *Annals* 2.37.2 (*ante limen curiae*).

Other public porticoes: Coarelli 1993b (*curia Pompei*, 24m x 20m), Panella 1999 (*porticus Liuiae*, 28m x 17m). Pompey’s portico: Plutarch *Brutus* 14.2 (στοὰ . . . ἐξέδραν ἔχουσα), Pliny *Natural History* 35.59 (*curia in porticu Pompei*), Suetonius *Diuus Iulius* 80.4, 81.3 (*in Pompei curiam*, with a *nemus* nearby); Nicolaus of Damascus *FGrH* 90 F130.82, Appian *Civil Wars* 2.115.481–2, Dio Cassius 44.16.2 (Senate meeting in στοά). Livia’s portico: Dio Cassius 68.10.2.

Evidence for libraries: details in Houston 2014.180–216, esp. 189–93 on Ephesus (main hall 16.72m x 10.92m) and 194–7 on Timgad. Minerva: Juvenal 3.219 (*hic libros dabit et loculos mediamque Mineruam*). *Baldacchino*: Last 1953.29.

137   Two Flavian halls: Balensiefen 2004, Iacopi and Tedone 2006, Carandini and Bruno 2008.213–9, Tucci 2013.286–91, Tomei 2014b.259–91. For the floor-space, I trust the dimensions given by Tucci 2013.286 (19.5m x 17.5m) over those given by Carandini and Bruno 2008.219 (21m x 19m), since the latter were determined to prove that all 600 senators could be accommodated (they allowed them a seating space of 45cm x 55cm each).

Singular noun decisive: as rightly pointed out by Richmond 1914.201 and Thompson 1981.338.

Current archaeological orthodoxy: as illustrated in Carandini and Carafa 2017 tables 70, 71, 282 (along with much baseless conjecture also presented as fact). But cf. Balensiefen 2004.103 and Pensabene 2017.2.99, who take *both* halls to be Augustan, and Carandini and Bruno 2008.213–9, who regard the north-eastern hall as a *curia* only, with separate library buildings to each side.

138   *Area Apollinis* identical with portico: as assumed nowadays, evidently on the strength of *FUR* frr. 20e-h (e.g., Carandini and Bruno 2008.221–2, Carandini and Carafa 2017 tab. 71). But see Rodriguez-Almeida 1981.99, where it is clear that the placing of the fragments depends on ‘la topografia finora conosciuta nelle vicinanze del tempio di Apollo Palatino’, and not vice versa.

Reluctant to admit: e.g., Carandini and Carafa 2012.243 = 2017.244, cf. 256 (‘the portico of the Danaids’ still supposedly extant in the Flavian and Severan periods).

An area very similar: i.e., 8268m², compared with about 8352m² for the portico of Livia (c. 116m x c. 72m) and about 15708m² for the portico of Octavia (c. 132m x c. 119m).

Current topographical literature: see above all *The Atlas of Ancient Rome* (Carandini and Carafa 2017 tables 70–2 and 282), where the space for the lateral wings is occupied by two separate ‘houses of Augustus’—one ‘public’, one ‘private’, both unattested, both the result of archaeological ‘free thinking’ (**2.3** above); for a corrective, see Wiseman 2009b, esp. 545 (‘an obstacle to historical understanding’).

139   Due process of law: Augustus *Res gestae* 2.1 (*iudiciis legitimis*), Appian *Civil Wars* 3.95.392 (νομῷ), Dio Cassius 46.48.2 (ἐν δίκῃ τινὶ).

Laurels and oak-wreath crown: Augustus *Res gestae* 34.2; Sutherland 1984.43 nos. 30–1, 47 nos. 78–9, 65 nos. 323–36, 86 no. 549 (*ob ciuis seruatos*), cf. Ovid *Tristia* 3.1.47–8.

9. PALATINE POETS

140   ‘Square Rome’: Festus 310L (*Quadrata Roma in Palatio ante templum Apollinis*), 312L (*saxo †minitus†*, where I propose to read *finitus*).

Notional centre: Solinus 1.18, cf. Zonaras 7.3, Tzetzes on Lycophron *Alexandra* 1232 (hut of Faustulus); Dionysius of Halicarnassus *Roman Antiquities* 2.5.1–2 (divine approval); Suetonius *Diuus Augustus* 7.2 (honorific name).

Pre-Augustan Palatine: Conon *FGrH* 26 F1.48.8 (καλύβη τις ἐν τῷ τοῦ Διὸς ἱερῷ). AD 41: Josephus *Jewish Antiquities* 19.75 (μικρόν τε πρὸ τοῦ βασιλείου καλύβης πηκτοῦ γενομένης), 19.90 (τὸ θέατρον, πηκτὸν . . . κατὰ ἕκαστον ἐνιαυτόν). Chance to strike: Josephus *Jewish Antiquities* 19.76 (πολλῶν μυριάδων ἀνθρώπων εἰς ὀλίγον χωρίον καθειργνυμένων).

Holiday for Augustus' birthday: Dio Cassius 51.19.2, 54.8.5, Degrassi 1963.80 (*fasti Maffeiani*). Dedication date of temple: Degrassi 1963.36–7, 194–5, 209 (*fasti Arualium, Amiternini, Antiates*). Games in honour of Actium: Dio Cassius 53.16, 54.19.8.

Watching stage performances: Tiro, quoted in Aulus Gellius 10.1.7 (*aedem . . . cuius gradus uicem theatri essent*); Cicero *De haruspicum responso* 24 (*ante templum in ipso Matris Magnae conspectu*), with Goldberg 1998.6–8. Other kinds of spectacle: Cicero *De imperio Cn. Pompei* 44, *Ad Atticum* 4.1.5.

Steps of Apollo temple: Ovid *Tristia* 3.1.59; the piazza pavement level was at 47.60 masl, the top of the podium on which the temple stood was at a little over 51.10 masl (Claridge 2014.149, figs. 4, 5). Temporary wooden terraces: *CIL* 6.32323.108, 156–7, 161 (*in theatro ligneo*), Vitruvius 5.5.7 (*publica lignea theatra*), Tacitus *Annals* 14.20.2 (*subitariis gradibus*), Servius on Virgil *Georgics* 3.24 (*componantur pegmata*).

Actors and dancers: Josephus *Jewish Antiquities* 19.94, Suetonius *Gaius* 57.4 (Catullus' *Laureolus* and a danced version of the tragedy *Cinyras*, AD 41); *Année Épigraphique* 1956.67.14 (a *pantomimus* dancer who won gold crowns dancing *in Palatio*, c. AD 200).

Famous for its poets: Velleius Paterculus 2.36.3, Martial 8.56. Performed in public: Horace *Satires* 1.4.36–8 and 73–8, 1.6.23, 1.10.37–9, *Epistles* 1.19.39–49 (with Wiseman 2015b.142–6), 2.2.95–6; Propertius 2.13.13–14; Ovid *Tristia* 4.10.57, *Ex Ponto* 4.2.34–5.

9.1 Horace

141 Poet's self-presentation: Horace *Odes* 3.1.3 (priest); 3.3.57–8, 3.6.1–6 (prophet). Addressed to Roman People: 3.6.1 (*Romane*); cf. 3.4.42, 3.5.1, 3.6.47 ('we').

Horace *Odes* 3.1.1–8:

odi profanum uulgus et arceo; | *fauete linguis: carmina non prius* | *audita Musarum sacerdos* | *uirginibus puerisque canto.* || *regum timendorum in proprios greges,* | *reges in ipsos imperium est Iouis,* | *clari Giganteo triumpho,* | *cuncta supercilio mouentis.*

Standard commentary: Nisbet and Rudd 2004.8. The god who led the Muses' song: e.g., Homer *Iliad* 1.603–4, [Homer] *Hymn to Apollo* 182–93, Hesiod *Shield of Herakles* 201–6, Pindar *Nemean Odes* 5.22–5. Conspicuous feature: Propertius 2.31.5–6.

Horace *Odes* 3.4.1–8:

descende caelo et dic age tibia | *regina longum Calliope melos,* | *seu uoce nunc mauis acuta* | *seu fidibus citharaque Phoebi.* || *auditis, an me ludit amabilis* | *insania? audire et uideor pios* | *errare per lucos, amoenae* | *quos et aquae subeunt et aurae . . .*

Muse of epic: *Anthologia Palatina* 9.504.1 (ἡρωίδος ἀοιδῆς); cf. Virgil *Aeneid* 9.525, Ovid *Metamorphoses* 5.337–40. Sacred groves: Propertius 4.6.70 (*lucus* at Apollo's temple), Solinus 1.18 (*silua quae est in area Apollinis*).

143 Horace *Odes* 3.4.37–48:

uos Caesarem altum, militia simul | *fessas cohortis abdidit oppidis,* | *finire quaerentem labores* | *Pierio recreatis antro.* || *uos lene consilium et datis et dato* | *gaudetis almae. scimus ut impios* | *Titanas immanemque turbam* | *fulmine sustulerit caduco,* || *qui terram inertem, qui mare temperat* | *uentosum, et urbes regnaque tristia* | *diuosque mortalisque turmas* | *imperio regit unus aequo.*

Settlement of veterans: Dio Cassius 51.4.5–6 (begun in 30 BC), Augustus *Res gestae* 15.3; Keppie 1983.73–82.

Three-day triumph: Virgil *Aeneid* 8.714, Livy *Epitome* 133, Macrobius *Saturnalia* 1.12.35 (*senatus consultum* of 8 BC), Degrassi 1947.344–5 (*fasti Barberiniani*), Suetonius *Diuus Augustus* 22, Dio Cassius 51.21.5–9.

Horace *Odes* 1.32.1–4, 13–16:

poscimur. siquid uacui sub umbra | lusimus tecum, quod et hunc in annum | uiuat et plures, age dic Latinum, | barbite, carmen ‖ . . . o decus Phoebi et dapibus supremi | grata testudo Iouis, o laborum | dulce lenimen medicumque salue | rite uocanti!

144   Horace *Odes* 1.31.1–4, 17–20:

quid dedicatum poscit Apollinem | uates? quid orat, de patera nouum | fundens liquorem? non opimae | Sardiniae segetes feraces ‖ . . . frui paratis et ualido mihi, | Latoe, dones et, precor, integra | cum mente, nec turpem senectam | degere nec cithara carentem.

Horace *Odes* 1.21.1–4, 13–16:

Dianam tenerae dicite uirgines, | intonsum, pueri, dicite Cynthium | Latonamque supremo | dilectam penitus Ioui. ‖ . . . hic bellum lacrimosum, hic miseram famem | pestemque a populo et principe Caesare in | Persas atque Britannos | uestra motus aget prece.

Horace *Odes* 4.15.1–8:

Phoebus uolentem proelia me loqui | uictas et urbes increpuit lyra, | ne parua Tyrrhenum per aequor | uela darem. tua, Caesar, aetas ‖ fruges et agris rettulit uberes | et signa nostro restituit Ioui | derepta Parthorum superbis | postibus . . .

Historical problem: Dio Cassius 54.8.3 (νεὼν Ἄρεως Τιμωροῦ ἐν τῷ Καπιτωλίῳ . . . καὶ ψηφισθῆναι ἐκέλευσε καὶ ἐποίησε), 55.10.2–8 (2 BC), Velleius Paterculus 2.100.2.

Dedicated at some other temple: Rich 1998.79–91; he limits the options to the three Jupiter temples on the Capitol, those of Optimus Maximus, Tonans, and Feretrius, but if Dio was mistaken that is an unnecessary restriction.

145   Hung with the spoils: Virgil *Aeneid* 8.721–2, Ovid *Tristia* 3.1.33–4.

9.2 Tibullus, Propertius, Ovid

Base of the cult statue: Suetonius *Diuus Augustus* 31.1 (*sub Palatini Apollinis basi*), with Wiseman 2014b.335: not (*pace* Zink 2012.398) in a crypt hollowed out of the podium.

Burned by the Sibyl: Varro *Divine Antiquities* fr. 56 Cardauns (Lactantius *Divine Institutions* 1.6.10, Servius on Virgil *Aeneid* 6.72), Dionysius of Halicarnassus *Roman Antiquities* 4.62.1–4, Aulus Gellius 1.19.

Burned in 83 BC: Fenestella *FRHist* 70 F19 (Lactantius *Divine Institutions* 1.6.14), Dionysius of Halicarnassus *Roman Antiquities* 4.62.5–6, Tacitus *Annals* 6.12.3. Newly purged survivors: Suetonius *Diuus Augustus* 31.1, Tacitus *Annals* 6.12.2.

Messalla Corvinus (Syme 1986.200–16): Velleius Paterculus 2.71.1 (Philippi), 2.112.1–2 (father of Messallinus). Changed sides: he was consul with Imp. Caesar in 31 BC, fought at Actium, and held a triumph from Gaul in September 27 BC. Orator: e.g., Horace *Ars poetica* 370–1, Tacitus *Dialogus* 18.2. Literary critic: Seneca *Controuersiae* 2.4.8 (*exactissimi ingenii . . . in omni studiorum parte*). Patron of poets: [Virgil] *Ciris* 54, *Catalepton* 9; [Tibullus] 3.8; Tibullus 1.1.53, 1.3.1, 2.1.31–6, 2.5.119–20.

Tibullus 2.5.1–12:

Phoebe faue, nouus ingreditur tua templa sacerdos: | huc age cum cithara carminibusque ueni. | nunc tu uocales impellere pollice chordas, | nunc precor ad laudes flectere uerba meas. | ipse triumphali deinctus tempora lauro, | dum cumulant aras, ad tua sacra ueni. | sed nitidus pulcherque ueni: nunc indue uestem | sepositam, longas nunc bene pecte comas, | qualem te memorant Saturno rege fugato | uictori laudes concinuisse Ioui. | tu procul euentura uides, tibi deditus augur | scit bene quid fati prouida cantet auis.

Since Tibullus died young (*iuuenis*, Domitius Marsus fr. 7.2 Courtney), this poem disproves Suetonius' assertion (*Diuus Augustus* 31.1) that the Sibylline books were placed in the temple only after Augustus' election as *pontifex maximus* in 12 BC.

Apollo and augury: cf. Horace *Odes* 1.2.32, *Carmen saeculare* 61–2, Virgil *Aeneid* 4.376.

146   Tibullus 2.5.23–8:

Romulus aeternae nondum formauerat urbis | moenia, consorti non habitanda Remo; | sed tunc pascebant herbosa Palatia uaccae | et stabant humiles in Iouis arce casae. | lacte madens illic suberat Pan ilicis umbrae | et facta agresti lignea falce Pales.

Romulus' wall specific to Palatine: Livy 1.7.3, Dionysius of Halicarnassus *Roman Antiquities* 1.88.2, 2.37.1; cf. Tacitus *Annals* 12.24.1, Aulus Gellius 13.14.2 (Romulus' *pomerium*). Eponymous goddess: Solinus 1.15 (*sunt qui uelint . . . a Pale pastorali dea . . . nomen monti adoptatum*).

Later in the poem: Tibullus 2.5.87. Under Apollo's gaze: Horace *Carmen saeculare* 65 (*si Palatinas uidet aequus aras*). Sister Diana: Tibullus 2.5. 121-2 (*adnue: sic tibi sint intonsi, Phoebe, capilli, | sic tua perpetuo sit tibi casta soror*).

Ancient family: Dionysius of Halicarnassus *Roman Antiquities* 2.46.3, 4.67.3, Plutarch *Numa* 5.1, *Publicola* 1.1 (time of Romulus); Cicero *Pro Flacco* 25, Valerius Maximus 2.4.5, 4.4.1, Pliny *Natural History* 36.112 (*primus consul*). Likely date: Syme 1986.230 ('As so often, ingenious or frivolous dallying with the poet ignores facts and disturbs history'); Messallinus' birth date is inferred from his consulship in 3 BC. 16 BC: Propertius 4.6.77 (cf. Dio Cassius 54.20.6), 4.11.66 (cf. Syme 1986.110, 250–2 on P. Scipio, consul in 16 BC).

Propertius 4.1.1–6:

hoc quodcumque uides, hospes, qua maxima Roma est | ante Phrygem Aenean collis et herba fuit; | atque ubi Nauali stant sacra Palatia Phoebo, | Euandri profugae procubuere boues. | fictilibus creuere deis haec aurea templa, | nec fuit opprobrio facta sine arte casa.

Cf. also 4.1.19 (festival of Pales).

Standard commentary: Hutchinson 2006.59; cf. 73 (no comment on the address to the *ciues* at 4.1.67), 130 (plural *credite* at 4.4.62 assumed to be addressed to readers). At 2006.13 Hutchinson regards 'the complete absence of the narrator-poet's voice from three of the poems' merely as evidence of 'radical discontinuity'; but what it surely attests is a poet composing dramatic texts that other performers could deliver.

Inference even more compelling: *pace* Hutchinson 2006.153 ('the poem does not present itself as written for an occasion'), 155 ('this is a metaphorical rite'). Cairns 1984.137–9 is excellent on the 'mythic hymn' genre, but even he shies away from the idea of actual performance: e.g., Cairns 1984. 133 ('the situation in which Propertius imagines it as being performed'), 141 ('Propertius, possibly imagining himself as a *choregus*'). This reluctance to allow the text to have been composed for public delivery seems to me an arbitrary restriction on our understanding of it.

147 Propertius 4.6.11–17:

Musa, Palatini referemus Apollinis aedem; | res est, Calliope, digna fauore tuo. | Caesaris in nomen ducuntur carmina; Caesar | dum canitur, quaeso Iuppiter ipse uaces. | est Phoebi fugiens Athamana ad litora portus, | qua sinus Ioniae murmura condit aquae, | Actia Iuleae Leucas monumenta carinae . . .

Caesar's name: cf. Propertius 2.1.42 for *Caesaris nomen* as an epic theme. Thanksgiving: Degrassi 1963.279 (*feriale Cumanum*), cf. 114–5 (*fasti Praenestini*), Ovid *Fasti* 1.587–616, Censorinus *De die natali* 21.8; Lacey 1996.88–96 for the sequence of events on 13–16 January 27 BC. Repeated use of *Augustus*: Propertius 4.6.23, 29, 38, 81.

Propertius 4.6.41–4:

'solue metu patriam, quae nunc te uindice freta | imposuit prorae publica uota tuae. | quam nisi defendes, murorum Romulus augur | ire Palatinas non bene uidit aues.'

Thalea: Ovid *Ars amatoria* 1.264, *Tristia* 4.10.56; cf. Virgil *Eclogues* 6.2, [Virgil] *Culex* 1. Comedy and mime: *Anthologia Palatina* 9.504.10, 505.7–8.

Read his poems to the People: Ovid *Tristia* 4.10.57–8. Public holidays and stage games: e.g., *Amores* 3.10 (*Cerialia*); cf. *Fasti* 4.187–90 (*Megalesia*), 4.417 (*Cerialia*), 5.190 (*Floralia*), with Wiseman 2015b.160.

Various parts of the city: Suetonius *Diuus Iulius* 39.1 (*regionatim urbe tota*), *Diuus Augustus* 43.1 (*uicatim et pluribus scaenis*).

Ovid *Ars amatoria* 2.1–2, 493–500, 509–10:

dicite 'io Paean' et 'io' bis dicite 'Paean': | decidit in casses praeda petita meos. | . . . haec ego cum canerem, subito manifestus Apollo | mouit inauratae pollice fila lyrae. | in manibus laurus, sacris induta capillis | laurus erat: uates ille uidendus adit. | is mihi 'lasciui' dixit 'praeceptor Amoris, | duc age discipulos ad mea templa tuos, | est ubi diuersum fama celebrata per orbem | littera, cognosci quae sibi quemque iubet | . . .' sic monuit Phoebus: Phoebo parete monenti; | certa dei sacro est huius in ore fides.

Cf. Servius on Virgil *Aeneid* 657 for *Paean* as *proprie Apollinis laudes*.

148 Ovid *Remedia amoris* 703–6:

consilium est quodcumque cano: parete canenti,| utque facis, coeptis, Phoebe saluber, ades.| Phoebus adest: sonuere lyrae, sonuere pharetrae;| signa deum nosco per sua: Phoebus adest.

> Cf. 251 (*noster Apollo*), 767 (*dux operis . . . Apollo*).

Ovid *Metamorphoses* 1.151–5:

neue foret terris securior arduus aether, | adfectasse ferunt regnum caeleste Gigantes | altaque congestos struxisse ad sidera montes. | tum pater omnipotens misso perfregit Olympum | fulmine et excussit subiectae Pelion Ossae.

Ovid *Metamorphoses* 1.168–76:

est uia sublimis, caelo manifesta sereno; | Lactea nomen habet, candore notabilis ipso. | hac iter est superis ad magni tecta Tonantis | regalemque domum. dextra laeuaque deorum | atria nobilium ualuis celebrantur apertis. | plebs habitat diuersa locis; hac parte potentes | caelicolae clarique suos posuere penates. | hic locus est quem, si uerbis audacia detur, | haud timeam magni dixisse Palatia caeli.

Marble chamber: 1.177 (*marmoreo . . . recessu*). Ovid insists on the contemporary parallels: 1.201 (*sanguine Caesareo*), 204 (*Auguste*); cf. 180 (*caesariem*).

Oak wreaths at Pythian games: 1.448–51. Oak wreath above Augustus' door: Ovid *Fasti* 4.953–4, *Tristia* 3.1.36, Augustus *Res gestae* 34.2, Dio Cassius 53.16.4.

Ovid *Metamorphoses* 1.557–65:

cui deus 'at quoniam coniunx mea non potes esse | arbor eris certe' dixit 'mea; semper habebunt | te coma, te citharae, te nostrae, laure, pharetrae. | tu ducibus Latiis aderis, cum laeta triumphum | uox canet et uisent longas Capitolia pompas. | postibus Augustis eadem fidissima custos | ante fores stabis mediamque tuebere quercum. | utque meum intonsis caput est iuuenale capillis, | tu quoque perpetuos semper gere frondis honores.'

149 Unique location: Ovid *Metamorphoses* 14.822–4 (*constitit in summo nemorosi colle Palati, | reddentemque suo non regia iura Quiriti | abstulit Iliaden*); contrast Ovid *Fasti* 2.491–2, Livy 1.16.1, Plutarch *Romulus* 27.6, *Numa* 2.1, *Camillus* 33.7, Florus 1.1.17, Solinus 1.20, *De uiris illustribus* 2.11.

Ovid *Metamorphoses* 15.861–5:

di, precor, Aeneae comites, quibus ensis et ignis | cesserunt, dique indigetes genitorque Quirine | urbis et inuicti genitor Gradiue Quirini, | Vestaque Caesareos inter sacrata penates | et cum Caesarea tu, Phoebe domestice, Vesta . . .

Inhabiting the residence: Ovid *Fasti* 4.951–2. Whole Palatine as *princeps'* residence: Dio Cassius 53.16.5–6.

God of music and poetry (Miller 2009.298–331): e.g., Tibullus 2.4.13, [Virgil] *Culex* 12, *Aetna* 4 (Apollo as *carminis auctor*).

9.3 Poetry and the Public

Suetonius *Diuus Augustus* 89.3:

ingenia saeculi sui omnibus modis fouit. recitantis et benigne et patienter audit, nec tantum carmina et historias sed et orationes et dialogos. componi tamen aliquid de se nisi et serio et a praestantissimis offendebatur, admonebatque praetores ne paterentur nomen suum commissionibus obsolefieri.

Misinterpreted by commentators: e.g., '*commissionibus*: contests of public speaking, at which praise of the emperor afforded an eminently suitable subject' (Carter 1982.199–200); 'here in the specific sense of adulatory, epideictic compositions (cf. *Cal.* 53.2) that had no lasting significance' (Wardle 2014.497). *Commissiones* could indeed be competitive exercises in the rhetorical schools (Suetonius *Gaius* 53.2, *De grammaticis* 17.1), but those were not under the praetors' jurisdiction.

150 Annual *ludi*: Dio Cassius 54.2.3–4 (praetors in charge from 22 BC), Juvenal 6.68–9 (none between the *plebeii* and the *Megalenses*); Balsdon 1969.248 for the total of days. Taking his turn: cf. Ovid *Fasti* 5.190 (*hoc quoque cum circi munere carmen eat*). Varied types: e.g., Phaedrus 5.5 (animal imitations), *Priapea* 27 (erotic dancing in the *circus*).

Horace *Satires* 1.10.37–9:

haec ego ludo | quae neque in aede sonent certantia iudice Tarpa | nec redeant iterum atque iterum spectanda theatris.

Horace *Epistles* 1.19.41–4:

non ego nobilium scriptorum auditor et ultor | grammaticas ambire tribus et pulpita dignor. | hinc illae lacrimae. 'spissis indigna theatris | scripta pudet recitare et nugis addere pondus' | si dixi, 'rides' ait 'et Iouis auribus ista | seruas.'

For the interpretation of the latter passage, see Wiseman 2015b.142–6.

Propertius 2.13.13–14:

haec ubi contigerint, populi confusa ualeto | fabula: nam domina iudice tutus ero.

Who was doing the judging: cf. Virgil *Eclogues* 4.58–9 (competing with Pan, *Arcadia iudice*). Valerius Cato: Gallus fr. 2.9 Courtney (*Kato, iudice te uereor*); Furius Bibaculus fr. 6 Courtney *(Cato grammaticus, Latina Siren, | qui solus legit ac facit poetas*). Maecius Tarpa: Cicero *Ad familiares* 7.1.1, Horace *Ars poetica* 387.

Ti. Claudius Tiberinus: *CIL* 6.10097 (*Ti. Claudius Esquilina Aug. Tiberinus hic situs est*), cf. 33960; Courtney 1995.120–1.

Humble priesthood: Porphyrio on Horace *Satires* 2.3.281 (*ab Augusto enim Lares, id est di domestici, in compitis positi sunt et libertini sacerdotes dati, qui Augustales appellati <sunt>*). There is no good reason to dismiss this evidence, as is the current fashion (Mouritsen 2011.251 n. 10, Flower 2017.288 n. 19); these *Augustales* must not be confused with the quite separate and much better attested *Augustales* in the towns of Italy and the western empire (but not Rome), on whom see Duthoy 1978, Ostrow 1990, Linderski 2007.179–83.

His own *Genius*: Ovid *Fasti* 5.145–6 (*mille Lares Geniumque ducis, qui tradidit illos, | urbs habet, et uici numina trina colunt*); cf. Fraschetti 1990.263–5, Galinsky 1996.301–4, Lott 2004.110–14, Wallace-Hadrill 2008.278–9. *Pace* Flower 2017.109 ('flippant'), 115 ('humor'), 328 ('playful or sarcastic'), Ovid's clear contemporary statement, confirmed by later evidence (e.g., *CIL* 6.449, 451 = *ILS* 3617, 3619), cannot simply be ignored.

7 BC: Degrassi 1947.285–6 (*Imp. Caesar August[us pontif. maxim.] cos. XI tribun. potes[t X] VII Lares Aug. mag. uici dedit*); for surviving compital altars erected by the *magistri uicorum*, see Galinsky 1996.302–10, Lott 2004.136–46, Wallace-Hadrill 2008.282–5. Unlike the *Augustales*, whose role was evidently sacerdotal, the *magistri uicorum* had administrative authority in the neighbourhoods (Suetonius *Diuus Augustus* 30.2, Dio Cassius 55.8.6–7).

Livia's first husband: Velleius Paterculus 2.75.1, 2.94.1; Suetonius *Tiberius* 3.1, 4.1–3.

151   *CIL* 6.10097:

tu quicumque mei ueheris prope limina busti, | supprime festinum, quaeso, uiator, iter. | perlege, sic numquam doleas pro funere acerbo; | inuenies titulo nomina fixa meo. | Roma mihi patria est, media de plebe parentes, | uita fuit nullis tunc uiolata malis. | gratus eram populo quondam notusque fauore, | nunc sum defleti parua fauilla rogi. | quis bona non hilari uidit conuiuia uoltu | atque meos mecum perui- gilare iocos? | quondam ego Pierio uatum monimenta canore | doctus cycneis enumerare modis, | doctus Maeonio spirantia carmina uersu | dicere, Caesareo carmina nota foro: | nunc amor et nomen superest de corpore toto, | quod spargit lacrimis maestus uterque parens. | serta mihi floresque nouos, mea gaudia, ponunt; | fusus in Elysia sic ego valle moror. | quot meat in stellis Delphin, quot Pegasus ales, | tot mea natales fata dedere mihi.

153   Professional entertainer: *pace* Courtney 1995.330 ('It is not clear exactly what profession [he] followed'); as Theodor Mommsen pointed out in his note on the original *CIL* publication, actors and performers were often enrolled in the *tribus Esquilina* (e.g., *CIL* 6.10103, 10105, 10107).

Hugely popular: Tacitus *Dialogus* 13.1–2. Everyone knew: Propertius 2.34.65–6, Donatus *Vita Vergili* 31 (Augustus' anxious enquiry). Augustus made sure: Donatus *Vita Vergili* 38-9.

Either is possible: Appian *Civil Wars* 2.102.424 states the purpose of the Forum Iulium ('for public business, not commerce'), and there is no evidence that it was ever used for entertainment; but in principle any open space could be so used on the N and NP days of the calendar (Wiseman 2015b.26–7).

154   Suetonius *Diuus Augustus* 53.2, 74:

in consulatu pedibus fere, extra consulatum saepe adaperta sella per publicum incessit. promiscuis saluta- tionibus admittebat et plebem, tanta comitate adeuntium desideria excipiens ut quendam ioco corripuerit, quod sic sibi libellum porrigere dubitaret 'quasi elephanto stipem'. . . . conuiuia nonnumquam et serius inibat et maturius relinquebat, cum conuiuae et cenare inciperent prius quam ille discumberet et permanerent digresso eo. cenam ternis ferculis aut cum abundantissime senis praebebat, ut non nimio sumptu ita summa comitate. nam et ad communionem sermonis tacentis uel summissim fabulantis prouocabat, et aut acroamata et histriones aut etiam triuiales ex circo ludios interponebat ac frequentius aretalogos.

Poetry readings: e.g., Nepos *Atticus* 14.1; cf. Varro *Menippean Satires* 340 Astbury, Cicero *Ad Atticum* 16.2.6, Juvenal 11.179–82.

'Honoured with his attention': Suetonius *Diuus Augustus* 45.3 (trans. D. Wardle).

Macrobius *Saturnalia* 2.7.17:

hac fabula et sagittas iecit in populum. eandem personam cum iussu Augusti in triclinio ageret, et intendit arcum et specula immisit. nec indignatus est Caesar eodem se loco Pyladi quo populum Romanum fuisse.

10. A MISCARRIAGE OF JUSTICE

10.1. Dynasty

155 Guardian of our affairs: Horace *Odes* 4.15.17–18 (*custode rerum Caesare*). Propaganda and cliché: Thomas 2011.260.

Oligarch arrogance: Sallust *Bellum Catilinae* 23.6, *Bellum Iugurthinum* 5.1, 31.2, 31.12, 64.1, 85.13, 85.19; cf. Cicero *Ad Atticum* 6.1.7 (Brutus), *Ad familiares* 11.28.3 (Matius on *optimates*). Citizen among citizens (see Wallace-Hadrill 1982 on *ciuilitas*): Suetonius *Diuus Augustus* 51–57, cf. Eutropius 7.8.4 (*ciuilissime uixit*).

Suetonius Diuus Augustus 53.1:

domini appellationem ut maledictum et obprobrium semper exhorruit. cum spectante eo ludos pronuntiatum esset in mimo 'o dominum aequum et bonum' et uniuersi quasi de ipso dictum exsultantes comprobassent, et statim manu uultuque indecoras adulationes repressit et insequenti die grauissimo corripuit edicto.

156 *Dominatio*: Augustus *Res gestae* 1.1 (*rem publicam a dominatione factionis oppressam in libertatem uindicaui*). Sharing the entertainment: Suetonius *Diuus Augustus* 45.1 for his enjoyment of shows (*studio spectandi ac uoluptate*). Dialogue by edicts: e.g., Suetonius *Diuus Augustus* 28.2, 31.5, 42.1–2, 56.1.

Horace *Epistles* 2.1.1–4:

cum tot sustineas et tanta negotia solus, | res Italas armis tuteris, moribus ornes, | legibus emendes, in publica commoda peccem | si longo sermone morer tua tempora, Caesar.

Death of Agrippa: Dio Cassius 54.28.1–3, cf. Pliny *Natural History* 7.45–6 ('in his 51st year').

Man of the common people: Velleius Paterculus 2.96.1, 2.127.1 (*nouitas familiae*); Seneca *Controuersiae* 2.4.13 (*paterna humilitas*), Seneca *De beneficiis* 3.32.4 (father unknown); cf. Pliny *Natural History* 35.26, 36.121 (policy of public ownership).

Seneca *Controuersiae* 2.4.13:

tanta autem sub diuo Augusto libertas fuit ut praepotenti tunc M. Agrippae non defuerint qui ignobilitatem exprobrarent . . . mihi uidetur admiratione dignus diuus Augustus, sub quo tantum licuit.

Cf. Suetonius *Diuus Augustus* 54–5 on freedom of speech.

Seneca knew: he wrote in old age (*Controuersiae* 1.pref.2) and died about AD 41 (Seneca *Consolatio ad Heluiam* 2.4). Gaius: Suetonius *Gaius* 23.1 (*Agrippae se nepotem neque credi neque dici ob ignobilitatem eius uolebat*); Seneca *De beneficiis* 2.12 (jewelled slipper).

Julia: Macrobius *Saturnalia* 2.5.8. Gaius and Lucius: Suetonius *Diuus Augustus* 56.2.

157 Dio Cassius 55.9.1–3:

ἰδὼν ὁ Αὔγουστος τόν τε Γάιον καὶ τὸν Λούκιον αὐτούς τε μὴ πάνυ, οἷα ἐν ἡγεμονίᾳ τρεφομένους, τὰ ἑαυτοῦ ἤθη ζηλοῦντας (οὐ γὰρ ὅτι ἁβρότερον διῆγον, ἀλλὰ καὶ ἐθρασύνοντο· ἐς γοῦν τὸ θέατρον ποτε καθ' ἑαυτὸν ὁ Λούκιος ἐσῆλθε) καὶ πρὸς πάντων τῶν ἐν τῇ πόλει, τὰ μὲν γνώμῃ τὰ δὲ κολακευομένους κἀκ τούτου ἔτι καὶ μᾶλλον θρυπτομένους (τά τε γὰρ ἄλλα καὶ ὕπατον τὸν Γάιον μηδὲ ἐς ἐφήβους πω τελοῦντα προεχειρίσαντο), ἠγανάκτησε, καὶ προσεπηύξατο μηδεμίαν τοιαύτην καιρῶν ἀνάγκην ὁποία ποτὲ αὐτὸν κατέλαβε γενέσθαι, ὥστε τινὰ νεώτερον εἰκοσιετοῦς ὑπατεῦσαι.

Nine years old: Dio Cassius 48.34.3 (Julia born 39 BC).

Designated as consul: Augustus *Res gestae* 14.1; *CIL* 6.3748 (Gaius), 6.900, 36908 (Lucius).

Astrologically perilous: Aulus Gellius 3.10.9 (quoting Varro's *Hebdomades*), 15.7.1–2.

Aulus Gellius 15.7.3:

praecipue diebus talibus, qualis est hodiernus, oculi mei requirunt meum Gaium, quem, ubicumque hoc die fuisti, spero laetum et bene ualentem celebrasse quartum et sexagesimum natalem meum. nam, ut uides, κλιμακτῆρα *communem seniorum omnium tertium et sexagesimum annum euasimus. deos autem oro ut mihi quantumcumque superest temporis, id saluis nobis traducere liceat in statu rei publicae felicissimo,* ἀνδραγαθούντων ὑμῶν καὶ διαδεχομένων *stationem meam.*

158 Deaths of Lucius and Gaius: Velleius Paterculus 2.102.2–3, Tacitus *Annals* 1.3.3, Dio Cassius 55.10a.6–9. Addressing the Roman People: Suetonius *Tiberius* 21.3 (*rei p. causa adoptare se eum pro contione iurauerit*). *Cohortes praetorianae*: e.g., Caesar *De bello Gallico* 1.40.14 (58 BC), Cicero *Ad familiares* 10.30.1–2 and 4–5 (43 BC), Appian *Civil Wars* 5.3.13 (42 BC); cf. Festus (Paulus) 249L (*praetoria cohors est dicta quod a praetore non discedebat*).

27 BC: Dio Cassius 53.11.5; Suetonius *Diuus Augustus* 49.1 (*partim in urbis partim in sui custodiam*). It seems unnecessarily pejorative to imagine 'the *Populus Romanus* . . . kept in order by the military police' (Wallace-Hadrill 2018.137).

Suetonius *Diuus Augustus* 49.1:

neque tamen umquam plures quam tres cohortes in urbe esse passus est easque sine castris, reliquas in hiberna et aestiua circa finitima oppida dimittere assuerat.

Cf. Tacitus *Annals* 4.5.3 (*nouem praetoriae cohortes*), Suetonius *Tiberius* 37.1 (*per hospitia dispersae*). Deputed command: Dio Cassius 55.10.10 (2 BC); *pace* Syme 1986.113, this is no reason to infer that 'Caesar Augustus was imposing a tight regime'.

Full of disasters: Pliny *Natural History* 7.149–50 (*iuncta deinde tot mala*); Dio Cassius 55.22.3 (earthquakes, flood, famine), 55.26.1 and 4 (famine, fire), 56.12.1 (famine), 56.23 (effect of the loss of Varus' army in Germany). Popular unrest: Dio Cassius 55.13.4 (AD 4), 55.27.1–3 (AD 6), 55.34.2 (AD 7), 56.28.4 (AD 13).

Equal to that of Augustus: Velleius Paterculus 2.121.1 (with Woodman 1977.210–11), Suetonius *Tiberius* 21.1.

159 Tacitus *Annals* 1.7.3 and 5:

nam Tiberius cuncta per consules incipiebat tamquam uetere re publica et ambiguus imperandi . . . sed defuncto Augusto signum praetoriis cohortibus ut imperator dederat; excubiae arma cetera aulae; miles in forum, miles in curiam comitabatur.

Cf. Woodman 1998.63–8, who offers a different punctuation and a different meaning for the first sentence; on reflection, I prefer the traditional reading, which preserves Tacitus' characteristic belief in Tiberius' dissimulation.

Brought together all nine cohorts: Tacitus *Annals* 4.2.1–2, Suetonius *Tiberius* 37.1, Dio Cassius 57.19.6–7 (AD 20). Retired in AD 26: Tacitus *Annals* 4.57.1 (Campania), 4.67.1–2 (Capri). Popularity a threat: namely Augustus' granddaughter Agrippina and her sons Nero Caesar and Drusus Caesar (Tacitus *Annals* 4.59.3–60.2, 4.67.3–4, 4.70.1–2, 5.3.1–2; Suetonius *Tiberius* 54.2, 55, 61.2).

After the fall of Sejanus: e.g., Tacitus *Annals* 6.19.2–3, 6.23.2–24.3, 6.47.3. Under Gaius: Josephus *Antiquitates* 19.32–42; e.g., Suetonius *Gaius* 32.1, Dio Cassius 59.26.3.

Josephus *Jewish Antiquities* 19.42 (Cassius Chaerea to M. Arrecinus Clemens):

δορυφόροι καὶ δήμιοι καθεστηκότες ἀντὶ στρατιωτῶν καὶ τὰ ὅπλα ταυτὶ φέροντες οὐχ ὑπὲρ ἐλευθερίας οὐδ᾽ ἀρχῆς τῶν Ῥωμαίων, ἀλλ᾽ ἐπὶ σωτηρίᾳ τοῦ δουλομένου τά τε σώματα αὐτῶν καὶ τὰ φρονήματα, μιαιόμενοι τῷ καθ᾽ ἡμέραν αἵματι σφαγῆς καὶ βασάνου τῆς ἐκείνων, μέχρι δή τις καὶ καθ᾽ ἡμῶν διακονήσεται τοιαῦτα Γαΐῳ.

Finding a new Caesar: Josephus *Antiquities* 19.162–5, 212–47; Suetonius *Diuus Claudius* 10, Dio Cassius 60.1–3. Huge bonus: Josephus *Antiquities* 19.247; Suetonius *Diuus Claudius* 10.4 (*primus Caesarum fidem militis etiam praemio pigneratus*) gives a lower figure, 15,000 *sesterces* = 3750 *denarii*; cf. Tacitus *Annals* 1.17.6 (praetorians got 2 *denarii* per day).

Withdrawing their loyalty: Suetonius *Nero* 47.1–2, 48.2; Dio Cassius 63.27.2b–3. Killed his successor: Tacitus *Histories* 1.5, 1.18, 1.40–3; Suetonius *Galba* 16.1, 19–20; Plutarch *Galba* 26.2–27.5; Dio Cassius 64.6.3–5.

160 Death of Vitellius: Suetonius *Vitellius* 17, cf. Tacitus *Histories* 3.85.

Senatus consultum de Cn. Pisone patre 46–7 (Damon and Takács 1999.20):

iam pridem numine diui Aug. uirtutibusq. Ti. Caesaris Aug. omnibus ciuilis belli sepultis malis.

10.2 The Great Historians

'Lawfully killed': e.g., Cicero *De oratore* 2.106, *Pro Milone* 8, *Brutus* 212, *Philippics* 8.13 (Ti. Gracchus); Cicero *Pro Milone* 72, 77, 79–80, Asconius 41C, 53–4C (P. Clodius); details in Wiseman 2009a.177–91.

Their view of Caesar: Cicero *Ad Atticum* 2.8.1, 2.9.1, 2.12.1, 2.13.2, 2.14.1, 2.17.1, 2.21.1, 2.24.3 (59 BC); *Ad Atticum* 7.5.4, 7.20.2, 8.2.4, 9.4.2, 9.13.4, 10.1.3, 10.4.2, 10.8.6, 10.12a.1 (50–49 BC); for the full Ciceronian evidence from letters after the Ides of March—e.g., *Ad Atticum* 14.14.4 (*iusto interitu tyranni*), 15.3.2 (*tyrannum iure optimo caesum*)—see Wiseman 2009a.201.

Gloried in his murder: e.g., Cicero *Ad Atticum* 14.4.2, 14.9.2, 14.12.2, 14.13.2, 14.22.2; *Ad familiares* 11.5.1, 11.7.2, 12.3.1; *De officiis* 3.19; *Philippics* 2.25, 2.117.

Brought up on Cicero: cf. Velleius Paterculus 2.66.5 (immortal name), Valerius Maximus 5.3.4 (*caput Romanae eloquentiae*); for inherited optimate views, cf. Velleius Paterculus 2.3.1–2, 2.6.2–3, Valerius Maximus 4.7.1, 7.2.6b, 9.4.3.

Josephus *Jewish Antiquities* 19.172–3:

ἐγὼ γὰρ τὰ παλαιὰ οἶδα ἀκοῇ παραλαβών, οἷς δὲ ὄψει ὁμιλήσας ἠσθόμην, οἵων κακῶν τὰς πολιτείας ἀναπιμπλᾶσιν αἱ τυραννίδες, κωλύουσαι μὲν πᾶσαν ἀρετὴν καὶ τοῦ μεγαλόφρονος ἀφαιρούμεναι τὸ ἐλεύθερον, κολακείας δὲ καὶ φόβου διδάσκαλοι καθιστάμεναι διὰ τὸ μὴ ἐπὶ σοφίᾳ τῶν νόμων, ἀλλ' ἐπὶ τῇ ὀργῇ τῶν ἐφεστηκότων καταλιπεῖν τὰ πράγματα. ἀφ' οὗ γὰρ Ἰούλιος Καῖσαρ φρονήσας ἐπὶ καταλύσει τῆς δημοκρατίας καὶ διαβιασάμενος τὸν κόσμον τῶν νόμων τὴν πολιτείαν συνετάραξεν, κρείσσων μὲν τοῦ δικαίου γενόμενος, ἥσσων δὲ τοῦ κατ' ἰδίαν ἡδονὴν αὐτῷ κομιοῦντος, οὐκ ἔστιν ὅ τι τῶν κακῶν οὐ διέτριψεν τὴν πόλιν.

Cf. *Antiquities* 19.187 ('in the hundredth year since they had been robbed of the republic', therefore since Caesar's consulship in 59 BC); for 'tyranny' and 'tyrannicide' see also *Antiquities* 19.63, 92, 155, 176–7, 187, 227, 230.

Tendentious travesty: all Caesar's powers and honours were voted to him by the Roman People (details in Wiseman 2009a.197–8) and the assassination 'tore up their votes' (Dio Cassius 44.1.1, τὰ ψηφισθέντα διεσκέδασε). The idea of Caesar motivated by his own whim is found already in Cicero (*Ad familiares* 9.16.3, *ne dicam libidine*).

161 Already a tyranny: Lucan *Pharsalia* 1.4, 1.86, 1.92, 1.109.

Lucan *Pharsalia* 1.126–8:

quis iustius induit arma | scire nefas. magno se iudice quisque tuetur: | uictrix causa deis placuit, sed uicta Catoni.

Elysium and Tartarus: *Pharsalia* 6.788 (Sulla), 795–9 (*popularia nomina*, including the Gracchi).

Tacitus' date of birth: inferred from his career (Birley 2000.234–6). Rich in disasters: Tacitus *Histories* 1.2.1 (*opus . . . opimum casibus*); for the date of the *Histories*, probably composed about AD 100–110, see Birley 2000.239–41.

Tacitus *Histories* 1.50.2:

captam totiens suis exercitibus urbem, uastitatem Italiae, direptiones prouinciarum, Pharsaliam Philippos et Perusiam ac Mutinam nota publicarum cladium nomina loquebantur.

Cf. Sallust *Bellum Iugurthinum* 5.2 for *uastitas Italiae*; but there is no sign in Tacitus of the 'challenge to the arrogance of the *nobilitas*' emphasised by Sallust in that passage.

Sulla in 88 BC: Livy *Epitome* 77, Velleius Paterculus 2.19.1, Appian *Civil Wars* 1.60.269, Plutarch *Sulla* 9.5–7. Caesar in 49 BC: Cicero *Ad Atticum* 7.3.5 and 7.7.6 (support of urban *plebs*), 8.3.4 (support of *multitudo*), 10.4.8 (*populi studium*). Young Caesar in 43: Appian *Civil Wars* 3.92.378–81.

Optimate slander: e.g., Cicero *De officiis* 3.84 (*ei regi . . . qui exercitu populi Romani populum ipsum Romanum oppressisset*); cf. Caesar *De bello ciuili* 1.22.5 on his enemies' *contumeliae*. Believed in Tacitus' time: cf. Suetonius *Diuus Iulius* 76.1 on Caesar's *dominatio* and why he was thought to have been 'justly killed' (*iure caesus*).

Tacitus *Histories* 1.50.2:

prope euersum orbem etiam cum de principatu inter bonos certaretur, sed mansisse C. Iulio, mansisse Caesare Augusto uictore imperium; mansuram fuisse sub Pompeio Brutoque rem publicam.

162 Tacitus *Histories* 2.38.1:

uetus ac iam pridem insita mortalibus potentiae cupido cum imperii magnitudine adoleuit erupitque; nam rebus modicis aequalitas facile habebatur. sed ubi subacto orbe et aemulis urbibus regibusue excisis securas opes concupiscere uacuum fuit, prima inter patres plebemque certamina exarsere. modo turbulenti tribuni, modo consules praeualidi, et in urbe ac foro temptamenta ciuilium bellorum.

Corrupting effect: cf. Sallust *Bellum Catilinae* 10 (esp. 10.3 *imperi cupido*), *Bellum Iugurthinum* 41. Oligarchy (*pauci*): Sallust *Bellum Catilinae* 20.7, 39.1, 58.11; *Bellum Iugurthinum* 3.4, 27.2, 31.2, 31.9, 31.19–20, 41.7, 42.1; *Histories* 1.12M, 1.55.23M, 3.48.6M. Crimes: Sallust *Bellum Iugurthinum* 42.1 (*paucorum scelera, nobilitas noxia*).

Schematic opposition: cf. Livy 6.38.13 (*usque ad memoriam nostram tribuniciis consularibusque certatum uiribus est*, on 368 BC).

Tacitus *Histories* 2.38.1:

mox e plebe infima C. Marius et nobilium saeuissimus L. Sulla uictam armis libertatem in dominationem uerterunt. post quos Cn. Pompeius occultior non melior, et numquam postea nisi de principatu quaesitum.

Just about supremacy: cf. Wallace-Hadrill 2018.10 ('a long-standing battle for personal dominance').

Tacitus *Annals* 1.1.1:

urbem Romam principio reges habuere; libertatem et consulatum L. Brutus instituit. dictaturae ad tempus sumebantur; neque decemuiralis potestas ultra biennium, neque tribunorum militum consulare ius diu ualuit. non Cinnae, non Sullae longa dominatio; et Pompeii Crassique potentia cito in Caesarem, Lepidi atque Antoni arma in Augustum cessere, qui cuncta discordiis ciuilibus fessa nomine principis sub imperium accepit.

Cf. Syme 1958b.304: 'The *Annales* from the opening words go to the limit of brevity and intensity.'
Tacitus *Annals* 1.1.3–2.1:

consilium mihi pauca de Augusto et extrema tradere, mox Tiberii principatum et cetera, sine ira et studio, quorum causas procul habeo. postquam Bruto et Cassio caesis nulla iam publica arma, Pompeius apud Siciliam oppressus exutoque Lepido interfecto Antonio, ne Iulianis partibus nisi Caesar dux reliquus.

163   Due judicial process: Augustus *Res gestae* 2.1, Appian *Civil Wars* 3.95.392, Dio Cassius 46.48.2. Elected and empowered: Appian *Civil Wars* 4.7.27, Dio Cassius 47.2.1–2 (triumvirate set up by tribunician law); Augustus *Res gestae* 1.4, Appian *Civil Wars* 4.8.31 (triumvirs elected).

Tacitus *Annals* 1.8.6:

die funeris milites uelut praesidio stetere, multum inridentibus qui ipsi uiderant quique a parentibus acceperant diem illum crudi adhuc seruitii et libertatis improspere repetitae, cum occisus dictator Caesar aliis pessimum aliis pulcherrimum facinus uideretur.

Liberators: e.g., Cicero *Ad Atticum* 14.12.2 (April 44 BC), *Philippics* 1.6; for Tacitus' favourable view, cf. *Annals* 1.76.2, 4.34–5.

Augustus' *dominatio*: Tacitus *Annals* 1.3.1, 1.10.1; cf. 1.2.1 (*seruitium*), 1.4.2 (his heirs as *domini* in waiting).

Late years of Domitian: Tacitus *Agricola* 45.1–2; Pliny *Epistulae* 3.11.3, *Panegyricus* 48.3–5. No understanding of politics: Tacitus *Histories* 1.89.1 (*uulgus et magnitudine nimia communium curarum expers populus*); cf. 2.61 (*stolidum uulgus*), 2.90.2 (*uulgus . . . uacuum curis et sine falsi uerique discrimine*).

As he sourly put it: Tacitus *Annals* 1.2.1 (*militem donis, populum annona, cunctos dulcedine otii pellexit*). 'Meditating Tacitus': Gibbon 2000.73 n.19.

164   Bimillennium exhibition: Giglioli 1938, Strong 1939; for the background, see Bosworth 2011.187–211. Fierce reaction: Syme 1939.viii–ix for the quotations; on *The Roman Revolution* (published 7 September 1939) and Syme's achievement in general, see the essays collected in Raaflaub and Toher 1990.

Gibbon invoked: 'historians [sometimes] fancy that the Principate of Augustus was genuinely Republican in spirit and in practice—a modern and academic failing. Tacitus and Gibbon knew better' (Syme 1939.3, citing *Annals* 1.2 and Gibbon's third chapter).

Exculpation: e.g., Syme 1939.4 ('their noble deed'), 58 ('to slay the tyrant'), 98 ('slain as a tyrant'); 'slay' is an evasive verb (it should be 'murder'). 'Liberators': the term is formally introduced at Syme 1939.57. Cf. also Syme 1939.56 on how they saw Caesar: 'His rule was far worse than the violent and illegal domination of Pompeius. The present was unbearable, the future hopeless. It was necessary to strike at once.' What violence and illegality had Pompey committed? No comment on Caesar's powers legally conferred, or the oath taken by all senators to preserve his safety (presented as a monarchic 'oath of allegiance' at Syme 1939.52).

Rabble, debauched by demagogues: Syme 1939.100; cf. 117 ('the superstitious mob'), 154 ('the dangerous and anachronistic liberties of the People'), 285 ('the corrupt plebs').

Precisely the theme: cf. Syme 1939.7 ('the rule of Augustus was the rule of a party'), 120 ('a faction may grow into something like a national party') ; his usual phrase, adjusting Tacitus, was 'the Caesarian party' (Syme 1939.55, 60 and passim). Unfriendly: Syme 1939.7. Inevitable: Syme 1939.9.

165 Pejorative tone: Syme 1939.2, 122, 130, 222, 287, 311. No moral distinction: Syme 1939.2 on Augustus as a chameleon ('colour changed, but not substance'). Least honest: Syme 1939.439. See Pelling 2015 for a brilliant analysis of 'the rhetoric of *The Roman Revolution*'.

Acknowledgment: 'There is a singular lack of adverse testimony from contemporary sources' (Syme 1939.4). Some special pleading was required (Syme 1939.323, 344): 'On all sides prevailed a conspiracy of decent reticence about the gap between fact and theory. It was evident: no profit but only danger from talking about it. . . . Nor did Agrippa speak for himself. Like the subtle Maecenas and the hard-headed Livia Drusilla, he kept his secret and never told his true opinion about the leader whom they all supported for Rome's sake.'

Sallust's account: Syme 1939.247–50; cf. Syme 1964.170–3 on *Bellum Iugurthinum* 41–2, 'schematic and defective'.

Cynical demagogues: 'The use of this weapon [the tribunate] became a mark of the politicians who arrogated to themselves the name of *populares*—often sinister and fraudulent, no better than their rivals, the men in power, who naturally invoked the specious and venerable authority of the Senate' (Syme 1939.15, citing Sallust *Bellum Catilinae* 38.3 and *Histories* 1.12M). He added a footnote (15 n. 2): 'There was no party of the *populares*: cf. H. Strasburger, in the articles "Optimates" and "Populares" (P-W, forthcoming)'; the reference is to Strasburger 1939 and Meier 1965, whose arguments are very vulnerable (Wiseman 2009a.29–30).

Optimate view: e.g., on Ti. Gracchus as 'the rash, self-righteous tribune [who] plunged into illegal courses' (Syme 1939.60), on the Marian 'party' forcing Sulla to march on Rome against his will (47), on the election of *popularis* consuls in 70 and 59 BC as 'violent usurpations' (38) 'subverting the constitution' (46), on the alliance of Pompey, Caesar, and Crassus as 'the end of the Free State' (36), on Caesar's championship of the expelled tribunes in 49 BC as a mere 'constitutional pretext' (48).

Party leaders: see respectively Syme 1939.61 ('his rule as party-leader [had] a personal and monarchic character') and 288 ('the last of the monarchic faction-leaders based his rule on personal allegiance'). For the 'parties' themselves, see Syme 1939.61–77 (Caesar's), 349–68 (Augustus').

Powerfully expressed: Syme 1958b.1 (usurpation), 1939.519 (violence and bloodshed), 1939.439 (despotic and murderous).

Recent examples: Harris 2016.96 (usurpation), 100 ('crafty tyrant', citing Gibbon), 105, 109; Alston 2015.228, 336; cf. 240 ('Augustan power depended not on law but on money and the potential for violence'). References to 'the Augustan regime' in modern scholarship should be regarded as *prima facie* evidence of prejudice.

Readers should also beware of the prejudicial treatment of Rome in Cartledge 2016.247–74, based not on contemporary sources but on a preconception that the republic was necessarily 'aristocratic-oligarchic' and Augustus necessarily 'monarchic'; Tacitus and Gibbon are invoked (270) to condemn him for 'democracy denied'. Atkins 2018.58–9 concurs; Wallace-Hadrill 2018.132–6 offers a more nuanced judgement, but still assumes that the young Caesar's rise to power was 'illegal and murderous' (133).

10.3 Epilogue

166 Obama farewell address, Chicago 10 January 2017 (New York Times transcript provided by the Federal News Service):

'For too many of us it's become safer to retreat into our own bubbles, whether in our neighborhoods, or on college campuses, or places of worship, or especially our social media feeds, surrounded by people who look like us and share the same political outlook and never challenge our assumptions. In the rise of naked partisanship and increasing economic and regional stratification, the splintering of our media into a channel for every taste, all this makes this great sorting seem natural, even inevitable.

And increasingly we become so secure in our bubbles that we start accepting only information, whether it's true or not, that fits our opinions, instead of basing our opinions on the evidence that is out there.

And this trend represents a third threat to our democracy. Look, politics is a battle of ideas. That's how our democracy was designed. In the course of a healthy debate, we prioritize different goals, and the different means of reaching them. But without some common baseline of facts, without a willingness to admit new information and concede that your opponent might be making a fair point, and that science and reason matter, then we're going to keep talking past each other.'

'Post-truth': see for instance D'Ancona 2017, Kakutani 2018.

BIBLIOGRAPHY

Alföldi 1965: Andrew Alföldi, *Early Rome and the Latins* (Jerome Lectures series 7). Ann Arbor: University of Michigan Press.

Alston 2015: Richard Alston, *Rome's Revolution: Death of the Republic and Birth of the Empire*. New York: Oxford University Press.

Ammerman 1990: Albert J. Ammerman, 'On the Origins of the Roman Forum', *American Journal of Archaeology* 94: 627–45.

Ammerman 1992: Albert J. Ammerman, 'Morfologia della valle fra Palatino e Velia', *Bollettino di archaeologia* 14–16: 107–11.

Ammerman 1995: Albert Jay Ammerman, 'Environmental Setting', in Carandini and Paolo Carafa (eds), *Palatium e Sacra Via I: Prima delle mura, l'età delle mura e l'età case arcaiche* (*Bollettino di archeologia* 31-33, Rome: Libreria dello Stato): 87-93.

Ammerman 1996: Albert J. Ammerman, 'The Comitium in Rome from the Beginning', *American Journal of Archaeology* 100: 121–36.

Ammerman 1998: Albert J. Ammerman, 'Environmental Archaeology in the Velabrum, Rome: interim report', *Journal of Roman Archaeology* 11: 213–23.

Ammerman 1999: A.J. Ammerman, 'Velabrum (environmental setting)', in Eva Margareta Steinby (ed.), *Lexicon Topographicum Urbis Romae* 5, T-Z (Rome: Quasar): 101–2.

Ammerman 2006: Albert Ammerman, 'Adding Time to Rome's *imago*', in Lothar Haselberger and John Humphrey (eds.), *Imaging Ancient Rome: Documentation—Visualization— Imagination* (JRA Supplement 61, Portsmouth RI): 297–308.

Ammerman 2009: Albert .J. Ammerman, 'Environmental Setting', in Russell T. Scott (ed.), *Excavations in the Area Sacra of Vesta (1987–1998)* (MAAR Supplementary volume 8. Ann Arbor: University of Michigan Press): 153–63.

Ammerman 2010: Albert J. Ammerman, 'Forum in Rome', in Michael Gagarin and Elaine Fantham (eds), *The Oxford Encyclopedia of Ancient Greece and Rome*, vol. 3 (New York: Oxford University Press): 212–22.

Ammerman 2016: Albert J. Ammerman, 'On Giacomo Boni, the Origins of the Forum, and Where We Stand Today', *Journal of Roman Archaeology* 29: 293–311.

Ampolo 2013: Carmine Ampolo, 'Il problema delle origini di Roma rivisitato: concordismo, ipertradizionalismo acritico, contesti. I', *Annali della Scuola Normale di Pisa* ser. 5, 5.1: 217–84.

Ampolo and Manfredini 1988: Carmine Ampolo and Mario Manfredini (eds), *Plutarco: Le vite di Teseo e Romolo*. Milan: Fondazione Lorenzo Valla.

Angelelli and Falzone 1999: Claudia Angelelli and Stella Falzone, 'Considerazioni sull'occupazione protostorica nell'area sud-occidentale del Palatino', *Journal of Roman Archaeology* 12: 5–32.

Angelelli and Falzone 2001: Claudia Angelelli and Stella Falzone, 'L'occupazione protostorica nell'area sud-ovest del Palatino', in Patrizio Pensabene and Stella Falzone (eds), *Scavi del Palatino I* (Studi miscellanei 32, Rome: L'Erma di Bretschneider): 65–77.

Arvanitis 2010: Nikolaos Arvanitis, *Il santuario di Vesta: la casa delle Vestali e il tempio di Vesta VIII sec. a.C.–64 d.C.* (Workshop di archeologia classica Quaderni 3). Pisa: Fabrizio Serra.

Ashby 1900: Thomas Ashby jr., 'Recent Excavations in Rome', *Classical Review* 14: 236–40.

Astin 1978: Alan E. Astin, *Cato the Censor*. Oxford: Clarendon Press.

Atkins 2018: Jed W. Atkins, *Roman Political Thought*. Cambridge: Cambridge University Press.

Augenti 1996: Andrea Augenti, *Il Palatino nel medioevo: Archeologia e topografia (secoli VI-XIII)* (BCAR Supplement 4). Rome: L'Erma di Bretschneider.

Augenti 2000: Andrea Augenti, 'Continuity and Discontinuity of a Seat of Power: The Palatine Hill from the Fifth to the Tenth Century', in Julia M.H. Smith (ed.), *Early Medieval Rome and the Christian West: Essays in Honour of Donald A. Bullough* (Leiden: Brill): 43–57.

Austin 1977: R.G. Austin (ed.), *P. Vergili Maronis Aeneidos Liber Sextus*. Oxford: Clarendon Press.

Balensiefen 2004: Lilian Balensiefen, 'Bibliotheca Palatina—Die Apollo-Bibliothek', in Adolf Hoffmann and Ulrike Wulf (eds), *Die Kaiserpaläste auf dem Palatin in Rom: Das Zentrum der römischen Welt und seine Bauten* (Mainz: von Zabern): 100–11.

Balsdon 1969: J.P.V.D. Balsdon, *Life and Leisure in Ancient Rome*. London: Bodley Head.

Barker and Jackson 1990: Felix Barker and Peter Jackson, *The History of London in Maps*. London: Barrie and Jenkins.

Baron 2013: Christopher A. Baron, *Timaeus of Tauromenium and Hellenistic Historiography*. Cambridge: Cambridge University Press.

Bartoli 1929: Alfonso Bartoli, 'Scavi del Palatino (Domus Augustana) 1926–1928', *Notizie degli scavi di antichità* 1929: 3–29.

Bartolini 1994: Fabio Bartolini, 'The Latin Shore', in Emanuela Bianchi (ed.), *Il Lazio di Thomas Ashby 1891–1930* (BSR Archive 4, Rome: Palombi): 193–215.

Battistelli 2001: Paola Battistelli, 'L'area sud-occidentale del Palatino tra il VI e il IV secolo a.C.', in Patrizio Pensabene and Stella Falzone (eds), *Scavi del Palatino I* (Studi miscellanei 32, Rome: 'L'Erma' di Bretschneider): 79–144.

Bauer 1993: H. Bauer, 'Cloaca, Cloaca Maxima', in Eva Margareta Steinby (ed.), *Lexicon Topographicum Urbis Romae* 1, A–C (Rome: Quasar): 288–90.

Beard, North, and Price 1998: Mary Beard, John North, and Simon Price, *Religions of Rome*, two volumes: 1 *A History*, 2 *A Sourcebook*. Cambridge: Cambridge University Press.

Berger-Doer 1992: Gratia Berger-Doer, 'Latona', *Lexicon Iconographicum Mythologiae Classicae* (Zurich: Artemis) 6.1: 267–72.

Bernard 2012: Seth G. Bernard, 'Continuing the Debate on Rome's Earliest Circuit Walls', *Papers of the British School at Rome* 80: 1–44.

Bettelli 1997: Marco Bettelli, *Roma, la città prima della città* (Studia archeologica 86). Rome: L'Erma di Bretschneider.

Birley 2000: Anthony R. Birley, 'The Life and Death of Cornelius Tacitus', *Historia* 49: 230–47.

Boatwright 1987: Mary Taliaferro Boatwright, *Hadrian and the City of Rome*. Princeton: Princeton University Press.

Boissier 1880: Gaston Boissier, *Promenades archéologiques: Rome et Pompéi* Paris: Hachette.

Boissier 1905: Gaston Boissier, *Rome and Pompeii: Archaeological Rambles*. London: Fisher Unwin.

Bosworth 2011: R.J.B. Bosworth, *Whispering City: Modern Rome and its Histories*. New Haven: Yale University Press.

Botschuyver 1935: Hendrik Johan Botschuyver (ed.), *Scholia in Horatium ΛΦΨ*. Amsterdam: van Bottenburg.

Braund 2000: David Braund, 'Learning, Luxury, and Empire: Athenaeus' Roman Patron', in David Braund and John Wilkins (eds), *Athenaeus and His World: Reading Greek Culture in the Roman Empire* (Exeter: University of Exeter Press): 3–22.

Brühl 1954: Carlrichard Brühl, 'Die Kaiserpfalz bei St. Peter und die Pfalz Ottos III auf dem Palatin', *Quellen und Forschungen aus italienischen Archiven und Bibliotheken* 34: 1–30.

Bruno 2010: Daniela Bruno, 'La fossa con ara romulea e la *Roma Quadrata* di Augusto', in Andrea Carandini (ed.), *La leggenda di Roma*, vol. 2 (Turin: Fondazione Lorenzo Valla): 287–96.

Brunt 1971: P.A. Brunt, *Italian Manpower 225 B.C.–A.D. 14*. Oxford: Clarendon Press.

Bucci 2014: Carlo Alberto Bucci, 'La casa di Augusto svela i suoi segreti', *Repubblica* 13 settembre 2014: http://www.repubblica.it/cultura/2014/09/13/news/casa_di_augusto

Buranelli 1989: Susanna Le Pera Buranelli, '28. Sacra Via', in *Archeologia a Roma nelle fotografie di Thomas Ashby 1891–1930* (British School at Rome Archive 2, Naples: Electa): 80–5.

Burn 1871: Robert Burn, *Rome and the Campagna: An Historical and Topographical Description of the Site, Buildings, and Neighbourhood of Ancient Rome*. Cambridge and London: Deighton, Bell.

Cairns 1984: Francis Cairns, 'Propertius and the Battle of Actium', in Tony Woodman and David West (eds), *Poetry and Politics in the Age of Augustus* (Cambridge: Cambridge University Press): 129–68.

Cameron 1970: Alan Cameron, *Claudian: Poetry and Propaganda at the Court of Honorius*. Oxford: Clarendon Press.

Cameron 2004: Alan Cameron, *Greek Mythology in the Roman World* (American Classical Studies 48). New York: Oxford University Press.

Campbell 2000: Brian Campbell, *The Writings of the Roman Land Surveyors* (JRS Monographs 9). London: Society for the Promotion of Roman Studies.

Cappelli 2000: Rosanna Cappelli, 'Questioni di iconografia', in Andrea Carandini and Rosanna Cappelli (eds), *Roma: Romolo, Remo e la fondazione della città* (Milan: Electa): 151–83.

Carafa 1998: Paolo Carafa, *Il Comizio di Roma dalle origini all'età di Augusto* (BCAR Supplement 5). Rome: L'Erma di Bretschneider.

Carandini 1990: Andrea Carandini, 'Il Palatino e il suo sistema di montes', in Mauro Cristofani (ed.), *La grande Roma dei Tarquini* (Rome: L'Erma di Bretschneider): 79–85.

Carandini 1997: Andrea Carandini, *La nascita di Roma: Dèi, Lari, eroi e uomini all'alba di una civiltà*. Turin: Einaudi.

Carandini 2000: Andrea Carandini, *Giornale di scavo: Pensieri sparsi di un archeologo*. Turin: Einaudi.

Carandini 2006a: Andrea Carandini (ed.), *La leggenda di Roma, volume I: Dalla nascita dei gemelli alla fondazione della città*. Milan: Mondadori.

Carandini 2006b: Andrea Carandini, *Remo e Romolo: Dai rioni dei Quiriti alla città di Romolo (775/750-700/675 a.C.)*. Turin: Einaudi.

Carandini 2007: Andrea Carandini, 'Archeologia e libero pensiero', *Workshop di archaeologia classica* 4: 11-15.

Carandini 2008: Andrea Carandini, *Archeologia classica: Vedere il tempo antico con gli occhi del 2000*. Turin: Einaudi.

Carandini 2010: Andrea Carandini, *Le case del potere nell'antica Roma*. Rome and Bari: Laterza.

Carandini 2011: Andrea Carandini, *Rome: Day One*. Princeton and Oxford: Princeton University Press. [Original edition 2007: *Roma: Il primo giorno*. Rome and Bari: Laterza.]

Carandini 2014: Andrea Carandini, *La Roma di Augusto in 100 monumenti*. Novara: UTET.

Carandini 2016: Andrea Carandini, *Angoli di Roma: Guida inconsueta alla città antica*. Rome and Bari: Laterza.

Carandini 2017: Andrea Carandini, *Antinomia ben temperata: Scavi nell'io e nel noi*. Milan: UTET.

Carandini and Bruno 2008: Andrea Carandini with Daniela Bruno, *La casa di Augusto dai "Lupercalia" al Natale*. Rome and Bari: Laterza.

Carandini and Cappelli 2000: Andrea Carandini and Rosanna Capelli (eds), *Roma: Romolo, Remo e la fondazione della città*. Milan: Electa.

Carandini and Carafa 1995: Andrea Carandini and Paolo Carafa (eds), *Palatium e Sacra Via I: Prima delle mura, l'età delle mura e l'età case arcaiche* (*Bollettino di archeologia* 31–33). Rome: Libreria dello Stato.

Carandini and Carafa 2012: Andrea Carandini with Paolo Carafa (eds), *Atlante di Roma antica: biografia e ritratti della città*. Milan: Mondadori Electa.

Carandini and Carafa 2017: Andrea Carandini with Paolo Carafa (eds), *The Atlas of Ancient Rome: Biography and Portraits of the City*. Princeton and Oxford: Princeton University Press.

Carettoni 1960: Gianfilippo Carettoni, 'Excavations and Discoveries in the Forum Romanum and on the Palatine During the Last Fifty Years', *Journal of Roman Studies* 50: 192–203.

Carettoni 1963: Gianfilippo Carettoni, 'La dimora Palatina di Augusto', *Capitolium* 38: 496–9.

Carettoni 1966–7: Gianfilippo Carettoni, 'I problemi della zona augustea del Palatino alla luce dei recenti scavi', *Atti della Pontificia Accademia Romana di Archeologia: Rendiconti* 39: 55–75.

Carettoni 1969: Gianfilippo Carettoni, 'The House of Augustus—1', *Illustrated London News* 20 September 1969: 24–5.

Carettoni 1983: Gianfilippo Carettoni, *Das Haus des Augustus auf dem Palatin*. Mainz: Philipp von Zabern.

Carter 1982: John M. Carter (ed.), *Suetonius: Diuus Augustus*. Bristol: Bristol Classical Press.

Carter 1996: John Carter (trans.), *Appian: The Civil Wars*. Harmondsworth: Penguin.

Cartledge 2016: Paul Cartledge, *Democracy: A Life*. Oxford: Oxford University Press.

Cassatella 1999: A. Cassatella, 'Venus et Roma, aedes, templum', in Eva Margareta Steinby (ed.), *Lexicon Topographicum Urbis Romae* 5, T-Z (Rome: Quasar): 121–3.

Castagnoli 1951–2: Ferdinando Castagnoli, 'Note di topografia romana', *Bullettino della commissione archeologica comunale di Roma* 74: 49–56.

Castagnoli 1964: Ferdinando Castagnoli, 'Sulla topografia del Palatino e del Foro Romano', *Archeologia classica* 16: 163–99.

Castagnoli 1977: Ferdinando Castagnoli, 'Cermalo', *Rivista di filologia* 105: 15–19.

Castagnoli et al. 1981: F(erdinando) C(astagnoli), C(airoli) F(ulvio) G(iuliani), P(aolo) S(ommella) and M(aria) F(enelli), 'La leggenda di Enea fondatore di Lavinium', in *Enea nel Lazio: archeologia e mito* (Rome: Fratelli Palombi): 155–271.

Cervesato 1913: Arnaldo Cervesato, *The Roman Campagna*. London: Fisher Unwin. [Original edition 1910: *Latina tellus: la campagna romana*. Rome: Mundus.]

Champlin 2003: Edward Champlin, *Nero*. Cambridge MA: Belknap Press.

Claridge 1998: Amanda Claridge, *Rome: An Oxford Archaeological Guide*. Oxford: Oxford University Press.

Claridge 2010: Amanda Claridge, *Rome: An Oxford Archaeological Guide*, ed. 2. Oxford: Oxford University Press.

Claridge 2014: Amanda Claridge, 'Reconstructing the Temple of Apollo on the Palatine Hill in Rome', in Chrystina Häuber, Franz X. Schütz, and Gordon M. Winder (eds), *Reconstruction and the Historic City: Rome and Abroad* (Beiträge zur Wirtschaftsgeographie München 6, Munich: Ludwig-Maximilians-Universität): 128–52.

Claridge 2018: Amanda Claridge, 'The Development of the City: An Archaeological Perspective', in Claire Holleran and Amanda Claridge (eds), *A Companion to the City of Rome* (Malden: Wiley Blackwell): 93–136.

Clarke 2008: Katherine Clarke, *Making Time for the Past: Local History and the Polis*. Oxford: Oxford University Press.

Coarelli 1983: Filippo Coarelli, *Il foro romano: periodo archaico*. Rome: Quasar.

Coarelli 1985: Filippo Coarelli, *Il foro romano: periodo repubblicano e augusteo*. Rome: Quasar.

Coarelli 1993a: F. Coarelli, 'Casa Romuli (Cermalus)', in Eva Margareta Steinby (ed.), *Lexicon Topographicum Urbis Romae* 1, A-C (Rome: Quasar): 241–2.

Coarelli 1993b: F. Coarelli, 'Curia Pompei, Pompeiana', in Eva Margareta Steinby (ed.), *Lexicon Topographicum Urbis Romae* 1, A-C (Rome: Quasar): 334–5.

Coarelli 1999: F. Coarelli, 'Roma Quadrata', in Eva Margareta Steinby (ed.), *Lexicon Topographicum Urbis Romae* 4, P-S (Rome: Quasar): 207–9.

Coarelli 2007: Filippo Coarelli, *Rome and Environs: An Archaeological Guide*. Berkeley and Los Angeles: University of California Press.

Coarelli 2011: Filippo Coarelli, *Le origini di Roma* (Storia dell'arte romana, vol. 1). Milan: Jaca Book.

Coarelli 2012: Filippo Coarelli, *Palatium: Il Palatino dalle origini all'Impero*. Rome: Quasar.

Coarelli 2013: Filippo Coarelli, *Argentum signatum: le origini della moneta d'argento a Roma* (Studi e materiali 15). Rome: Istituto Italiano di Numismatica.

Coarelli 2016: Filippo Coarelli, *I mercanti nel tempio. Delo: culto, politica, commercio* (Tripodes 16). Athens: Scuola Archeologica Italiana di Atene.

Coleman 2006: Kathleen M. Coleman (ed.), *M. Valerii Martialis Liber Spectaculorum*. Oxford: Oxford University Press.

Conventi 2004: Marta Conventi, *Città romane di fondazione* (Studia archeologica 130). Rome, L'Erma di Bretschneider.

Cooley 2009: Alison E. Cooley, *Res Gestae Divi Augusti: Text, Translation, and Commentary*. Cambridge: Cambridge University Press.

Cosmo 1990: Silvano Cosmo, 'Aspetti topologici e topografici degli Orti farnesiani come premessa alla conservazione ambientale', in *Gli Orti farnesiani sul Palatino* (Roma antica 2). Rome: École française de Rome and Soprintendenza archeologica di Roma.

Courtney 1993: Edward Courtney (ed.), *The Fragmentary Latin Poets*. Oxford: Clarendon Press.

Courtney 1995: E. Courtney (ed.), *Musa lapidaria: A Selection of Latin Verse Inscriptions* (American Classical Studies 36). Atlanta: Scholars' Press.

Crawford 1974: Michael H. Crawford, *Roman Republican Coinage*. Cambridge: Cambridge University Press.

Crawford 1994: Jane W. Crawford (ed.), *M. Tullius Cicero: The Fragmentary Speeches* (American Classical Studies 33). Atlanta: Scholars' Press.

Crawford 1996: M.H. Crawford (ed.), *Roman Statutes* (BICS Supplement 64), vol. 1. London: Institute of Classical Studies.

Cristofani 1990: Mauro Cristofani (ed.), *La grande Roma dei Tarquinii: catalogo della mostra*. Rome: L'Erma di Bretschneider.

Curtis 2011: Paul Curtis (ed.), *Stesichoros's Geryoneis* (Mnemosyne Supplement 333). Leiden: Brill.

Damon and Takács 1999: Cynthia Damon and Sarolta Takács (eds), 'The *Senatus consultum de Cn. Pisone patre*: Text, Translation, Discussion', *American Journal of Philology* 120: 1–162.

D'Ancona 2017: Matthew D'Ancona, *Post Truth: The New War on Truth and How to Fight Back*. London: Ebury.

Davies and Finglass 2014: M. Davies and P.J. Finglass (eds), *Stesichorus: The Poems* (Cambridge Classical Texts and Commentaries 54). Cambridge: Cambridge University Press.

De Angelis 2010: Francesco de Angelis, 'The Emperor's Justice and Its Spaces in Rome and Italy', in Francesco de Angelis (ed.), *Spaces of Justice in the Roman World* (Columbia Studies in the Classical Tradition 35, Leiden: Brill): 127–59.

Degrassi 1937: Atilius Degrassi (ed.), *Inscriptiones Italiae*, XIII *Fasti et elogia*, fasc. 3 *Elogia*. Rome: Libreria dello stato.

Degrassi 1947: Atilius Degrassi (ed.), *Inscriptiones Italiae*, XIII *Fasti et elogia*, fasc. 1 *Fasti consulares et triumphales*. Rome: Libreria dello stato.

Degrassi 1963: Atilius Degrassi (ed.), *Inscriptiones Italiae*, XIII *Fasti et elogia*, fasc. 2 *Fasti anni Numani et Iuliani*. Rome: Istituto poligrafico dello stato.

Dilke 1971: O.A.W. Dilke, *The Roman Land Surveyors: An Introduction to the* Agrimensores. Newton Abbot: David & Charles.

Du Quesnay 1977: I.M. le M. Du Quesnay, 'Virgil's Fourth *Eclogue*', *Papers of the Liverpool Latin Seminar 1976* (Arca 2, Liverpool: Francis Cairns): 25–99.

Duthoy 1978: Robert Duthoy, 'Les *Augustales', in Wolfgang Haase (ed.), *Aufstieg und Niedergang der römischen Welt* 2.16.2 (Berlin and New York: De Gruyter): 1254–1309.

Eck 1997: Werner Eck, '*Cum dignitate otium*: Senatorial *domus* in Imperial Rome', *Scripta Classica Israelica* 16: 162–90.

Filippi 2004: Dunia Filippi, 'La *domus regia*', *Workshop di archeologia classica* 1: 101–21.

Filippi 2005: Dunia Filippi, 'Il Velabro e le origini del Foro', *Workshop di archeologia classica* 2: 93–115.

Flower 2017: Harriet I. Flower, *The Dancing* Lares *and the Serpent in the Garden: Religion at the Roman Street Corner*. Princeton: Princeton University Press.

Forsythe 1994: Gary Forsythe, *The Historian L. Calpurnius Piso Frugi and the Roman Annalistic Tradition*. Lanham MD: University Press of America.

Fowler 2013: Robert L. Fowler, *Early Greek Mythography*, vol. II: *Commentary*. Oxford: Oxford University Press.

Fraschetti 1990: Augusto Fraschetti, *Roma e il principe*. Roma and Bari: Laterza.

Fraschetti 1996: A. Fraschetti, 'Montes', in Eva Margareta Steinby (ed.), *Lexicon Topographicum Urbis Romae* 3, H-O (Rome: Quasar): 282–7.

Fraschetti 2005: Augusto Fraschetti, *The Foundation of Rome*. Edinburgh: Edinburgh University Press. [Original edtion 2002: *Romolo il fondatore*. Rome and Bari: Laterza.]

Fraser 2008: Christian Fraser, 'House of Augustus Opens to Public', BBC News 9 March 2008: http:// news.bbc .co.uk/1/hi/world/europe/7286305.stm

Fulminante 2014: Francesca Fulminante, *The Urbanization of Rome and Latium Vetus: From the Bronze Age to the Archaic Era*. Cambridge: Cambridge University Press.

Gabba 1963: Emilio Gabba, 'Il latino come dialetto greco', in *Miscellanea di studi alessandrini in memoria di Augusto Rostagni* (Turin: Bottega di Erasmo): 188–94.

Gabba 2000: Emilio Gabba, *Roma arcaica: storia e storiografia*. Rome: Edizioni di storia e letteratura.

Galinsky 1981: Karl Galinsky, 'Augustus' Legislation on Morals and Marriage', *Philologus* 125: 126–44.

Galinsky 1996: Karl Galinsky, *Augustan Culture: An Interpretive Introduction*. Princeton: Princeton University Press.

Gargola 2017: Daniel J. Gargola, *The Shape of the Roman Order: The Republic and Its Spaces*. Chapel Hill: University of North Carolina Press.

Gibbon 1984: Edward Gibbon, *Memoirs of My Life* (ed. Betty Radice). Harmondsworth: Penguin.

Gibbon 2000: Edward Gibbon, *The History of the Decline and Fall of the Roman Empire* (ed. David Womersley). Harmondsworth: Penguin.

Giglioli 1938: Giulio Quirini Giglioli (ed.), *Mostra Augustea della romanità: catalogo*. Rome: Colombo.

Goldberg 1998: Sander Goldberg, 'Plautus on the Palatine', *Journal of Roman Studies* 88: 1–20.

Goldberg and Manuwald 2018: Sander M. Goldberg and Gesine Manuwald, *Fragmentary Republican Latin I* (LCL 294). Cambridge MA and London: Harvard University Press.

Gow and Page 1968: A.S.F. Gow and D.L. Page (eds), *The Greek Anthology: The Garland of Philip and Some Contemporary Epigrams*, 2 volumes. Cambridge: Cambridge University Press.

Grandazzi 1997: Alexandre Grandazzi, *The Foundation of Rome: Myth and History*. Ithaca and London: Cornell University Press. [Original edition 1991: *La Fondation de Rome: Réflection sur l'histoire*. Paris: Les belles lettres.]

Grandazzi 2008: Alexandre, *Alba Longa: histoire d'une légende* (Bibliothèque des Écoles françaises d'Athènes et de Rome 336). Rome: École française de Rome.

Gros 2001: Pierre Gros, *L'architecture romaine du début du III*e *siècle av. J.C. à la fin du Haut Empire*, vol. 2 *Maisons, palais, villas et tombeaux*. Paris: Picard.

Gros 2003: Pierre Gros, 'Le bois sacré du Palatin: une composante oubliée du sanctuaire augustéen', *Revue archéologique* n.s.1: 51–66.

Gros 2009: Pierre Gros, 'Les limites d'un compromis historique: de la *domus* vitruvienne à la maison augustéenne du Palatin', in Frédéric Hurlet and Bernard Mineo (eds), *Le Principat d'Auguste: Réalités et representations du pouvoir: Autour de la Res publica restituta* (Rennes: Presses Universitaires de Rennes): 169–85.

Gruen 1990: Erich S. Gruen, *Studies in Greek Culture and Roman Policy* (Cincinnati Classical Studies 7). Leiden: E.J. Brill.

Guarducci 1971: Margherita Guarducci, 'Enea e Vesta', *Mitteilungen des Deutschen Archäologischen Instituts: Römische Abteilung* 78: 73–118.

Gurval 1995: Robert Alan Gurval, *Actium and Apollo: The Politics and Emotions of Civil War*. Ann Arbor: University of Michigan Press.

Hall 2014: Jonathan M. Hall, *Artifact and Artifice: Classical Archaeology and the Ancient Historian*. Chicago: University of Chicago Press.

Hansen 1996: William Hansen, *Phlegon of Tralles' Book of Marvels*. Exeter: University of Exeter Press.

Harris 2016: W.V. Harris, *Roman Power: A Thousand Years of Empire*. Cambridge: Cambridge University Press.

Haselberger, Romano, and Dumser 2002: Lothar Haselberger, David Gilman Romano, and Elisha Ann Dumser, *Mapping Augustan Rome* (JRA Supplementary Series 50). Portsmouth, RI: Journal of Roman Archaeology.

Henige 2009: David Henige, 'Impossible to Disprove yet Impossible to Believe: The Unforgiving Epistemology of Deep-Time Oral Tradition', *History in Africa* 36: 127–234.

Heyworth and Morwood 2011: S.J. Heyworth and J.H.W. Morwood, *A Commentary on Propertius, Book 3*. Oxford: Oxford University Press

Hoffmann and Wulf 2004: Adolf Hoffmann and Ulrike Wulf, in Adolf Hoffmann and Ulrike Wulf (eds), *Die Kaiserpaläste auf dem Palatin in Rom: Das Zentrum der römischen Welt und seine Bauten* (Mainz: von Zabern): 153–72.

Hofter 1988: Mathias Hofter, 'Porträt', in *Kaiser Augustus und die verlorene Republik* (Mainz: von Zabern): 291–343.

Holloway 1994: R. Ross Holloway, *The Archaeology of Early Rome and Latium*. London: Routledge.

Hölscher 1988: Tonio Hölscher, 'Historischer Reliefs', in *Kaiser Augustus und die verlorene Republik* (Mainz: von Zabern): 351–400.

Hopkins 2016: John North Hopkins, *The Genesis of Roman Architecture*. New Haven and London: Yale University Press.

Horsfall 1972: Nicholas Horsfall, 'Varro and Caesar: Three Chronological Problems', *Bulletin of the Institute of Classical Studies* 19: 120–8.

Houston 2014: George W. Houston, *Inside Roman Libraries: Book Collections and Their Management in Antiquity*. Chapel Hill: University of North Carolina Press.

Hubbard 1974: Margaret Hubbard, *Propertius*. London: Duckworth.

Hutchinson 2006: Gregory Hutchinson (ed.), *Propertius Elegies Book IV* (Cambridge Greek and Latin Classics). Cambridge: Cambridge University Press.

Iacopi 1995: I. Iacopi, 'Domus: Augustus (Palatium)', in Eva Margareta Steinby (ed.), *Lexicon Topographicum Urbis Romae* 2, D-G (Rome: Quasar): 46–8.

Iacopi 2007: Irene Iacopi, *La casa di Augusto: Le pitture*. Verona: Electa.

Iacopi and Tedone 2006: Irene Iacopi and Giovanna Tedone, 'Bibliotheca e porticus ad Apollinis', *Mitteilungen des Deutschen Archäologischen Instituts: Römische Abteilung* 112: 351–78.

Johnson 1983: Anne Johnson, *Roman Forts of the 1st and 2nd centuries AD in Britain and the German Provinces*. London: A. & C. Black.

Jordan 1874: Henri Jordan (ed.), *Forma urbis Romae regionum xiiii*. Berlin: Weidmann.

Kakutani 2018: Michiko Kakutani, *The Death of Truth*. London: William Collins.

Kaster 1995: Robert A. Kaster (ed.), *C. Suetonius Tranquillus* De Grammaticis et Rhetoribus. Oxford: Clarendon Press.

Keppie 1983: Lawrence Keppie, *Colonisation and Veteran Settlement in Italy 47–14 BC*. London: British School at Rome.

Klyne and Liljenstolpe 2000: Allan Klyne and Peter Liljenstolpe, 'Where to Put Augustus? A Note on the Placement of the Prima Porta Statue', *American Journal of Philology* 121: 121–8.

Koortbojian 2006: Michael Koortbojian, 'The Bringer of Victory: Imagery and Institutions at the Advent of Empire', in Sheila Dillon and Katherine E. Welch (eds), *Representations of War in Ancient Rome* (Cambridge: Cambridge University Press): 184–217.

Krause 2004: Clemens Krause, 'Die Domus Tiberiana– Vom Wohnquartier zum Kaiserpalast', in Adolf Hoffmann and Ulrike Wulf (eds), *Die Kaiserpaläste auf dem Palatin in Rom: Das Zentrum der römischen Welt und seine Bauten* (Mainz: von Zabern): 32–58.

Krautheimer 1980: Richard Krautheimer, *Rome: Profile of a City, 312–1308*. Princeton: Princeton University Press.

Lacey 1996: W.K. Lacey, *Augustus and the Principate: The Evolution of the System* (ARCA 35). Leeds: Francis Cairns.

Lanciani 1883: Rodolfo Lanciani, 'Dell'Atrio di Vesta', *Notizie degli scavi di antichità* 1883: 468–80.

Lanciani 1888: Rodolfo Lanciani, *Ancient Rome in the Light of Recent Discoveries*. Boston and New York: Houghton, Mifflin.

Lanciani 1893: Rodolfo Lanciani, *Pagan and Christian Rome*. London: Macmillan.

Lanciani 1897: Rodolfo Lanciani, *The Ruins and Excavations of Ancient Rome*. London: Macmillan.

Lanciani 1901: Rodolfo Lanciani, *The Destruction of Ancient Rome: A Sketch of the History of the Monuments*. London: Macmillan.

Lanciani 1988: Rodolfo Lanciani: *Notes from Rome* (ed. Anthony L. Cubberley). London: British School at Rome.

La Rocca 2013: Eugenio La Rocca (ed.), *Augusto*. Milan: Electa.

Last 1953: Hugh Last, 'The *Tabula Hebana* and Propertius II, 31', *Journal of Roman Studies* 43: 27–9.

Le Gall 1953: Joël Le Gall, *Le Tibre fleuve de Rome dans l'antiquité*. Paris: Presses universitaires de France.

Leigh 2000: Matthew Leigh, 'Founts of Identity: The Thirst of Hercules and the Greater Greek World', *Journal of Mediterranean Studies* 10: 125–38.

Lenoir 1979: Maurice Lenoir (ed.), *Pseudo-Hygin: Des fortifications du camp*. Paris: Les Belles Lettres.

Linderski 1986: Jerzy Linderski, 'The Augural Law', in Hildegard Temporini and Wolfgang Haase (eds), *Aufstieg und Niedergang der Römischen Welt* 2.16 (Berlin and New York: De Gruyter): 2146–312.

Linderski 2007: Jerzy Linderski, *Roman Questions II* (Heidelberger Althistorische Beiträge und Epigraphische Studien 44). Stuttgart: Franz Steiner.

Llewellyn 1970: Peter Llewellyn, *Rome in the Dark Ages*. London: Faber and Faber.

Lott 2004: J. Bert Lott, *The Neighborhoods of Augustan Rome*. Cambridge: Cambridge University Press.

Lugli 1965: Giuseppe Lugli, *Studi minori di topografia antica*. Rome: De Luca.

Lugli 1970: Giuseppe Lugli, *Itinerario di Roma antica*. Milan: Periodici Scientifici.

Malloch 2013: S.J.V. Malloch (ed.), *The Annals of Tacitus Book 11* (Cambridge Classical Texts and Commentaries 51). Cambridge: Cambridge University Press.

Marsden 1980: Peter Marsden, *Roman London*. London: Thames and Hudson.

Martyn 2004: John R.C. Martyn (trans.), *The Letters of Gregory the Great* (Medieval Sources in Translation 40), vol. 3. Toronto: Pontifical Institute of Medieval Studies.

Marucchi 1906: Horace Marucchi, *The Roman Forum and the Palatine*. Paris and Rome: Desclée Lefebvre.

Mattingly and Sydenham 1926: Harold Mattingly and Edward A. Sydenham, *The Roman Imperial Coinage*, vol. 2. London: Spink.

Meier 1965: Christian Meier, 'Populares', *Paulys Realencyclopädie der classischen Altertumswissenschaft* Supplementband 10: 549–615.

Middleton 1885: J. Henry Middleton, *Ancient Rome in 1885*. Edinburgh: Black.

Middleton 1892: J. Henry Middleton, *The Remains of Ancient Rome*, vol. 1. London and Edinburgh: Black.

Millar 1977: Fergus Millar, *The Emperor in the Roman World (31 BC–AD 337)*. London: Duckworth.

Millar 2000: Fergus Millar, 'The First Revolution: Imperator Caesar, 36-28 BC', in *La révolution romaine après Ronald Syme: Bilans et perspectives* (Entretiens sur l'antiquité classique 46, Geneva: Fondation Hardt): 1–30.

Miller 2009: John F. Miller, *Apollo, Augustus, and the Poets*. Cambridge: Cambridge University Press.

Mirsch 1882: Paullus Mirsch, 'De M. Terenti Varronis antiquitatum rerum humanarum libris XXV', *Leipziger Studien zur classischen Philologie* 5: 1–144.

Mocchegiani Carpano 1984: Claudio Mocchegiani Carpano, 'Il Palatino sotterraneo', in Roberto Luciani (ed.), *Roma Sotterranea* (Rome: Palombi): 185–99.

Morton 1957. H.V. Morton, *A Traveller in Rome*. London: Methuen.

Mouritsen 2011: Henrik Mouritsen, *The Freedman in the Roman World*. Cambridge: Cambridge University Press.

Mouritsen 2017: Henrik Mouritsen, *Politics in the Roman Republic*. Cambridge: Cambridge University Press.

Nicholls 2013: Matthew Nicholls, 'Roman Libraries as Public Buildings in the Cities of the Empire', in Jason König, Katerina Oikonomopoulou, and Greg Woolf (eds), *Ancient Libraries* (Cambridge: Cambridge University Press): 261–76.

Nicolet 1999: Claude Nicolet, 'Napoléon III et l'histoire romaine', in Tomei 1999: ix–xxi.

Nijboer et al. 1999–2000: A.J. Nijboer, J. van der Plicht, A.M. Bietti Sestieri, A. De Santis, 'A High Chronology for the Early Iron Age in Central Italy', *Palaeohistoria* 41/42: 163–76.

Nisbet and Rudd 2004: R.G.M. Nisbet and Niall Rudd, *A Commentary on Horace: Odes Book III*. Oxford: Oxford University Press.

North 2008: J.A. North, 'Caesar at the Lupercalia', *Journal of Roman Studies* 98: 144–60.

North and McLynn 2008: J.A. North and Neil McLynn, 'Postscript to the Lupercalia: From Caesar to Andromachus', *Journal of Roman Studies* 98: 176–81.

Orlin 1997: Eric M. Orlin, *Temples, Religion and Politics in the Roman Republic* (*Mnemosyne* Supplement 164). Leiden: Brill.

Osborne 1987: John Osborne (trans.), *Master Gregorius: The Marvels of Rome* (Medieval Sources in Translation 31). Toronto: Pontifical Institute of Medieval Studies.

Ostrow 1990: S.E. Ostrow, 'The *Augustales* in the Augustan Scheme', in Kurt A. Raaflaub and Mark Toher (eds), *Between Republic and Empire: Interpretations of Augustus and His Principate* (Berkeley: University of California Press): 364–79.

Pais 1906: Ettore Pais, *Ancient Legends of Roman History*. London: Swan Sonnenschein.

Palmer 1978: Robert E.A. Palmer, 'Severan Ruler-Cult and the Moon in the City of Rome', *Aufstieg und Niedergang der römischen Welt* 16.2 (Berlin and New York: De Gruyter): 1085–1120.

Panciera 2006: Silvio Panciera, *Epigrafi, Epigrafia, Epigrafisti: Scritti vari editi e inediti (1956–2005) con note complementari e indici* (Vetera 16). Rome: Quasar.

Panciera 2007: Silvio Panciera, '*Domus Augustana*', in Anna Leone, Domenico Palombi, and Susan Walker (eds), *Res Bene Gestae: Ricerche di storia urbana su Roma antica in onore di Eva Margareta Steinby* (LTUR Supplement 4, Rome: Quasar): 293–308.

Panella 1999: C. Panella, 'Porticus Liviae', in Eva Margareta Steinby (ed.), *Lexicon Topographicum Urbis Romae* 4, P-S (Rome: Quasar): 127–9.

Papi 1999: Emanuele Papi, 'Scalae Anulariae', in Eva Margareta Steinby (ed.), *Lexicon Topographicum Urbis Romae* 4, P-S (Rome: Quasar): 238–9.

Paris, Bruni, and Roghi 2014: Rita Paris, Silvia Bruni, and Miria Roghi (eds), *Rivoluzione Augusto: l'imperatore che riscrisse il tempo e la città*. Milan: Electa.

Pelling 2015: Christopher Pelling, 'The Rhetoric of *The Roman Revolution*', *Syllecta Classica* 26: 207–47.

Pensabene 1998: Patrizio Pensabene, 'Vent'anni di studi e scavi dell'Università di Roma "La Sapienza" nell'area sud-ovest del palatino (1977–1997)', in Carlo Giavarini (ed.), *Il Palatino: area sacra sud-ovest e Domus Tiberiana* (Studia archaeologica 95, Rome: L'Erma di Bretschneider): 1–154.

Pensabene 2002: Patrizio Pensabene, 'Venticinque anni di ricerche sul Palatino: i santuari e il sistema sustruttivo dell'area sud-ovest', *Archeologia classica* 53: 65–136.

Pensabene 2017: Patrizio Pensabene, *Scavi del Palatino 2: Culti architettura e decorazioni* (Studi miscellanei 39), two volumes. Rome: L'Erma di Bretschneider.

Pensabene and D'Alessio 2006: Patrizio Pensabene and Alessandro D'Alessio, 'L'immaginario urbano: spazio sacro sul Palatino tardo-repubblicano', in Lothar Haselberger and John Humphrey (eds), *Imaging Ancient Rome: Documentation—Visualization—Imagination* (*JRA* Supplement 61, Portsmouth RI: JRA): 30–49.

Pensabene and Gallocchio 2011: Patrizio Pensabene and Enrico Gallocchio, 'Contributo alla discussione sul complesso augusteo palatino', *Archeologia classica* 52: 475–87.

Pensabene and Gallocchio 2013: Patrizio Pensabene and Enrico Gallocchio, 'Alcuni interrogativi sul complesso augusteo palatino', *Archeologia classica* 54: 557–82.

Pinza 1910: Giovanni Pinza, 'Il tempio di Apollo Palatino', *Bullettino della Commissione archeologica comunale di Roma* 38: 3–41.

Platner and Ashby 1929: Samuel Ball Platner and Thomas Ashby, *A Topographical Dictionary of Ancient Rome*. London: Oxford University Press.

Poucet 2000: Jacques Poucet. *Les rois de Rome: Tradition et histoire*. Brussels: Académie Royale de Belgique.

Powell 2008: Anton Powell, *Virgil the Partisan: A Study in the Re-integration of Classics*. Swansea: Classical Press of Wales.

Raaflaub and Toher 1990: Kurt A. Raaflaub and Mark Toher (eds), *Between Republic and Empire: Interpretations of Augustus and His Principate*. Berkeley: University of California Press.

Ramsey and Licht 1997: John T. Ramsey and A. Lewis Licht, *The Comet of 44 B.C. and Caesar's Funeral Games* (American Classical Studies 39). Atlanta: Scholars' Press.

Ravaglioli 1981: Armando Ravaglioli (ed.), *Tidmarsh-Brewer: Roma 1888 veduta panoramica*. Rome: Roma Centro Storico.

Rich 1998: J.W. Rich, 'Augustus's Parthian Honours, the Temple of Mars Ultor and the Arch in the Roman Forum', *Papers of the British School at Rome* 66: 71–128.

Rich and Williams 1999: J.W. Rich and J.H.C. Williams, '*LEGES ET IVRA P.R. RESTITVIT*: A New Aureus of Octavian and the Settlement of 28–27 BC', *Numismatic Chronicle* 159: 169–214.

Richardson 1992: L. Richardson, jr, *A New Topographical Dictionary of Ancient Rome*. Baltimore and London: Johns Hopkins University Press.

Richmond 1914: O.L. Richmond, 'The Augustan Palatium', *Journal of Roman Studies* 4: 193–226.

Richter 1901: Otto Richter, *Topographie der Stadt Rom* (Handbuch der klassischen Altertums-Wissenschaft 3.3.2). Munich: Beck.

Ridgway 1992: David Ridgway, *The First Western Greeks*. Cambridge University Press.

Ridgway 1996: David Ridgway, 'Greek Letters at Osteria dell'Osa', *Opuscula Romana* 20: 87–97.

Roccos 1989: Linda Jones Roccos, 'Apollo Palatinus: The Augustan Apollo on the Sorrento Base', *American Journal of Archaeology* 93: 571–88.

Rodriguez Almeida 1981: Emilio Rodriguez Almeida, *Forma urbis marmorea: Aggiornamento generale 1980*. Rome: Quasar.

Rosa 1865: P. Rosa, 'Scavi del Palatino', *Annali dell'Instituto di corrispondenza archeologica* 37: 346–67.

Royo 1985: M. Royo, 'Le Palatin', in *Roma Antiqua: Envois des architectes français (1788–1924): Forum Colisée Palatin* (Rome: Académie de France): 304–55.

Russell 2016: Amy Russell, *The Politics of Public Space in Republican Rome*. Cambridge: Cambridge University Press.

Santangeli Valenzani 2017: Riccardo Santangeli Valenzani, 'The End of the Ancient City', in Andrea Carandini with Paolo Carafa (eds), *The Atlas of Ancient Rome: Biography and Portraits of the City* (Princeton and Oxford: Princeton University Press): 116–21.

Santoro 1989: P. Santoro, 'Alcuni frammenti di ceramica arcaica provenienti da Caere', in *Atti II congresso internazionale etrusco (Firenze 1985)*, vol. 2 (Rome, G. Bretschneider): 961–6.

Sasso d'Elia 1995: L. Sasso D'Elia, 'Domus Augustana, Augustiana', in Eva Margareta Steinby (ed.), *Lexicon Topographicum Urbis Romae* 2, D-G (Rome: Quasar): 40–5.

Schoener 1898: Reinhold Schoener, *Rome* (trans. Mrs Arthur Bell). London and New York: Low, Marston and Charles Scribner's Sons.

Schürer 1973: Emil Schürer, *The History of the Jewish People in the Age of Jesus Christ*, vol. 1 (rev. ed.). Edinburgh: T. & T. Clarke.

Scott-Kilvert 1979: Ian Scott-Kilvert (trans.), *Polybius: The Rise of the Roman Empire*. Harmondsworth: Penguin.

Sider 1997: David Sider, *The Epigrams of Philodemos: Introduction, Text, and Commentary*. New York: Oxford University Press.

Simon 1984: Erika Simon, 'Apollo', *Lexicon Iconographicum Mythologiae Classicae* (Zurich: Artemis) 2.1: 363–464.

Smith and Cornell 2013: C.J. S[mith] and T.J. C[ornell], 'Origo gentis Romanae', in T.J. Cornell (ed.), *The Fragments of the Roman Historians* vol. 1 (Oxford: Oxford University Press): 96–101.

Solin 1983: Heikki Solin, 'Varia onomastica: V. Κλεῖκλος', *Zeitschrift für Papyrologie und Epigraphik* 51: 180–2.

Sorrell and Birley 1970: Alan Sorrell and Anthony Birley, *Imperial Rome*. London: Lutterworth Press.

Squire 2011: Michael Squire, *The Iliad in a Nutshell: Visualizing Epic on the Tabulae Iliacae*. Oxford: Oxford University Press.

Strasburger 1939: H. Strasburger, 'Optimates', *Paulys Realencyclopädie der classischen Altertumswissenschaft* 18.1: 773–98.

Strong 1939: Eugénie Strong, '"Romanità" Throughout the Ages', *Journal of Roman Studies* 29: 137–66.

Studniczka 1910: Franz Studniczka, 'Zur Augustusstatue der Livia', *Römische Mitteilungen* 25: 27–55.

Sumner 1971: G.V. Sumner, 'A Note on Julius Caesar's Great-Grandfather', *Classical Philology* 71: 341–4.

Sutherland 1984: C.H.V. Sutherland, *The Roman Imperial Coinage*, revised ed., vol. 1. London: Spink.

Syme 1937: Ronald Syme, 'Who Was Decidius Saxa?', *Journal of Roman Studies* 27: 127–37.

Syme 1939: Ronald Syme, *The Roman Revolution*. Oxford: Clarendon Press.

Syme 1958a: Ronald Syme, 'Imperator Caesar: A Study in Nomenclature', *Historia* 7: 172–88.

Syme 1958b: Ronald Syme, *Tacitus*. Oxford: Clarendon Press.

Syme 1964: Ronald Syme, *Sallust* (Sather Classical Lectures 33). Berkeley: University of California Press.

Syme 1979: Ronald Syme, *Roman Papers*, vols. 1–2. Oxford: Clarendon Press.

Syme 1986: Ronald Syme, *The Augustan Aristocracy*. Oxford: Clarendon Press.

ten Brink 1855: B. ten Brink, *M. Terentii Varronis locus de urbe Roma*. Utrecht: van der Post.

Testa 2012: Alessandro Testa, 'Verità del mito e verità della storia: una critica storico-religiosa a recenti ipotesi sui *primordia* di Roma', *Mediterranea* 9: 195–231.

Thomas 1988: Richard F. Thomas (ed.), *Virgil Georgics: vol. 2 Books III–IV* (Cambridge Greek and Latin Classics). Cambridge: Cambridge University Press.

Thomas 2011: Richard F. Thomas (ed.), *Horace Odes Book IV and Carmen Saeculare* (Cambridge Greek and Latin Classics). Cambridge: Cambridge University Press.

Thompson 1981: David L. Thompson, 'The Meetings of the Roman Senate on the Palatine', *American Journal of Archaeology* 85: 335–9.

Tomei 1999: Maria Antonietta Tomei, *Scavi francesi sul Palatino: Le indagini di Pietro Rosa per Napoleone III* (Roma antica 5). Rome: École française de Rome and Soprintendenza archeologica di Roma.

Tomei 2000: Maria Antonietta Tomei, 'I resti dell'arco di Ottavio sul Palatino e il Portico delle Danaidi', *Mélanges de l'École française de Rome (Antiquité)* 112: 557–610.

Tomei 2014a: Maria Antonietta Tomei, 'Augusto sul Palatino', in Carlo Gasparri and Maria Antonietta Tomei, *Museo Palatino: le collezioni* (Milan: Electa): 25–45.

Tomei 2014b: Maria Antonietta Tomei, *Augusto sul Palatino: Gli scavi di Gianfilippo Carettoni, appunti inediti (1955–1984)*. Milan: Electa.

Tomei 2014c: Maria Antonietta Tomei, 'Il Museo Palatino rinnovato per il bimillennario augusteo', in Carlo Gasparri and Maria Antonietta Tomei, *Museo Palatino: le collezioni* (Milan: Electa): 11–23.

Tomei 2014d: M(aria) A(ntonietta) T(omei), 'Lastre filliti policrome', in Carlo Gasparri and Maria Antonietta Tomei, *Museo Palatino: le collezioni* (Milan: Electa): 150–61.

Tomei and Filetici 2011: Maria Antonietta Tomei and Maria Grazia Filetici (eds), *Domus Tiberiana: scavi e restauri 1990–2011*. Milan: Electa.

Torelli 1987: Mario Torelli, 'Culto imperiale e spazi urbani in età flavia: dai rilievi Hartwig all'arco di Tito', in *L'Urbs: espace urbain et histoire (Iᵉʳ siècle av. J.-C— IIIᵉ siècle ap. J.-C.)* (CEFR 98, Rome: École française de Rome): 563–82.

Torelli 2014: Mario Torelli, 'Il Palatium: Realtà e ideologia dei luoghi di potere', in Carlo Gasparri and Maria Antonietta Tomei, *Museo Palatino: le collezioni* (Milan: Electa): 47–61.

Tortorella 2000: Stefano Tortorella, 'L'adolescenza dei gemelli, la festa dei *Lupercalia* e l'uccisione di Amulio', in Andrea Carandini and Rosanna Cappelli (eds), *Roma: Romolo, Remo e la fondazione della città* (Milan: Electa): 244–55.

Tortorella 2013: Stefano Tortorella, 'Lastre Campana con figurazioni simmetriche', in Eugenio La Rocca (ed.), *Augusto* (Milan: Electa): 226–7.

Tucci 2013: Pier Luigi Tucci, 'Flavian Libraries in the City of Rome', in Jason König, Katerina Oikonomopoulou, and Greg Woolf (eds), *Ancient Libraries* (Cambridge: Cambridge University Press): 277–311.

Usener 1912: Hermann Usener, *Kleine Schriften*, vol. 1. Leipzig and Berlin: Teubner.

Vaglieri 1907: D. Vaglieri, 'Regione X: scoperte al Palatino', *Notizie degli scavi* 1907: 185–205.

Valentini and Zucchetti 1940: Roberto Valentini and Giuseppe Zucchetti (eds), *Codice topografico della città di Roma*, vol. 1. Rome: Istituto Storico Italiano per il Medio Evo.

Van Deman 1923: Esther Boise Van Deman, 'The Neronian Sacra Via', *American Journal of Archaeology* 27: 383–424.

Van Deman 1925: Esther Boise Van Deman, 'The Sacra Via of Nero', *Memoirs of the American Academy in Rome* 5: 115–26.

Vella 2010–11: Alessandro Vella, 'Due nuovi frammenti di un calendario marmoreo dalla via Ardeatina a Roma: considerazioni epigrafiche e riflessioni sulla topografia del Campidoglio', *Atti della Pontificia Accademia Romana di Archeologia: Rendiconti* 83: 335–78.

Villedieu 1997: Françoise Villedieu (ed.), *La Vigna Barberini I: Histoire d'une site* (Roma antica 3). Rome: École française de Rome.

Villedieu 2007: Françoise Villedieu (ed.), *La Vigna Barberini II: Domus, palais impérial et temples* (Roma antica 6). Rome: École française de Rome.

Virgili 1999: P. Virgili, 'Vicus Iugarius', in Eva Margareta Steinby (ed.), *Lexicon Topographicum Urbis Romae* 5, T-Z (Rome: Quasar): 169–70.

Viscogliosi 1999: A. Viscogliosi, 'Porticus Octaviae', in Eva Margareta Steinby (ed.), *Lexicon Topographicum Urbis Romae* 4, P-S (Rome: Quasar): 141–5.

Von Rohden and Winnefeld 1911: Hermann von Rohden und Hermann Winnefeld, *Architektonische römische Tonreliefs der Kaiserzeit*. Berlin and Stuttgart: W. Spemann.

Wallace-Hadrill 1982: Andrew Wallace-Hadrill, 'Civilis Princeps: Between Citizen and King', *Journal of Roman Studies* 72: 32–48.

Wallace-Hadrill 2008: Andrew Wallace-Hadrill, *Rome's Cultural Revolution*. Cambridge: Cambridge University Press.

Wallace-Hadrill 2018: Andrew Wallace-Hadrill, *Augustan Rome*, ed. 2. London: Bloomsbury.

Walsh 2010: P.G. Walsh (ed.), *Augustine De Civitate Dei (The City of God) Books VI & VII*. Oxford: Aris & Phillips.

Walter 1969: Hermann Walter, *Die 'Collectanea rerum memorabilium' des C. Iulius Solinus* (*Hermes* Einzelschriften Heft 22). Wiesbaden: Franz Steiner.

Ward Perkins 1951: John Ward Perkins, 'Tripolitania and the Marble Trade', *Journal of Roman Studies* 41: 89–104.

Wardle 2014: J. Wardle, *Suetonius: Life of Augustus*. Oxford: Oxford University Press.

Weinstock 1971: Stefan Weinstock, *Divus Julius*. Oxford: Clarendon Press.

Weiss 1969: Roberto Weiss, *The Renaissance Discovery of Classical Antiquity*. Oxford: Blackwell.

Werner 2004: Klaus Werner, 'Antikenschutz und Antikendokumentation am Beispiel einer bislang unbekannten Grabung Sicinio Capizucchis', in Adolf Hoffmann and Ulrike Wulf (eds), *Die Kaiserpaläste auf dem Palatin in Rom: Das Zentrum der römischen Welt und seine Bauten* (Mainz: von Zabern): 144–52.

West 2013: M.L. West, *The Epic Cycle: A Commentary on the Lost Troy Epics*. Oxford: Oxford University Press.

West 2015: M.L. West, 'Epic, Lyric, and Lyric Epic', in P.J. Finglass and Adrian Kelly (eds), *Stesichorus in Context* (Cambridge: Cambridge University Press): 63–80.

Whitley 1943: Margaret Whitley, 'Excavations at Chalbury Camp, Dorset, 1939', *Antiquaries Journal* 23: 98–121.

Wickham 2015: Chris Wickham, *Medieval Rome: Stability and Crisis of a City, 900–1150*. Oxford: Oxford University Press.

Winter 2009: Nancy A. Winter, *Symbols of Wealth and Power: Architectural Terracotta Decoration in Etruria and Central Italy, 640–510 BC* (MAAR Supplement 9). Ann Arbor: University of Michigan Press.

Wiseman 1995: T.P. Wiseman, *Remus: a Roman Myth*. Cambridge: Cambridge University Press.

Wiseman 1998: T.P. Wiseman, *Roman Drama and Roman History*. Exeter: University of Exeter Press.

Wiseman 2001: T.P. Wiseman, 'Reading Carandini', *Journal of Roman Studies* 91: 182–93.

Wiseman 2004a: T.P. Wiseman, *The Myths of Rome*. Exeter: University of Exeter Press.

Wiseman 2004b: T.P. Wiseman, 'Where was the *Noua uia*?', *Papers of the British School at Rome* 72: 167–83.

Wiseman 2004–6: T.P. Wiseman, 'Andrea Carandini and *Roma Quadrata*', *Accordia Research Papers* 10: 103–26.

Wiseman 2008: T.P. Wiseman, *Unwritten Rome*. Exeter: University of Exeter Press.

Wiseman 2009a: T.P. Wiseman, *Remembering the Roman People: Essays on Late-Republican Politics and Literature*. Oxford: Oxford University Press.

Wiseman 2009b: T.P. Wiseman, 'The House of Augustus and the Lupercal', *Journal of Roman Archaeology* 22: 527–45.

Wiseman 2010: T.P. Wiseman, 'The City That Never Was: Alba Longa and the Historical Tradition', *Journal of Roman Archaeology* 23: 433–9.

Wiseman 2011: T.P. Wiseman, 'Vesta and *Vestibulum*: An Ovidian Etymology', *Scholia* 20: 72–9.

Wiseman 2012a: T.P. Wiseman, '*Roma Quadrata*, Archaic Huts, the House of Augustus, and the Orientation of Palatine Apollo', *Journal of Roman Archaeology* 25: 371–87.

Wiseman 2012b: T.P. Wiseman, 'Where did they live (e.g., Cicero, Octavius, Augustus)?', *Journal of Roman Archaeology* 25: 656–72.

Wiseman 2013a: T.P. Wiseman, *The Death of Caligula: Josephus* Ant. Iud. *XIX 1–273, Translation and Commentary*. Liverpool: Liverpool University Press.

Wiseman 2013b: T.P. Wiseman, 'The Palatine, from Evander to Elagabalus', *Journal of Roman Studies* 103: 234–68.

Wiseman 2014a: T.P. Wiseman, 'Popular Memory', in Karl Galinsky (ed.), *Memoria Romana: Memory in Rome and Rome in Memory* (MAAR Suppl. 10, Ann Arbor: University of Michigan Press): 43–62.

Wiseman 2014b: T.P. Wiseman, 'The Temple of Apollo and Diana at Rome', *Oxford Journal of Archaeology* 33: 327–38.

Wiseman 2015a: T.P. Wiseman, 'Rome on the Balance: Varro and the Foundation Legend', in D.J. Butterfield (ed.), *Varro Varius: The Polymath of the Roman World* (Cambridge Classical Journal Supplement 39, Cambridge): 93–122.

Wiseman 2015b: T.P. Wiseman, *The Roman Audience: Classical Literature as Social History*. Oxford: Oxford University Press.

Wiseman 2016: T.P. Wiseman, *Julius Caesar* ('Pocket Giants'). Stroud: The History Press.

Wiseman 2017: T.P. Wiseman, '*Iuppiter Stator in Palatio*: A New Solution to an Old Puzzle', *Mitteilungen des Deutschen Archäologischen Instituts, Römische Abteilung* 123: 13–45.

Woodman 1977: A.J. Woodman (ed.), *Velleius Paterculus: The Tiberian Narrative (2.94–131)* (Cambridge Classical Texts and Commentaries 19). Cambridge: Cambridge University Press.

Woodman 1998: A.J. Woodman, *Tacitus Reviewed*. Oxford: Clarendon Press.

Zanker 1983: Paul Zanker, 'Der Apollontempel auf dem Palatin: Ausstattung und politische Sinnbezüge nach der Schlacht von Actium', in *Città e architettura nella Roma imperiale* (Analecta Romana Instituti Danici Suppl. 10, Odense: Odense University Press): 21–40.

Zanker 1988: Paul Zanker, *The Power of Images in the Age of Augustus* (Jerome Lectures 16). Ann Arbor: University of Michigan Press.

Zanker 2004: Paul Zanker, 'Domitians Palast auf dem Palatin als Monument kaiserlicher Selbstdarstellung', in Adolf Hoffmann and Ulrike Wulf (eds), *Die Kaiserpaläste auf dem Palatin in Rom: Das Zentrum der römischen Welt und seine Bauten* (Mainz: von Zabern): 86–99.

Zevi 1995: Fausto Zevi, 'Demarato e i re "corinzi" di Roma', in A. Storchi Marino (ed.), *L'incidenza dell'antico: studi in memoria di Ettore Lepore*, I (Naples: Luciano editore): 291–314.

Zink 2012: S. Zink, 'Old and new archaeological evidence for the plan of the Palatine temple of Apollo', *Journal of Roman Archaeology* 25: 388–402.

Zink 2015: Stephan Zink, 'The Palatine Sanctuary of Apollo: The Site and Its Development, 6th to 1st c. B.C.', *Journal of Roman Archaeology* 28: 358–70.

Ziółkowski 2004: Adam Ziółkowski, *Sacra Via Twenty Years After* (Journal of Juristic Papyrology, Supplement 3). Warsaw: Raphael Taubenschlag Foundation.

Ziółkowski 2015: Adam Ziółkowski, 'Reading Coarelli's *Palatium*, or the *Sacra via* yet again', *Journal of Roman Archaeology* 28: 569–81.

Ziółkowski 2016: Adam Ziółkowski, 'Le débat moderne sur le tracé de la course des Luperques', *Revue des Études Latines* 94: 21–43.

GENERAL INDEX

INDEX OF PASSAGES